First Things

First Things

The Maternal Imaginary
in Literature, Art, and Psychoanalysis

Mary Jacobus

Routledge
New York / London

Published in 1995 by
Routledge
29 West 35th Street
New York, NY 10001

Published in Great Britain by
Routledge
11 New Fetter Lane
London, EC4P 4EE

Copyright © 1995 by Routledge

Printed in the United States of America on acid-free paper.

Library of Congress Cataloging-in-Publication Data

Jacobus, Mary.
    First Things: The Maternal Imaginary in Literature,
    Art, and Psychoanalysis / Mary Jacobus.
        p.   cm.
    Includes bibliographical references and index.
    ISBN 0–415–90383-1. ——ISBN 0–415–90384–X (pbk.)

    1. Psychoanalysis and literature. 2. Pyschoanalysis and art. 3. Psychoanalysis and
    feminism. 4. Femininity (Psychology) 5. Women and psychoanalysis. 6. Mothers
    in Literature. 7. Myth in literature. 8. Mothers in Art.
    I. Title

PN56.P92J33   1995
809 .93353–dc20   95–17589
                                                        CIP

For my children, Frances and Josiah,
and in memory of my mother,
Diana Longstaff Jacobus,
with love

CONTENTS

Acknowledgments

I am grateful to the Society for the Humanities at Cornell University for a Faculty Fellowship during 1986–87, when this book began to take shape, and to the Guggenheim Foundation for the award of a Guggenheim Fellowship during 1988–89 which allowed me to begin work in earnest. Three chapters, "Malthus, Matricide, and the Marquis de Sade," "Replacing the Race of Mothers: AIDS and *The Last Man*," and "Portrait of the Artist as a Young Dog," were originally written as the Alexander Lectures, and delivered, along with " ' 'Cos of the Horse': The Origin of Questions," under the umbrella title of "First Things" at the University of Toronto in the autumn of 1991. I am grateful for the opportunity to have shared them with a Canadian audience. I am also grateful to the President and Fellows of St. John's College, Cambridge, for an appointment as Visiting Scholar during 1993, which provided me with valuable time in which to complete this book. A brief stay as guest professor at the Center for Feminist Research and Gender Studies, University of Aarhus, Denmark, in fall 1992, occasioned the writing of "In Love with a Cold Climate: Travelling with Wollstonecraft" for a Scandinavian audience.

A number of essays included in this book have appeared elsewhere: "Freud's Mnemonic: Screen Memories and Feminist Nostalgia," was first published as part of a special issue on women and memory in *Michigan Quarterly Review* 26 (Winter 1987), and some of the Freud material in "'The Third Stroke: Reading Woolf with Freud," in *Grafts: Feminist Cultural Criticism*, edited by Susan Sheridan (London and New York: Verso, 1988); "In Parenthesis: Immaculate Conceptions and Feminine Desire," in *Body/Politics: Women and the Discourses of Science*, edited by Mary Jacobus, Evelyn Fox Keller, and Sally Shuttleworth (London and New York: Routledge, 1989); "Russian Tactics: Freud's 'Case of Homosexuality in a Woman' " in a special issue on Freud in *GLQ: A Journal of Lesbian and Gay Studies* 2 (1995); " 'Tea Daddy': Poor Mrs. Klein and the Pencil Shavings" in a special Klein issue of *Women: A Cultural Review* 1 (1990); and "Incorruptible Milk: Breast-feeding and the French Revolution" in *Rebel Daughters: Women and the French Revolution*, edited by Sarah E. Melzer and Leslie W. Rabine (New York: Oxford University Press, 1991. Copyright © 1992 by the University of California Humanities Institute; reprinted by permission of Oxford University Press, Inc.). I am grateful for permission to revise and reprint them here.

I am also grateful for permission to quote from the collection *Her Soul beneath the Bone: Women's Poetry on Breast Cancer*, edited by Leatrice H. Lifshitz (Urbana and

Chicago: University of Illinois Press, 1988) and to quote Tess Enroth's "Consultation" in full. This material, ©1988 by the Board of Trustees, is used with the permission of Illinois Press. Finally, I am grateful to Chatto & Windus and the Melanie Klein Tust for permission to reproduce Richard's drawings from Melanie Klein's *Narrative of a Child Analysis* (London: Virago Press, 1989). Copyright © The Melanie Klein Trust, 1961.

Among the many friends and colleagues who have contributed directly or indirectly to the writing of this book at different stages, whether by their conversation, by listening, by their comments, or by their support, I would like to mention in particular: Gillian Beer, Rachel Bowlby, Cynthia Chase, Jonathan Culler, Peggy Dieter, Zillah Eisenstein, Carol Gilligan, Sander Gilman, Sally Greaves, Evelyn Fox Keller, Karen Klitgaard, Daphne Lambert, Dorothy Mermin, Juliet Mitchell, Reeve Parker, Naomi Segal, Elaine Showalter, and Sally Shuttleworth. I owe a special debt to the members of the Cambridge Women's Reading Group (1992–93) and to participants in Cornell graduate seminars over the past ten years who have helped me to think more clearly and further by their own energy, commitment, and subtlety of mind.

I am grateful to Kathleen Adler and Tamar Garb, and to the Mount Holyoke College Art Museum for assistance in matters concerning Berthe Morisot; to Malcolm Bowie for helping me grapple with the opacity of Mallarmé's prose; to Margaret Webster at the Cornell Art and Architecture Visual Resources Center; and to Rachel Roze and Katie Louise Thomas for assistance in the final stages of preparing the manuscript. Finally, I would like to thank my editor, William P. Germano, for encouraging (and waiting for) this book, and Christine Cipriani for seeing it through to press.

First Things is dedicated to my children, from whom I have learned much along the way (including how to order my priorities), and whose own inquiries have sometimes influenced mine. I owe a special debt to my daughter, Frances, who wrote about Morisot as a woman Impressionist before I did, and to my son, Josiah, who still sometimes asks me questions. Since *First Things* are last things too, this book is also dedicated to the memory of my mother, who did not live to see its publication, and who has had more to do with its writing than either she or I will ever know.

Note: The writings of Freud quoted in the text and notes are from *The Standard Edition of the Complete Psychological Works of Sigmund Freud*, ed. James Strachey, 24 vols. (London: Hogarth Press, 1953–74), cited as *SE*, with volume and page number.

Preface

The inception of this book coincided with a number of influential books on the body published during the second half of the 1980s.[1] I thought of myself then as writing yet another "body" book—specifically, a book on literature, psychoanalysis, and the maternal body (rather than, for instance, on the historical, social, or scientific construction of the maternal body). But as time passed, the maternal body came to seem altogether too embodied, too taken-for-granted, and too material an entity for the essays I found myself writing. This is not to say that the body in question turned out to be entirely disembodied or textualized, or immune to the pressures of the times. Contemporary issues and historical events (the debate over surrogate motherhood, AIDS phobia, and breast cancer, the population increase during the eighteenth century, the French Revolution, and World War II) kept returning me to the effects of texts and ideologies on actual bodies. But my real subject is what I have called "the maternal imaginary"—a portmanteau phrase sufficiently capacious to contain Freud's writing on screen memory, Mary Shelley's futuristic plague novel, Klein's analytic work with children, or Berthe Morisot's Impressionism.

This is not a book about the body—any more than it is a book about motherhood or mythic mothers. But it is about how such myths are born and about the ideological work they do. My subject (insofar as anything so various, multiform, and pervasive as the maternal imaginary can be said to be, or have, a "subject") is the fantasmatic mother who may or may not possess reproductive parts, nurturing functions, and specific historical or material manifestations; but who exists chiefly in the realm of images and imagos (whether perceived or imagined), mirroring and identifications, icons and figures; who is associated sometimes with feminist nostalgia, sometimes with ideological mystification; who surfaces in connection with melancholia, matriphobia, and matricide, and plays a key part in Kristevan theories of signification; who figures prominently in the writings of Melanie Klein, where terms such as splitting, identification, and projection analyze a repertoire of activities involving fantasized attacks on, and reparations to, the maternal body; who gives the breast its cultural power (whether in French Revolutionary iconography, nineteenth-century Realist painting, or *fin de siècle*

iii

Impressionism) and incites the imagination to linger on the hallucinatory breast, the lost breast, or the idea of a good feed.

The "First Things" of my title are the earliest, unformed yet vitally informing phantasies that shape the infant's emergence as a subject; the first "Thing" is Julia Kristeva's maternal thing, the not-yet object of an emerging, chaotic not-yet subject. Although *First Things* is primarily a book of literary and cultural criticism that makes excursions into art history, it is preoccupied throughout by psychoanalytic theory. I have thought of myself as writing about both signs and psychoanalysis, and about the relations between them. My texts may be written or visual, contemporary or historical; but throughout I assume that literary criticism and psychoanalysis are mutually illuminating and imbricated practices. Psychoanalytic theory is my tool but, at times, a tool that is subjected to criticism; it also provides a rich resource for exploring the maternal imaginary as it surfaces in Freud's remembering and conceiving; in Kristeva's writing of melancholia; in Klein's narratives of child analysis; and in the development of post-Kleinian object-relations theory.

First Things begins with Freud and ends with Wilfred Bion; its informing presences are Kristeva and Klein. The trajectory reflects my own during the writing of this book, as well as a shift in contemporary psychoanalytic feminism—turning away from the Lacanian return to Freud, and beyond the feminist critique of Freud, toward Kleinian accounts that emphasize the mother and the freight of unconscious phantasies and feelings she brings in her train. In Part 1, Freud's oedipal myth jostles with the feminist countermyth of preoedipal origins, legislates the relations between maternity and errant desire, or defines passion between women as a daughter's disappointed desire for her father. Part 2 moves from Freud to Kristeva. Lacan's sacred trinity (Symbolic, Imaginary, Real) tends to oppose the Symbolic to the regressive, narcissistic, mother-identified Imaginary. By contrast, Kristeva emphasizes the Imaginary as a discursive semiotic system whose presence is implicated at all levels of symbolic activity. The essays in Part 2 draw on Kristeva's writing about abjection and melancholia to explore love, hate, and the transfer of affect. Part 3, rereading Klein with Kristevan hindsight, attempts to recover her missing theory of signs. Kleinian theory posits both a persecutory, paranoid-schizoid, and a reparative depressive phase in the infant, which not only structures psychic life from the outset but continues to shape the adult psyche, while also continually threatening to return it to its beginnings. Wilfred Bion, building on Klein's theories, provides the basis for a speculative theory of thinking (and linking); taking maternal reverie as the model for the analytic situation, Bion suggests that thought comes into being from the relation between a preconception (an empty thought), a conception, and the infant's frustration by an absent breast. Part 4 ends with this speculation.

Surprisingly, essays written over a period of years have turned out to speak to one another, even when their point of departure or theoretical focus seem markedly different. In Part 1, "Freud's Mnemonic: Screen Memories and Femininist Nostalgia" and "In Parenthesis: Immaculate Conceptions and Feminine Desire" open the question of the maternal imaginary by way of Freud's thinking about himself and his mother, feminist mythmaking, and attempts to subsume feminine sexuality under the sign of maternity. Although they belong to the earliest stage of my thinking about the maternal imaginary, I have chosen to include these essays under the heading of "Preconceptions" (my own as well as Freud's) because of the ground-clearing work that they perform. In "Russian Tactics: Freud's 'Case of Homosexuality in a Woman,'" the resistance of Freud's homosexual girl prompts a rereading of her suicidal passion for a mother figure; her refusal to "know" (a resistance in which Freud himself is implicated) leads to the discovery of his attempt to think the unthinkable: the lesbian body.

The "Melancholy Figures" of Part 2 are the dead or absent mothers who figure, metaphorically, in writing by Wollstonecraft, Malthus, Sade, and Mary Shelley. "In Love with a Cold Climate: Travelling with Wollstonecraft" reads transference love as resistance, reflecting on the relation of contemporary feminism to a foremother whose amatory melancholia represents the negative and unassimilable aspect of Wollstonecraft's legacy. In "Malthus, Matricide, and the Marquis de Sade," the mother figures as an uncontrollable source of reproductive anxiety; she must be punished or dis-invaginated in order to rid the masculine subject of unmanly melancholia and secure the closure of the libertine text. Reading Malthusian population discourse and Sade together reveals their common matriphobic subtext. Linking AIDS phobia and the infectiousness of grief, "Replacing the Race of Mothers: AIDS and *The Last Man*" argues that the discourse of melancholia enables the consolidation of an authorial subject through Shelley's identification with a dead mother, while also allowing her to memorialize the lost immunity of unborn children.

Part 3, "The Origin of Signs," focuses on the relation between Klein's analysis of the unconscious phantasies of early childhood and children's sign-making activities—their language, play, interminable questions, stories, and drawings.

Lacan's seminar on the Imaginary returns to Klein (rather than Freud) for an account of the child's first entry into language and his insertion into the oedipal scene. "'Tea Daddy': Poor Mrs. Klein and the Pencil Shavings" asks what is at stake in this return, arguing that Klein's metaphoricity (rather than her literalness) emerges from the encounter. "'Cos of the Horse': The Origin of Questions" explores the linguistic and rhetorical role of questions in Freud's inquiry into little Hans's phobia and in Klein's analysis of little Fritz; Kristeva's narrative of phobic signs (her rereading of the case of little Hans) makes language itself the hero of the tale. With Klein's "Portrait of the Artist as a Young Dog"—a case history that makes extensive use of a child's drawings—the origins of signs becomes the untold story of Klein's maternal archaeology, which is also the narrative of a child at war.

Part 4, "Theory at the Breast," focuses on representations of the breast in Enlightenment and Revolutionary France, surgical iconography, and *haute bourgeoise* culture of the 1890s. In "Incorruptible Milk: Breast-feeding and the French Revolution," the breast becomes a figure for Republican attempts to purify signs—for the hallucinatory satisfactions of state-authorized ideology. "Baring the Breast: Mastectomy and the Surgical Analogy" reflects on Freud's surgical analogy and its use in psychoanalytic art history; the medical context that produced the cathartic talking cure also produced the radical mastectomy. In contrast to the heroic pathos of Thomas Eakins's painting of a mastectomy operation, women's contemporary mastectomy poetry bares the lost breast as a holding operation. "Narcissa's Gaze: Berthe Morisot and the Filial Mirror" juxtaposes Morisot's reflections on middle age with her portraits of her adolescent daughter, tracing the relations between painting and thinking, between narcissism and artistic filiation. Morisot's reinvention of modernity in the image of a feminine subject gives rise to the speculation that thinking itself may depend on a lost breast.

In *First Things*, specific literary, psychoanalytic, or visual texts have been the occasion for a series of linked inquiries, explorations, and speculations. While theoretical concerns are always at stake, for the most part I have addressed them indirectly, hoping that textual and visual pleasure are compatible with the rigors of theoretical inquiry; I have preferred immersion, even empathy, to metatheory. Although I am indebted to contemporary work in cultural studies, queer theory, gender studies, the history of science, and feminist art history (to name only a few of the studies currently being pursued under the heading of literary study), my approach is first of all that of a psychoanalytically inclined feminist literary critic. *First Things* begins with a woman poet's quest for something "that could re-member us." It ends with a woman painter thinking forward through her daughter. In tracing this trajectory, the first things of this book are both found and lost, and thinking begins.

1. For instance, Leo Bersani's psychoanalytic *The Freudian Body: Psychoanalysis and Art* (New York: Columbia University Press, 1986), Emily Martin's anthropological *The Woman in the Body: A Cultural Analysis of Reproduction* (Boston: Beacon Press, 1987), the "Representations" collection edited by Catherine Gallagher and Thomas Laqueur as *The Making of the Modern Body: Sexuality and Society in the Nineteenth Century* (Berkeley, Los Angeles, and London: University of California Press, 1988), Zillah Eisenstein's *The Female Body and the Law* (Berkeley, Los Angeles, and London: University of California Press, 1988), the collection of 1986 English Institute essays edited by Elaine Scarry as *Literature and the Body: Essays on Populations and Persons* (Baltimore and London: Johns Hopkins University Press, 1988), the collection edited by Mary Jacobus, Evelyn Fox Keller, and Sally Shuttleworth as *Body/Politics: Women and the Discourses of Science* (New York and London: Routledge, 1990), and Thomas Laqueur's *Making Sex: Body and Gender from the Greeks to Freud* (Cambridge, MA, and London: Harvard University Press, 1990)—to name only a few.

Part I

Preconceptions

Freud's Mnemonic

Screen Memories and Feminist Nostalgia

*There is a joking saying that "Love is homesickness." Whenever a man
dreams of a place or a country and says to himself, while he is still
dreaming: "this place is familiar to me, I've been here before," we may
interpret the place as being his mother's genitals or her body.*

— Sigmund Freud, "The Uncanny," 1919 (SE 17.245)

*But in fact we were always like this,
rootless, dismembered: knowing it makes the difference.
Birth stripped our birthright from us
so early on
and the whole chorus throbbing at our ears
like midges, told us nothing, nothing
of origins, nothing we needed
to know, nothing that could re-member us.*

—Adrienne Rich, "Transcendental Étude."[1]

JOKING APART, in what mythic place could we at once re-find the maternal body
and re-member ourselves? In his essay on Leonardo da Vinci, Freud compares childhood memories to the memories preserved in a nation's myths (SE 11.83–84).
While myths may be a means of access to what childhood memories screen, they
may also be said to produce and structure memory itself. Freud's writing on screen
memory reminds us that memory is a form of representation, and that representations reproduce sexual ideology (historically determined myths), just as "woman"

is itself an ideologically determined representation. In Freud's writing, woman serves not only as a mnemonic for sexual difference, but as a reminder of an oedipal "case" or story that is Freud's own. What part is played by the memory of a woman—specifically, the mother—in the Freudian representation of sexual difference? The workings of memory, as Freud himself put it, are always "tendentious." What, then, is the relation between the myth of psychoanalysis and the representations we call "memories"—between the theory of sexual difference produced by Freudian psychoanalysis and the childhood memories it uses to buttress this theory? Finally, another question arises: Is the feminist attempt to recover the memory (specifically, memory of the mother) beneath the myth—the contemporary feminist excavation of what Freud himself called the "Minoan-Mycenaean" or preoedipal phase screened by the Hellenic oedipal—a form of nostalgia?[2] In its desire to ground femininity on the bedrock not of Freudian penis envy but of the body of the mother, some versions of feminism may have risked forgetting that every theory is grounded on a fictional moment and that nostalgia itself is a form of *Nachträglichkeit* or retroactive construction. The statement that "this place is familiar to me, I've been here before," would then gesture not so much toward a lost mother country as toward the myth that has also sustained feminist revisions of Freudian theory—the "memory" of imaginary oneness with the body of the mother, a feminist myth of origins whose function, in Rich's phrase, is to "re-member us."

i: *"The difference between* m *and* n*"*

In Freud's writing about "screen memory," memory and the mother are intimately associated from the start. In *The Psychopathology of Everyday Life* (1901), Freud devoted a chapter to the topic of "Childhood Memories and Screen Memories," which he later substantially revised to include some of his own memories. By "screen memories," he means memories that preserve, associatively, not an ostensible "content" but something that is "screened off" or unavailable to consciousness. This associative link always involves a chronological distortion. Either the manifest content derives from a later (unconscious) experience—the "memory" being in this case retroactively recovered or retrospectively constructed—or a recent experience serves to inscribe repressed content dating back to earliest childhood, and, as it were, *"displaced forward"* (SE 6.43–44). Alternatively, a screen memory may hide something that is contemporary or contiguous in time. Either way, the status of memory is put in question. Instead of being a recovery of the past in the present, it always involves a revision, reinscription, or re-presentation of an ultimately irretrievable past. The past ceases to be the proper referent of memory; rather, memories "refer" (improperly—that is, metaphorically or metonymically) to the unconscious. Memory, then, becomes a mode of "reproduction" (Freud's term) like any other, one that resembles dreaming not only in its distortions and displacements but in its paradoxical relation to a forgetting that is always, though unconscious, deliberate and purposive. Just as a dream represents the fulfillment of a repressed wish, so a memory represents a contradictory desire—not the wish to remember, but the wish to forget.

In his correspondence with Fliess, which provides a running commentary on the self-analysis carried on with particular intensity between May and mid-October 1897, Freud specifies that the element responsible for repression "is always what is feminine." "In every instance," he insists, "repression starts from the feminine aspect." [3] We might translate this as follows: "What gets repressed is femininity." At stake in these memories (Freud's own) is nothing less than childhood sexuality, which for Freud is always oedipal rather than preoedipal; hence, we might say that these memories preserve the repressive inscription of sexual difference. What gets repressed is precisely "the feminine" or the child's bisexuality—if you like, the mother's desire in him as well as his desire for the mother. Freud tells us that he was first alerted to "the tendentious nature" of memory by the striking fact that memories preserved from earliest childhood appear to be (his term) "indifferent." The word "indifferent" recurs in his account of "Screen Memories" with troubling insistence. What is an "indifferent" memory? Could it be one in which the inscription of sexual difference has been elided or repressed, and along with it not simply sexuality but what Freud terms "the feminine"? This infantile amnesia is for Freud the "strange riddle" that (no less than the riddle of femininity) perplexes the analytic self-interpreter. The key to it, he claims, may unlock our understanding of other amnesias, those purposive forgettings which provide the basis for all neurosis.

To prove his point, Freud tells an anecdote which turns on the displacement of sexual difference onto the ostensibly indifferent scene of writing:

> A man of twenty-four has preserved the following picture from his fifth year. He is sitting in the garden of a summer villa, on a small chair beside his aunt, who is trying to teach him the letters of the alphabet. He is in difficulties over the difference between *m* and *n* and he asks his aunt to tell him how to know one from the other.

His aunt points out to him that the *m* has a whole piece more than the *n*—the third stroke. There appeared to be no reason for challenging the trustworthiness of this childhood memory; it had, however, only acquired its meaning at a later date, when it showed itself suited to represent symbolically another of the boy's curiosities. For just as at that time he wanted to know the difference betweem *m* and *n*, so later he was anxious to find out the difference between boys and girls, and would have been very willing for this particular aunt to be the one to teach him. He also discovered then that the difference was a similar one—that a boy, too, has a whole piece more than a girl; and at the time when he acquired this piece of knowledge he called up the recollection of the parallel curiosity of his childhood. (SE 6.48)

In this classic representation of sexual difference ("The *m* has a whole piece more than the *n*"), binary opposition leads to asymmetry; *m* has something that *n* lacks, "a whole piece more," or an extra "member," although to be without it is to be less than whole. That this asymmetrical structure—the minimal difference between two adjacent characters, a difference characterized as feminine lack—determines the entire phallocentricity of the Freudian inscription of sexual difference hardly needs underlining, though Freud's own italics place the emphasis there. Figuring sexual difference as a hierarchy of plus or minus underlines the castrating cost for women of "the third stroke."

But why the imbrication of sexual difference in the scene of writing? At the very point where the possibility of self-inscription arises, and with it the self-division and self-dispersal figured by writing itself, anxiety about sexual differentiation enters in. Freud implies that the difference between *m* and *n* only becomes significant (no longer "indifferent") for the boy at a later stage, when his sexual curiosity and desire have become aroused and focused on his aunt (an obvious mother substitute). But to write is already to have acceded to the inscription of sexual difference—to the Oedipus complex and to the anxieties about loss of wholeness that Freud calls castration anxiety. *La plume de ma tante*, in Lacanian terms at least, would have it that all subjects are "castrated," whether *avant* or *à la lettre*, irrespective of anatomical gender. Inscription can never be regarded as indifferent, any more than the screen memories of childhood can. Rather, the scene of writing "screens" not only castration anxiety, but the differentiating ban on the mother and the traumatic discovery (for both boys *and* girls) that the mother lacks a penis. When it comes to the phallic signifier, lack is the lesson taught to all subjects. This anxious discovery is managed in Freud's asymmetrical account by placing femininity on the side of lack, just as the stories boys tell themselves manage castration anxiety by projecting the loss of what they still possess onto what little girls have never had.

Freud's overdetermined anecdote turns out to be an exemplary "mnemonic" for the child's passage through the Oedipus and castration complexes. The hidden story of screen memory is nothing other than the inscription of sexual difference. In this scene, the swift reconsolidation of masculine identity occurs by reference to a woman (an aunt) who stands in for the always-absent mother, and hence for the structure of oedipal desire (rivalry with the father for possession of the mother). The aunt lacks what the boy wants; she teaches him his own desire. At this point it may be instructive to follow Freud's own trajectory in *The Psychopathology of Everyday Life*, moving via his preliminary "mnemonic" (notice how aptly, by an accident of language, *m* and *n* figure in this term) to Freud himself. In his 1907 revisions to *The Psychopathology of Everyday Life*, the subject of screen memory initiates a series of autobiographical memories that uncover Freud's own earliest childhood encounters with sexual difference. These recollections specifically concern his mother. Preceding the ostensibly "indifferent" scene of writing by many years, they prove to be of particular significance for Freud himself, since they lead to the momentous "discovery" of the Oedipus complex on which Freud's entire theory of sexuality comes to depend. In these autobiographical memories, what is forgotten or repressed, and thereby rendered "indifferent," turns out to be not only sexual difference or the oedipal ban on desire for the mother, but theoretical desire—the founding desire of psychoanalysis.

"Shut up already" (words apocryphally attributed to the Jewish mother) could serve as a mnemonic for the repressed inscription of the mother in Freud's writing. Desire for the mother must give way to the law of the Father in the Freudian account of the universality of the Oedipus and castration complexes. Yet these crucial "memories" reveal an intriguing interpretive structure. When the forty-two-year-old Freud turns to his (now elderly) mother for an explanation of certain childhood memories involving her and his old nurse, she provides unexpected illumination ("threw a flood of light on the childhood scene," as Freud puts it; *SE* 6.51). Her symbolic confinement, it turns out, has served to screen from memory her reproductive capacity, her maternal "confinement." "Mother" becomes the name for closet-memory, in the sense that we speak of "closet-drama"—the unacted drama that has its life in the mind, or on the page of the unconscious where memories (whether of past or present) are inscribed. "Mother" is the ostensible referent of these closet memories, yet it is only by making an extra-textual appeal to her as an entirely contingent witness that Freud is able to establish the universal structures at work in screen memory. What is the status of the mother? Is she a content, or rather, as he seems to imply, an interpretative structure? We might suspect that Freud's mnemonic is a reminder, not of a "what" (the mother) but of a "how"—the process whereby sexual difference gets inscribed in the prehistory of the subject.

In a recollection that circumstancial evidence dates back to his third year, Freud sees himself "standing in front of a cupboard ['*Kasten*'— in his first translation, he calls it a wardrobe, '*Schrank*'] demanding something and screaming, while [his] half-brother . . . held it open. Then suddenly [his] mother, looking beautiful and slim, walked into the room, as if she had come in from the street" (*SE* 6.50). These, Freud makes clear, were his own words for describing the scene. He does not know whether his half-brother (his senior by twenty years) wanted to open or shut the cupboard, why he himself was crying, or what the arrival of his mother had to do with the brouhaha. Only after considerable analytic efforts does he bring to light the fact that he had "missed his mother, and had come to suspect that she was shut up in this wardrobe or cupboard." When he discovers that the cupboard is empty, he begins to scream: "This is the moment that my memory has held fast; and it was followed at once by the appearance of my mother" (*SE* 6.50). How, Freud wonders, did the child get the idea of looking for his absent mother in the cupboard? The answer seems to lie in the dreams that Freud had during the period of self-analysis occupying him in 1897 and that he recorded in his contemporary correspondence with Fliess.

These dreams concerned not only Freud's mother, but the other woman in his early life, his elderly nurse. His nurse, it transpires, had been charged with a series of petty domestic thefts during his mother's confinement and had therefore also suddenly disappeared—in the punning words of Freud's elder half brother, she had been "boxed up" ["*eingekastelt*"—sent to jail] just as Freud's own mother had been "confined" for the birth of a daughter, two-and-a half years younger than little Sigmund. As Freud puts it, "The sudden disappearance of the nurse had not been a matter of *indifference* to [him]" (my italics), any more than he had been indifferent to the reappearance of his mother, her slimness now restored. Freud adds in a footnote that the two-and-a-half-year-old Sigmund was "full of mistrust and anxiety that his mother's inside might conceal still more children. The wardrobe or cupboard was a symbol for him of his mother's inside." In addition, just as he suspects the older brother ("who . . . had taken his father's place as the child's rival") of having "boxed up" the nurse, so he suspects him of having played a part in introducing the new baby into his mother's inside; hence, it may be his brother who is responsible for her "confinement." Neither the disappearance of his nurse nor the reappearance of his mother were "matters of indifference" at all. On the contrary, what their closeting figures is the child's repressed recognition of his mother's sexuality, along with his own guilty relation to it (like his nurse, he wants to appropriate what is not his). In other words, Freud finds "in my own case too, falling in love with the mother and jealousy of the father, *and I now regard it as a universal event of early childhood.*"[4] The discovery of this maternal skeleton in the family cupboard is not only the culminating insight of Freud's self-analysis, but the founding moment of his theory of sexuality. The oedipal myth emerges to at once interpret and universalize the meaning of his childhood memory. Where mother was, there psychoanalysis shall be.

And what about myth itself? Does the inscription of a remembered (*autobiographical*) self provide independent evidence of the myth of psychoanalysis, or is it rather that the Oedipus myth structures the autobiographical memory? Is a myth a content or, like the mother, "a universal event"—an interpretive structure? Does a myth reinterpret the prehistory of the gendered subject in the light of a theory of origins that we are in the habit of calling "mother"? What is the status of an oedipal theory that has itself been described as the central "myth" of psychoanalysis? The persistent but unacknowledged punning on insides and outsides points to an indeterminate structure: the mother is both inside the cupboard, its shut-up or repressed content, and the cupboard itself—the "inside" that contains the baby (inside its inside). Freud simply tells us that the child's disappointment at finding the cupboard empty represents "affect in the wrong place" (*SE* 6.51–52 n.); he should have looked somewhere else. The mother is always absent, lost, or sequestered, and always doubly inscribed—both contained and container, both the content of memory and the structure that produces "mother" as its meaning (both what is repressed and the mode of repression itself). This game of hide-and-seek for a lost object, or double inscription, is repeated in the form of Freud's narrative. On one hand, he pursues his self-interpretation by way of associated dream material, in quest of what it contains. On the other hand, he solves the problem of interpretation by asking his mother, now grown old, about the nurse's misdeeds ("This information threw a flood of light on the childhood scene, and so enabled me to understand it." *SE* 6.51). The mother is at once the figure closeted in the unconscious and she who holds open the door to it. She both is, and guarantees, an originating "truth." Simultaneously inside and outside, she ends by putting in question the very concepts of inside and outside—of content as opposed to structure. How, then, can a myth that is a content be differentiated from a myth that is a structure? As literary critics, we are accustomed to the idea that structure determines meaning, and that there is no content apart from the container. We might also ask where this leaves not just the mother, but the founding myth of Freudian psychoanalysis. Psychoanalysis itself starts to look like an open-and-shut case ("shut up already")—as thoroughly predetermined as the difference between *m* and *n*.

Freud's original sequence of dream memories in the letters to Fliess offers another angle on the emergence of his theoretical concerns. During their correspondence, Freud frequently invokes Fliess's notion of male periodicity, especially in the context of his own "periodic" creativity and stagnation as a psychoanalytic theorist.[5] One might mention in passing that both men are much concerned with the engendering of (their own) children and with their wives' pregnancies and reproductive cycles. In a searching and speculative article on the relation between "*Mater*," "nannie," and the discovery of the Oedipus complex, Jim Swan argues that Freud's "discovery" should be read in the light of the dream memories he communicated to Fliess (in other words, read in the light of the autobiography of Freud's own unconscious). The Oedipus complex, for Swan, refers to the content of Freudian memory. Swan focuses his attention on the two mothers (the loving *Mater* and the scornful nannie) who recur in Freud's dreams, arguing that their respective qualities get redistributed between the pure mother and the authoritarian father of the Oedipus complex.[6] More to my point, he emphasizes the old nurse's role as Freud's first seducer, his "prime originator" ("she was my teacher in sexual matters," he tells Fliess).[7] She, not the mother, is blamed for arousing and shaming him, even though the pure mother is the first object of his desires. Freud abandons the seduction theory in his famous letter to Fliess of September 21, 1897, substituting for it the theory of infantile fantasy, but he allows this bit of autobiography to stand. Moreover, it reemerges much later in the essays on femininity, when Freud argues that the mother or her substitute, the nurse, is the girl's first seducer—actually, and not in the realm of fantasy. The seductive mother will not go quietly; significantly (as has often been remarked) Freud could only tackle the question of femininity after the death of his own mother.

But a different reading of the connection between Freudian theory and Freudian autobiography is possible. What nannie steals from *Mater* is guilt. Whose guilt? Freud's identification with the nurse, who stole money from him but whom he incorrectly remembered as having induced him to steal ("she made me steal zehners [ten-kreuzer coins] to give them to her"),[8] is bound up with his current anxieties about getting money from his patients for bad treatment, just as his nannie got money from him in return for bad treatment of him. But his mother steps in to revise the memory—actually the nurse stole money from him. The proper interpretation (according to Freud) is that he improperly takes money from the mother of a doctor. That is, he says, "I=she, and the mother of the doctor equals my mother."[9] "I= she" is the bizarre equation here. "I" (equals nurse) take something from *Mater*. What nurse actually takes from *Mater* is not so much the guilt of seduction as his wish to seduce or steal her for himself. One could go further. Among Freud's memories of his nannie is that of having been washed in reddish water in which she had previously bathed herself. This telling memory of menstrual blood—the mother's menstrual blood, presumably, since the nurse herself is "elderly"—obviously purifies the mother at nannie's expense; but it also confirms the strange identity of "she=I." As in the Freud-Fliess correspondence, the menstruating woman infects the man; the mother's womb is always getting inside the child when it, or she, ought rather to be his place of origin. From this point of view, Freud's memory of his shut-up mother is a screen memory for the way in which every child contains maternal desire inside its inside. As masculinity is inhabited by repressed femininity, so the oedipal myth is haunted by its repressed preoedipal other. For Freud himself, the preoedipal only becomes visible as the buried or repressed "content" of the myth of psychoanalysis when he turns to the question of femininity, naming the mother as the first seducer, not of the boy but of the girl—the daughter whose prior inscription under the letter *n* renders her history one of hypothetical deprivation rather than threatened castration. This is the mythic history of forgotten mother-daughter relations to which Adrienne Rich's "Transcendental Etude" refers when it commemorates the mother as bedrock. With its nostalgia for maternal origins and its retroactive revision of psychoanalysis—its excavation of a buried Minoan-Mycenaean preoedipal region—this is also the myth that has generated some of the most influential contemporary attempts to provide a feminist version of the founding myth of psychoanalysis.

ii. The Dandelion Phantasy

Freud's other extended discussion of screen memory occurs in an essay of 1899 to which he refers obliquely in a letter of January 3, 1899, again in the context of his own self-analysis, "a small bit" of which (he tells Fliess) "has forced its way through and confirmed that fantasies are products of later periods and are projected back from what was then the present into earliest childhood."[10] Freud's essay on "Screen Memories" begins by considering the arbitrary and fragmentary nature of childhood recollections, insisting that "precisely what is important is repressed and what is indifferent retained" (SE 3.306). Under the cloak of an assumed persona, playing the parts of both analyst and analysand, Freud offers a first-person narrative that is generally assumed to be autobiographical. His narrative singles out a scene which "appears to [him] fairly indifferent." Freud-as-analysand goes on, "I cannot understand why it should have become fixed in my memory. Let me describe it to you" (SE 3.311). What follows is an interpetive dialogue between the ideal analyst (Freud) and his ideal analysand (Freud), focused on a scene that comes to be known as "the dandelion phantasy":

> I see a rectangular, rather steeply sloping piece of meadow-land, green and thickly grown; in the green there are a great number of yellow flowers—evidently common dandelions. At the top end of the meadow there is a cottage and in front of the cottage door two women are standing chatting busily, a peasant-woman with a handkerchief on her head and a children's nurse. Three children are playing in the grass. One of them is myself (between the age of two and three); the two others are my boy cousin, who is a year older than me, and his sister, who is almost exactly the same age as I am. We are picking the yellow flowers and each of us is holding a bunch of flowers we have already picked. The little girl has the best bunch; and, as though by mutual agreement, we—the two boys—fall on her and snatch away her flowers. She runs up the meadow in tears and as a consolation the peasant-woman gives her a big piece of black bread. Hardly have we seen this than we throw the flowers away, hurry to the cottage, and ask to be given some bread too. And we are in fact given some; the peasant-woman cuts the loaf with a long knife. In my memory the bread tastes quite delicious— and at that point the scene breaks off. (SE 3.311)

At the outset, Freud-as-analysand confesses himself baffled. Does the emphasis lie on the little boys' "disagreeable behaviour to the little girl"? Is it the yellow color of the dandelions? The taste of the bread, made especially delicious by a child's appetite? Color and taste seem exaggerated, almost hallucinatory; there is "something not quite right about this scene" (SE 3.312). Later, it emerges that two episodes have been grafted together as one. Further skillful questioning by Freud-as-analyst elicits the information that this "memory" first emerged at the age of seventeen, when the young Freud returned to the country where he had spent his early childhood. This return also led to his "first calf-love" (SE 3.313) for a fifteen-year-old girl who was wearing a yellow dress when they met. He is indifferent now to her, as he is to dandelions. But *was* the color that of dandelions? No, "more of a yellowish brown, more like the colour of wallflowers." Another flower—found in the Alps, similar to the dandelion but dark yellow—"would exactly agree in colour with the dress of the girl I was so fond of." The alpine reference dates the emergence of the "screen memory" as belonging to a still later period, placing on it the time-stamp of his first acquaintance with alpine scenery.

This was another occasion that "stirred up in [Freud] the impressions of childhood." As a young man, now a medical student, he visits his uncle and meets again the two children in his childhood "memory," the boy and girl cousins. This time he does not fall in love with his girl cousin. Instead, the fantasy is projected onto his father and uncle, who (Freud believes) had hopes that he and his cousin might marry and settle down in some practical walk of life. Not until later, when struggling to make a living (as in the time-present of his self-analysis) does Freud reflect that his father had meant well in this plan for his son. The delicious bread he remembers from childhood corresponds to the idea of the comfortable life he would have led if he had married his cousin and gone into business with his uncle. As Freud the analyst puts it, "Throwing away the flowers in exchange for bread strikes me as not a bad disguise for the scheme your father had for you: you were to give up your unpractical ideals and take on a 'bread-and-butter' occupation" (SE 3.315). The adolescent fantasy and the young man's rebellious rejection of the life planned for him by his father have been superimposed on one another to create a childhood memory that screens his unacknowledged desires. The "memory" actually belongs to the time of Freud's struggles to establish himself as "a newly-fledged man of science" (SE 3.314). Though the scene may be genuine, it is charged with impressions and thoughts from a later date—including, though Freud does not say say so, the present. Its hallucinatory vividness comes from this freight of unconscious desire.

But Freud's self-analysis does not stop there. The yellow flowers remain to be explained as "a representation of love," and "taking flowers away from a girl means to deflower her" (*SE* 3.316). This is a scene of rape—a bold unconscious fantasy beneath the bashfulness of the seventeen-year-old and the rebellious indifference of the student. As Freud remarks, "it is precisely the coarsely sensual element in the phantasy which explains why it does not develop into a *conscious* phantasy but must be content to find its way allusively and under a flowery disguise into a child-hood scene" (*SE* 3.317). Why a childhood scene, though? For the sake of its innocence, perhaps; or, alternatively, because of the rules governing repression and the covering over of repressed thoughts and wishes by strategically employed childhood memories. "Screen memory" allows the repressed thought to become conscious, albeit in a censored form. On the one hand repressed desire emerges as a metaphor (picking flowers), and on the other hand it emerges as a visual image (bread). A final question remains. Is the whole "dandelion phantasy" nothing but a retrospective construction? No, Freud allows it to be genuine—"there is a memory trace the content of which offers the phantasy a point of contact" (*SE* 3.318). A prior inscription subsequently acquired the superscription which accounts for its vividness. "In your case," Freud tells himself, "the childhood scene seems only to have had some of its lines engraved more deeply: think of the over-emphasis on the yellow and the exaggerated niceness of the bread" (*SE* 3.318). And as proof of the genuineness of the scene, he adduces its unexplained, contingent residue—the two little boys, the peasant-woman, and the nurse.

But there is another residue of "the dandelion phantasy," its unexplored and unacknowledged pathos (unacknowledged by Freud, that is). Perhaps there is more to be said, both on Freud's own account and with respect to the founding myth of psychoanalysis. Freud's recollections concern himself as son. But by the time of his self-analysis, he was also a father. The rejected counter-movement of his own psychoanalytic thinking at this period, as witnessed by the letters to Fliess, involved the allegations of his hysterical women patients that they had actually been seduced by their fathers—allegations that he subsequently came to view as a manifestation of unconscious desire. Giving up the "seduction theory" as an explanation for hysteria was the first step in the crucial break between psychoanalysis and empirical or positivistic science. For disillusioned Freudians like Jeffrey Masson, this constitutes an act of bad faith on the part of a Freud, who was overanxious to distance himself from the disturbing actualities of medical malpractice (the bloody affair of Emma's nose)[11] and the historical reality of nineteenth-century child abuse; it represents the desire of the theorist to ignore what lay under his own nose. But it is possible to impugn Freud for his sexual politics without losing sight of the radical effects of psychoanalytic theory. Its rejection of unmediated, one-to-one causal connections between the contingencies of personal, family, and national history on one hand and the unconscious on the other is what has proved most enduring, as well as most disturbing, about psychoanalysis in general, but particularly with regard to theorizing sexual difference. Femininity, psychoanalysis tends to suggest, is neither the sum of women's social oppression, nor predicated biologically or anatomically on the body. An alternative, feminist reading of Freud's dandelion phantasy might proceed, not by reinstituting the literal intervention of seduction (as Masson does) but rather by interrogating the text of memory as a seduction myth.

Freudian theory is often said to have a "blind spot" in relation to femininity. Freud's appropriation of Greek myth also has a blind spot, an oedipal blindness. Nineteenth-century Hellenism, the cultural determinant of Freud's psychoanalytic mythmaking, offers one route to uncovering the hidden sexual biases of cultural history as well as providing a less ad hominem indictment of Freudian theory than Masson's. Freud's letter to Fliess of May 31, 1897, records a dream about having "overaffectionate feelings for Mathilde" (his daughter), "only she was called Hella; and afterward I again saw 'Hella' before me, printed in heavy type."[12] Hella, it appears, was the name of Freud's American niece. But his daughter Mathilde, Freud tells us, might also be called "Hella" because "she recently shed bitter tears over the defeats of the Greeks. She is enthralled by the mythology of ancient Hellas." She is a young Greek girl, in love with the past of Greek myth. For Freud, the dream "shows the fulfilment of my wish to catch a *Pater* as the originator of neurosis" (the word "originator," incidentally, is the one that Freud had also used to describe his seductive nurse). One might say that Freud's dream fulfills his wish to find the seduction theory true (even at the cost of accusing himself), despite the fact that he was on the verge of letting it go. But what about this allusion to "the mythology of ancient Hellas"—the mythology that came so readily to hand soon afterwards when Freud moved, by way of his memories of mother, nurse, and cupboard, to the conviction of the universality of the Oedipus complex and to his abandonment of the seduction theory. Freud's denial of the role of the parent as seducer and his corresponding emphasis on the unconscious desires of the child depend on the privileging of one myth (the oedipal) over another (call it the preoedipal). The residual pathos of the dandelion phantasy may not be merely a matter of repressed autobiography; rather, it may be a sign that what this memory screens is the unexplored myth of psychoanalysis to which feminists have appealed in their quest for lost mother-daughter relations. This cultural myth makes the dandelion phantasy into what Freud calls a *"universal event of early childhood,"* or a "universal" feminist memory.

What else but the rape of Proserpine by Pluto is so calculated as to make those yellow flowers bloom with hallucinatory brightness—what but this mythic seduction underwrites the archetypal violence and sacrificial pathos of the scene? "As though by mutual agreement, we—the two boys—fall on her and snatch away her flowers. She runs up the meadow in tears." Ovid's *Metamorphoses* book 5 and *Fasti* 4 both provide versions of the rape of Proserpine. *Metamorphoses* is brief enough to quote as an illustration of the powerful literary motif that gives the dandelion phantasy its resonance and its freight of more than autobiographical affect, making it a poignant glimpse of the loss of preoedipal innocence as it affects, not sons, but daughters:

> There spring is everlasting. Within this grove Proserpine was playing, and gathering violets or white lillies. And while with girlish eagerness she was filling her basket and her bosom, and striving to surpass her mates in gathering, almost in one act did Pluto see and love and carry her away: so precipitate was his love. The terrified girl called plaintively on her mother and her companions, but more often upon her mother. And since she had torn her garment at its upper edge, the flowers which she had gathered fell out of her loosened tunic; and such was the innocence of her girlish years, the loss of her flowers even at such a time aroused new grief.[13]

The account in Ovid's *Fasti* gives still greater prominence to Proserpine's flower picking (in some versions of the story her flowers are poppies, emblem of forgetfulness). And who sees Proserpine gathering flowers? "Her father's brother," Pluto (brother of Jupiter). For "father's brother," or uncle, we have to read "father" in at least one of Freud's *Studies on Hysteria* from the same period ("Katharina," for instance, which he later acknowledged had screened an incestuous seduction attempt on the part of a father).[14] This is not to say that Freud consciously or unconsciously "screens" the father's (uncle's) part in the dandelion phantasy, but rather that— just as the work of memory may be "tendentious"—all appropriations of myth in a theoretical context are tendentious, motivated at least as much by the wish to forget as by the wish to remember.

Selecting the Oedipus myth as his vantage point for undoing the empiricism of psychiatric medicine, Freud simultaneously writes into his theory the sexual politics that consigns the preoedipal to forgetfulness. His inability to "read" the dandelion phantasy as a screen for paternal desire reveals the tendency, or tendentiousness—its masculinist and patriarchal self-interest—that has rendered psychoanalysis traditionally suspect to feminists. This ideological and theoretical bias goes along with the equally suspect tendency to claim as universal and timeless what is gender-specific and historically determined—the product of power relations that are gender-marked. Sociological defenses of Freud would want to see patriarchal rapine as the hidden but accurate model of relations between the sexes, with incest as the unacknowledged and repressed "norm" of heterosexuality inscribed in the bourgeois family. My intention, however, is not to abandon the realm of psychoanalysis for a sociological account of the oppressive functioning of gender relations in patriarchal culture (but neither is it to privilege the myths of Hellenic culture as timelessly universal). Rather, what intrigues me is the way in which literature provides the pre-text for psychoanalytic theory. Scratch a screen memory and you find a myth; scratch a myth and you find literature. But literature too has a historical context. One might speculate that in humanist high culture, Sophoclean tragedy ranks above Ovidean retelling of myth. In this literary or textual economy, the male actor gets assigned to tragedy (a "strong" form that normalizes violent contingency as moral justice) while the female actress gets assigned to pathos (a "weak" form that makes passive suffering aesthetically acceptable). The question one might well ask is whether feminist criticism has unwittingly adopted this literary pathos as its own pervasive matrilinear fiction.

The story that Freud "forgets"—the story screened by the Oedipus myth—is not simply the story of the preoedipal, but the main narrative of a nostalgic feminism. The dandelion phantasy screens the rape of the girl child (Proserpine/Kore) from her mother (Ceres/Demeter) by the patriarchal father (Pluto/Hades). In psychoanalytic terms, this is the dark underside of the Oedipus complex, or rather, the price paid by women for the civilizing effect of the Oedipus complex on men. The story could be summarized as the girl's rejection of her mother for failing to equip her with a penis and the forcible transfer of love from her first maternal object to a heterosexual love object, by way of incestuous desire for the father. Adrienne Rich in *Of Woman Born: Motherhood as Experience and Institution* (1976) calls this rupture of mother-daughter relations in the interests of patriarchal society "the great unwritten story": "Before sisterhood, there was the knowledge—transitory, fragmented, perhaps, but original and crucial—of mother-and-daughterhood."[15] *Of Woman Born* is a history of bodily expropriation underwritten by the myth of the mother's mourning for her lost daughter and the daughter's mourning for the loss of her nurturing mother. Though there may be strategic effectiveness in the use to which the myth is put by both Rich and, before her, by Phillis Chesler in *Women and Madness* (1973), I want to question not only its implicit psychic utopianism (Can women ever be whole? Can mothers and daughters ever be united in a sacramental "mother-and-daughterhood" without going back to the womb?) but also its status as universal feminist "memory." Rich's ecological feminism urges us to rethink, by an act akin to remembering, our alienated relations to our bodies, our war-torn world, and our natural resources. Chesler—the Cassandra-like voice of the professional feminist therapist—is a bearer of bad news about the institution of psychiatry, recalling the lives lost to madness in a culture where femininity enjoins mental illness, self-division, and passivity. Even as they indict the institutional effects of patriarchy on women's bodies and minds, both Rich and Chesler imply the possibility of a utopian state in which our relations to the body could be unalienated, and our psychic state whole.

Mothers and myths of origins have the same function, which may in the end be to remind us that something is always lost in stories of the constitution of the subject, whether we call it the body or an undivided self. Feminism has tried to supply this lack by making the mother the unremembered heroine of the psychoanalytic text—she who would make it whole if we could only tell the entire unexpurgated story. Both Chesler and Rich make highly politicized appeals to the Eleusinian cult of Demeter as a source of authority for their own writing. But even as they mobilize the mythic mother for their respective politics, Chesler and Rich perpetuate a new myth. For Chesler, Demeter has lost her daughters to marriage, patriarchy, and psychiatric rape; this is the narrative of a fall.[16] For Rich, the earth mother conjures into being a utopian vision of lost maternal power regained.[17] In the writing of both, the feminist restoration of sanity and strength would come by way of a form of memory remarkably like the fantasy which Freud calls "the phallic mother," the figure of a woman who (still) possesses the phallus. This would be the story of "*m*," the mother whose immunity from castration (according to Freud's own theory) has the function of assuaging masculine castration anxiety. Paradoxically, the mother-centered feminist narrative developed by Rich and Chesler as an alternative to Freud's father-centered narrative risks reinscribing the fiction of the uncastrated woman who defends against castration anxiety—but does so at the price of denying sexual difference. If the mother is phallic, then there is nothing but masculinity after all; women are really men. To re-member the phallic mother is to forget the lesson of originary dismemberment recalled in another pregnant line of Rich's poem: "But in fact we were always like this, / rootless, dismembered."

iii. Expropriating Myth

Is there, then, no way for feminists to answer Woolf's call to "think back through our mothers" without falling into the fetishist's refusal of sexual difference—no way to read the myth of Proserpine, as it were, "beyond Oedipus"? In an essay called "Beyond Oedipus: The Specimen Story of Psychoanalysis," Shoshana Felman calls attention to Freud's self-analysis in the Fliess correspondence ("the specimen story") as "a new way of writing one's autobiography, by transforming personal narration into a pathbreaking theoretical discovery."[18] As Felman goes on to point out, "the discovery that emerges out of the narration is itself referred back to a story that confirms it: the literary drama of the destiny of Oedipus." Like the mother in the cupboard, the structure is at once circular and self-contained ("Myth in Freud is not . . . external to the theory; but the very vehicle of theory"[19]). In her Lacanian reading of the Oedipus story, what Felman sees as the internal splitting of theory—its break with itself and its origins—is embodied by myth itself, the element in theory that simultaneously "expropriates it from its truth, and at the same time founds it as 'a fictitious truthful structure.'" Psychoanalytic theory involves the expropriation of the myth that founds it. Accordingly, Felman reads the myth of Oedipus not as "the myth of the possession of a story, but the myth . . . of the dispossession by the story."[20] In the production of knowledge or "science," she insists, there is always a moment of such necessary forgetting ("insofar as it embodies its own forgetting . . . the Oedipus myth constitutes the science of psychoanalysis"). Psychoanalysis can only (mis)take itself for a science when it "*forgets* the fictive, generative, moment of its birth, when it forgets that its owes its creativity—the production of its knowledge—to a myth."[21] The expropriation of the Oedipus myth embodies the misremembering of just such a founding or generative fiction in Freudian theory.

The myth "screened" by the Oedipus story (the rape of Proserpine) is a story of rape or expropriation. The story of Prosperpine and Ceres (Kore and Demeter) could also be read—"expropriated"—as a myth of the alienation between the myth and itself, or the necessary breach between the theory and the fiction on which it is founded. In the story as it is often read, expropriation and division are naturalized and put to generative purposes; the girl must leave her mother if she is to become a mother in turn. This is the consoling face of the mythic rape that serves to found heterosexist patriarchy. The story of Proserpine might thus be read as the myth that unpacks the function of the Oedipus myth in psychoanalytic theory, which is to convert a fictional hypothesis into a universal law of the (masculine) subject while erasing the question of mother-daughter relations. All theory is expropriated myth, all myth expropriated memory. But memory itself (as we have seen) is only myth. There is no unified, self-complete, undivided theory (nor, for that matter, is there a true memory); both theory and memory fold back on themselves to reveal a rift—something not self-identical. The implications of this rift are important for psychoanalytic theory in general, since they serve to undermine the idea of any pure or unitary moment, truth, or origin. But they are also important for feminist psychoanalytic theory, since they call into question the notion of a preoedipal phase of unmediated mother-child relations. There never was a prior time, or an unmediated relation for the subject (whether masculine or feminine), except as the oedipal defined it retroactively. The mother is already structured as division by the oedipal; no violent separation can be envisaged without an aura of pathos, because separation is inscribed from the start ("Birth stripped our birthright from us . . .").

But to say that there is a problem with the sustaining fantasy of a good-enough mother who might undo the daughter's rape (with Rich) or save her from the mental institutions of patriarchal power (with Chesler) is not to disavow its powerful nostalgia. As feminists, we cannot deny this yearning for a lost past any more than we can overlook the pathos of the dandelion phantasy. Nostalgia, indeed, may be regarded not only as a powerful symptom, but as one peculiarly enjoined on women and therefore worth investigating. Freud invokes nostalgia in relation to masculine fantasies of recovering the mother's body in his essay on "The Uncanny" ("'Love is homesickness'"). Could there be a sense in which nostalgia relates specifically to femininity? Writing of Lacan's classic essay "The Signification of the Phallus," Jane Gallop emphasizes the significance of the word "nostalgia" for Lacan himself. Lacan makes the castration complex for both men and women (boys and girls) turn on the perception of the mother's lack—she has no phallus; she is already divided (she has no third member)—rather than making it arise, as in more orthodox Freudian accounts, in response to desire for the mother and paternal prohibitions on incest. Only in the light of this perceived lack does castration take on its psychic reality for boys, and penis envy for girls. But where desire is joined to threat for the boy, it is joined to nostalgia for the girl.[22] As Gallop puts it, "the boy's fear of losing what he has as the mother lost hers" is matched by "the female's regret for what she does not have (any longer)"; the boy's fear is matched by feminine nostalgia. "Man's desire will henceforth be linked by law to a menace; but woman's desire will legally cohabit with nostalgia."[23] The usual distinction is between threat on one hand and deprivation on the other. Lacan's rereading of Freud unexpectedly substitutes the term "nostalgia" for the deprivation generally associated with the operation of the castration complex on women. Gallop reads Lacan's essay autobiographically, in the light of Lacan's own nostalgia for the earlier moment in psychoanalytic theory that provides the starting point for his discussion of sexual difference, the "great debate" of 1928–32 over feminine sexuality. In this doubling of autobiographical and theoretical concerns, she finds something that takes Lacan not so much "beyond Oedipus" (as in Felman's reading of Freud) as beyond the stalemate over penis envy—back, in short, to femininity. The Lacanian "return to Freud" is not only nostalgic, but produces a redefinition of feminine desire as nostalgia.

Gallop defines nostalgia as something that accompanies a moment of retrospection; as "*Nachträglicheit*"—"Nostalgia here is a regret for a lost past that occurs as a result of a present view of that past moment." Similarly, the nostalgia of penis envy "does not simply accompany the moment of castration, but rather is a retroactive effect . . . . It is not that the girl experiences loss but rather that, looking back . . . she feels regret."[24] Memory (of what has never been lost) is constitutive of nostalgia—just as one might say that the oedipal is constitutive of the preoedipal; or, as Gallop writes, "Loss is inferred on the basis of a retrospective view that sees the past as fuller than the present. Something must have been lost." Freudian theory says that this perception of loss on the part of the girl is perceived loss of the phallus that the boy (still) has; feminist theory (in turn and in reaction) prefers to see this retrospective perception of loss as mourning for the lost mother. Gallop goes on to point out that "*nostalgie*," in its French form, is primarily defined as (1) haunting regret for one's native land, or homesickness; and (2) melancholy regret, or unsatisfied desire. In the essay on "The Uncanny," Freud claims that, psychoanalytically speaking, homesickness is longing to return to the lost home (womb) of the mother (sense 1). But unless she is fantasized as the phallic mother, the mother is always lost, the subject forever abroad. Or, as Gallop puts it,

> the discovery that the mother does not have the phallus means that
> the subject can never return to the womb. Somehow the fact that
> the mother is not phallic means that the mother as mother is lost
> forever, that the mother as womb, homeland, source, and ground-
> ing for the subject is irretrievably past. The subject is hence in a
> foreign land, alienated. [25]

For Lacan, desire itself is always the offshoot of a need that "finds itself alienated"—always a state of melancholy or unsatisfied desire (sense 2). This alienated
need is the nostalgia of feminism. Paradoxically, it is a nostalgia rooted in the
desire to forget the irretrievability of "the mother as mother"; the mother (the
phallus) is not only always lost but never possessed, always a sign of alienation.

When Rich's "Transcendental Etude" speaks of homesickness—"*Homesick for
myself, for her*"—the term is synonymous with desire ("the fluted vault of desire").
Desire for the mother is desire doubled, the revelation of unlimited desire between
women—"two women, eye to eye / measuring each other's spirit, each other's /
limitless desire." In Rich's poem, the Vermont landscape is "Hesperidean," a green
and paradisal world, its young deer not yet menaced by weekend hunters. This is
the very note of nostalgia, or what Rich calls the melodic "ground-note" of infancy
("the simple line / of a woman's voice singing a child / against her heart"). Women's
"homesickness for a woman, for ourselves" provides the ground for this imaginary
memory of the mother's lullaby. But Rich's poem goes on to speak of the inevitabil-
ity, for the survivor intent on forging a new language, of "the cutting-away of an
old force that held her / rooted to an old ground." This uprooting is what Rich
elsewhere, and more politically, calls "the will to change." If we were always "rootless, dismembered," at least "knowing it makes the difference." But in what sense,
we may be entitled to ask, is Rich's étude "transcendental"? Ostensibly its movement beyond knowledge is a movement back to the experiential (but for Felman,
we may recall, "the narrative movement of the myth is precisely that which always
takes us—if we dare go with it—*beyond itself*").[26] Although science or knowledge
as Felman defines them can never lay claim to their truth (or we to ours), still the
truth of literature exceeds itself. There could be a saving rift in Rich's natural
bedrock, the bedrock of her concluding image.

The last movement of "Transcendental Etude" opens with a simile that is also
a narrative: "as if a woman quietly walked away / from the argument. . . ." Walking
away from the argument means, here, patiently turning over the personal detritus

of memory that compose a woman's life ("bits of yarn, calico and velvet scraps," shells, skeins of milkweed, petunia petals, seaweed, cats' whiskers, bird feathers). These are "the finest findings"—the mnemonics or *objets trouvés*—in which a woman "finds herself" where she is not, or no longer. Memory is less "found" than fabricated out of such stuff. Consciousness is a patchwork rather than a seamless web. "Such a composition has nothing to to with eternity," or with wholeness; it has to do with temporality and fragments. What sustains a life imagined in these terms is not "the will to mastery" (or so Rich argues, ever tenacious of her theme) but the will to change—the deeply held beliefs that tug the poem apart even as Rich tries to pull it harmoniously together ("pulling the tenets of a life together / with no mere will to mastery"). While I question Rich's too-dichotomized privileging of lived experience over will-to-mastery, and of feminine particularity over masculine transcendence (not least because such privileging is at odds with the always thought-driven movement of her own mind and poetry), I want to expropriate her poem as a reminder that the text of memory is a mnemonic for remaking, or making over, the past—"the many-lived, unending / forms" in which, as women, we both find and lose our forgotten selves. Memory in Rich's poem is a mnemonic for the will to change, or feminist politics in its retrospective, nostalgic mode. Feminist nostalgia, after all, looks back not only to what feminism desires, but to what it desires different, and differently, both now and in the future.[27]

1. Adrienne Rich, *The Dream of a Common Language* (New York: Norton, 1978).

2. See "Female Sexuality," 1931 (SE 21.226).

3. Jeffrey Moussaieff Masson, *The Complete Letters of Sigmund Freud to Wilhelm Fliess* (Cambridge, MA, and London: Harvard University Press, 1985), 246.

4. Masson, *Complete Letters*, 272.

5. Ibid., 270.

6. See Jim Swan, "*Mater* and Nannie: Freud's Two Mothers and the Discovery of the Oedipus Complex," *American Imago* 31 (1974): 33.

7. Masson, *Complete Letters*, 268–69.

8. Ibid., 269.

9. Ibid., 269.

10. Ibid., 338.

11. Ibid., 116–27.

12. Ibid., 249.

13. Ovid, *Metamorphoses*, trans. Frank Justus Miller (London: William Heinemann, 1916), 2: 265–67.

14. See *SE* 2.134 n.

15. Adrienne Rich, *Of Woman Born: Motherhood as Experience and Institution* (New York: Norton, 1976), 225.

16. See Phyllis Chesler, *Women and Madness* (New York: Avon, 1973), xiv–xxiii.

17. Rich, *Of Woman Born*, 238–40.

18. Shoshana Felman, "Beyond Oedipus: The Specimen Story of Psychoanalysis," in *Jacques Lacan and the Adventure of Insight* (Cambridge, MA: Harvard University Press, 1987), 100–101.

19. Felman, "Beyond Oedipus," 151.

20. Ibid., 153.

21. Ibid., 157–58.

22. Jane Gallop, *Reading Lacan* (Ithaca and London: Cornell University Press, 1985), 145.

23. Gallop, *Reading Lacan*, 146.

24. Ibid.,147.

25. Ibid.,148.

26. Felman, "Beyond Oedipus," 158.

27. For a corrective reading of Rich's "Transcendental Etude," see Teresa de Lauretis, *The Practice of Love: Lesbian Sexuality and Perverse Desire* (Bloomington and Indianapolis: Indiana University Press, 1994), 167–71. Noting the elision of maternal and lesbian desire in my reading (and a revealing misquotation), de Lauretis directs her argument about "the maternal imaginary" against "a long history of equivocation on sexual difference between women that not only orthodox psychoanalysis but also the greater part of feminist theory persistently disallows" (*The Practise of Love*, 171). While I would not equate the "carnal enigma" in Rich's poem with sexual difference *between* women (Rich herself gave us the term "lesbian continuum"), it would be hard to miss seeing that this is a lesbian love poem. De Lauretis's remarks on memory and deferred action (*Nachträglichkeit*) are particularly apposite to a more extended reading of "Transcendental Etude" in terms of a fantasmatic relation to the mother than I have attempted here.

2

In Parenthesis
Immaculate Conceptions and Feminine Desire

A PARENTHESIS, according to the Oxford English Dictionary is both "An explanatory or qualifying word, clause, or sentence inserted into a passage with which it has not necessarily any grammatical connexion," and a rhetorical figure—"A passage introduced into a context with which it has no connexion, a digression"; a figure defined by Puttenham as a "figure of tolerable disorder." The gap between feminine desire and conception, and between conception and maternal desire, constitutes just such a disordering figure. What it disorders is our sense of a unified, coherent subject; it confronts us instead with the irreducibility of a body that is only metonymically linked to desire. The disordering figure—the intrusion of biology into the psychic realm—applies ultimately to sexuality itself, viewed as a threshold between the psychic and the somatic. An earlier age than ours tended to believe that feminine pleasure and conception went together; but as Thomas Laqueur has argued persuasively, a divorce was effected at the end of the century of Enlightenment, when medical science could no longer link the two.[1] I want to argue that this divorce has a specifically disordering effect on conceptions of the feminine subject; and that attempts to remarry feminine pleasure, or desire, and conception, are motivated not only by the wish to reappropriate femininity under the aspect of maternity, but also by a fundamentally theological imperative to maintain the integrity of the subject.

I will be discussing three "scenes" or narratives of reproduction that bear on the distinction between feminine desire and conception. My first is Heinrich von Kleist's "The Marquise of O——" (1808), in which Kleist reads the pregnant body as a sign of unconscious feminine desire despite his portrayal of sexuality as a disordering figure; my second narrative involves Freud's difficulty in accounting for feminine sexuality at all in *Three Essays on the Theory of Sexuality* (1905) and his final reliance on a teleology derived from masculine sexuality; my third instance is the contemporary debate about surrogate motherhood prompted in America by the Mary Beth Whitehead case, read in the light of Pope John Paul II's pronouncements on artificial fertilization and reproduction and Julia Kristeva's analysis of the cult of the Virgin Mary. My aim in linking these three representations of femininity—one literary, one psychoanalytic, and one theological—is to suggest not only the traditional difficulty in specifying feminine desire without appropriating it to maternity (and hence, ultimately, to paternity), but also the problems that arise even when science, in the guise of contemporary biomedical technology, seems finally to have succeeded in freeing feminine pleasure from reproduction. Politically, women have everything to gain from this separation—the right to pleasure without conception, the right to bodily self-determination (whether to contraception or abortion), the right even to surrogacy itself. But this is not to refuse the implications of sexual difference as they manifest themselves in the reproductive process—in the asymmetry between male fertilization and female pregnancy. To take the example of surrogacy, to treat the sperm donor and the surrogate mother as if they were comparable is to reproduce not equality but a traditional, deeply engrained inequality in the position of women vis-à-vis reproduction, discourse, and even the law, as the notorious Baby M. case reveals. For all their unconventional routes to motherhood, I will argue, the Marquise of O——, the Virgin Mary, and Mary Beth Whitehead (Baby M.'s biological mother) figure in a discourse of maternity that is bound to reproduce the Law of the Father.

i. An Oedipal Romance

The main action of Kleist's story "The Marquise of O——" takes place literally "in parenthesis," while the marquise herself is unconscious. A young widow, "a lady of unblemished reputation and the mother of several well-brought-up children,"[2] is surprised by a rabble of Russian soldiers who have stormed the citadel commanded by her father. Just as they are about to gang rape her, she is rescued by a gallant Russian officer, a count, who seems to her like "an angel sent from heaven" (p. 69), addresses her in French, and leads her to safety. Kleist's narrative continues: "stricken speechless by her ordeal, she now collapsed in a dead faint. Then—[the dash marks a missing parenthesis] the officer instructed the marquise's frightened servants, who presently arrived, to send for a doctor; he assured them that she would soon recover, replaced his hat and returned to the fighting" (p. 70). The would-be gang rapists are identified and summarily shot. But before the widow or her family can express their gratitude to the Russian count, he is misreported as having been killed in action; his (supposedly) last words are: "Giulietta! This bullet avenges you!" (p. 73). (Giulietta is the marquise's name.)

Kleist's narrative begins some months later, when the marquise inserts an advertisement in the newspapers to the effect "that she had, without knowledge of the cause, come to find herself in a certain situation; that she would like the father of the child she was expecting to disclose his identity to her; and that she was resolved, out of consideration for her family, to marry him" (p. 68). Kleist's source for the young widow's situation is an anecdote from Montaigne's essay "Of drunkenness" about a French village woman (also a widow) who finds herself unaccountably pregnant. She announces her willingness to marry the father, whereupon a young farmhand of hers comes forward, declaring

> that he had found her, one holiday when she had taken her wine
> very freely, so fast asleep by her fireplace, and in so indecent a pos-
> ture, that he had been able to enjoy her without waking her.[3]

Kleist turns Montaigne's bucolic anecdote into a story of inexplicable passion over-laid by refined sentiment and high familial drama. But the bottom line is the same—a woman's unwitting conception of a child as a result of acquaintance rape. Moreover, in Kleist's story the rape takes place in the space of a narrative absence, not outside nature but outside consciousness. Like a parenthesis, the sexual act resulting in conception is without grammatical or logical connection to its context. Who has lost control here, we might ask—the widow, the Russian count, or Kleist himself? What is the status of a sexual encounter that not only takes place while one party is unconscious and the other in a state of sexual transport, but which must be banished from the story itself?

"The worst condition of man," writes Montaigne, "is when he loses knowl-edge and control of himself."[4] Drunkenness in Montaigne's essay is an instance of the will overcome by passion. Yet drinking in Montaigne's essay is also placed on the side of pleasure and desire, connected both with the dizzy exploits of war and with the poet's imaginative frenzy—with a form of madness defined as "any trans-port, however laudable, that transcends our own judgment and reason; inasmuch as wisdom is an orderly management of our soul."[5] By implication at least, the type of madness is not so much drunkenness as sexuality—sexuality defined as a figure for disorder of the soul. Montaigne asks (in Horace's words) "if wine can storm the very fort of wisdom".[6] In Kleist's story the storming of a fortress leads to the storming of a woman; clearly the exploits of war and the transports of sexual desire are adjacent. Kleist has the count make amends for "the one ignoble action he had committed in his life" (p. 77) by returning unexpectedly to press his suit on the marquise and her astonished family—without, however, confessing his crime ("All were agreed that . . . he seemed to be accustomed to taking ladies' hearts, like fortresses, by storm" [p. 79]). Although reluctant at first, the young widow (as yet unaware of her pregnancy) finally consents to an engagement; but before the marriage can take place, the count leaves on official business. To her consternation, the marquise's pregnancy meanwhile becomes evident; her father points a gun at her and she quits his house for her country estate, taking her children with her. This is how things stand when the count returns to claim the marquise as his wife, undeterred by the pregnancy that he alone has suspected all along. The newspaper advertisement with which the story opens leaves him no option but to reveal himself to her and her family as her repentant rapist—whereupon she furiously refuses to marry him.

Montaigne's "Of drunkenness" goes some way towards explaining how the gallant Russian count might have rescued the marquise from gang rape only to ravish her himself. Kleist, in fact, tells us more about what motivates the Russian count than about the nature of the marquise's desire for him; indeed, coherent motivation is precisely what she lacks (she has a body instead). We gain access to the count's unconscious processes through the vision of a swan that haunts him during the delirium of his supposedly fatal wound. He remembers

> an occasion on which he had once thrown some mud at this swan, whereupon it had silently dived under the surface and re-emerged, washed clean by the water; that she had always seemed to be swimming about on a fiery surface . . . but that he had not been able to lure her towards him. (p. 82)

We hardly need Freud's observations on "A Special Type of Choice of Object made by Men"(1910) to recognize that the Russian count is in the grip of a fantasy that compels him at once to idealize, to debase, and to rescue the woman he loves: "These various meanings of rescuing in dreams and phantasies can be recognized particularly clearly when they are found in connection with water," writes Freud.

"A man rescuing a woman from the water in a dream means that he makes her a mother, which . . . amounts to making her his own mother" (*SE* 11.174). But what about the marquise's fantasy—*her* unconscious desire? Critics usually come up with the rapist's apology: she must have wanted it anyway.[7] Is it rather the marquise's body that plays the part of the feminine unconscious in Kleist's story? And if she has a body instead of an unconscious, then the marquise is not a desiring subject in the same sense as the count; the only desiring subject in the story becomes a masculine one.

From the marquise's ambivalence and agitation at the count's tumultuous wooing, we might suspect no more than we do from the Russian officer's flushed face after his original rescue of the marquise. In her case, however, the body "knows" what is excluded from both her consciousness and Kleist's narrative. What it knows is glossed by the well-known Freudian formula: child = penis. Before the count's whirlwind courtship, the marquise and her mother have exchanged some frank women's talk. The marquise is suffering from mysterious spells of nausea, giddiness, and fainting fits. She confides to her mother: " 'If any woman were to tell me that she had felt just as I did a moment ago when I picked up this teacup, I should say to myself that she must be with child' " (p. 74). Her mother jokes that "she would no doubt be giving birth to the god of Fantasy." The marquise replies (also jokingly) "that at any rate Morpheus, or one of his attendant dreams, must be the father" (p. 74). Soon after this, the Russian count returns from the dead, "his face a little pale, but looking as beautiful as a young god" (p. 74). If this makes him Morpheus, the marquise is indeed about to give birth to "the god of Fantasy"—the fantasy he has engendered in her. The Russian count dreams of making her a mother (in Freudian terms). By the same token, does the marquise dream of making him a (that is, her) father, the father of her fantasy? In the last resort, the count's function in Kleist's narrative is to give her meaning as a woman—filling her empty O with his child. But what she signifies is *his* (masculine) desire. The fulfillment of this desire rounds off the story with its domestication of sexuality-as-reproduction, or happy ending.

In Kleist's narrative, the progress of the marquise's pregnancy amounts to a discourse of the maternal body—the site where the feminine unconscious speaks. After the count has won her consent to the marriage and departed on his official mission, the marquise begins to notice "an incomprehensible change in her figure" (p. 85). She calls in a doctor, and "jestingly told him what condition she believed herself to be in" (p. 86). When he confirms her diagnosis she is outraged, threatening to report him to her father. As he leaves in a huff, she pleads: " 'But, Doctor, how is what you say possible?' " The doctor replies "that she would presumably not expect him to explain the facts of life to her" (p. 86). Yet this seems to be the case; after the doctor's visit the marquise tells her mother that although her conscience is clear, she must now consult a midwife: " 'A midwife!' exclaimed the commandant's wife indignantly, 'a clear conscience and a midwife!' And speech failed her"(p. 88)—just as words had failed Kleist at the crucial moment that engendered his story. Either the marquise has invented "a fable about the overturning of the whole order of nature" (p. 89), or (as the midwife puts it) "young widows who found themselves in her ladyship's position always believed themselves to have been living on desert islands" (p. 90); here the marquise faints for the second time. "With a faltering voice," the marquise then asks the midwife "what the ways of nature were, and whether such a thing as an unwitting conception was possible." Not in her case, replies the midwife; "with the exception of the Blessed Virgin, it had never yet happened to any woman on earth" (p. 91).

An attentive reader of Kleist's story knows by this stage that the marquise conceived her child not outside the realm of nature, but in the parenthetical moment that is excluded both from her consciousness and from Kleist's story. In Kleist's own discourse, it seems that feminine sexuality, however mediated, can never fully submit to textuality. The woman's body—the hollow, open "O——" signified by the marquise's name—remains the site of something at once undecidable and contradictory, in excess of narrative.[8] Just as desire interrupts consciousness as a wordless rift—as madness rather than reason—so conception gives rise to the absurd nonsense that the marquise must talk to herself, her mother, her doctor, and her midwife. Kleist could have specified exactly what took place between the marquise and her rescuer if he wished to do so. Why then his reticence—a reticence that mimes the marquise's double consciousness (that she is pregnant, but that her pregnancy is either a joke or a miracle)? I want to suggest not simply that Kleist saw in Montaigne's bucolic anecdote the potential for a highly wrought Romantic drama of feminine denial and silenced desire, but rather, that feminine sexuality in Kleist's story can only be recuperated for narrative under the aegis of an oedipal conception familiar to modern readers from the writings of Freud.

The unwritten story in "The Marquise of O——" is not so much rape as a difficulty (analogous to Freud's) in accounting for feminine sexuality at all. Kleist solves the problem, as Freud was to do a century later, by subordinating femininity to the Law of the Father. When the count presents himself in answer to the marquise's newspaper advertisement, the marquise—in her father's words, "hysterical"—no longer sees him as an angel, but as a devil. We might take the commandant's adjective seriously for a moment. Hysteria, for Freud, means body language, the conversion of unconscious sexual desire into physical symptoms, of which hysterical pregnancy is one. Dora's hysterical pregnancy occurs exactly nine months after delivering her slap of rejection to Herr K.—a hysterical pregnancy interpreted by Freud as the wish that things had gone otherwise, and ultimately as displaced desire for the father. What is the marquise's "hysterical" predicament in Kleist's story? Like Dora's rejection of Herr K., her refusal of the count when he reveals himself as the father of her child could be read as masking unacknowledged desire for the father. The subtext of Kleist's story would thus equate feminine desire and oedipal desire, making this the informing ideological narrative that is placed in parenthesis from the start.

I want to turn for support to a scene depicting the reunion of the marquise and her father, surely among the most extravagant scenes in the story. When the marquise places her advertisement in the newspaper, her mother decides that the time has come for reconciliation. Convincing herself of the marquise's innocence by a simple ruse, she brings the marquise back to the paternal home. A tearful scene ensues between father and daughter; the commandant's wife leaves them alone together, and when we next see them, the marquise "with her head thrown back and her eyes tightly shut, was lying quietly in her father's arms, while the latter, with tears glistening in his wide-open eyes, sat in the armchair, pressing long, ardent, avid kisses on to her mouth, just like a lover!" (p. 107). Here the father acts the part of the battle- and desire-drunk count (perhaps the marquise has fainted again). In an obvious sense, this later scene stands in for the passionate sexual encounter that Kleist had consigned to the parenthesis at the start of his story. But the model of feminine desire that we glimpse here is unmistakably oedipal—the wish not to be, but to have the child of her father which (in the Freudian narrative) impels the little girl into the Oedipus complex, into heterosexuality and finally, faute de mieux, into maternity. It is not just that Kleist must transform feminine desire into maternal desire in order to meet the conditions of representability, rather the height of representable passion turns out to be an oedipal encounter between father and (fantastically pregnant) daughter. Kleist's story seems to suggest that every unconscious desire will yield up at the moment of its conception not simply the masculine desire to turn a woman into a mother, but the feminine desire that is all too readily subsumed under the sign of the daughter's unconscious desire for her father's child. In Kleist's story, the disordering figure of sexual trans-port is not only chanelled toward reproduction, but ultimately ordered by the Law of the Father.

ii. Instincts and Their Vicissitudes

Freud's difficulty in conceptualizing feminine desire as other than oedipal, and maternal desire as other than desire for the penis, scarcely needs elaborating.[9] I want now to recapitulate the story that he himself calls "Instincts and their Vicissitudes" (the title of his 1915 essay) and that he tells at greater length in the earlier, much revised *Three Essays on the Theory of Sexuality*. This is a story not unlike Kleist's "Marquise of O——" in suggesting, contradictorily, the perverse and disordered qual-ity of sexuality—its objectlessness and its severence from reproductive aim—while superimposing on this original aberrancy a teleology whereby the sexual instinct is always in quest of normative biological reproduction. Freud argues that the sexual instinct at first wanders eccentrically from the paths laid down by the organism, but that in the end, it aims purposively at the continuance of the species by way of hetero-sexual intercourse. That purposiveness might be called the romance of the penis; like all romantic quests, its parentheses and digressions are finally ordered by a telos or end that organizes Freudian theory into a coherent narrative about the relation between sexual desire and reproduction.

For Freud, instinct ("*Trieb*"), biologically considered, lies "on the frontier between the mental and the somatic" (*SE* 14.121–22); instinct itself, however, is already a psychical representation.[10] As far as mental life is concerned, nothing is really outside the realm of (psychosexual) representation. Yet the problem of biol-ogy remains—surfacing for women in the contentious region of penis envy, the bedrock of femininity that for Freud himself finally constituted "a biological fact."[11] For men, biology surfaces in the special case of sexual reproduction. The story told by *Three Essays on the Theory of Sexuality* reveals with particular clarity the diffi-culty of talking about sexual instincts (that is, psychical representations) without falling back into talking about the body, and the masculine body at that. To some recent commentators, however, *Three Essays* also contains the story that cannot be told by Freud himself—a story about what defeats (phallic) representation, chal-lenges teleology, and puts the subject itself in question.

In *The Freudian Body*, Leo Bersani describes sexual excitement, in terms that recall Kleist, as a state when "the organization of the self is momentarily disturbed by sensations of affective processes somehow 'beyond' those compatible with psychic organization."[12] Desire, in Bersani's words, is for "what nearly shatters us, and the shattering experience is, it would seem, *without any specific content*—which may be our only way of saying that the experience cannot be said, that it belongs to the nonlinguistic biology of human life." Psychoanalysis becomes for Bersani "the unprecedented attempt to psychologize that biology [and] to coerce it into discourse."[13] Sexual desire paradoxically unsettles our sense of what it is to be desiring subjects, shattering both consciousness and discourse: psychoanalysis attempts a linguistic recuperation of biology, forcing the body to speak even in parenthesis (the parenthesis that Kleist consigns to narrative silence). We could read "The Marquise of O——" in this light, as an unprecedented attempt to psychologize "the nonlinguistic biology of human life" and coerce it into discourse; an attempt, however, that stumbles into banality precisely where Freud himself does, on the frontier between psychic shattering and the body, the threshold of the unconscious and of biology.

The first of Freud's *Three Essays on the Theory of Sexuality*, "The Sexual Aberrations," consists of a radical onslaught on sexuality, designed to "loosen the bond that exists in our thoughts between instinct and object" (*SE* 7.148). Not only is the sexual instinct independent of an object, but its aim, too, swerves from "the union of the genitals in the act known as copulation" (*SE* 7.149) into paths of perversion or deferral that constitute a veritable map of body surfaces, space, and orifices—skin, mouth, anus, even eye. Typically, the so-called perversions either extend erotogenicity beyond the anatomical regions of the body specifically designed for sexual reproduction, or linger on the intermediary stages without pressing on toward the goal of sexual intercourse (an apt definition of sexuality's end-less diffusion).[14] When in his second essay Freud turns to "Infantile Sexuality," we find that the model for adult sexuality is infantile thumb-sucking, an activity detached from the original somatic function it imitates. While thumb-sucking "attaches itself to"—props itself upon ("*entsteht in Anlehnung an*")—a vital somatic function (feeding), it is no longer linked to the taking of nourishment, but rather to fantasy. Infant auto-eroticism is propped on the mother; adult sexuality is propped on childhood auto-eroticisim and polymorphous perversity. The Lacanian account of sexual desire—in excess of any possible satisfaction, wandering metonymically from one object to another—develops the implications of what is most radical in Freud's *Three Essays*.

In the last of his three essays, Freud attempts finally to account for the normative chanelling of sexuality into reproduction. It is at this point that teleology reenters his story as the romance of the penis. What he calls "The Transformations of Puberty" consist less in rediscovering a lost sexual object than in finding a new heterosexual object and replacing sexual aimlessness with a sexual purpose. But what might such a purpose be *for women*? By this point in *Three Essays*, Freud has had to fall back on a self-admittedly unsatisfactory (and certainly outdated) masculine sexual economy that he calls "the discharge of the sexual products," one in which "the sexual instinct is now subordinated to the reproductive function" (*SE* 7.207). But as Freud himself is forced to acknowledge, an economy of sexual products leaves out of account (among others) children, castrati, and, above all, women; how can the theory be made to fit a nonmasculine genital apparatus? Freud never answers this question. Instead, his account swerves towards a version of "end-pleasure" as opposed to "fore-pleasure" (his terms) resolutely focused on a teleology of the penis. "The finding of an object" means that, "in a man, the penis, which has now become capable of erection, presses forward insistently towards the new sexual aim—penetration into a cavity in the body which excites his genital zone" (*SE* 7.222); just so, presumably, the Russian count pressed forward insistently to penetrate the hollow O figured by the marquise's body. Women, by contrast, are left in Freud's account with the problem of (reproductively nonfunctional) clitoral pleasure, or else with the propensity to vaginal frigidity that a puzzled Freud came to view as "intimately related to the essence of femininity" (*SE* 7.221).

Since the only function of the clitoris, according to Freud, is that of "pine shavings . . . kindled in order to set a log of harder wood on fire" (*SE* 7.221), feminine pleasure must remain forever on the side of what Freud calls "fore-pleasure" rather than "end-pleasure"; or, if you like, on the side of perverse rather than purposive sexuality. In an earlier passage, Freud has seen the "average uncultivated woman" as tending naturally toward the condition of the prostitute, which is that of infantile sexuality, or polymorphous perversity.[15] Feminine sexuality, therefore, comes to occupy an anomalous and contradictory position in Freud's thinking in *Three Essays*. Either feminine sexual pleasure (that is, clitoral pleasure) is repressed altogether as the high price of conforming to phallic needs, or it is permanently consigned to the realm of the perverse and the aimless (the infantile and polymorphous perversity that Freud associates especially with the prostitute). In short, it remains unaccountable because it can never be fully subsumed into a penile telos—it undoes the happy ending of Freud's romance while forever threatening to disjoin sexuality from reproduction.

Where does this leave women vis-à-vis not just sexual pleasure, but maternal desire? The answer will be cast in entirely oedipal terms when Freud returns a quarter of a century later to the mystery of femininity, and tries to account for the question of both feminine and maternal desire in terms of the unconscious wish to possess the father's penis (= baby). It is this instinct—this "psychical representation"—that forms the specifically feminine subplot to the masculine romance of the penis. A teleology of feminine sexuality is finally achieved by way of archaeology; maternal desire becomes the overlay of infantile penis envy. "In this way," Freud concludes, "the ancient masculine wish for the possession of a penis is still faintly visible through the femininity now achieved" (*SE* 22.128). Freud's drastic solution (penis envy) not only accounts for what is specific and problematic in the girl's passage through the Oedipus complex as he defines it; his solution also provides a retrospective explanation for what would otherwise be unaccountable in "the transformations of puberty"—namely, the connection for women (as opposed to men) between sexuality and reproduction. Yet for all his later attempts to marry maternal desire to an oedipal construction of femininity, Freud's radical perception about the perverse errancy of feminine sexuality continues to undermine his story, much as the parenthetical moment of radical disorder in Kleist's story undermines the Romantic reproductive telos of "The Marquise of O——". Reading Freud and Kleist together, we glimpse in the parentheses of a masculine economy the possibility of a feminine sexuality so radically disjoined from reproduction as to create a rift in both subjectivity and narrative. The parenthetical figure of femininity makes nonsense of both their stories.

iii. The Holy Family

My third scene for the disjunction between feminine pleasure and procreation involves the one represented by science itself, in the form of the contemporary application of biomedical technology to human reproduction. The theological issues involved in the formation of what sociologists have termed "the artificial family"[16]—the practice of AID (artificial insemination by donor), IVF (in vitro fertilization), and surrogacy—are not in themselves new, since they abut on earlier debates about artificial birth control. The same definitions of the individual (the subject) and of marriage (sexuality) that have traditionally underpinned the opposition of the Catholic Church to contraception and abortion now underpin its opposition to artificial reproduction. I want, however, to suggest that the theological debate about artificial reproduction and fertilization also bears on questions of subjectivity and language, and that these may be evident in the drama played out in the American courts during recent years about what has come to seem (and not only for feminists) the most problematic way to form an artificial family, namely, surrogate motherhood.

Ironically, the first artificial family was the Holy Family. The Virgin Mary herself constitutes the most famous (not to say miraculous) instance of the surrogacy arrangement, at least in the New Testament. Even Catholics would have to concede that God himself set a precedent for third-party intervention between husband and wife. Historians of the cult of the Virgin Mary have pointed out that the Virgin Birth was from the outset a vexed question, even for Christians, and sometimes had to be defended against scurrilous stories (presumably on the lines of Montaigne's bucolic anecdote). The most ingenious of the myths about the origin of Christ (Origen's, in fact) was that he was conceived through the ear by means of the logos at the Annunciation—a case of apostrophic conception ("Hail Mary . . ."). But when one thinks about it, this theory is no odder than the more familiar view that an androgynous Holy Spirit disguised as a dove descended on the Virgin Mary. Reproductively speaking, the Virgin's role becomes that of sublime incubator for the Word; or else, as theories of reproduction changed, provider of the material or bodily element necessary for the Incarnation.[17] In time, it also became standard Catholic doctrine to deny not only any loss of virginity on Mary's part but any taint of original sin attending her own birth, in a doctrinal *mise en abime* of purification. The dogma of the Immaculate Conception finally became official in the middle of the nineteenth century, when Pope Pius IX settled the question for good. [18] The age that gave birth to modern feminism and to psychoanalysis also officially consecrated femininity under the sign of a sacred Mother—firmly subordinated, however, to God the Father.

In "Stabat Mater," her essay on the cult of the Virgin Mary, Julia Kristeva argues that the twentieth-century decline in religion has left women without an available discourse of maternity. She asks: what can the (now attenuated) cult of the Virgin Mary tell us about the social and psychic function of the fantasy of motherhood? The distinctively Kristevan aspect of her inquiry is the claim that this fantasy has a specific function in relation to language. Kristeva defines the "maternal" as "an identity catastrophe that causes the Name to topple over into the unnameable that one imagines as femininity, non-language or body."[19] In Marian iconography, milk and tears become "the metaphors of non-speech, of a 'semiotics' that linguistic communication does not account for."[20] Kristeva glimpses in the Virgin Mother "the tremendous territory hither and yon of the parenthesis of language"—something extralinguistic and heterogenous that tends to "re-establish what is non-verbal . . . a signifying disposition that is closer to the so-called primary processes," or to the unconscious—in other words, a return of the (preoedipal) repressed within the Symbolic (the Kristevan "semiotic").[21] This is a form of prelinguistic signification mapped on the body itself in the preoedipal realm where the mother's care for the infant's body installs borders and separations. The mother in Kristevan discourse has a status not unlike that of Freud's "instinct"; she is posited as a psychic representation on the frontier between the mental and the somatic, "a strange fold that changes culture into nature, the speaking subject into biology." As such, she poses a dangerous threat to the notion of subjectivity itself. The cult of the Virgin Mary finally illustrates Kristeva's underlying thesis that "Belief in the mother is rooted in fear, fascinated with a weakness—the weakness of language."[22] Religion, she argues, attempts to overcome this fear by recuperating heterogeneity, via the maternal, for the symbolic system known as the Word—a move that Kristeva is swift to detect since it resembles, paradoxically, her own.

Given its doctrine on marriage, the family, and the rights of the unborn, the Catholic Church was bound to come out strongly against all forms of artificial reproduction.[23] Pope Paul VI in *Humanae Vitae* (1968) rejected any attempt "which would pretend to separate, in generation, the biological activity in the personal relation of the married couple." Or, as Pope Pius XII had already written in a prophetic moment,

> To reduce the shared life of a married couple and the act of married love to a mere organic activity for transmitting semen would be like turning the domestic home, the sanctuary of the family, into a biological laboratory.[24]

(Or like turning the uterus into a petri dish.) Pope John Paul II's more recent "Instruction on Respect for Human Life in its Origins and on the Dignity of Procreation—Replies to Certain Questions of the Day" (1987) simply applies to the current debate formulations derived from these earlier papal statements on contraception and abortion. What is not immediately obvious, however, is why the papal "Instruction" should also involve considerations that are in the last resort linguistic. I want to argue that the Catholic stance on artificial reproduction reflects the same fear that, in Kristeva's analysis, gives rise to the cult of the Virgin mother. The document states in its introduction that the Church's intervention in the field of artificial reproduction is inspired by love for both man and Christ "as she [sic] contemplates the mystery of the Incarnate Word" (note the traditional gendering of the Church). [25] In a text from which the maternal body is otherwise conspicuously absent, we should not be surprised to find the womb or "maternal receptacle" (Kristeva's phrase) functioning here as "a permanent lining" (a necessary complement or supplement) to theological contemplation of the Incarnate Word.

By way of establishing first principles, the papal "Instruction" sets out the relation of what it calls "Anthropology" to "Procedures in the Biomedical Field"—anthropology here defined as "a proper idea of the nature of the human person in his [sic] bodily dimension," which proves to be that of a "'unified totality'" (the phrase is Pope John Paul II's own), or a nature "at the same time corporal and spiritual."[26] Any intervention involving the human body therefore implicates what the papal "Instruction" glosses as "the person himself in his concrete reality." The Pope's argument about artificial reproduction is underwritten by the Church's mission to safeguard this notion of personhood, indivisibly corporeal and spiritual. To admit the possibility of intervention at the level of conception is to threaten—to shatter or disorder—a theory of the subject founded on a traditional unity-in-duality (body and soul as two-in-one). God alone has the right to undo the subject, thus conceived; the same argument applies to abortion. But notice how the body has been re-appropriated. With Kristeva in mind, we might suspect that papal insistence on the importance of the corporeal has the function of recuperating heterogeneity (the Kristevan semiotic, or maternal lining) for the Word in the face of an anxiety about its symbolic poverty. It is the mother—the Virgin Mary—who makes the Word "Incarnate."

The language of "Instruction on Respect for Human Life" becomes most charged with respect to marital relations. AID, we are told, does not "conform to the dignity of the couple and to the truth of marriage" because "it objectively deprives conjugal fruitfulness of its unity and integrity," bringing about "a rupture between genetic parenthood, gestational parenthood, and responsibility for upbringing" that "threatens the unity and stability of the family."[27] Surrogacy is the type of such separation, since it "sets up, to the detriment of families, a division between the physical, psychological, and moral elements which constitute those families."[28]

For the parents, the family is constituted by conjugal fidelity; for the child, it is constituted by continuity between biological and social parenting.[29] Given this definition, it's not surprising that the papal document should have most to say about its ban on "homologous" artificial fertilization (in which both sperm and egg come from the marriage partners themselves, rather than from a third party), even though, on the face of it, "homologous" artificial fertilization seems to contradict neither principle. The argument turns on the connection between procreation and "the conjugal act" (here we are back with Pope Paul VI's 1968 encyclical, *Humanae Vitae*).[30] "The meanings of the conjugal act" (the signified of marriage) and "the goods of marriage" (the signifier) can never be arbitrarily disjoined. Like its view of the subject, the Catholic concept of sexuality depends on that of bodily unity-in-duality, "inseparably corporal and spiritual." What the document calls " 'the language of the body' " (quoting from Pope John Paul II himself), must involve both "spousal meanings" and "parental" ones, sexuality inseparably joined to procreation in a shatterproof subject rather than a petri dish.[31]

In effect, the papal "Instruction" produces a regulated system of signification in which the "goods" of marriage must have only unitary, unambiguous "meanings," and "the language of the body" refers to a specifically theological view of the speaking and desiring subject. "Fertilization achieved outside the body of the couple [i.e., of the woman's body] remains by this very fact deprived of the meanings and the values which are expressed in the language of the body and in the union of human persons."[32] This amounts to saying that artificial reproduction is meaningless—or, alternatively, that meaning can only be unitary and self-identical. Arguably, the underlying threat posed by AID, IVF, and surrogacy is precisely their threat to the Word, since they destabilize imbricated notions of the subject and of language that sustain the entire theological edifice. If goods and meanings are not self-identical—if bodies and words can drift apart, or personal identity ceases to be unified by divine cement, or signifiers and signifieds turn out to have arbitrary rather than natural or God-given relations—then not only does language become an artificial system, but God himself has to be read as mere (phallo) logocentrism. The papal "Instruction" can finally be seen as an attempt to hold the line not just on artificial reproduction but on the subject, and not just on the subject but on language too. Their fragmentation threatens to reveal the disjoined relation between sexuality and reproduction (the radical insight of Freud's *Three Essays*), or the arbitrary relation betwen "goods" and "meanings" (the radical insight of poststructuralist theories of language since Saussure).

Papal views about the organic and spiritual unity of both subjects and signs which sustain the ban on artificial reproduction are unlikely to cut much ice either with poststructuralists or with contemporary feminists of whatever persuasion. But on one issue, that of surrogacy, feminists themselves are deeply divided. Whatever their view of commercial surrogacy, they are understandably reluctant to claim that a mother's biological tie to her baby differs from that of a father. It smacks of essentialism, not to say biologism. But (it might well be argued), the surrogate mother gives up not jut an egg but a baby—nine months' worth of gestation and all that it entails, both physical and psychic. Defenders of surrogacy rejoin sharply (with Judge Sorkow in the Baby M. case) that women have as much right to sell their wombs as men have to sell their sperm. What we see here, however, is not equality with men, but rather a surfacing of the patriarchal thinking that reduces the role of the biological mother to mere provider of a nurturing uterus. As Lee Salk put it, in his role as spokesperson for paternal rights, "The role of parents was achieved by a surrogate uterus and not a surrogate mother";[33] this is what you might call the synecdotal view of surrogacy (part for whole, or the equation of uterine function and maternity) with which feminist historians of the relations between women and the body are all too familiar.[34] Despite the fact that on some level such arguments resonate with feminist views that motherhood is artificially constructed or "reproduced" rather than biologically constituted, they still illustrate once more the socially controlling function that Kristeva ascribes to the cult of the Virgin Mary—its apparent empowering of women, but only at the price of ultimate containment. Although superficially liberated from the confines of the patriarchal family and conjugal fidelity by "the virginal maternal" (Kristeva's phrase), the surrogate mother is finally subsumed under the Law of (God) the Father, or Dr. Salk as the champion of paternal rights.[35]

In other words, the commissioning father in a surrogacy agreement occupies the traditional position of God, and Mary Beth Whitehead was caught up in a battle that was equally obscure to her and to the legal experts on either side of the case—one, moreover, that she was bound to lose, at least initially, given the privileging of the Father in any system of representation that inscribes paternal, oedipal, or divine desire as primary. By shifting the emphasis from the contractual to the custodial—by treating a disputed surrogacy agreement like any other custody squabble—the judge concerned in the Baby M. case may have hoped to offload one set of highly prejudicial concerns connected with biology; but in the process other concerns arose, of which the most obvious were social and economic. Less obvious, however, but equally pervasive, is the ideological subtext that traditionally privileges the father as property holder, as meaning maker, and as desiring subject. It is no accident, in other words, that hot on the heels of the revelation that Mary Beth Whitehead was once a high-school dropout, a welfare mother, and a go-go dancer came testimony to the effect that she was defective as a subject—that she suffered (as the experts claimed) from a variety of so-called personality disorders: narcissism, impulsiveness, lack of contact with reality, overinvolvement with her children, failure to keep appointments for psychological counseling, and, above all, inability to tell the truth, or a duplicitous relation to language (the Sterns' lawyer in the Baby M. case is on record as having set out to prove her "a liar"). The implication is that anyone who agreed to surrogacy in the first place had ceded her claims to full personhood in the papal sense, becoming, as Mary Beth Whitehead herself vividly complained, a mere uterus on legs, and a liar as well.

The only acceptable conception—the only good surrogate uterus—is the one that does away with feminine desire altogether; in any event, the woman loses out. Either she goes quietly and gets her fee plus the everlasting gratitude and forgetfulness of the commissioning couple, or, if she changes her mind, she seems doomed to be the loser in a custody case by virtue of lacking paternal authority. As Kristeva puts it, more abstractly, "Christianity does associate woman with the symbolic community, but only provided they keep their *virginity*. Failing that, they can atone for their carnal *jouissance* with their martydom."[36] Arguably, any feminine subject who permits herself to be identified primarily in terms of a maternal function has put herself in the same position as either the Virgin Mary or Mary Beth Whitehead. And yet, a refusal to acknowledge that one constituent of women's social and economic oppression, as well as of feminine specificity, comprises the intimately intertwined physical, psychic, and social meanings that we know as "maternity" risks ignoring the real nonequivalence of the reproductive process for men and for women. The distinction between femininity and maternity may be crucial for a feminist politics of the body, but recognition of the biological noncomparability of paternity and maternity is equally crucial for any nondiscriminatory social and juridical inscription of sexual difference.[37] Even as women refuse the traditional equation of femininity and motherhood, they may be compelled to make some claims under the sign of maternity in order to protect themselves in the workplace, under the law, and—as I've tried to argue by way of these differing narratives of conception—in the face of the subtle but powerful workings of paternalist sexual ideologies and the symbolic systems that sustain them.

*   *   *

Postscript: The original judgement that stripped Mary Beth Whitehead of her parental rights so that Baby M. could be legally adopted by the commissioning "mother" has since been overturned. Mary Beth Whitehead now has recognized parental rights; she did not, however, get Baby M.—an outcome that reminds us that in an era famous for proclaiming the sanctity of family values, some families are holier than others.

1.   "Near the end of the century of Enlightenment, medical science and those who relied upon it ceased to regard the female orgasm as relevant to generation. Conception, it was held, could take place secretly, with no tell-tale shivers or signs of arousal." Thomas Laqueur, "Orgasm, Generation, and the Politics of Reproductive Biology," in *The Making of the Modern Body: Sexuality and Society in the Nineteenth Century* (Berkeley, Los Angeles, and London: University of California Press, 1987), 1.

2.   Heinrich von Kleist, *The Marquise of O—— and Other Stories*, trans. David Luke and Nigel Reeves (Harmondsworth: Penguin, 1978), 68. Subsequent page references in the text are to this edition.

3.   *The Complete Works of Montaigne*, trans. Donald M. Frame (Stanford: Stanford University Press, 1948), 246.

4.   Ibid., 245.

5.   Ibid., 251.

6.   Ibid., 249.

7.   See, for instance, James M. McGlathery, *Desire's Sway: The Plays and Stories of Heinrich von Kleist* (Detroit: Wayne State University Press, 1983), 81–84 and n. An essay whose publication postdates the original appearance of this one interestingly explores the story of rape as a masculine battleground; see Susan Winnett, "The Marquise's 'O' and the Mad Dash of Narrative," in *Rape and Representation*, ed. Lynn A. Higgins and Brenda R. Silver (New York: Columbia University Press, 1991), 67–86.

8.   See Mary Poovey, " 'Scenes of an Indelicate Character': The Medical 'Treatment' of Victorian Women," in *Uneven Developments: The Ideological Work of Gender in Mid-Victorian England* (Chicago: The University of Chicago Press, 1988), 24–50, for the ways in which the debate provoked by the use of chloroform on women similarly made it the site of contradiction or undecidability. Poovey cites a number of cases where women, while unconscious under the influence of chloroform, shocked medical practitioners with their manifest eroticism—one woman, for instance, reenacting in childbirth "those preliminaries which had led her to the state in which [her medical attendants] now beheld her" (*Uneven Developments*, 31, 211 n).

9.   See, for instance, "Femininity" in *New Introductory Lectures on Psycho-Analysis*, 1933 (*SE* 22.112–35).

10. See also an addition to the 1915 edition of *Three Essays on the Theory of Sexuality*, where Freud refers to instinct as "the psychical representative of an endosomatic, continuously flowing source of stimulation. . . . The concept of instinct is thus one of those lying on the frontier between the mental and the physical" (*SE* 7.168). Elsewhere, however, Freud distinguishes between instinct and its psychical representative; see *SE* 14.112–13. For another discussion of Freud's concept of "*Trieb*," see also Jean Laplanche, *Life and Death in Psychoanalysis*, trans. Jeffrey Mehlman (Baltimore and London: Johns Hopkins University Press, 1976), 8–14.

11. See "Analysis Terminable and Interminable," 1937 (*SE* 23.252).

12. Leo Bersani, *The Freudian Body: Psychoanalysis and Art* (New York: Columbia University Press, 1986), 38.

13. Ibid., 39–40.

14. See *SE* 7.150.

15. "In this respect children behave in the same kind of way as an average uncultivated woman in whom the same polymorphously perverse disposition persists. Under ordinary conditions she may remain normal sexually, but if she is led on by a clever seducer she will find every sort of perversion to her taste, and will retain them as part of her own sexual activities. Prostitutes exploit the same polymorphous, that is, infantile, disposition for the purposes of their profession" (*SE* 7.191).

16. See, for instance, R. Snowden and G. D. Mitchell, *The Artificial Family: A Consideration of Artificial Insemination by Donor* (London: George Allen & Unwin, 1981); see also R. Snowden, G. D. Mitchell, and E. M. Snowden, *Artificial Reproduction: A Social Investigation* (London: George Allen & Unwin, 1983) for a study of the social implications of artificial reproduction.

17. See Marina Warner, *Alone of All Her Sex: The Myth and the Cult of the Virgin Mary* (New York: Alfred A. Knopf, 1976), 34–49.

18. See Warner, *Alone of All Her Sex*, 236–37. See also *The Dogma of the Immaculate Conception: History and Significance*, ed. Edward Dennis O'Connor, C.S.C. (Notre Dame, Indiana: University of Notre Dame Press, 1958).

19. *The Kristeva Reader*, ed. Toril Moi (New York: Columbia University Press, 1986), 162.

20. Ibid., 174.

21. Ibid., 174–75.

22. Ibid., 175.

23. A comic side to the debate is provided by unofficially sanctioned techniques for circumventing the outright ban on artificial fertilization such as the use of a perforated condom; for instance the technique known as GIFT—"Gamete Intra-Fallopian Transfer"—involves extracting an egg, placing it near sperm cells in a catheter and then inserting both into the uterus: "Some Catholics have judged the technique acceptable provided that masturbation is not involved in collection of the sperm. A perforated condom is used during intercourse, with the sperm retrieved from the condom afterward." See marginal discussion and comment by Cardinal Joseph Ratzinger and Father Bartholomew Kiely, "Instruction on Respect for Human Life in Its Origin and on the Dignity of Procreation," *Origins: NC documentary service* 16, no. 40 (1987): 699–700.

24. See Peter Singer and Deane Wells, *Making Babies: The New Science and Ethics of Conceptions*

(New York: Charles Scribner's Sons, 1985), 38. Similarly, the Archbishop of Canterbury's 1945 commission into the practice of AID had recommended that it should be a criminal offense, presumably on the grounds of its implications for marriage; see Snowden and Mitchell, *The Artificial Family*, 15.

25. "Instruction on Respect for Human Life in Its Origin and on the Dignity of Procreation," *Origins* 16, no.40 (1987): 699; subsequent quotations are from this text.

26. Ibid., 700; the quotation is from apostolic exhortation *Familiaris Consortio* (1982).

27. Ibid., 705.

28. Ibid., 705.

29. One surprising implication of the papal "Instruction" is that it should by rights ban adoption too in the interests of consistency—surely an irony in the light of the advocacy of adoption by right-to-lifers as an alternative to abortion.

30. Ratzinger and Keily, "Instruction," 705; Pope Paul VI, Encyclical Letter *Humanae Vitae* (1968).

31. Ratzinger and Keily, "Instruction," 706; General Audience on January 16, 1980: *Insegnamenti di Giovanni Paolo II*.

32. Ratzinger and Keily, "Instruction," 706.

33. Gannett News Service, *Ithaca Journal*, February 11, 1987.

34. See, for instance, Ann Oakley, *The Captured Womb: A History of the Medical Care of Pregnant Women* (Oxford: Basil Blackwell, 1984).

35. See Oakley, *The Captured Womb*, 142: "[monotheism] represents the paternal function: patrilinear descent with transmission of the name of the father . . . is caught in the grip of an abstract symbolic authority which refuses to recognise the growth of the child in the mother's body."

36. *The Kristeva Reader*, 145–46.

37. See Zillah Eisenstein, *The Female Body and the Law* (Berkeley, Los Angeles, and London: University of California Press, 1988), 190–224, and, for the Baby M. case, 192–94. As Eisenstein writes, in a lucid account of the political and economic inequalities of surrogacy, "Treating the biological father as equal in importance to the biological mother in questions of custody may seem like a progressive shifting of the discourse of sex equality. But . . . such treatment can be only partially interpreted as progressive, because surrogacy is constructed within an engendered legal and social system. In surrogacy arrangments thus far, the phallus takes the form of the economically privileged father as the more able parent . . . . This issue demonstrates a truth about all sex-specific legislation: we cannot talk about distinguishing the female from the mother's body in abstraction, that is, outside the context of power that construct's a woman's options" (*The Female Body and the Law*, 194). For another contestatory discussion of the issues involved in surrogacy and its bearing on the concept of motherhood, see Juliette Zipper and Selma Sevenhuijsen, "Surrogacy: Feminist Notions of Motherhood Reconsidered," in *Reproductive Technologies: Gender, Motherhood and Medicine*, ed. Michelle Stanworth (Cambridge: Polity Press, 1987), 118–38.

3

Russian Tactics
Freud's "Case of Homosexuality in a Woman"

The impression one had of her analysis was not unlike that of a hypnotic treatment, where the resistance has in the same way withdrawn to a certain boundary line, beyond which it proves to be unconquerable. The resistance very often pursues similar tactics—Russian tactics, as they might be called—in cases of obsessional neurosis.

—Sigmund Freud, "The Psychogenesis of a Case of Homosexuality in a Woman," 1920 (SE 18.163)

THE "RUSSIAN TACTICS" of my title are Freud's code-name for the strategies employed by resistance in the face of psychoanalytic enlightenment. As he writes of his "beautiful and clever" eighteen-year-old patient in "The Psychogenesis of a Case of Homosexuality in a Woman" (1920), "the resistance ha[d] . . . withdrawn to a certain boundary line [*Grenze*, or frontier], beyond which it prove[d] to be unconquerable" (SE 18.163).[1] Freud's Russian analogy has a pre-history. It goes back twenty years to a period when Russia, viewed from the perspective of German enlightenment, would have been the symbol of an unreformed autocracy intent on protecting itself from new and alien ideas (especially German ideas).[2] In *The Interpretation of Dreams* (1900), Freud had written of a "ruthless" censorship that "acts exactly like the censorship of newspapers at the Russian frontier, which allows foreign journals to fall into the hands of the readers whom it is its business to protect only after a quantity of passages have been blacked out" (SE 5 (II). 529). Still earlier, he wrote to Fliess in 1897:

> Have you ever seen a foreign newspaper which has passed the
> Russian censorship at the frontier? Words, whole clauses and sen-
> tences are blacked out so that what is left becomes unintelligible.
> A *Russian censorship* of this kind comes about in psychoses and
> produces the apparently meaningless deliria. (SE 1.273)[3]

Freud's prerevolutionary analogy points not only to a similar time-lag in his thinking about female homosexuality but to a blockade of information at the frontier of
his own psychoanalytic inquiry—a resistance that may equal his patient's.

Poised at the opening of the great debate over the question of female sexuality which occupied both male and female analysts during the 1920s, "A Case of
Homosexuality in a Woman" looks back to the precursor text of twenty years
before, Freud's "Fragment of an Analysis of a Case of Hysteria" (1901).[4] Another
spirited young hysteric handed over to Freud by her exasperated father, Dora notoriously broke off the analysis, confronting Freud himself with his failure to recognize
both the nature of the transference and her homosexuality; as he writes in his
famous afterthought, "I failed to discover in time . . . that her homosexual (gynae-
cophilic) love for Frau K. was the strongest unconscious current in her mental
life" (SE 7.120 n). This time, however, Freud is the one who breaks off the analysis when he discovers "the sweeping repudiation of men" which his patient has
transferred to him: "As soon . . . as I recognized the girl's attitude to her father, I
broke off the treatment and advised her parents that . . . it should be continued by
a woman doctor" (SE 18.164). In an attempt to explain her decisive turn toward
homosexuality, Freud suggests that the girl has "retired in favour of someone else"
(SE 18.158, 159 n)—her mother. Just as the disappointed girl turns away from her
father, Freud himself could be said to "retire in favour" of a female analytic rival.[5]
Is it too much to suggest that he too had "withdrawn to a certain boundary line"—
a line beyond which a resistant psychoanalysis might also prove to be unconquerable?
The identification here would be not so much the obvious one between Freud and
the girl's baffled, angry father, as the one between Freud and the girl herself, whose
"resistance"—her willed refusal to know—revives the Russian analogy at the contested frontier of female homosexuality.

Freud boasts at the outset of the unbrokenness of his narrative; the case, he says,
allows him to trace the origin and development of female homosexuality "with
complete certainty and almost without a gap" (*lückenlos*; SE 18.147), despite sup-
pressions that are "easily to be explained by the medical discretion necessary in

discussing a recent case" (SE 18.147). But Freud observes later on that "the information received by our consciousness about our erotic life is especially liable to be incomplete, full of gaps [lückenhaft], or falsified" (SE 18.167). His own production of psychoanalytic knowledge contains similar gaps and falsifications in the face of unwelcome information. I want to explore Freud's representation of what he calls "the mystery of homosexuality" under three interconnected headings: the "psychogenesis," not of homosexuality, but of passion; the "enigma of suicide" (the phrase is Freud's); and what he calls the "deliria" of censorship, or the apparent meaninglessness that he had earlier identified with psychosis. I will argue that this unconcealed censorship—the Russian tactics that Freud associates with the girl's own resistance—becomes especially evident in the delirious finale of "A Case of Homosexuality in a Woman," where the operations of the Freudian unconscious and those of the sex-change operation converge at the imaginary site of the lesbian body.

i. The Lady and the Tramp

Freud's patient, a young woman of the *haute bourgeoisie [aus sozial hochstehender Familie]*—referred to throughout as "the girl" (*das Mädchen*)—has aroused her parent's displeasure by her open adoration of "a certain 'society lady' ['*aus der Gesellschaft*'] about ten years older than herself." Her parents insist that "in spite of her distinguished name, this lady was nothing but a *cocotte [kokotte]*." Freud himself calls her a "*demi-mondaine*" [*Halbweltdame*] placing the term "lady" in quotation marks—for the lady is also a tramp, whose sexuality belongs in the public domain. According to the girl's parents, she is well known to be living on intimate terms with a married woman while carrying on promiscuous affairs with a number of men. The girl loses no opportunity of displaying her devotion—hanging about outside the lady's door and sending her flowers—as well as openly flaunting her attachment by accompanying her about the streets in the vicinity of her father's workplace ("she did not scruple to appear in the most frequented streets in the company of her undesirable friend," SE 18.148). But despite her courtship, the girl has apparently been unable, in Freud's euphemistic term, to "succeed in satisfying her passion"—a matter on which he makes his prognosis partly dependent. Interestingly, the word "passion" (rendered throughout Freud's text as *Leidenschaft*) is used not only in apposition to the girl's genital sexuality ("her genital chastity, if one may use such a phrase, had remained intact," SE 18.153), but apropos of the fatal attraction—"a consuming passion"—that makes her neglect her studies, social functions, and friends of her own age in pursuit of the "undesirable" lady.

Freud treats the girl's passion as the sign of a masculine identification. Her adoration for the lady is like that of a courtly lover: "the girl had adopted the characteristic masculine type of love," he tells us, "'Hoping little and asking for nothing'" ("*che poco spera e nulla chiede*"—the quotation is from Tasso's *Gerusalemme Liberata*).[6] In this it resembles "the first passionate adoration of a youth for a celebrated actress whom he regards as far above him, to whom he scarcely dares lift his bashful eyes" (*SE* 18.160). The quotation from Tasso reminds us that courtly love can be regarded not just as a sign of humility, but as a form of distraction—"devoted" in another sense, for these particular lovers in Tasso's poem risk immolation. Not only that, but the girl's choice of a sexually debased love object and her wish to "rescue" her mimic the one described in Freud's "Special Type of Choice of Object Made by Men" (1910), where "it is a necessary condition that the loved object should be in some way or other 'of bad repute' sexually—someone who really may be called a *cocotte*" (*SE* 18.161). [7] But when it comes to Freud's discussion of the ways in which the girl resembles her father and his list of the girl's "masculine" intellectual attributes—"her acuteness of comprehension and her lucid objectivity, *in so far as she was not dominated by her passion*" (*SE* 18.154; my italics)—he tends to associate passion, to the contrary, with an aberration: she is masculine in her passion, but her passion makes her *less* masculine, *less* like her father. Passion turns out to be a form of masquerade (of courtly love, of masculinity) whose meaning is reversed—much as Lacan alleges, apropos of "the phallic mark of desire," that "virile display itself appears as feminine."[8] In Freud's gender scheme, it is masculine to desire the lady, but feminine to make a virile display of phallic desire. Loving a woman as a man might do (Freud's earlier definition of Dora's "gynaecophilia") takes on the paradoxical appearance of femininity.

Freud traces the "special type of choice of object made by men" back to maternal attachment: the mother, not the father, is the original object of passion. The girl may have given up her father and "retired in favour of her mother," but it turns out that her earlier love objects had all been substitute mothers anyway—schoolteachers or the "women between thirty and thirty-five whom she had met with their children during summer holidays" (*SE* 18.156), and whom she could identify with her own mother. Her present lady-love is just such a substitute for the mother who had recently given birth to a much younger child.[9] Freud describes this current in her feelings ("one that we may unhesitatingly designate as homosexual") as "a direct and unchanged continuation of an infantile fixation on her mother" (*SE* 18.168). Strong maternal attachment leads not only to "a special type of choice of object" but to homosexuality in men (later on in the case, Freud reminds us "that homosexual men have experienced a specially strong fixation on their mother," *SE* 18.171)—and, apparently, in women too. What would it mean for a woman to repudiate the strength of her fixation on her mother, instead of repudiating her father, as this girl does? The answer, presumably, is the normative outcome of the feminine Oedipus complex—namely, the castration anxiety that ensures the girl's repudiation of her first love object (the mother) in favor of a heterosexual object (the father) and his symbolic substitute (penis = baby). But this particular girl ("A spirited girl, always ready for romping and fighting") has "brought along with her from her childhood a strongly marked 'masculinity complex'" and "a pronounced envy for the penis." As Freud puts it, bluntly, "She was in fact a feminist" (*SE* 18.169). Rebelling against the lot of woman, she has come particularly to dislike the idea of having a baby, which would provide the only cure for penis envy known to Freud; as we have seen, he attributes the decisive homosexual turn and timing of the girl's choice of object to her disappointment when her father gives this precious penis substitute to her mother instead of her ("it was not *she* who bore the child, but her unconsciously hated rival, the mother," *SE* 18.157). Whereupon she "foreswears" Freudian womanhood altogether—repudiating not just her father but "her wish for a child, her love of men, and the feminine role in general."

As Freud sums up the perverse trajectory of disappointed womanhood, "She changed into a man and took her mother in place of her father as the object of her love" (*SE* 18.158). This is his definition of female homosexuality, insofar as he offers one. But his definition risks conflating two distinct aspects of psychic life: *identification* and *object-choice*. Has the girl *identified* with her father in choosing her maternal love object, or has she never really yielded up that prior maternal object in the first place? And what is the relation between this subsequent paternal identification and the earliest emergence of the maternal object-choice that Freud takes as a given? A footnote signals the slippage: "It is by no means rare," Freud writes, "for a love-relation to be broken off through *a process of identification* on the part of the lover with the loved object, a process equivalent to a kind of regression to narcissism" (*SE* 18.158 n; my italics). In identifying with her father, the girl not only "regresses" to her orginal love object, the mother, but to an earlier form of identification too. We know that narcissistic object-choice underlies all others for Freud. Her regression-through-identification serves to confirm what Freud has implied throughout: that all object-choice is narcissistic in origin, and that the prototype for later identifications is the narcissistic form of identification that actually occurs prior to object-choice proper. If the psychogenesis of both sexuality and homosexuality can be traced back to maternal fixation, the wonder is that all men aren't homosexual, and all women too—indeed, as Freud himself acknowledges, they may well be: "a very considerable measure of latent or unconscious homosexuality can be detected in all normal people" (*SE* 18.171).[10] On this deconstructive note, Freud lets his case rest: "It is not for psycho-analysis to solve the problem of homosexuality" (*SE* 18.171).

Before leaving the "lady," however, I want to note what amounts to an implicit feminine identification on Freud's own part. Determined to combat his daughter's homosexuality "with all the means in his power," the girl's father turns to psychoanalysis despite (in Freud's words) "the low estimation in which [it] is so generally held in Vienna" (*SE* 18.149). Even the girl treats Freud with some *hauteur*:

> Once when I expounded to her a specially important part of the theory, once touching her nearly, she replied in an inimitable tone, 'How very interesting', as though she were a *grande dame* being taken over a museum and glancing through her lorgnon at objects to which she was completely indifferent. (*SE* 18.163)

This indifference to the "objects" in Freud's psychoanalytic gallery—and above all to the tour guide himself—suggests Freud's sensitivity to the social standing of his Viennese profession; however veiled by "medical discretion," he too, like the lady, threatens to bring sexuality out of the home into the public domain. Readers of Dora's case history will recall Freud's preoccupation with the sources of Dora's sexual knowledge, which he traces not only to her undercover reading but to an oral source—Frau K., her father's mistress, and Dora's homosexual love object.[11] She knows very well, she tells Freud, "that there was more than one way of obtaining sexual gratification" (*SE* 7.47). In "A Case of Homosexuality in a Woman," the girl similarly tells Freud that

> she meant to marry, but only in order to escape her father's tyranny and to follow her true inclinations undisturbed. As for the husband, she remarked rather contemptuously, she would easily deal with him,

and besides, one could have sexual relations with a man and a woman at one and the same time. (*SE* 18.165)

The source of her knowledge is none other than "the example of the adored lady." Even more than the woman doctor in whose favor Freud "retires," the lady turns out to be a rival authority on lesbian and bisexual matters. What's more, there is no "indifference" with regard to *this* object. The most telling aspect of Freud's emphasis on the girl's "passion" for the lady is her contrasting dis-passion for psychoanalysis, her indifference to Freud himself. Freud's story of a woman spurned—a girl made vengeful by "the disappointment she had suffered from her father" (*SE* 18.164)—looks uncomfortably like a displaced inversion of his own. Hell hath no fury like a father spurned. But an obscure "something" remains to be explained in the depth of her father's bitter reaction ("There was something about his daughter's homosexuality that aroused the deepest bitterness in him," *SE* 18.149). This mysterious "something," I suggest, is the father's own "feminine" identification, aroused and implicated by the daughter's homosexuality—the troubling feminine identification that characterizes both Freud's countertransference and his resistance.

ii. The Enigma of Suicide

According to Freud, the lady only begins to treat the girl "in a more friendly manner" when she provides "unmistakable proof of serious passion" by attempting suicide. As the girl obviously intends, her father eventually encounters her and her beloved in the street, passing them "with an angry glance which boded no good"—whereupon "the girl rushed off and flung herself over a wall down the side of a cutting onto the suburban railway line which ran close by" (*SE* 18.148). Freud remarks that the girl's suicide attempt improves her position with both the lady and her parents, who are all forced to take her passion seriously. Later he rehearses the episode, this time offering a fresh explanation—first hers, then his:

She went for a walk with [the lady] one day in a part of the town and at an hour at which she was not unlikely to meet her father on his way from his office. So it turned out. Her father passed them in the street and cast a furious look at her and her companion, about whom he had by that time come to know. A few moments later she flung herself into the railway cutting. The explanation she gave of the immediate reasons determining her decision sounded quite plausible. She had confessed to the lady that the man who had given them such an irate glance was her father, and that he had absolutely forbidden their friendship. The lady became incensed at this and ordered the girl to leave her then and there, and never again to wait for her or to address her—the affair must now come to an end. In her despair at having thus lost her loved one for ever, she wanted to put an end to herself. (SE 18.161–62)

Uncovering "another and deeper explanation," Freud calls the attempted suicide both "the fulfillment of a punishment (self-punishment) and the fulfillment of a wish." The wish fulfilled by this "fall" is "the wish to have a child by her father, for now she 'fell' through her father's fault" (SE 18.162; Freud's reading turns on the word *niederkommen*, meaning both "to fall" and "to be delivered of a child").[12] But the girl's suicide also reveals her unconscious, vengeful death wishes against both her father (for impeding her love) and her mother (for becoming pregnant with her little brother). The connecting link, according to Freud, is the double prohibition uttered by the irate father and the incensed lady: "the affair must now come to an end."

It is in this connection that Freud invokes "the enigma of suicide." Absorbing "all that is enigmatic" in the girl's homosexuality (SE 18.161), suicide stands in for "the mystery of homosexuality" while again bringing the matter of narcissistic identification and object-choice to the fore. Freud explains suicide as an attempt to kill an object with whom the subject has identified herself ("turning against [oneself] a deathwish which had been directed at someone else," SE 18.162). In "Mourning and Melancholia" (1917), written three years before the "Case of Homosexuality in a Woman," Freud has a similar solution to "the riddle of the tendency to suicide" (SE 14.252). The melancholic ego, he says, can only kill itself by treating itself as an object. But the violence directed against itself is a manifestation of the hostility representing the ego's original reaction to objects—a reaction that is strictly speaking pre-objectal. Freud had originally offered this explanation of suicide in "Instincts and their Vicissitudes" (1915). Here he says that when the object first makes its appearance, during the stage of primary narcissism, "indifference" to the external world coincides with "unpleasure"; only at this stage does the opposite to loving, i.e., hating, emerge. But as Freud points out, "loving" has not one but *three* opposites: hating, being loved, and indifference—or rather, rearranged in a developmental sequence, (1) indifference, (2) hating, and (3) being loved.[13] Indifference is a special case of hate, having first appeared as its forerunner (much as homosexuality is a special case of object-choice, having first appeared as maternal attachment). Put differently, as ego is to the external world, so love is to indifference; and as pleasure is to unpleasure, so love (the quest for pleasure) is to hate (self-preservation).[14] Love and hate only become opposites at the point of genital organization. The upshot, in Freud's account, is that "Hate, as a relation to objects, is older than love" (*SE* 14.139). The "enigma of suicide" turns out to be the enigma of passion, whose regressive forms are hate and, earlier still, indifference.

The girl's attempted suicide (the act of violence she directs against herself and her father) therefore tells the story of passion's origins in a prior "indifference." Posing as a *grande dame*, the girl at once masks hatred as indifference and regresses to hate's forerunner, the unpleasure with which all external stimuli were originally regarded. The play of glances in Freud's narrative—the *grande dame*'s indifferent glance through her lorgnon, the father's "angry glance" [*Blick*] as he passes his daughter in the street—stages a narcissistic drama. In "Mourning and Melancholia," Freud had written that frustrated object-choice regresses to narcissism, enshrining "a preliminary stage of object-choice" (*SE* 14.249) characterized by narcissistic identification. This substitution of narcissistic identification for object love—the transformation of object loss into ego loss—is the key to melancholia (as he puts it epigramatically, "the shadow of the object [falls] upon the ego" *SE* 14.249). Being in love and attempting suicide represent two alternate ways in which the ego may be overwhelmed by the object. In *Black Sun: Depression and Melancholia* (1987), Kristeva argues that the affective and aesthetic elaborations of melancholia preserve the "pre-" of object relations. Prior to the Oedipus complex and its resolution—prior, that is, to both the splitting and the prohibition that constitute subjectivity and gender—melancholia implicates the in-difference of un- or dis-passion.[15] The subject of melancholia is an improper subject, an "abject" insufficiently differentiated from its not-yet-object—what Kristeva calls the maternal "Thing" that will be (but is not yet) the mother. The interest (and the difficulty) of Kristeva's account of melancholia lies in the specificity of its implications for women. I want to pursue these implications briefly in connection with the "Case of Homosexuality in a Woman."

Kristeva suggests that women's "specular identification with the mother" and their "introjection of the maternal body and self" are more immediate, and hence more problematic, than men's. Because of this primary narcissistic identification, she asserts, it is more difficult for women to turn matricidal drive into saving representation—more difficult, in other words, for women to symbolize (i.e., to mourn a lost object). This failure at the level of symbolization tends to trap the feminine subject in the incorporatory psychosis of melancholia, addicted as she is to the maternal, pre-objectal Thing. Hence the destructive drive that women, more than men, turn against themselves ("the melancholy woman is the dead one that has always been abandoned within herself").[16] Depression and even suicide take the place of mourning. Only by an act of symbolic matricide can the maternal object be lost and found again, "transposed," as Kristeva puts it, "by means of an unbelievable symbolic effort."[17] The extra symbolic effort demanded of women becomes for Kristeva the defining asymmetry between the sexes. While heterosexual men and homosexual women can recover the lost maternal object as erotic object, finding an erotic object other than the primary maternal object (i.e., a heterosexual object) involves *for heterosexual women* "a gigantic elaboration"—a symbolic elaboration—far greater than men are called upon to undertake in the interests of their own heterosexuality. Freud implies that femininity is a high-risk condition for neurosis, given women's difficulties in negotiating the Oedipus complex: Kristeva implies that women are similarly at risk for melancholia given their primary maternal identification. If female homosexuality looks like the path of least resistance in the face of the disproportionate difficulty of this symbolic undertaking, the "enigma of suicide" represents the psychotic outcome when that path is blocked, and incorporation has to take the place of erotic cathexis.

In Freud's narrative, the girl identifies with her father, turning his angry and punitive glance on herself. A Kristevan narrative points instead to the melancholy that *Black Sun* defines as *"impossible mourning for the maternal object."*[18] The girl is overwhelmed by the Thing. But there is a difficulty here for feminism. Freud claims that her suicide attempt signals "her attitude of defiance and revenge against her father," much as in "Mourning and Melancholia" he detects "a mental constellation of revolt" in his melancholy patients' complaints and self-reproaches (*SE* 14.248). One obvious objection to the Kristevan reading is that it leaves no scope for the girl's defiance—"She was in fact a feminist"—to exert political leverage on the symbolic realm embodied by her heterosexist father and Freudian theory.[19] Where Freud equates the mystery of female homosexuality with the enigma of suicide, Kristeva seems to make female homosexuality a flight from female psychosis. But this may be to misread Kristeva, for whom the Symbolic is always accompanied and disrupted by its failures, and for whom psychosis is as much a mode of signification as a pathology. If the performance of homosexuality unsettles the masquerade of heterosexuality, psychosis (defined as the failure to symbolize) points to the precariousness of the symbolic realm while providing a permanent record within the subject of the immense price paid for admission. This is not to romanticize female homosexuality as a spanner in the symbolic works (much as hysteria was also romanticized by earlier feminist psychoanalytic criticism). Rather, Freud's text of female homosexuality can be read as uncovering this pre-history of the (failed) institution of (heterosexual) boundaries—boundaries that are constantly being breached in the present tense (as well as past tense) of the subject's psychic narrative. I want to turn, finally, to this narrative; or rather, to the cut (at once a literal trace and a trace of the literal) that disrupts Freud's own story with a form of signification that it is tempting to call "psychotic" in this specialized Kristevan sense.

iii. The Unkindest Cut

According to Freud's Russian analogy, censorship (i.e., resistance) produces "apparently meaningless deliria" (*Delirien*—elsewhere defined as delusional structures of thought).[20] In *The Interpretation of Dreams*, "deliria" are "the work of a censorship which no longer takes the trouble to conceal its operation." Just as the girl in "A Case of Homosexuality in a Woman" is at once "too open" and "full of deceitfulness" (*SE* 18.148), the censored (resistant) text is characterized by its blatantly unconcealed deception: "instead of collaborating in producing a new version that shall be unobjectionable, it ruthlessly deletes whatever it disapproves of, so that what remains becomes quite disconnected" (*SE* 5.529). Its cuts are brutally visible. Freud's textual analogy is striking, not least in associating the disruption of meaning with psychosis (as he had written in the letter to Fliess, "A Russian censorship of this kind comes about in psychoses" (*SE* 1.273). The psychotic text contains the disconnected traces of impossible meanings. At the end of Freud's "Case of Homosexuality in a Woman," the unconcealed operations of the censor are preserved in the very objectionableness of its representation of female homosexuality. Disconnection—the sign of "deliria" or psychosis—openly defeats Freud's boasted attempt to trace a coherent "psychogenesis" of female homosexuality ("almost without a gap," *lückenlos*). The cut that we glimpse in the girl's enigmatic suicide attempt surfaces in Freud's closing discussion of Steinach's sex-change operations, where the operations of the Freudian unconscious and those of castration converge on the fantasmatic lesbian body.

Confronted with the double prohibition uttered by both father and lady ("the affair must now come to an end," *SE* 18.162), the girl flings herself into a railway cutting—in German, *Einschnitt* (*der Stadtbahn*). Freud discusses the meaning of her "fall" (her imaginary pregnancy) in terms of her simultaneous wish for fulfillment and punishment. But the meaning of the "cutting" remains unexplored. The "enigma" of her suicide implies both what it covers and what the girl herself does not recover from—the literalness of the cut into which she flings herself when her father "cuts" her in the street with his furious glance. Metaphorically speaking, such a cut is equivalent to castration—the castration that the girl is forced to recognize in both herself and her mother, according to Freud's account of the feminine Oedipus complex, thereby setting in motion the girl's repudiation of the castrated mother (as opposed to the boy, for whom castration anxiety, by contrast, brings about a resolution of the Oedipus complex). Flinging herself into the breach, you might say, the girl identifies herself in a literal sense—a psychotic sense—with both cutting and cut. Contrary to Freud's assertion, she identifies with what she hasn't got (rather than with what the father has). Her refusal to be the phallus for the man—the symbol of his desire—identifies her in a literal fashion with the psychoanalytically prescribed lack that is enjoined on her. By improperly literalizing the symbolic castration that assigns her to her proper place within a heterosexualized oedipal structure, the girl makes visible the hideous literalness of the oedipal narrative. Freud and her father tell her: "you just don't get it [i.e., the phallus], and you never will." To which the girl makes her suicidal reply, aiming it at both her father and the lady who ventriloquizes his prohibition: "*you* just don't get it [i.e., understand], and you never will." Freud misrecognizes the disconnected meaning(lessness) of her reply, just as he had once failed to recognize Dora's homosexuality in his preoccupation with what, for him, would compensate the girl for her castration—her imaginary pregnancy. But Freud also tells us that the girl is "always reserved in what she said about her mother" (*SE* 18.149). What is this "reserve" in the relations between mother and daughter, and how does it bear on the matter of castration?

According to Freud, while her father is chagrined by his daughter's homosexuality, her mother's "attitude towards the girl was not so easy to grasp" (*SE* 18.149). Far from being incensed, she even "enjoyed her daughter's confidence concerning her passion." This is the more surprising because she treats her daughter harshly in contrast to her sons and sees her as a rival ("still youthful herself, [she] saw in her rapidly developing daughter an inconvenient competitor," SE 18.157). Freud's cynical implication is that the mother acquiesces in her daughter's homosexual object-choice because it leaves all the men to her ("The mother herself still attached great value to the attentions and the admiration of men," SE 18.158). But if we take a leaf out of Melanie Klein's book, there may be another way to view the mother's acquiescence. In "The Effects of Early Anxiety-Situations on the Sexual Development of the Girl" (1932), Klein follows Freud in viewing female homosexuality as a form of masculine identification.[21] The specifically Kleinian turn consists in viewing castration anxiety in terms of the girl's sadistic fantasies, for instance, of the destruction of her mother by her father's dangerous penis. The result may be the wish to "restore her mother by means of a penis with healing powers," reinforcing her homosexuality—especially if she believes herself to have been successful in castrating her father (like the girl in Freud's "Case," who "realized how she could wound her father and take revenge on him," SE 18.159). In a footnote, Klein goes on: "If her homosexuality emerges in sublimated ways only, she will . . . protect and take care of other women (i.e., her mother), adopting in these respects a husband's attitude towards them."[22] What is the girl's devotion to the "lady" if not just such a sublimated form of caretaking? No wonder, then, that when the lady echoes her father's thunderous prohibition ("the affair must now come to an end"), the girl experiences her rejection as the unkindest cut of all. Where else can she go but over the wall?

Freud's "Case of Female Homosexuality in a Woman" closes with a deliberate aporia. "It is not for psycho-analysis," he says, "to solve the problem of homosexuality" (SE 18.171). Now the enigma is not suicide, but the mystery of the homosexuality whose psychogenesis Freud had initally claimed to trace "with complete certainty." Freud dismisses the popular stereotype of female homosexuality (as he parodically represents it, " 'a masculine mind, irresistibly attracted by women, but, alas! imprisoned in a feminine body' "). For him there is no freakish "third sex." All that psychoanalysis can do is to throw light on the choice of object; it cannot even elucidate "what in conventional . . . phraseology is termed 'masculine' and 'feminine' " (SE 18.171); this is the domain of biology. Yet Freud's text takes a disconcerting turn at this point, alluding to "the remarkable transformations that Steinach has effected in some cases by his operations" (SE 18.171). Freud seems to take his distance from the drastic intervention of surgical sex-change, noting that Steinach has operated on "the condition . . . of a very patent physical 'hermaphroditism'" (*SE* 18.170–71). "Any analogous treatment of female homosexuality," he says, "is at present quite obscure." Indeed, he regards a physical "cure" for female homosexuality that involves the removal of supposedly "hermaphroditic" ovaries as patently impractical (SE. 18.172). Interestingly, Freud had updated *Three Essays on the Theory of Sexuality* (1905) in 1920, the same year as the "Case of Homosexuality in a Woman," with a long footnote on the biological experiments performed by the controversial endocrinologist Eugen Steinach ("Experimental castration and subsequently grafting the sex-glands of the opposite sex").[23] Freud counters Steinach's notion of a "cure" for homosexuality by resurrecting the theory of bisexuality (which he goes out of his way to attribute to Fliess). "Psycho-analytic research," he insists, "is most decidedly opposed to any attempt at separating off homosexuals from the rest of mankind as a group of a special character" (*SE* 7.145 n). But his running commentary on Steinach suggests an undisclosed engagement with the experimental field of endocrinology.

In 1923, Freud himself underwent a small operation on his testicles (technically, "a ligature of the vas deferens on both sides," or a vasectomy) known as "the Steinach operation"—a fashionable procedure identified with none other than Eugen Steinach.[24] Supposedly restorative of fading sexual potency (Freud hoped it might improve "his sexuality, his general condition and his capacity for work"), the operation was also thought to have rejuvenating effects on aging males and possibly to mobilize the body's resources against cancer (at this time Freud was subject to repeated invasive procedures to combat cancer of the mouth).[25] It is as if, at the end of "A Case of Homosexuality in a Woman," Freud has suddenly caught a glimpse of the surgically modified body—the castrated body—and looked away. In his strangely compressed punchline, the mystery of female homosexuality, like the enigma of suicide, returns to haunt the Freudian text in the form of an inoperable lesbian body. Here is Freud's closing sentence:

> A woman who has felt herself to be a man, and has loved in masculine fashion, will hardly let herself be forced into playing the part of a woman, when she must pay for this transformation, which is not in every way advantageous, by renouncing all hope of motherhood. (*SE* 18.172)

What female homosexual would submit to the knife on these terms? Freud leaves her, caught on the horns of a cruel dilemma—between the rock of hermaphroditic ovaries and the hard place of irremediable penis envy, unalleviated by "all hope of motherhood" (the only known Freudian cure for the neurosis of femininity). In the half-glimpsed, disavowed violence of this Steinach-induced fantasy, Freud allows us to see the sadistic operations of the unconscious. As the girl's act of homosexual resistance breaches the frontiers of Freudian knowledge, "A Case of Homosexuality in a Woman" produces a new domain of unthinkability within the very frontiers of psychoanalytic theory—a moment of repudiation (at once of femininity and of homosexuality) inserted by way of Steinach's experiments. Who is to say on which side of this contested frontier one would rather be—with the rhetoric of Freud's psychoanalytic aporia (the knowledge he refuses, since "It is not for psycho-analysis to solve the problem of homosexuality"), or the literalness of the girl's resistance (her defiant refusal to know)?[26]

1. For the German text of "Über die Psychogenese eines Falles von Weiblicher Homosexualität," see *Gesammelte Werke*, 18 vols. (Frankfurt: S. Fischer, 1960), 12.271–302.

2. See Marianna Tax Choldin, *A Fence around the Empire: Russian Censorship of Western Ideas under the Tzars* (Durham, NC: Duke University Press, 1985). In 1906, a statute granted the Russian press its "freedom"; see Charles A. Rund, *Fighting Words: Imperial Censorship and the Russian Press, 1804–1906* (Toronto: University of Toronto Press, 1982); foreign censorship continued, however, until 1917.

3. For the original (and highly charged) context in which Freud first makes his "Russian analogy," see *The Complete Letters of Sigmund Freud to Wilhelm Fliess*, ed. Jeffrey Moussaieff Masson (Cambridge, MA, and London: Harvard University Press, 1985), 287–89.

4. For an excellent earlier discussion of "A Case of Homosexuality in a Woman" and the Dora connection, see Mandy Merck, "The train of thought in Freud's 'Case of Homosexuality in a Woman,'" reprinted in *Perversions* (New York: Routledge, 1993), 13–32; Merck's essay, the first feminist attempt to engage with this case, originally appeared in *m/f* 11/12 (1986): 35–46. See also Jacqueline Rose, "Dora—Fragment of an Analysis," in *Sexuality in the Field of Vision* (London: Verso, 1986), 34–35, and, for recent discussions, Judith Roof, *A Lure of Knowledge: Lesbian Sexuality and Theory* (New York: Columbia University Press, 1992), 177, 210–15; Noreen O'Connor and Joanna Ryan, *Wild Desires and Mistaken Identities: Lesbianism and Psychoanalysis* (London: Virago Press, 1993), 30–46; and Diana Fuss, "Fallen Women: 'The Psychogenesis of a Case of Homosexuality in a Woman,'" in *Identification Papers* (New York and London: Routledge, 1994), 57–82.

5. As Mandy Merck points out; see "Train of Thought," 30.

6. "*Che . . . poco spera e nulla chiede*" (*Gerusalemme Liberata*, canto 2, st. 16). The line describes Olindo's love for Sophronia; in Fairfax's translation, "he full of bashfulnes and truth, / Lov'd much, hop'd little, and desired nought . . . ." The passage continues: "Thus lov'd, thus serv'd

he long, but not regarded, / Unseene, unmarkt, unpitied, unrewarded"; see *Godfrey of Bulloigne*, ed. Kathleen M. Lea and T. M. Gang (Oxford: Clarendon Press, 1981), bk. 2, st. 16.

7. See *SE* 11.165–75.

8. See "The Meaning of the Phallus," *Feminine Sexuality: Jacques Lacan and the école freudienne*, ed. Juliet Mitchell and Jacqueline Rose (New York: Norton, 1985), 85. Lacan is discussing Joan Rivière's essay on masquerade in the context of male and female homosexuality. Compare Judith Butler, "Imitation and Gender Subordination," in *Inside/Out: Lesbian Theories, Gay Theories*, ed. Diana Fuss (New York and London: Routledge, 1991), 22–33, for homosexuality as an imitation that exposes heterosexuality ("an imitation of an imitation, a copy of a copy").

9. Freud notes that motherhood itself ceases to be a sine qua non for the girl because it is difficult to combine with another precondition—her (heterosexual) feelings for her brother; see *SE* 18.156.

10. Or, as Jacqueline Rose puts it, "either the girl is neurotic (which she clearly is not) or all women are neurotic (which indeed they might be)"; see "Dora," 35.

11. Freud identifies "a second and *oral* source of information . . . I should not have been surprised to hear that this source had been Frau K. herself" (*SE* 7.105 n); later, he concludes: "I ought to have guessed that the main source of [Dora's] knowledge of sexual matters could have been no one but Frau K." (*SE* 7.120 n).

12. See *SE* 18.162 n.

13. See "Instincts and their Vicissitudes," *SE* 14.135–36, 135 n.

14. See *SE* 14.136.

15. Judith Butler's otherwise interesting account of what she calls "the melancholia of gender" is problematized by her failure to recognize this undifferentiated state (in both the pre-subject and the pre-object); regarding the melancholy of gender as the melancholy of lost gender identifications leaves out of account the fact that in Freud's (and Kristeva's) account of melancholia, what is preserved is a pre-objectal, that is preoedipal (hence pregender) form of identification; see *Gender Trouble: Feminism and the Subversion of Identity* (New York and London: Routledge, 1990), 57–65, and compare also "Imitation and Gender Subordination," 13–31.

16. Julia Kristeva, *Black Sun: Depression and Melancholia* (New York: Columbia University Press, 1989), 28–29, 30; see also the case histories in "Illustrations of Feminine Depression" (*Black Sun*, 69–94).

17. Ibid., 28.

18. Ibid., 9.

19. Compare Butler's critique of Kristeva in *Gender Trouble*, 79–93 passim.

20. See "Notes upon a Case of Obsessional Neurosis" (1909), *SE* 10.164, 222.

21. In doing so, Klein however also associates herself with Karen Horney, Joan Riviere, and Ernest Jones; see *The Psycho-Analysis of Children*. trans. Alix Strachey (London: Virago, 1989), 212 n, 213 n, 214 n, 215 n.

22. Ibid., 216 n.

23. The extensive footnote on homosexuality to which his comments on Steinach belong represents

a running commentary on successive additions to *Three Essays on The Theory of Sexuality* dated 1910, 1915, and 1920; see *SE* 7.144–47 nn.

24. See Peter Gay, *Freud: A Life for Our Time* (New York and London: Norton, 1988), 426. For contemporary claims about the rejuvenating effects of the Steinach operation, and for its scientific status at the time, see Sharon Romm, *The Unwelcome Intruder: Freud's Struggle with Cancer* (New York: Praeger, 1983), 73–85; interest in the operation, which was very new at the time it was performed on Freud, peaked during the 1920s and 1930s. See also Eugen Steinach, *Sex and Life: Forty Years of Biological and Medical Experiments* (New York: Viking Press, 1940) for an account of Steinach's life and work and, for a brief discussion of "experimental" hermaphrodites and "congenital" homosexuality, Steinach, 83–92.

25. See *A Life for Our Time*, 426; the quotation is from Ernest Jones, *The Life and Works of Sigmund Freud* (New York: Basic Books, 1953–57), 3: 98–99. For an account of Freud's cancer surgery, see Max Schur, *Freud: Living and Dying* (New York: International Universities Press, 1972), 347–66.

26. Compare the closing aporia of Merck's essay: "And who shall we say was more reluctant to make the journey?" ("The train of thought in Freud's 'Case of Homosexuality in a Woman,'" 32)— more evidence of the way Freud's scrupulously evenhanded text tends to be weighed in the balance and found wanting by feminist readers.

Part II

Melancholy Figures

4

In Love with a Cold Climate
Travelling with Wollstonecraft

I am very far from thinking love irresistible.

—Mary Wollstonecraft, *Thoughts on the Education of Daughters* (1787)

To the well-educated layman . . . things that have to do with love are incommensurable with everything else; they are, as it were, written on a special page on which no other writing is tolerated.

—Sigmund Freud, "Observations on Transference Love," 1915 (SE 12.160)

"A BOOK OF TRAVELS that so irresistably seizes on the heart, never, in any other instance, found its way from the press."[1] This was William Godwin's response, after her death, to the irresistibility of Wollstonecraft's *Letters Written during a Short Residence in Sweden, Norway, and Denmark* (1796). In his own *Memoirs of the Author of A Vindication of The Rights of Woman* (1798), he writes as if reading her lightly fictionalized, semiautobiographical travel book had been enough to make him fall romantically in love with her—although this was not, in fact, the case.[2] But Godwin would certainly have been familiar with the story of Wollstonecraft's desertion by her American lover, Gilbert Imlay, at the time he read them (*Memoirs*, 256). He seems also to have recognized that her romantic melancholia was, to use his own term, "calculated"; that is, a form of literary affect capable of transfer:

If ever there was a book calculated to make a man in love with its author, this appears to me to be the book. She speaks of her sorrows, in a way that fills us with melancholy, and dissolves us in tenderness. . . . Affliction had tempered her heart to a softness almost more than human; and the gentleness of her spirit seems precisely to accord with all the romance of unbounded attachment. (*Memoirs*, 249)

Such literary falling in love occurs in Wollstonecraft's own writing, notably in her posthumously published novel *The Wrongs of Woman* (1798), in which the heroine, Maria, falls in love with a fellow prisoner after reading the marginalia in his copy of Rousseau's *La Nouvelle Héloïse*. Later, he proves to be as unreliable a sentimentalist as the real life Imlay. Beware of sentimentalism, seems to be Wollstonecraft's message; beware especially of the sentimentalist you meet over a book by Rousseau. The romance of transference-lovers, seemingly written on a special page, turns out to be inscribed in the general history of women's oppression.

In fact, it was Wollstonecraft herself who sent Godwin the third volume of *La Nouvelle Héloïse* in the summer of 1796.[3] Wollstonecraft called Rousseau the "Prometheus of Sentiment," and in an earlier letter to Imlay she had described herself as having been "always half in love" with him.[4] Rousseau continues to be a touchstone, even in the aftermath of her love affair with Imlay. In a moment of trepidation, shortly after they had become lovers, Wollstonecraft tells Godwin that if necessary she would be content to become once more "a *Solitary Walker*"— a reference to *Les Rêveries du promeneur solitaire* whose influence shapes her literary self-representation as a too-solitary female wanderer.[5] Judging from Godwin's response to *Letters Written during a Short Residence*, Wollstonecraft's campaign to sentimentalize him was successful even before they began (in her words) to "woo philosophy" together. And after her death, Godwin himself experienced, in retrospect, "all the romance of unbounded attachment" for Wollstonecraft. In *Mourning and Melancholia* (1917), Freud observes that suicidal melancholy and "being most intensely in love" are two sides of the same narcissistic predicament (*SE* 14.252). Confronted by the evidence of Imlay's desertion, Wollstonecraft had attempted suicide both before and after her Scandinavian journey. Godwin, by contrast, tried to keep her alive after her death by immersing himself in her writings, occupying her study, and idealizing her as a female Werther "endowed with the most exquisite and delicious sensibility" (*Memoirs*, 242).[6]

In Love with a Cold Climate

Godwin's response to Wollstonecraft's travel book eroticizes the condition of feminine sorrow—reminding us that the Romantic trope of the deserted woman is predicated on the spectacle of her suffering. His arousal depends (like the sadist's) on sympathetic identification with the "delicious sensibility" whose literary articulation had seized his heart in Wollstonecraft's travel book. It was, of course, Godwin himself who made public Wollstonecraft's orginal love letters to Imlay in his edition of the *Posthumous Works*; this was a love triangle. Scholars have speculated that Coleridge's knowledge of Wollstonecraft's desertion by Imlay also gave rise to the exotic "woman wailing for her demon-lover" in the deep romantic chasm of "Kubla Khan" (belonging to 1797).[7] When woman wails, Romantic man either splits into the tenderly dissolved (Godwin) or else turns dissolute (Imlay). But Godwin's tendresse reveals more than erotic capture by the literature of feminine suffering, or by rivalrous triangulation with Wollstonecraft's sentimental past. Rather, his falling in love provides a diagnostic insight into the psychic hinterland occupied by Wollstonecraft's Scandinavian letters. Read as a sustained inquiry into amatory melancholia—the condition of being unhappily in love—they offer an account of feminine melancholia that is not only "calculated" in its literary effects, but also, I want to argue, historically specific. "The romance of unbounded attachment" was bounded by the history of the French Revolution.

Godwin was not alone in responding to *Letters Written during a Short Residence* with the language of love; contemporary reviewers similarly regarded her sorrows as those of a sentimental heroine (and a wandering mother) in distress.[8] The young Robert Southey, for instance, wrote enthusiastically that "She has made me in love with a cold climate, and frost and snow, with a northern moonlight."[9] Falling in love again . . . The recurrence of these phrases may point to something unexplored in our own reading of Wollstonecraft. It is tempting to recall Freud's comparison of transference to "new editions or facsimiles" of old impulses and phantasies (SE 7.116). The bicentennial of the publication of Wollstonecraft's *Vindication of the Rights of Woman* (1792) highlighted Wollstonecraft's continuing appeal to modern feminists, while also raising the question of feminism's transferential relations to her writing. If we are indeed Wollstonecraft's daughters, as modern (or, at any rate, British) feminists are wont to claim—if we can still read her founding text of liberal feminism as a first edition of our own contemporary concerns—it also seems worth asking how we position ourselves in relation to her romantic distress and her literary melancholia. Feminism's modern romance with Wollstonecraft recapitulates the contemporary response to her travel book in the

1790s. But must we repeat Godwin's erotic capture, "falling in love" again, or is there another way to read her melancholia? Alternatively, like Mary Shelley, must we construct Wollstonecraft as a (literally) dead mother? It may not be far-fetched to connect Wollstonecraft's exploration of the relation between love, death, and melancholia with a later response to her book, Mary Godwin Shelley's *Frankenstein; or, the Modern Prometheus* (1818), in which the extinction of love takes the Modern Prometheus to a northern death, pursued by his abject and unloved creation. What if—a speculation I will return to briefly at the end—another "dead mother" is involved at the site of a transference whose meaning is also (Freud warns us) that of resistance? I want to begin to answer these questions by turning over what Wollstonecraft calls "a new page in the history of [her] own heart" (*A Short Residence*, p. 122) before attempting to sketch the historical relations between her melancholy and her feminism. At the same time, I will outline a tentative genealogy of the feminist melancholia that links Wollstonecraft, her daughters, and her readers at the common site of transference and maternity.

i. "A New Page in the History of My Own Heart"

In the same letter in which she refers to being half in love with Rousseau, Wollstonecraft teases Imlay for his commercial preoccupations and reproaches him for having insufficient respect for the imagination: "I could prove to you in a trice that it is the mother of sentiment," she threatens. "Imagination," she goes on, "is the true fire, stolen from heaven, to animate this cold creature of clay."[10] Wollstonecraft's feminized Promethean imagery makes imagination ("the mother of sentiment") a maternal spark. A number of similar allusions to Prometheus recur in her Scandinavian letters (some quite playful). For instance, Wollstonecraft reflects that while "Prometheus alone stole fire to animate the first man," and "love is generally termed a flame," nowadays "his posterity need not supernatural aid to preserve the species" (*A Short Residence*, 116). A recent and enthusiastic mother herself, travelling alone with her one-year-old daughter, Wollstonecraft could afford to joke about the loveless preservation of the species. Elsewhere during her travels she grumbles about the uncooperative peasants of Sweden as "half alive beings, who seem to have been made by Prometheus, when the fire he stole from heaven was so exhausted, that he could only spare a spark to give life, not animation, to the inert clay" (*A Short Residence*, 156). Men who live so close to subsistence level ("so near the brute creation") have "little or no imagination . . . to fructify the faint glimmerings of mind" (*A Short Residence*, 65). Throughout her Scandinavian letters, Wollstonecraft maintains an implicit contrast between herself and the unimaginative or commercial people she encounters. Imagination and sentiment mother, animate, and fructify, as opposed to the "embruting" commercial spirit (or the loveless sexuality) which Wolstonecraft increasingly comes to identify with her former lover, Imlay, the imaginary recipient of her travel letters.[11] Commerce embrutes the mind: imagination (and travel too) brings it to life.

As Godwin observed, "it is of the very essence of affection, to seek to perpetuate itself"; *Memoirs*, 245). Wollstonecraft's letters seem written as much to keep her own love alive as to make their recipient fall in love (again). Writing from Sweden shortly after her arrival, Wollstonecraft offered Imlay a brief disquisition on the importance of love in her psychic economy. "Love," she insists, "is a want of my heart."

> I . . . find, that to deaden is not to calm the mind—Aiming at tranquillity, I have almost destroyed all the energy of my soul . . . . Despair, since the birth of my child, has rendered me stupid—soul and body seemed to be fading away before the withering touch of disappointment.[12]

"Nothing," Wollstonecraft concludes, "can extinguish the heavenly spark." Love is a "want" of her heart (a lack? a demand?). Despair has rendered her stupid, subject to the "fading" that Ernest Jones calls "aphanisis," or the disappearance of sexual desire, and associates specifically with women's fear of separation from a loved object.[13] But for Lacan, "aphanisis" means not so much the fear of seeing desire disappear as something altogether more "lethal"—"the level at which the subject manifests himself in this movement of disappearance," or "the *fading* of the subject." This fading (on the side of death rather than life) is an effect of the division of the subject in signification, so that "when the subject appears somewhere as meaning, he is manifested elsewhere . . . as disappearance."[14] Love and travel keep Wollstonecraft from fading in the face of a loss which is not so much loss of the loved object, or even loss of desire, as loss of meaning. She writes that her mind "is at present painfully active," that even the "agony" of unrequited love affords her pleasure, representing as it does the only "spark of hope . . . yet alive in [her] forlorn bosom" (a Promethean spark, presumably).[15] A few weeks later she tells Imlay: "I cannot endure the anguish of corresponding with you—if we are only to correspond. No; if you seek for happiness elsewhere, my letters shall not interrupt your repose. *I will be dead to you.*"[16] Ceasing to correspond means death to the letter. Wollstonecraft's travel book, begun as a journal alongside her letters to Imlay, can be read as a writer's defense against fading; as a matter of life and death.

Travelling as Imlay's wife and legal representative in an attempt to sort out his tangled business affairs (and perhaps to give him a convenient respite from her reproachful presence in London), Wollstonecraft seems to have spent the trip in a state of prolonged despair over the failure of her hopes for revolutionary domestic intimacy with Imlay: "I never wanted but your heart," she told him, after her return from Scandinavia and her second suicide attempt.[17] The Rousseauian *promeneuse solitaire* of the Scandinavian letters represents a literary solution to "the want" of Imlay's heart and the want of her own; Wollstonecraft becomes identified with a self-sufficient discourse of love that defies the threat of affective and erotic extinction ("I will be dead to you") posed by the failure of her "correspondence" with Imlay.[18] Soon after arriving in Sweden, Wollstonecraft announced to Imlay: "I am more alive, than you have seen me for a long, long time. I have a degree of vivacity, even in my grief, which is preferable to the benumbing stupour that, for the last year, has frozen up all my faculties."[19] This is the note she strikes early on in *Letters Written during a Short Residence*. Writing at midnight without a candle during the short northern night, she contrasts her wakefulness with the sleeping landscape: "What, I exclaimed, is this active principle which keeps me still awake? . . . emotions that trembled on the brink of extacy and agony gave a poignancy to my sensations, which made me feel more alive than usual" (*A Short Residence*, 69). While the long Swedish winter keeps the people "sluggish" (a favorite word), their children loaded with smelly flannels even in summer, their women fat and indolent, Wollstonecraft portrays herself as "more alive than usual." By contrast, she at times views other people—other peoples—with the hostile, not to say xenophobic eye of the frustrated eighteenth-century traveller.

Often the only lively consciousness in this northern climate appears to be Wollstonecraft's own. Characteristically awake while her travelling companions sleep, she "contemplated . . . a night such as [she] had never before seen or felt":

> The very air was balmy, as it freshened into morn, producing the most voluptuous sensations. A vague pleasurable sentiment absorbed me, as I opened my bosom to the embraces of nature; and my soul rose to its author, with the chirping of the solitary birds, which

began to feel, rather than see, advancing day. . . . The grey morn,
streaked with silvery rays, ushered in the orient beams,—how
beautifully varying into purple!—yet, I was sorry to lose the soft
watery clouds which preceded them. (*A Short Residence*, 94)

"I saw the sun—and sighed," she concludes. "Absorbed" by sentiment, her bosom
is embraced by nature, her soul by God—signalling a pleasurable regress to "voluptuous sensations" in the arms of an imaginary combined parent that predates the
threat of oedipal sexuality. Coming on the heels of this voluptuous all-embrace,
Wollstonecraft's exhalation, "I saw the sun—and sighed," makes sense in the light
of her speculation, earlier in the same letter, that pursuit of the sun had originally
led to the peopling of the earth by northern tribes. Her sigh marks an acknowledgment
of her return to a modern world in which loveless preservation of the species can
take place without the intervention of Prometheus. This is what love in a cold
climate has come to, she seems to say.

Despite its ostensible function to guarantee uninterrupted, Rousseauian reverie,
the northern landscape (like its "sluggish" people) often serves as a projection of
Wollstonecraft's inner depression and numbness—"the benumbing stupour that,
for the last year, has frozen up all [her] faculties." Her reveries are apt to be disturbed
by bad smells (the "detestable evaporation" of herrings, for instance); even nature—
appropriated by the Rousseauian subject as a sign of its own self-sufficiency—contains
traces of the abject, or the dullness of lost meaning. On one occasion, she writes
in full summer that "The current of life appeared congealed at the source: all were
not frozen, for it was summer, you remember; but every thing appeared so dull,
that I waited to see ice, in order to reconcile me to the absence of gaiety" (*A Short
Residence*, 88). Wollstonecraft's northern metaphor literalizes the pathetic fallacy
of her earlier letter of complaint to Imlay: "How am I altered by disappointment! . . . Now I am going towards the North in search of sunbeams!—Will any
ever warm this desolated heart? all nature seems to frown—or rather mourn with
me. —Every thing is cold—cold as my expectations!"[20] Failed latter-day
Prometheanism leaves the northern landscape drained of warmth and life. Bearing
the marks of her own abjection, it functions as the melancholic underside of her
hectic pursuit of love in a cold climate.

The image of the human body in a state of repulsive preservation provokes
one of the most disturbing passages in *Letters Written During a Short Residence*.

Meditating on the Norwegian custom of embalming bodies, Wollstonecraft vents her disgust at "the human form when deprived of life":

> A desire of preserving the body seems to have prevailed in most countries of the world. . . . When I was shewn these human pet-rifications, I shrunk back with disgust and horror. "Ashes to ashes!" thought I—"Dust to dust!"—If this be not dissolution, it is some-thing worse than natural decay. . . . nothing is so ugly as the human form when deprived of life, and thus dried into stone, merely to pre-serve the most disgusting image of death. . . . Life, what art thou? Where goes this breath? this *I* so much alive? . . .—What will break the enchantment of animation?—For worlds, I would not see a form I loved—embalmed in my heart—thus sacrilegiously han-dled!—Pugh! my stomach turns. (*A Short Residence*, 108–109)

Confronted by the petrified human form ("the most disgusting image of death"), Wollstonecraft's writing becomes violently visceral ("Pugh! my stomach turns"). Her response, registered as a moment of textual semiosis ("Pugh!"), dramatizes the fantasy of abjection that Kristeva, in *Powers of Horror*, associates particularly with the maternal body and with the earliest stages of differentiation from the mother or the threat of "dissolution."[21]

It is hardly surprising that this moment should return, uncannily, in the most famous of all mother-daughter literary transactions, where the corpse of a dead love ("a form I loved—embalmed in my heart") comes to life as the embodiment of maternal failure. Mary Shelley took *Letters Written during a Short Residence* with her on her first European journey, after eloping with Percy Shelley.[22] Later, when she came to imagine Frankenstein's death-bringing, anti-Promethean mode of engendering in *Frankenstein; or, The Modern Prometheus*, she recapitulated her mother's outbust of revulsion at "something worse than natural decay." Her gothic tale takes its nightmarish inception from the moment Frankenstein falls asleep, after disgustedly contemplating his hideous handywork, only to dream that he is embrac-ing the corpse of his dead mother. His dream is a prelude to the animation of a Being made up entirely of the embalmed body parts of corpses. As Shelley writes of this horrific creation, in a seemingly unintentional pun, "A mummy again endued with animation could not be so hideous as that wretch"—apparently recalling the mum-mies to which Wollstonecraft compares the embalmed Norwegian corpses in her

Scandinavian letters ("The teeth, nails and skin were whole, without appearing black like the Egyptian mummies") (*A Short Residence*, 109). Significantly, the revenge of this unloved child on his maker—a new Prometheus for whom electricity, not love, brings clay to life—is to pursue Frankenstein ever further into the frozen arctic waste where they perish.

But this passage from Wollstonecraft's Scandinavian letters signals more than the transferential encounter between a literary mother and the daughter who had known her only through her writings and Godwin's *Memoirs*. Underlying the hideous materiality of petrified bodies is the image of a dead love that has been encrypted in the melancholy ego.[23] Wollstonecraft ends by musing about future perfectibility, in contrast to this melancholic embalming of the past. She concludes:

> Thinking of death makes us tenderly cling to our affections—with more than usual tenderness, I therefore assure you that I am yours, wishing that the temporary death of absence may not endure longer than is absolutely necessary. (*A Short Residence*, 109)

In the light of Wollstonecraft's horror at love's petrified body, we might be justified in reading this tender clinging as a clinging to love itself—a refusal to let love die, as much as the wish to overcome a separation that she calls "the temporary death of absence." When Godwin asked, shrewdly enough, "Why did she thus obstinately cling to an ill-starred unhappy passion?" (her passion for Imlay), he answered "Because it is of the very essence of affection, to seek to perpetuate itself" (*Memoirs*, 245). He might have added that she clung obstinately to her passion for Imlay because even an ill-starred passion is better than no passion at all. Keeping the image of the absent object alive guarantees the continued life of the subject, so completely has it become identified with the object. Worse than "the temporary death of absence," worse than losing the object of one's love, the death of love threatens the subject with loss of meaning altogether. Without her passion for the imaginary Imlay, Wollstonecraft seems to say, she might as well be a corpse; without her love letters, she would be dead (to him). Musing on "the fear of annihilation," she exclaims: "I cannot bear to think of being no more—of losing myself—though existence is often but a painful consciousness of misery" (*A Short Residence*, 112). The thought of her own death threatens to disrupt the text, as she demands, in a series of broken rhetorical questions: "Life, what art thou? Where goes this breath?

this *I*, so much alive?" The melancholic lover of life keeps going by thinking about dying.

Expelling an incorporated dead object in order to keep the "I" alive ("Pugh!"), Wollstonecraft turns at this nadir of her journey from the regressive and impoverished ego of the melancholic—narcissistically identified with the lost object—to something like mourning; this is the work that, for Freud, frees the ego to love once more. The mummified body is replaced by the other loved bodies from whom her travels have separated her. The first of these bodies belongs to the dead Fanny Blood, "a dear friend, the friend of [her] youth" (*A Short Residence*, 100). Hers is the "warbling" voice she still hears during her wanderings, functioning as the guarantee of a living sensibility in nature itself. The second body is that of her namesake—the infant Fanny Imlay, "the fire of whose eyes . . . still warms [Wollstonecraft's] breast" (*A Short Residence*, 100). Little Fanny, a form "embalmed in [her] heart," is not only a living memorial to Fanny Blood, but a constant reminder of Wollstonecraft's own capacity to feel—"still too young to ask why starts the tear, so near akin to pleasure and pain" (*A Short Residence*, 100), she nonetheless mirrors Wollstonecraft's continuing susceptibility to tears (and to pleasure too). Wollstonecraft not only imagines her daughter blushing, but later blushes at her own memories—presumably, the memory of Fanny's engendering:

> Tokens of love which I have received have rapt me in elysium—purifying the heart they enchanted.—My bosom still glows.—Do not saucily ask, repeating Sterne's question, "Maria, is it still so warm!". . . Sufficiently, O my God! has it been chilled by sorrow and unkindness—still nature will prevail—and if I blush at recollecting past enjoyment, it is the rosy hue of pleasure heightened by modesty, for the blush of modesty and shame are as distinct as the emotions by which they are produced. (*A Short Residence*, 111)

With the help of Sterne's *Sentimental Journey*, Wollstonecraft insists that recalling past sexual pleasure keeps her warm in the face of present "sorrow and unkindness." Refusing to relegate sexuality to the realm of shame, her still-blushing body provides an antidote to Imlay's desertion (death by absence), while the erotic tear ("so near akin to pleasure and pain") is redefined as the "balm" of mourning.

In the course of Wollstonecraft's travels, the eroticized, blushing body of the lover is converted into that of a mother.[24] The tearful relation of mother to child—

the bosom "heav[ing] with a pang at the thought which only an unhappy mother could feel" (A Short Residence, 158)—is Wollstonecraft's imaginary substitute for her relation to a cold and unfeeling lover; this is no ordinarily sexual "pang," although it may still be an erotic one. At the start of her travels, Wollstonecraft sheds tears while preserving a flower ("heart's ease") in "a letter that had not conveyed balm to [her] heart" (A Short Residence, 67). The mother-child embrace provides the tearful "balm" that Imlay's letters refuse. In the same letter, "a tear drop[s] on the rosy cheek [she] had just kissed" (A Short Residence, 69); later, she dreams that "[Her] little cherub was again hiding her face in [her] bosom" (A Short Residence 127). Balm and tears, or embalming in the heart—a tearful process of affective memorialization—are never far apart. Through her juxtaposition of maternal bosom and blushes, mother and infant daughter, tears and balm, Wollstonecraft posits an imaginary alternative to the deadly petrification at the heart of melancholia. Apropos of the narcissistic origin of poetical fictions, she observes that "In solitude, the imagination bodies forth its conceptions unrestrained, and stops enraptured to adore the beings of its own creation" (A Short Residence, 119). Little Fanny represents just such a narcissistic "being of [her] own creation." Like the Scandinavian letters, she is both a living memorial ("embalmed in the heart") and the balm itself; and like writing, she stands between her mother and death.

ii. "Hapless Woman! What a Fate is Thine!"

Wollststonecraft's feminism breaks in on this production of a maternal imaginary as the mark of difference between playing and being a child. On one hand the woman, "who [has] received the cruellest of disappointments" (an allusion to Imlay's infidelity), and on the other, the child, whose tears are without anguish: "I play the child, and weep at the recollection . . . yet never did drops of anguish like these bedew the cheeks of infantine innocence" (A Short Residence, 189). She plays the child in weeping, but her tears are not those of a child. When Wollstonecraft reflects on her daughter's future, in the context of their first parting during her Scandinavian journey, she does so "as a female" for whom the cultivation of sensibility is necessarily connected with "dread":

> You know that as a female I am particularly attached to her—I
> feel more than a mother's fondness and anxiety, when I reflect on
> the dependent and oppressed state of her sex. I dread lest she

73

should be forced to sacrifice her heart to her principles, or principles to her heart. With trembling hand I shall cultivate sensibility,
and cherish delicacy of sentiment . . . I dread to unfold her mind,
lest it should render her unfit for the world she is to inhabit—
Hapless woman! what a fate is thine! (*A Short Residence*, 97)

Feminist sensibility is divided against itself, like heart and principles, the cultivation of one depending on the sacrifice of the other. Wollstonecraft ventriloquizes
her reader's complaint against the obsessive idée fixe of a wronged woman ("Still
harping on the same subject, you will exclaim") in order to rebut the complaint with
a reminder of women's collective class oppression: "How can I avoid it, when most
of the struggles of an eventful life have been occasioned by the oppressed state of
my sex: *we reason deeply when we forcibly feel*" (*A Short Residence*, 171; my italics).
The hand that cultivates sensibility trembles from forced feeling; the oppressed
state of her sex generates an excess of sensibility ("I feel *more* than a mother's fondness and anxiety"). For Wollstonecraft, it seems, feminist subjectivity is being
forced to feel, not only one's own division, but too much, and too much as a woman;
and not only to feel for one's daughter, but for women in general. The internally
divided relation of mother and daughter becomes the basis for a gender-specific mode
of identification and a precarious, expensive subjectivity.

Elsewhere in the Scandinavian letters, Wollstonecraft projects her sense of the
oppression of women as a class onto a historical figure, "The unfortunate Matilda."
Queen Caroline Matilda (1751–75), sister of George III of England, was married
at fifteen to mad King Christian VII of Denmark, and died in exile at the age of
twenty-four. In concert with the royal physician, Struensee, the probable father of
her daughter, Matilda was able to initiate a comparatively liberal and reformed
regime until her imprisonment and Struensee's brutal beheading. All this was comparatively recent history when Wollstonecraft visited Copenhagen, where she was
annoyed to find Matilda being censured for the enlightened child-rearing practices that she herself had advocated. She writes that she was haunted by Matilda's
story, believing her the victim not so much of her love affair with Struensee, but
of her premature attempts to bring about social and political reforms in Denmark:

I am now fully convinced that she was the victim of the party she
displaced, who would have overlooked, or encouraged, her attachment, had her lover not, aiming at being useful, attempted to

overturn some established abuses before the people, ripe for the change, had sufficient spirit to support him when struggling in their behalf. Such indeed was the asperity sharpened against her, that I have heard her, even after so many years have elapsed, charged with licentiousness . . . for her very charities, because she erected amongst other institutions, an hospital to receive foundlings. (A Short Residence, 166)

Wollstonecraft goes out of her way to defend Matilda for "an error common to innovators, in wishing to do immediately what can only be done by time" (A Short Residence, 166). Her zeal in defending Matilda can be ascribed to her own republican politics. But Wollstonecraft clearly also identified with her—not only as the mother of an illegitimate daughter (and as a woman similarly "charged with licentiousness" for an extra-marital affair in the face of her arranged marriage), but as an earlier example of the woman of spirit who tried to reform the world before it was ready.

Wollstonecraft writes in the post-Revolutionary *apologia* with which she ends her book that "An ardent affection for the human race makes enthusiastic characters eager to produce alteration in laws and governments prematurely" (A Short Residence, 198). The passage is often read as a pulling back from the principles of the French Revolution in the wake of the Jacobin bloodbath that Wollstonecraft had witnessed firsthand. But taken in conjunction with her reflections on Queen Matilda, it suggests rather that Wollstonecraft recognized a link between her own enthusiastic prematurity and the failure of the revolutionary experiment on which she herself had embarked in France in the form of her failed domestication with Imlay. Towards the end of *Letters Written during a Short Residence*, Wollstonecraft, "growing bitter," turns against the imaginary recipient of her letters. He becomes the "embruted" man of commerce, the reader who resists her book:

But you will say that I am growing bitter, perhaps, personal. Ah! shall I whisper to you—that you—yourself, are strangely altered, since you have entered deeply into commerce—more than you are aware of—. . . . Nature has given you talents, which lie dormant, or are wasted in ignoble pursuits. (A Short Residence, 191)

"Cassandra," she writes darkly, "was not the only prophetess whose warning voice has been disregarded" (*A Short Residence*, p. 193). This is the closest Wollstonecraft comes to denouncing Imlay directly. By this time Wollstonecraft's Scandinavian journey was at an end; Imlay remained a resistant reader and had failed to meet her at Hamburg, despite her hopes. She blames his defection on "speculation"—on the spirit of the age: "to business, as it is termed, every thing must give way . . . and all the endearing charities of citizen, husband, father, brother, become empty names." And again, "But to commerce, everything must give way; profit and profit are the only speculations—'double—double, toil and trouble'" (*A Short Residence*, 193, 194). What would it take to make the names of "citizen, husband, father, brother" full names instead of empty ones, or to take the troubled doubling out of the profit motif? Presumably, the idealistic, new-masculine revolutionary sensibility that Imlay had once seemed to embody.

But Imlay, whose tangled business affairs Wollstonecraft had been tending during her own journey, has come to represent instead a commercial traveller. The failed venture that had brought Mary Wollstonecraft to Scandinavia was the mysterious disappearance of a ship called the *Maria and Margaretha* (named after Mary Wollstonecraft and Fanny's devoted French nursemaid, Marguerite), into which Imlay had sunk a substantial investment in the form of a cargo of bullion; like others at the time, Imlay had been engaged in running the British blockade of France by importing goods under the flag of the neutral Scandinavian countries—whose delicate balance of neutrality and commercial support for revolutionary France came to an end with the bombardment of Copenhagen.[25] Earlier in their relationship, Wollstonecraft had blamed Imlay's commercial speculations for keeping them apart. Now she blames commerce in general for the entire aftermath of the French Revolution: "The interests of nations are bartered by speculating merchants" (*A Short Residence*, 195). Her glimpse behind the scenes at Imlay's import-export dealings has exposed "the mean machinery which has directed many transactions of moment." This is the same rhetoric we find in her *Historical and Moral View of the French Revolution* (1794), which ends by denouncing "The destructive influence of commerce."[26] A sentimental traveller in Imlay's commercial world, Wollstonecraft is forced to bring sensibility into the political domain: "Why should I weep for myself?" she demands. Instead, she should weep for the bartered interests of nations.

Despite Wollstonecraft's politically correct optimism (her faith in "the grand causes which combine to carry mankind forward, and diminish the sum of human misery" (*A Short Residence*, 198), the sum of her own revolutionary hopes has also come to nothing. Wollstonecraft's speculation in love has left her, as well as Imlay, close to bankruptcy. In the fragmentary jottings that conclude her travels, her world is progressively divested of significance; travel becomes "vanity," the cliffs of Dover "insignificant," her wanderings designed "literally speaking, to kill time" (*A Short Residence*, 197). Informed readers can complete the fragmentary narrative of her homecoming with her second, more serious suicide attempt when she arrives in London (the first preceded her journey to Scandinavia). But what part does "commerce" play in this melancholy, unwritten dénouement? Why does woman wail so loudly for her commercial lover? And when Godwin calls *Letters Written during a Short Residence* "a book calculated to make a man in love with its author" (*Memoirs*, 249), what were the gains that Wollstonecraft accrued to herself by so publicly lamenting the sorrows of a deserted revolutionary feminist? One answer to these questions is that more than Wollstonecraft's own emotional investment had gone astray during the period of her love affair with Imlay. Freud is right to remind us that mourning and melancholia may both be reactions, not only to the loss of a loved person, but to "the loss of some abstraction which has taken the place of one, such as one's country, liberty, an ideal, and so on" (*SE* 14.243).

At the start of Wollstonecraft's Scandinavian travels she alludes to "the horrors [she] had witnessed in France, which had cast a gloom over all nature" (*A Short Residence*, 68). After her firsthand experience of Robespierre's France, her Scandinavian journey represents a retreat from the tumultuous and "unnatural fermentation" of the French Revolution, whose amorality and opportunism were now embodied by Imlay. Her withdrawal into the reflective pose of the *promeneuse solitaire* (written in the wake of her politically engaged *Historical and Moral View of . . . the French Revolution*) enacts the same retreat from the theater of politics to the private, affective sphere that also occurs during the mid-1790s in Wordsworth. Both were disaffected by Robespierre, yet alienated from the England that Wollstonecraft describes as dominated by "Aristocracy and fanaticism" (*A Short Residence*, 121). Unlike Wollstonecraft, however, Wordsworth did not choose to acknowledge—in public at least—that the turn taken by revolutionary history had also separated him from his own French lover and her illegitimate daughter. The comparison with Wordsworth casts new light on Wollstonecraft's visibility as a woman lamenting her desertion, and even on her self-representation as an unmarried mother. In *The Prelude*, Wordsworth was later to figure the French Revolution in terms of an unmarried mother separated from her lover with his autobiographical roman à clef, "Vaudracour and Julia." In book 9 of *The Prelude*, the fictional lovers fall victim to the ancien régime rather than to the new post-Revolutionary order, but their story is similarly infected by Wordsworth's personal and political malaise during the mid-1790s. Wollstonecraft's Scandinavian letters, in other words, can be seen as at once a gender-specific and a historically specific response to the failure of the revolutionary imagination which confronted Girondist sympathizers like herself and Wordsworth at the time.

In its own way, Wollstonecraft's love affair with Imlay had been a political project—an attempt at domesticated romance, eschewing legal marriage, in a period of revolutionary optimism.[27] The collapse of their relationship and their separation demand to be seen in the larger context of the separation between France, England, and America under the military and mercantile pressures of competing empires. The exotic setting of Coleridge's "deep romantic chasm" obscures a European site. Woman wails for her democratic lover (Imlay was, after all, a democrat) against the background of European revolutionary upheaval. Wollstonecraft's Scandinavian letters can be read not only as an autobiographical inquiry into "the history of [her] own heart," but as a chapter in the history of the relations between sensibility, feminism, and the revolutionary era they inhabit. If we still fall in love with the author of *Letters Written during a Short Residence in Sweden, Norway, and Denmark* today, it may not be only because a melancholy, politically incorrect *promeneuse solitaire* unexpectedly retains her appeal for latter-day romantic daughters. It may also be because we can claim Wollstonecraft as the mother of the contemporary feminism whose much disputed founding slogan reminds us that the personal is, indeed, always political—that even the history of feminine melancholia intersects with the bartered interests of nations. Like Godwin, and like Mary Shelley, we necessarily read Wollstonecraft's writings posthumously and find our own meanings there. But, as so often, we find that she has travelled this country before us.

* * *

Freud observes of transference-love that, to the layman at least, "things that have to do with love are incommensurable with everything else; they are, as it were, written on a special page on which no other writing is tolerated" (*SE* 12.160). But to the psychoanalyst, "the outbreak of a passionate demand for love is largely the work of resistance" (*SE* 12.162). Falling in love is always falling in love again—

always a matter of "new editions of old feelings or fantasies aroused in the analysis." This form of resistance, according to Freud, is likely to occur where especially troubling material threatens to emerge in the analysis; in particular, transference resistances accompany the reexperiencing of the repressed object-relations of earliest childhood.[28] Mary Shelley's *Frankenstein* offers itself as one figure for the effects of early maternal deprivation. But *Letters Written during a Short Residence* already provides a figure of maternal deprivation in Fanny Imlay. In an essay called "The Dead Mother," André Green explores the transferential effects produced by a mother who is dead in the sense of having withdrawn into melancholia and depression—not literally absent, or dead as Wollstonecraft was for her second daughter, Mary Shelley, but dead as she might have been for the depressed infant Fanny: *"The essential characteristic of this depression is that it takes place in the presence of the object, which is itself absorbed by a bereavement."*[29] For Green, the melancholic mother produces an impossible mourning visible only in the transference—in the affective blank, or contentless mourning, that marks the site of her burial; even melancholia is secondary to the "'blank' anxiety which expresses a loss that has been experienced on a narcissistic level."[30] Those who have experienced such a loss (here Green's language interestingly recapitulates the language of Wollstonecraft's travel book) are numbed and frozen, "complain[ing] of being cold even in the heat. . . . they feel chilled by a funereal shiver, wrapped in their shroud." For them the mother is embalmed: "The subject's entire structure aims at a fundamental fantasy: to nourish the dead mother, to maintain her perpetually embalmed."[31] Green's essay permits one to reread the frozen landscape and embalmed corpses of Wollstonecraft's travel book as metaphors for a psychic predicament that implicates not the absent lover, but the "dead" or melancholic mother.

In *Letters Written during a Short Residence*, the infant Fanny functions as a marker for the psychic terrain of the absent mother. Falling in love with Wollstonecraft—finding her travel book "irrestistible"—signals a transferential effect that could be read, paradoxically, as an effect of resistance. Transference-love resists "the death of absence." What resists, taking the form of transference, is the problem of mourning that Green locates in the empty space of the dead mother—not "the psychical consequences of the real death of the mother, but rather that of an imago . . . brutally transforming a living object, which was a source of vitality for the child, into a distant figure, toneless, practically inanimate."[32] This figure is the dead "mummy" of Wollstonecraft's Scandinavian letters. Located at the heart of her travel book, the dead mother reminds us not so much

that Wollstonecraft's pursuit of love in a cold climate may have been activated by
an originary maternal depression; and not so much that Fanny (who herself committed suicide as a young woman) was the daughter of a depressed mother who had
attempted suicide twice during her infancy; but rather, that when we fall in love
(again) with Wollstonecraft's writing, we may be signalling our own resistance to
being Wollstonecraft's daughters. As heirs to her melancholia as well as her feminism, we are bound to resist (or fall in love with) her legacy of impossible mourning.
In Wollstonecraft's travel book, her own resistance takes the form of the "*quest for
lost meaning*" (Green again) that is figured by her melancholy pursuit of love in a
cold climate. But the same quest also informs our inquiry into Wollstonecraft's
meaning for feminism today. Green glosses this quest for meaning as "a patched breast,
a piece of cognitive fabric which is destined to mask the hole left by [the dead
mother], while secondary hatred and erotic excitation teem on the edge of an abyss
of emptiness."[33] This is why Wollstonecraft must at once love Imlay and hate him,
at once embalm the memory of Fanny Blood and cling to the pleasure-giving form
of Fanny Imlay. But it may also be why we still find Wollstonecraft's travel book
irresistible. *Letters Written during a Short Residence* tells us not only about the history of feminism, not only about Wollstonecraft's amatory melancholia, but about
the condition of being unmothered, when maternal depression and oppression
coincide. Providing a genealogy of mother-daughter melancholia, it also preserves
Wollstonecraft, our dead mother, where we can best memorialize her—at once
dead and present, in her writing.

1. Mary Wollstonecraft, *A Short Residence in Sweden, Norway and Denmark* and William Godwin,
    Memoirs of the Author of The Rights of Woman, ed. Richard Holmes (Harmondsworth, UK:
    Penguin, 1987), 249. Subsequent references in the text to Wollstonecraft's *A Short Residence*
    and Godwin's *Memoirs* are to this edition.

2. Godwin read Wollstonecraft's travel book in January 1796, six months before they actually
    became lovers. See *Collected Letters of Mary Wollstonecraft*, ed. Ralph M. Wardle (Ithaca and
    London: Cornell University Press, 1979), 46; and William St. Clair, *The Godwins and the
    Shelleys: The Biography of a Family* (London: Faber and Faber, 1989), 161.

3. *Collected Letters*, 331. Vol. 3 of William Kenrick's much reprinted translation of *Eloisa, or a
    series of original letters* (London, 1761) describes Julie's happily married domestication with
    the philosophic M. Wolmar.

4. *Collected Letters*, 263.

5. Ibid., 337. In her excellent account of Mary Wollstonecraft's *Letters Written during a Short
    Residence*, however, Mary A. Favret has argued for a subtle revision of Rousseau, from solitude

to the social; see Mary A. Favret, *Romantic Correspondence: Women, Politics and the Fiction of Letters* (Cambridge: Cambridge University Press, 1993), 96–132. Favret's chapter, "Mary Wollstonecraft and the Business of Letters," is virtually alone in dealing with the letter form of Wollstonecraft's Scandinavian travels as a significant fictional and political device. See also Mitzi Myers, "Mary Wollstonecraft's *Letters Written . . . in Sweden*: Toward Romantic Autobiography," *Studies in Eighteenth-Century Culture* 8 (1979): 165–85; and Gary Kelly, *Revolutionary: Feminism: The Mind and Career of Mary Wollstonecraft* (London: Macmillan, 1992), 171–95.

6. For the *Memoirs* as Godwin's "self-therapy," see Mitzi Myers, "Godwin's *Memoirs* of Wollstonecraft: The Shaping of Self and Subject," *Studies in Romanticism* 20 (1981): 299–316, especially 306–307.

7. For an interesting recent reconsideration of this debt, see Jane Moore, "Plagiarism with a Difference: Subjectivity in 'Kubla Khan' and *Letters Written during a Short Residence in Sweden, Norway and Denmark*," in *Beyond Romanticism*, ed. Stephen Copley and John Whale (London and New York: Routledge, 1992), 140–59.

8. See, for instance, *Monthly Mirror* 1 (1796): 287 ("an unhappy mother, wandering through foreign countries with her helpless infant"); quoted by Favret, *Romantic Correspondence*, 129.

9. Letter of March 13, 1797; see William Godwin, *Memoirs of Mary Wollstonecraft*, ed. W. Clark Durant (London and New York: Constable & Co Ltd, 1927), 306–307. Southey also paid tribute to Wollstonecraft in his dedication to "The Triumph of Woman": " The lilly cheek, the 'purple light of love,' / The liquid lustre of the melting eye,— Mary! of these the Poet sung"; *Poems* (Bristol: Joseph Cottle, 1797), 3. For other smitten readers of Wollstonecraft's travels, see St. Clair, *The Godwins and the Shelleys*, 161–62, and Moore, "Plagiarism with a Difference," 145. More recently Richard Holmes echoes this language of love in his introduction to the Penguin edition of Wollstonecraft's travels and Godwin's *Memoirs*; Wollstonecraft "fell in love with" Norway, while her travel letters are "a vivid piece of self-portraiture, the kind of thing with which Godwin . . . fell in love" (*A Short Residence*, 19, 20).

10. *Collected Letters*, 263.

11. Ibid., 263, 274.

12. Ibid., 302.

13. See Ernest Jones, "Early Development of Female Sexuality" (1927), in *Papers on Psycho-Analysis*, 5th ed. (London: Baillière, Tindall & Cox, 1950), 438–51.

14. Jacques Lacan, *The Four Fundamental Concepts of Psycho-Analysis*, ed. Jacques-Alain Miller, trans. Alan Sheridan (New York: W. W. Norton & Company, 1978), 207–208, 218.

15. *Collected Letters*, 306.

16. Ibid., 309; my italics.

17. Ibid., 318. By embarking on her book, Wollstonecraft was also taking a step toward financial independence, hoping to "discharge all my obligations of a pecuniary kind" (*Collected Letters*, 306).

18. See Favret, *Romantic Correspondence*, 96–132 for the metaphorical implications of both "correspondence" and "commerce"; Favret engages both the politics and the financial aspects of Wollstonecraft's Scandinavian letters.

19. *Collected Letters*, 303.

20. Ibid., 298.

21. "The abject . . . confronts us . . . within our personal archeology, with our earliest attempts to release the hold of *maternal* entity even before existing outside of her"; see Julia Kristeva, *Powers of Horror: An Essay on Abjection*, trans. Leon S. Roudiez (New York: Columbia University Press, 1982), 13.

22. See St. Clair, *The Godwins and the Shelleys*, 366. Mary Shelley reread Godwin's *Memoirs*, the letters to Imlay, and *A Short Residence* during June 1820, the anniversary of the death of her son William; see *The Journals of Mary Shelley*, ed. Paula R. Feldman and Diana Scott-Kilvert (Oxford: Clarendon Press, 1987), 2: 649, 684.

23. For an account of the "encrypted" or incorporated mourning that constitutes melancholia, see Nicholas Abraham and Maria Torok, "Mourning *or* Melancholia: Introjection *versus* Incorporation," in *The Shell and the Kernel*, ed. and trans. Nicholas Rand (Chicago and London: University of Chicago Press, 1994), 125–38.

24. For an interesting account of "maternal regression," drawing on Chodorow and Klein, in relation to Wollstonecraft's use of the pictureque, see Jeanne Moskal, "The Picturesque and the Affectionate in Wollstonecraft's *Letters from Norway*," *Modern Language Quarterly* 52 (1991): 263–94, especially 266–68.

25. For the full story of Imlay's Scandinavian debacle and Wollstonecraft's attempts to effect an out-of-court settlement, see Per Nyström, "Mary Wollstonecraft's Scandinavian Journey," *Acts of the Royal Society of Arts and Sciences of Gothenburg, Humaniora* 17 (1980), especially 16–32. Imlay's original investment may have represented an attempt to raise the £1,000 necessary for his and Wollstonecraft's projected emigration to America.

26. See *Mary Wollstonecraft: Political Writings*, ed. Janet Todd (London: William Pickering, 1989), 385.

27. See Kelly, *Revolutionary Feminism*, 140–70 for this period in Wollstonecraft's life and thought and what Kelly calls Wollstonecraft's "vanguardist revolutionary conjugality with Imlay." Wollstonecraft had been registered by Imlay as his wife with the American consul so that she could escape imprisonment (along with other English revolutionary sympathizers in Paris like Helen Maria Williams) after the decree of August 1793; unlike Britain, America was not at war with France.

28. See Sigmund Freud, "An Autobiographical Study" (1925): "The transference . . . is resolved by convincing [the patient] that in his transference attitude he is *re-experiencing* emotional relations which had their origin in his earliest object-attachments during the repressed period of his childhood" (*SE* 20.43).

29. André Green, "The Dead Mother," in *On Private Madness* (Madison, CT: International Universities Press, 1986), 149; Green's italics.

30. Ibid., 146.

31. Ibid., 156–57, 162.

32. Ibid., 142.

33. Ibid., 152.

5

Malthus, Matricide, and the Marquis de Sade

Taking the population of the world at any number, a thousand millions, for instance, the human species would increase in the ratio of — 1, 2, 4, 8, 16, 32, 64, 128, 256, 512, etc. and subsistence as — 1, 2, 3, 4, 5, 6, 7, 8, 9, 10, etc. In two centuries and a quarter, the population would be to the means of subsistence as 512 to 10: in three centuries as 4096 to 13, and in two thousand years the difference would be almost incalculable.

—Malthus, An Essay on the Principle of Population (1798)[1]

MADAME DE SAINT-ANGE — *Do you know, Dolmancé, that by means of this system you are going to be led to prove that totally to extinguish the human race would be nothing but to render Nature a service?* DOLMANCÉ — *Who doubts of it, Madame?*

—Sade, Philosophy in the Bedroom (1795)[2]

IN THE PANIC-STRICKEN IMAGININGS that accompany both pre- and post-Malthusian thinking about population growth, population and plague are inseparable. Either plague threatens to wipe out the gains of prosperity that were generally thought (until Malthus's time) to accompany increased population; or else population increase itself becomes the plague of hungry nations (our contemporary post-Malthusian anxiety). Panic about an epidemic of unchecked reproduction brings with it, as its shadow, the nightmare of a world unable to sustain its inhabitants and emptied of people altogether. As the first modern demographer to bring statistics to bear on forecasting the human condition, Malthus's contradictory achievement was to unleash, simultaneously, the terror of too many and too few.[3] Fear of unbearable multitudes and fear of extinction occupy the same, overcrowded space in the Malthusian imaginary. The momentum of geometrical progression underwhelms us (so to speak) with the startling result that incalculability equals nothing in the end. This folding back on itself of the imaginary logic of population growth is the paradigm that I want to explore in Malthus's *Essay on the Principle of Population* (1798).

Malthus and the Marquis de Sade make strange bedfellows. But the same reproductive anxieties haunt their writing. The numbers of babies abandoned to the *Enfants trouvés*, or foundling hospitals, by the poor of late eighteenth-century France during the decades leading up to the French Revolution—years when the population was rising, although not so sharply as in England—gave poignant and controversial visibility to population growth during Sade's own lifetime.[4] *Philosophy in the Bedroom* (1795), published a few years before Malthus's essay in the wake of the French Revolution, preaches population control in the face of an abjectly multiplying poor.[5] For Sade's aristocratic libertine, Dolmancé, state institutions of benevolence (the *Enfants trouvés*) are merely the source from which "spews forth into society a swarm of new-made creatures whose unique hope resides in your purse" (p. 216). Dolmancé goes on to demand: "Does anyone fear France's depopulation? Ha! dread not." But "dread" is the operative word. For all his libertine frivolity, Dolmancé *does* dread. This is not only a political dread that it's tempting to connect with the French Revolution, but a psychic dread whose origins are more obscure. On one level, what is at stake is the survival of republican systems. As Dolmancé warns us, "in no matter what political organization, whenever the size of the population exceeds what is strictly necessary to its existence, that society languishes" (p. 216). But on the psychic level, the issue is the survival of the libertine self. Monarchy needs slaves, but His Majesty the Ego must reign alone in Sade's libertine republic: "Beware of too great a multiplication in a race whose every member is sovereign, and be certain that revolutions are never but the effect of a too numerous population" (p. 336). The survival of the post-(sexual-)revolutionary order demands the purging of the reproductive body politic, as Sade puts it, "from the cradle" (p. 336).

A subversive political economist, Sade's Dolmancé is also a canny libertine philosopher who reveals the unsaid in Malthus's domesticized sexual economy. *Philosophy in the Bedroom* can be read as a no-holds-barred disquisition on population, but it incidentally provides an education in what Malthus represses entirely, namely, the possibility of separating sexual pleasure from reproduction. The anti-sentimental education given to Dolmancé's willing fifteen-year-old pupil—aptly named Eugénie—comprises, among other things, a manual on late eighteenth-century methods of birth control. Since Sade's physiology of female sexuality is modelled on men's, his radical solution is to render disposable what women have in excess, which is both maternity and one hole too many (for the sodomite, that is). If all women were men, the need for population control would be obviated; in the meantime, sodomy offers at once pleasure and prophylaxis. The imaginary economy of Malthus's *Essay* is based on the notion of exchange—sexuality equals reproduction. In Sade's seminal economy, by contrast, the circulation of both sexual and discursive pleasure depends on the liberal expenditure of body fluids (not for nothing have Sade's editors called *Philosophy in the Bedroom* among his most "seminal" works; p. 181). The conspicuous, nonproductive expenditure of semen forms the climactic coup de théâtre of the libertine's everchanging sexual scenarios. But it is important that this expenditure should have no results—that it bear no risk of being converted into babies. Conception would represent the bourgeois accumulation which both the republican and the aristocrat despise, or else the "national defect" of overpopulation embodied by the abject "swarm of new-made creatures" draining both the nation's purse and the libertine's psyche.

At the core of the Sadeian libertine's blackly ironic philosophy is the identification between the immoralist's restlessness and republican insurrection. The fictional political pamphlet embedded in the boudoir setting of *Philosophy in the Bedroom*—"Yet Another Effort, Frenchmen, If You Would Become Republicans"— was sufficiently Republican to be detatched from its context and published separately during the Revolution of 1848. Read, as it were, "straight," the pamphlet mounts a powerful anti-familial case for sexual liberation (unusually, extended to women— on certain terms—as well as to men), while arguing for the recognition of prostitution, sodomy, and male homosexuality as legitimate social and sexual practices. Sade's intentions in writing this pamphlet are notoriously hard to gauge, given the extremity to which it takes Revolutionary ideas; as he puts it, "Republican mettle calls for a touch of ferocity" (p. 333). But even if this were not the case, the pamphlet's context in the libertine dialogues of *Philosophy in the Bedroom* would put a kink in Sade's political philosophy. Dolmancé's elaborately choreographed *tableaux vivants*—the ever varying sexual practices and "positions" which embody his libertine theories— locate the sources of Sadeian pleasure in something other than irony, even if a measure of humor attends his demonstrations.[6] Sadeian pleasure, it hardly needs saying, involves the discursive elaboration of pain and usually takes the body of a woman as its text. In *Philosophy in the Bedroom*, the maternal body is the prime site for this sadistic elaboration. It is worth asking why discursive pleasure should focus on the mother, and why Sade's libertine inquiry demands the closing of the maternal body to effect its own closure—a question to which I will return in my own dénouement.

Along with their underlying fear of women's reproductive capacities, Malthus and Sade share the suspicion that female sexuality may elude the order and the specular capture of their respective modes of philosophic inquiry.[7] Both the *Essay* and Sade's *Philosophy in the Bedroom* associate the question of women's visibility with the need to restrain their sexuality. Sadeian women are supposed to ejaculate ("discharge") just as men do—but invisibly. Hence the only legible signs of women's pleasure are marks of pain on the surface of the female body: "Pleasure's effects, in women, are always uncertain. . . . hence, pain must be preferred, for pain's telling effects cannot deceive" (p. 252). In the Sadeian imaginary, sexuality is a sign-system inscribed on a feminine surface with pen, whip, and even needle. The phobic object of Sade's libertine imaginary is the interior of the reproductive body that forever threatens to elude his legible system. *Philosophy in the Bedroom* culminates in a vicious matriphobic phantasy designed to put a stop to reproduction at its source. Instead of being inseminated, a mother's body is literally sewn up—disinvaginated. The pain inscribed on the maternal body can be read as the libertine's revenge on women for their resistance to the specular system that underpins the libertine's philosophy and orders his psychic identity. Sewing up the problem of the mother at once renders feminine sexuality seamless—closing the question—and fantasmatically halts reproduction. Casting out sexual difference and the threat of maternity in one radical operation, the libertine constitutes himself as sovereign ego at the expense of the mother. *Philosophy in the Bedroom* exposes the matriphobic sexual politics that underlie *An Essay on the Principle of Population*, while bringing to light the connections between visibility, restraint, and punishment that are more discreetly encoded in Malthus's domestication of the population problem.

i: "She Makes Hungry Where Most She Satisfies"

In Malthus's *Essay*, the figure of the reproductive woman surfaces to subvert both the rhetoric of intellectual inquiry and the narrative of population control. Malthus's final chapter reminds us that passions and physical wants combine to awaken the mind and accentuate the desire for knowledge. "Every part of nature," he asserts, "seems . . . to offer inexhaustible food for the most unremitted inquiry." Nature, the proper object of inquiry, is also what feeds it. Here Malthus invokes Shakespeare's Cleopatra: "Custom cannot stale / Her infinite variety" (p. 211). But Malthus is paying nature a backhanded compliment. Placed as it is in the mouth of an ever hungry inquirer, the quotation puts him as much at the mercy of his desires as Shakespeare's imperial fool, Anthony. Here is the relevant, often quoted passage:

> Age cannot wither her, nor custom stale
> Her infinite variety: other women cloy
> The appetite they feed; *but she makes hungry*
> *Where most she satisfies . . .*
> (*Anthony and Cleopatra* 2.2.243–46; my italics)

How are we to read this allusion to a hunger-inducing nature? It is tempting to view it as entirely, if unintentionally, consistent with the paradoxical law of nature promulgated by Malthus's *Essay*—that hunger, or famine, will always outrun plentiful resources. In other words, "she" (nature) makes hungry where most she multiplies. Or, in Malthus's classic formula, "The perpetual tendency in the race of man to increase beyond the means of subsistence is one of the general laws of animated nature which we can have no reason to expect will change" (p. 199). Enough food will always mean too many bodies; the resources that can support more people rapidly become scarce resources overtaxed by the hungry many.

Malthus's basic proposition—that although resources are finite, population growth is potentially infinite without the checks of plague, famine, and war—has been called "the dismal theorum." His melancholy argument (the ineradicability of human suffering, the impossibility of achieving a perfect state of society) mounts an explicit political critique of Godwinian utopianism, while challenging Godwin's mistrust of social institutions. Nature, Malthus asserts, will always counter the effects of social reform or the abolition of political injustice with its own disasterous logic. The effect of Malthus's allusion to Cleopatra is even stranger when you consider that Malthus's other main proposition is the impossibility of extinguishing sexual passion. Where Godwin claimed, implausibly, that sexual passion would wither away in a state of perfected Reason, Malthus saw sexuality as the ultimate spanner in the works. His hidden figure for this problem is the other woman—the reproductive woman who resists domestication and social control. Other women may cloy the appetitite they feed, but *this* other woman—the embodiment of Otherness—will always leave you hungry, ruining both empires and men. Cleopatra surfaces as a version of the figure who often accompanies discussions of population and plague—the woman, here an alien or foreign one, who produces unwanted babies or covertly transmits infection. The allusion to Cleopatra marks the borders of an invasive difference. Difference, in fact, turns out to be what is at stake in the paragraph that follows, where Malthus makes his case for a Christian view of divine creative intentions in terms of the aestheticized body of a woman. The offensive underside of Cleopatra's "infinite variety" has to be overlooked, he argues, in the interests of the whole:

> Infinite variety seems, indeed, eminently her [i.e., nature's] characteristic feature. The shades that are here and there blended in the picture give spirit, life, and prominence to her exuberant beauties, and those roughnesses and inequalities, those inferior parts that support the superior, though they sometimes offend the fastidious miscroscopic eye of short-sighted man, contribute to the symmetry, grace, and fair proportion of the whole. (p. 211)

In this naming of nature's parts, Malthus simultaneously deploys and denies sexual difference. A natural fetishist, he is willing to overlook the "offence" of the inferior parts in the interests of a superior wholeness whose proportions conveniently reflect the outlines of masculine desire.

The fastidious microscopic eye of shortsighted man recalls no one so much as Gulliver, disgustedly contemplating the skin blemishes of Brobdingnagian ladies. Malthus's justification for God's design unsettlingly rejects Gulliver's microscopic eye only to end up sounding like the inquirer satirized in Swift's *A Tale of a Tub* for preferring "a perpetual Possession of being well Deceived." The symmetry, grace, and fair proportion of an idealized, class-specific feminine body can hardly stand up to being undressed, let alone flayed. Malthus's unwitting reminiscence of Swift's self-betrayed philosophic inquirer points to the tradition of inquiry to which the *Essay on the Principle of Population* belongs. Among other things, it can be read as an essay on the principle of modern philosophic inquiry itself, underwritten by Newtonian theology in contrast to Godwin's Cartesian legacy.[8] How is the rational inquirer to preach not political justice (like Godwin) but divine justice, in the face of nature's incorrigible faults? If social engineering works against the "natural" checks of plague and famine, or the man-made check of war, what is to prevent the Christian moral philosopher from falling prey to despair? For Malthus, one answer is manly exertion, but another is the manliness of daring to look truth in the face: "the most baleful mischiefs," he writes, "may be expected from the *unmanly* conduct of not daring to face truth because it is unpleasing" (p. 199; my italics). To be unmanned by the unpleasing aspect of the reproductive natural body—the offensive body of a woman—sounds perilously like being afflicted by castration anxiety. Facing it involves either adopting the fetishist's stance or successfully resolving the Oedipus complex—that is, maintaining the status quo, which is just what Malthus's political opponents accused him of doing. This is not to argue that the *Essay* is a manifestation of the unconscious of social-scientific inquiry, or that when science unveils nature it always encounters castration anxiety.[9] Rather, I want to point out that when he opposes manliness to despair, Malthus tries to take the dismalness out of his theorem by constructing a gender system.

In Malthus's domestic economy, it is women who pay the price for what Godwin called "things as they are" (the title of his novel, *Things as They Are; or, The Adventures of Caleb Williams,* 1794). Malthus's solution to the population problem is to feminize it, and then to manage it via the voluntary "restraint" which he equates with the newly emerging historical phenomenon of companionate middle-class marriage. By a sleight of hand familiar to students of domestic ideology (and especially to readers of Jane Austen), managing family size turns out to mean marrying prudently within one's means. Malthus's well-known objection to Godwin's *Enquiry concerning Political Justice* (1793) was his focus on institutions as the source of all social ills and political injustice. Godwin envisages, in particular, an end to the institution of marriage; as Malthus paraphrases Godwin, marriage would be replaced by "the commerce of the sexes established upon principles of the most perfect freedom" (p. 135). In Godwin's scenario, Malthus points out, "it would be of little consequence . . . how many children a woman had or to whom they belonged" (p. 135) since support would be spontaneously forthcoming from society. Such a state of affairs, Malthus observes, would be highly favorable to population growth—doing away with one powerful deterrent to marriage (what he calls dourly its "irremediableness"), while promoting early coupling and removing any anxieties about child support. As a result, Malthus writes, "I do not conceive that there would be one woman in a hundred, of twenty-three, without a family" (p. 136). "Conceived" like this, the Godwinian population would rapidly exceed resources, leading to the very want and misery that (for Malthus) human institutions such as marriage exist to regulate. As Malthus goes on to argue, property rights would still have to be rationed and respected in a situation of finite resources, unless "some mysterious interference of heaven" were to strike men with impotence and women with barrenness. And in order to police the responsibility for maintaining one's offspring, something not very different from the institution of marriage would have to come into operation.

Here Malthus shows his hand. For him, the burden of sexuality is unevenly shouldered by men and women; women are to blame for any glitches in the system. As he puts it: "The view of these difficulties presents us with a very natural origin of the superior disgrace which attends a breach of chastity in the woman than in the man" (pp. 141–42). Lacking the resources to support her own children, a woman abandoned by a man who was under no contractual obligation to support his offspring would have have to turn to society for help, or let her children starve. And since "it would be highly unjust to punish so natural a fault by personal restraint or infliction, the men might agree to punish it with disgrace" (p. 142). In other words, unmarried mothers must be punished with disgrace in order to make men shoulder their reproductive and familial responsibilities. Malthus argues that because feminine unchastity—that is, pregnancy—is "more obvious and conspicuous in the woman" than in the man, it can be punished more effectively. Ancient origins are wheeled in to explain, if not entirely justify, the inequities of modern sexual ideology:

> The offence is beside more obvious and conspicuous in the woman, and less liable to any mistake. The father of a child may not always be known, but the same uncertainty cannot easily exist with regard to the mother. Where the evidence of the offence was most complete, and the inconvenience to the society at the same time the greatest, there it was agreed upon that the large share of the blame should fall. . . . That a woman should at present be almost driven from society for an offence which men commit nearly with impunity, seems to be undoubtedly a breach of natural justice. But the origin of the custom, as the most obvious and effectual method of preventing the frequent recurrence of a serious inconvenience to a community, appears to be natural, though not perhaps perfectly justifiable. (p. 142)

By Malthus's own admission, the most peculiar relic of this hypothetical past is that although upper-class women are least likely to become conspicuously unchaste outside marriage, they are the ones who have most completely internalized the ideological demand that the *Essay* codes, delicately, as "female delicacy." Malthus's functionalist explanation of the origin of the double standard legitimates social injustice by associating punishment with visibility. Society, he implies, can only be upheld by the painful, if not "perfectly justifiable," inscription of archaic traces on the bodies and minds of women.

Malthus, unlike Godwin, is willing to salvage sexual pleasure—in a fashion. A given in his domestic economy, along with the economic dependence of women on men, is that women are the objects of masculine desire. In the face of Godwin's claim that passion between the sexes will be extinguished in a perfect society, Malthus, by contrast, argues sentimentally that the love of women leads to virtue ("Virtuous love . . . [is] . . . most powerfully calculated to awaken the sympathies of the soul, and produce the most exquisite gratifications," p. 147). Next after the mind-awakening effects of inquiring into nature come the sympathy-awakening effects and exquisite gratifications of "virtuous love"—for a heterosexual object, it goes without saying. Malthusian man, in fact, really prefers the company of women to reading books: "I have very frequently taken up a book and almost as frequently gone to sleep over it; but when I pass an evening with a gay party, or a pretty woman, I feel alive, and in spirits, and truly enjoy my existence" (p. 166). Strip the commerce of the sexes of their attendant pleasures, as Godwin urges, and what remains? Malthus replies: "[Godwin] might as well say to a man who admired trees: strip them of their spreading branches and lovely foliage, and what beauty can you see in a bare pole?" (p. 14). Viewed by the light of Godwinian reason, a woman is no more than a poor bare pole: "It is 'the symmetry of person, the vivacity, the voluptuous softness of the temper, the affectionate kindness of feelings, the imagination and the wit' of a woman that excite the passion of love, and not the mere distinction of her being female" (p. 148). Malthus is making an argument for pleasure along Burkean lines. Burke's *Reflections on the Revolution in France* (1790) had invoked the paraphernalia of inherited authority—royalty, patriarchy, and chivalry— to protect Marie Antionette from an imaginary rape in her own bed: Malthus invokes the contingencies of upper-class social intercourse between civilized men and women who possess the conventional attributes of their class.[10] But his philosophy of the drawing room unexpectedly brings to light the hidden connections between sentimentalism and libertinage.

ii. "Something Else as Unnatural"

Although popular Malthusianism became synonymous with ideas about family limitation in the nineteenth century, Malthus himself never considers birth control directly, except by way of a mystifying allusion to Condorcet's scandalous twin solutions—"promiscuous concubinage, which would prevent breeding, or . . . something else as unnatural" (p. 124; presumably, infanticide or abortion).[11] The only alternatives Malthus himself can envisage are vice (sex outside marriage—mysteriously without reproductive consequences) or virtue (sex within marriage). But marriage itself—equally mysteriously—constitutes a form of prophylaxis, since Malthus makes it synonymous with moral restraint, or at any rate with deferral. It is worth asking how Malthus depicts marriage, given his representations of the painfully disgraced unmarried mother, on one hand, and the pleasure of socially constituted relations between the sexes, on the other. His anxious portrait of marriage à la mode turns out to have more to do with the idea of limited resources in the household than with limited resources in the world. The Malthusian family is strikingly class-specific.[12] Apart from a future of mass starvation, the most vividly imagined Malthusian fate in the *Essay on the Principle of Population* is one of downward mobility. Malthus was derided by Godwin for instructing the poor to calculate how many children they could support before embarking on marriage. But Malthusianism is really the creed of an emerging nineteenth-century class phenomenon—the man of liberal education and limited means, faced with the impossibility of maintaining his family in the style of his inherited class position. In Godwin's derisive paraphrase, "Two or three hundred pounds *per annum* legally secured to the parties and their heirs for ever, I should think might do."[13] Frances Ferguson has shrewdly pointed out that the thought of a woman unhappy because married beneath herself is ultimately Malthus's most powerful prophylactic. Once again, crediting women with the capacity to suffer becomes a way to enforce masculine responsibilities.[14]

The woman dragged down by maternity—a woman by definition déclassée—stands in for the generalized anxiety about downward mobility in Malthus's *Essay*:

> A man of liberal education, but with an income only just sufficient to enable him to associate in the rank of gentleman, must feel absolutely certain that if he marries and has a family he shall be obliged, if he mixes at all in society, to rank himself with moder-

ate farmers and the lower class of tradesman. The woman that a man of education would naturally make the object of his choice would be one brought up in the same tastes and sentiments with himself and used to the familiar intercourse of a society totally different from that to which she must be reduced by marriage. Can a man consent to place the object of his affection in a situation so discordant, probably, to her tastes and inclinations? Two or three steps of descent in society, particularly at this round of the ladder, where education ends and ignorance begins, will not be considered by the generality of people as a fancied and chimerical, but a real and essential evil. (p. 90)

"Can a man consent to place the object of his affections in a situation so discordant . . . ?" Surely not. Just as women are more visibly disgraced by pregnancy than men who fail in their child-support payments, so women who marry men without means are more pitiably "reduced" than their husbands. Whether married or unmarried, women are punishable by the visible marks of pity or disgrace. A certain morbid pleasure attends this spectacle of female suffering (not, Malthus insists, "fancied and chimerical, but a real and essential evil"). Imagined like this, as the Sadeian libertine imagines his victim's suffering, female consciousness marks the boundaries of Malthus's thinking on sexuality. The unimaginable alternatives—whether nonreproductive sex outside marriage or nonreproductive sex within it—are equally erased under the heading of "vice," whose traditional partner, we know from fictions other than Malthus's own, is the "misery" inflicted on women who break the laws of marriage. "Let other pens dwell on guilt and misery," writes Jane Austen at the end of *Mansfield Park* (1814)—a novel notably preoccupied with the nuances of class mobility and errant feminine desire.

Vice names the missing term in these two Malthusian narratives (the story of the disgraced unmarried mother, and the story of the downwardly mobile married mother). Malthus nowhere invokes, except in the moral language of "restraint," the reproductive intervention we know as contraception. Twenty years later, at a time when Francis Place was campaigning to publicize simple contraceptive methods like the sponge, Percy Shelley's notebooks contain a jotted comment on the "Malthus principle":

The sexual intercourse by no means presents, as has been supposed, the [?] horrendous alternative of a being to be invested with existence for whom there is no subsistence, or the revolting expedients of infanticide and abortion. Any student of anatomy must be aware of an innocent, small and almost imperceptible precaution by which all consequences of this kind are prevented, and the ends of an union of two persons of the opposite sexes in every other respect fulfilled. . . . It is curious to remark how few medical men of any considerable science have more children than they can comfortably maintain.[15]

"Any student of anatomy must be aware. . . ." Not Malthus, evidently; or not in print. The effect of this drastic repression in the *Essay* is that (whatever her marital status) a woman's sexuality is unimaginable in terms other than maternity, while sexual pleasure (which we might naively think of as "the ends of an union of two persons of the opposite sexes") is entirely subsumed into reproduction. "Vice" therefore marks not just one, but two significant elisions in Malthus's argument—not only contraception, but sexual pleasure in excess of reproductive ends. Because women are always threatening to become mothers—because reproduction is the "obvious and conspicuous" manifestation of feminine sexuality—mothers are the latent cause of overpopulation which lurks even within the prudently married, companionate, prophylactic family. It is for this that women are to be so much pitied and so much punished, whether married or unmarried, in the unconscious of Malthus's text. Chanelling female reproduction into marriage turns out to be only a partial solution after all. Hence Malthusian marriage must not only be economically viable, but subject to a "restraint" that is imposed especially on the poor—as contemporary critics of Malthus like Hazlitt were swift to point out—and, above all, on women.[16] The *Essay on the Principle of Population* reveals as its underlying principle Malthus's coupling of the offensive visibility of pregnancy with the fantasy of women's unlimited reproductive tendencies. Nature's checks on population growth are plague and famine: Malthus's checks on women's reproductive tendencies are the visible marks of disgrace and pity.

In this punitive construction of gender relations, reproduction becomes the nexus for a wealth of unstated anxieties that may have less to do with numbers or with actual material resources than with economic considerations. A historical, class-contextualized reading of Malthus's *Essay* might even diagnose the threat of over-population as a response to the visible concentration of resources in the hands of a newly proliferating mercantile class; wealth in the hands of the few means poverty for the rapidly multiplying artisan population that was necessary to service a consumer society and an emerging industrial economy. From being a sign of national wealth, reproduction becomes the sign of wealth accumulated via a system of unequal exchange—a famine economy in which the rich get richer, while the poor get children. But reading the *Essay* as a disquisition on the relations between class anxieties and domestic ideology leaves out of account a different economy altogether—a system designed to restrain both sexuality and signs themselves. The *Essay* yields a pervasive fantasy that economic exchange could be successfully regulated alongside reproduction. The figure for the threat that the accumulation of individual wealth poses to the prosperity of nations (envisaged by Malthus as predominently agricultural wealth), and perhaps also to the wisdom of the educated classes (their unearned cultural wealth), are consumer luxuries—"The fine silks and cottons, the laces, and other ornamental luxuries of a rich country" (p. 193). For Malthus, the conversion of agricultural wealth (viewed as the harvest of productive labor) into conspicuous consumption (viewed as the profits of nonproductive labor) adds nothing to the collective wealth of a nation: "The consumable commodities of silks, laces, trinkets, and expensive furniture, are . . . the revenue only of the rich" (p. 195). The shift from agriculture to commerce puts an end to an era in which agrarian wealth could be imagined as universal, or at least national—as a means of suppporting the many, rather than (as in reality it was) concentrated in the hands of the few.[17] As Catherine Gallagher has convincingly argued, Malthus cannot admit to the possibility of a nonproductive form of labour that is not immediately converted into the means of subsistence. Nonreproductive labor is the economic equivalent of nonreproductive sexuality.[18]

Luxuries, therefore, have a dual function in Malthus, standing for both a nonproductive system of commercial exchange and a sexual economy in which pleasure might be divorced from reproduction. But Malthus also found it hard to reconcile himself to the issue of paper currency during the early years of the nineteenth century, fearing that paper money might proliferate without reference to any increase in actual wealth.[19] Only the imaginary routing of desire into reproduction—like an economy in which all labor is productive labor—could fend off proliferation and the exhaustion of finite resources. In the same way, only a real equivalency between signs and things (paper and bullion) could prevent incalculable inflation in the cost of food. Or, as Malthus wrote in his essay on "Depreciation of Paper Currency"

(1811), "every kind of circulating medium, as well as every other kind of commodity, is necessarily depreciated by excess, and raised in value by deficiency, compared with the demand, without reference either to confidence or intrinsic use."[20] Formulated this way, the problem is not just one of excess or deficiency, but the collapse of reference when divorced from either absolute standards or use-value ("without reference either to confidence or intrinsic use"). Sexuality freed up from a circuit of exchange—no longer tied to reproduction—is like paper currency, a sign-system associated for Malthus with unstable reference. The "something else as unnatural" that haunts Malthusian discourse could be read as the trace of his own prophylactic attempt to check the unlimited reproduction of signs (or paper currency), along with babies, by means of a violent repression of the figural—the "unmanly" or prostituted face of the truth. This violence underlies the "restraint" that is Malthus's means of regulating a reproductive world wishfully imagined in terms of a past agrarian economy, where the fantasy of exact equivalency orders relations between signs and things, labor and subsistence, sexuality and reproduction. As Mary Shelley put it in 1820, writing to a woman friend: "I could say a great many things to prove to you that a woman is not a field to be continually employed either in bringing forth or enlarging grain—but I say only, take care of yourself."[21] Underlying Malthus's *Essay on the Principle of Population* is his nostalgic attachment to a lost golden age when women knew their reproductive place, men could afford to reap the harvest, and women did not have to take care of themselves.[22]

iii: Bedroom Philosophy

"*Malthusianiser*" means, in French, "to practice birth control." Mary Shelley strikes the note usually assigned by Sade in *Philosophy of the Bedroom* to his female libertine, Madame de Saint-Ange, whose job is to initiate the ingenuous Eugénie into the mysteries and varieties of sexual pleasure. She also instructs Eugénie, in some detail, in available late eighteenth-century contraceptive methods—not only a multiplicity of sexual practices involving bodily orifices and surfaces that carry no risk of pregnancy, but sponges and condoms, and, of course, abortion.[23] For Dolmancé, Eugénie's other chief instructor, the horror of reproduction is scandalously figured in the prophylactic he recommends, namely, sodomy. In the guise of Nature's immoral advocate, Dolmancé argues that Nature can be as devoutly worshipped at a site of nonreproductive sexuality as elsewhere. His rationale is not only the pleasures of sodomy for and among men, but—ostensibly at least—its pleasures for women, along with the fact that it conveniently does away with the risk of pregnancy. Dolmancé, however, makes it clear that his first inclination is for men; the expendability of all women, not just mothers (not to mention the disposable Sadeian baby), underpins his libertine philosophy. Women are necessary in order to cement homoerotic sexual relations "between men," but a world without mothers would do away with the population problem altogether. In Dolmancé's endlessly inventive sexual scenarios, the female body is inundated by a seminal flow directed anywhere but into "the vessel of reproduction." Once discharged, semen becomes waste (one stage direction has Eugénie "spewing forth the fuck from her mouth and her ass"), sometimes orally consumed by its producer in a perfect circuit of nonproductive consumption. Instances of natural waste and nonproductivity abound in Dolmancé's ingenious libertine discourse. For him, there is nothing unnatural about waste since the spillage of "spermatic liquid" occurs all the time ("were nature miserly about this so precious sap, 'twould never be but into the vessel of reproduction she would tolerate its flow," p. 275). In contrast to the nostalgic exchange economy implied by the Malthusian text, Sadeian economics privilege a "spend" economy with zero return.

The ultimate end of this economy, at once desired and deferred, would be total self-expenditure. The function of waste in Sade's bedroom philosophy is to shore up libertine identity in the face of the self-annihilation that accompanies the end of all pleasure. Seminal emission defends the libertine against nothingness by its repeated rituals of "pollution"—Dolmancé's term for the many masturbatory acts that take place in the philosophic bedroom. This pollution is not so much self-pollution as aggressive pollution of the other. The essence of libertinism is its solitude, its wasting of the other in order to constitute a sovereign self. Underlying the witty speciousness of the reckless libertine spender is a darker and more melancholy vision—not just the abjection of the other, but the expendability of the entire human race. As Sade's Republican pamphlet puts it, "The human species must be purged from the cradle" (p. 336)—throwing the baby out with the spermatic bathwater. Nothing is sacred, not even life: "Let us make no mistake about it," declares Dolmancé, "propagation was never one of [Nature's] laws, nothing she ever demanded of us. . . . Why! what difference would it make to her were the race of men entirely to be extinguished upon earth, annihilated!" (p. 276). Fantasies of murderous destruction return at intervals to haunt this savagely Watteauesque text. *Philosophy in the Bedroom* reveals the dependence of a developed sexual discourse on leisure—

not for nothing is its setting the boudoir—as well as the deferral (up to a point) of satisfaction; but it also reveals the problematic dependence of Sadeian pleasure on cruelty. By proximity at least, serial sex is linked with the psychic onslaught enacted by the serial murderer against his love objects; abandoned and betrayed, he rages at maternal absence and avenges himself on surrogate maternal bodies. This may explain why, of all the murders envisaged by Sade's libertine educators, the idea of matricide is the one that recurs most obsessively.

Early on, Eugénie confesses to a loathing for her mother, whom she refers to as "an abominable creature I have long wished to see in her grave" (p. 239). We are led to believe that her instructress, Madame de Saint-Ange, has already done away with her own mother. Egged on by her libertine coaches, Eugénie becomes an enthusiastic participant in her mother's degradation and torture. Sade makes it clear that the mother is the object of abomination in exact proportion to her conventional sacredness—indeed, that her sacredness may be nothing more than the sublimation of what was once abject in an attempt to close off the psychic chaos with which she threatens to undo the infant subject. A Kristevan reading of the mother's abomination points not so much to an oedipal scenario (the castration anxiety aroused by what she is supposed to lack), but to the precarious emergence of the improper, pre-objectal subject. I want to pursue this reading in relation to my discussion of the Sadeian subtext in Malthus, since it throws light, not only on the horror of reproduction, and not only on the matriphobia that accompanies it, but on the place of phobia in general in the discourses of population and libertinage. Here is Kristeva, in *Powers of Horror*, on what she calls "the horror within," or "the horrors of maternal bowels":

> The body's inside . . . shows up in order to compensate for the collapse of the border between inside and outside. It is as if the skin, a fragile container, no longer guaranteed the integrity of one's "own and clean self" but, scraped or transparent, invisible or taut, gave way before the dejection of its contents. Urine, blood, sperm, excrement then show up in order to reassure a subject that is lacking its "own and clean self." The abjection of those flows from within suddenly becomes the sole "object" of sexual desire—a true "ab-ject" where man, frightened, crosses over the horrors of maternal bowels and, in an immersion that enables him to avoid coming face to face with an other, spares himself the risk of castration.[24]

For Kristeva, the lack of an "own and clean self"—the impossibility of ever guaranteeing one's discreteness, of successfully maintaining an effective barrier between inside and outside, or between one's own body and another's (typically, the mother's)—lies at the heart of phobia and abuts on its neighbor, sexual desire. With the displacement of affect onto the phobic object, a symbolic system of sorts emerges to bind anxiety, serving to reassure the subject by safeguarding its boundaries.

In this symbolic system, waste (urine, blood, sperm, excrement) becomes the substitute for an unnameable fear, which is at once the fear of nothing and the anguished want of a proper object. Kristeva glosses this nonobject as the "Thing," or rather, no-thing, which stands in for the maternal—the abject, preobjectal mother. Abjection shifts the emphasis from an oedipalized matriphobia associated with castration anxiety toward the earliest processes of subject formation, while also helping to account for something else, namely, the pleasurable effects of the Sadeian text. Disgust, horror, perversity, even murderousness, inseparable as they are from phobic matter, become a means to trace and retrace the saving surfaces not just of the skin as fragile container, but of language and signifying systems. As such, they mingle fascination and repulsion, terror and reassurance. Every imagined seminal ejaculation, each exclamation of pleasure, the proliferation of *tableaux vivants*, signs themselves—whether on the printed page or painfully inscribed on the body—defend against the chaos of no-meaning by demarcating the dangerous boundary between the proper and the abject. The horrifying finale of Sade's *Philosophy in the Bedroom* represents just such a moment where boundaries are violently inscribed on the body of the text. The excision of the maternal body brings the endlessly inventive theorizing of libertine philosophy to a close, as well as providing a dénouement for the intertwined, merged, and confounded knot of sexual bodies that constitutes the polymorphously perverse imaginary of libertine "practice." The final scene of *Philosophy in the Bedroom* involves a representation of the hemming in of the inside of a maternal body that Kristeva calls "desirable and terrifying, nourishing and murderous, fascinating and abject."[25] This is a seam that must be sewn up in the interests of constituting both libertine identity and the libertine text.

The sewing up of Eugénie's mother—already revealed as an abused, oppressed, and pitiably betrayed wife (a wife "discordantly" situated, to use Malthus's language, if ever there was one)—takes place after she has been humiliated, beaten unconscious, sexually assaulted, sodomized, and infected with the pox. Her bodily closure is not only the final act of violence committed against her, but a symbolic cordoning off of the maternal body—the ultimate contraceptive measure. She can no longer infect men or give birth to babies (the punishment is tailor-made to fit the crime). The sewing operation is performed by Eugénie, the monstrously over-achieving pupil who outdoes her immoral teachers (as she boasts, "at one stroke incestuous, adulteress, sodomite, and all that in a girl who only lost her maiden-head today! . . . What progress, my friends!" p. 359). Associated as it is with the useless labors of *la jeune fille bien élevée*, Eugénie's needle becomes a weapon with which she kills off "at one stroke" not only domestic ideology but her imaginary sibling rivals, the unborn babies who lurk in the maternal insides: "Spread your thighs, Mama," she commands, "so I can stitch you together—so that you'll give me no more little brothers and sisters" (p. 363). But lest we should think that only a daughter can hate her mother this much, Dolmancé sews her up behind once Eugénie has sewed her up in front. Female buttocks—at first the target of mascu-line fondling and pleasurable penetration—become the target of masculine aversion and penetration of a different kind (the stage direction runs, "he drives his needle into at least twenty places," p. 365). But as the flow of semen joins the flow of blood to complete the ritual of maternal pollution, Dolmancé's coup de théâtre unex-pectedly turns into an anticlimax. According to the stage directions, "The group disperses" (p. 366). In Dolmancé's words, "All's been said." The dispersal of atti-tudes, like the exhaustion of words, suggests that what the libertine dreads most of all, and must keep on postponing, is the final expenditure that brings with it the death of desire—or rather, the weakness that originally precedes the birth of desire. As Dolmancé laments, "why must weakness succeed passions so alive?" (p. 366). He might have asked, "and precede them too?"

Weakness written on the masculine body translates into cruelty inflicted on the body of a woman—in this case, the submissive body of an exasperatingly exemplary wife and mother who begs her tormentor's pardon, just as she submitted to her husband's blows. *Philosophy in the Bedroom* incidentally reveals patriarchy's mis-sion to be the disciplining of women's bodies and minds to the practice and internalization of suffering (no wonder Malthusian marriage and motherhood are a sorry business). But for the libertine, the impossibility of warding off weakness while enjoying the pleasures of spending constitutes the essential double bind. It is this psychic knot, above all, that the mother is called on to untie. If both pleasure and cruelty lead to weakness, no amount of deferral can avert the moment of bankruptcy when phobic desire collapses back into the nameless fear that underlies it—the neg-ativity of death-drive, in contrast to "passions so alive." This is the deathliness of a drive that as yet lacks life-giving objects, attaching itself, in passing, to "abjects." In Kristeva's account, the subject is saved by the displacement of drive onto these phobic not-yet-objects, the convenient repositories of loathing or repressed desire. As she puts it, phobia is the ceaseless elaboration of signs, powered by a drive economy in want of an object.[26] At the end of *Philosophy in the Bedroom*, Dolmancé can look back with satisfaction on the day's work—"Well, we've had an active day. I never dine so heartily, I never sleep so soundly as when I have during the day, sufficiently befouled myself with what our fools call crimes" (p. 367). His satisfaction at a day well spent derives from having made crime pay, in the form of what amounts to a symbolic discourse of befoulment. Self-pollution finds its displaced object of desire in the cruel text embroidered on the surface of the maternal body. The borders of Kristeva's maternal Thing are reinscribed at the end of *Philosophy in the Bedroom* as the defensive gesture of a phobic subject confronted by the death of desire.

*   *   *

Domestic restraint in Malthus and Sade's drastic solution to the population problem could both be read as defenses against the threat of infinite self-dispersal. If there is danger in numbers, there is even more in incalculability. The statistical forecasts that marked the start of the second decade of an officially recognized epidemic, AIDS, represent a similarly phobic attempt to find safety in numbers.[27] I want to risk a moment of painful closure on my own account by drawing a parallel between the historically specific discourse of population and contemporary AIDS discourse— what might almost be called a lesson of history, handed down to us by one of Malthus's most virulent critics. For the republican Hazlitt, Malthus's real target was "the bugbear of Modern Philosophy"—by which he meant not simply Godwinian philosophy, but a reformist social and political agenda. [28] The threat posed by Malthusian doctrine was not only its tendency to discriminate against an already oppressed poor but its tendency (in spite of Malthusian manliness) to encourage inertia in the face of hopelessly computed odds. Although Malthus himself insisted that evil existed as a spur to activity rather than an incitement to despair, the melancholy inference of the *Essay* remained; any attempt to improve the human condition would merely lead to a speedier, more calamitous exhaustion of resources. The progressive sexual politics of AIDS cultural activism was born out of the need to contest just such discrimination, inertia, and hopelessness—to go beyond prophylaxis, *laissez-faire*, or genocidal despair. The common characteristic of Malthusian doctrine and AIDS phobia are their underlying melancholia; matriphobia and homophobia turn out to be near neighbors. As the site of reproduction, the maternal body becomes a privileged focus for the mechanisms that produce and discipline relations among pleasure, knowledge, and power; on its docility depends the docility of the species (hence the regulatory controls that Foucault calls "*a biopolitics of the population*").[29] Unstitching the textual body opens a less cruel but no less pointed political inquiry into the fabric that Godwin, denouncing the seamless ideology of his own times, called "things as they are"—an ideology resistant both to the politics of change and to cultural activism.

1. Thomas Robert Malthus, *An Essay on the Principle of Population and A Summary View of the Principle of Population*, ed. Antony Flew (Harmondsworth, UK: Penguin, 1970), 75–76. Subsequent page references in the text are to this edition.

2. *The Marquis de Sade: The Complete Justine, Philosophy in the Bedroom, and other writings*, ed. and trans. Richard Seaver and Austryn Wainhouse (New York: Grove Press, 1966), 230–31. Subsequent page references in the text are to this edition.

3. For Malthus's achievement as a demographer and the debate surrounding the *Essay*, see, for instance, Patricia James, *Population Malthus: His Life and Times* (London: Routledge and Kegan Paul, 1979), especially 55–69, 116–36, 369–82; see also Peter Laslett, "Gregory King, Robert Malthus, and the Origins of English Social Realism," *Populations Studies* 39 (1985): 351–62.

4. For population growth in England, see Colin McEvedy and Richard Jones, *Atlas of World Population History* (Harmondsworth, UK: Penguin, 1978), 42–56; and E. A. Wrigley and R. S. Schofield, *The Population History of England, 1541–1871* (Cambridge, MA, and London: Harvard University Press, 1981). See also E. A. Wrigley and R. S. Schofield, "English Population History from Family Reconstitution: Summary Results, 1600–1799," *Population Studies* 37 (1983): 183–84; and J. A. Goldstone, "The Demographic Revolution in England: A Re-examination," *Population Studies* 40 (1986): 30–31. For the abandonment of children by the poor of France during the late eighteenth century, see O. H. Hufton, *The Poor of Eighteenth-Century France 1750–1789* (Oxford: Oxford University Press, 1974), 329–49.

5. See Lynn Hunt, *The Family Romance of the French Revolution* (London: Routledge, 1992), 124–50, for an illuminating discussion of *Philosophy in the Bedroom* in the context of pornographic writing and gender issues during the immediately post-Revolutionary period; and, for Sade's relation to eighteenth-century parodies of sensibility, R. F. Brissenden, "La Philosophie dans le boudoir; or, A Young Lady's Entrance into the World," *Studies in Eighteenth Century Culture* 2 (1972): 113–41.

6. See also Lucienne Frappier-Mazur, "The Social Body: Disorder and Ritual in Sade's *Story of Juliette*," in *Eroticism and the Body Politic*, ed. Lynn Hunt (Baltimore and London: Johns Hopkins University Press, 1991), 131–43 for the rituals of the Sadeian orgy.

7. See Thomas Laqueur, *Making Sex: Body and Gender from the Greeks to Freud* (Cambridge, MA,

and London: Harvard University Press, 1990), 193–243, for the relation between reproductive narratives and representation from the mid-eighteenth century on.

8. For Malthus's rhetorical self-positioning in the tradition of Newtonian scientific inquiry, rather than the Cartesian tradition of intellectual inquiry with which he associates Godwin, see Arthur E. Walzer, "Logic and Rhetoric in Malthus's *Essay on the Principle of Population*, 1798," *Quarterly Journal of Speech* 73 (1987): 1–17.

9. See Ludmilla Jordanova, "Nature Unveiling Before Science," in her *Sexual Visions: Images of Gender in Science and Medicine* (Madison: University of Wisconsin Press, 1989), 87–110, for the pervasive gendering of nature and science.

10. Malthus argues that Godwin's tactic—depriving the magnet of its most essential causes of attraction and then calling it weak—is no answer to the history of human passion; by his reckoning, population can only be checked by unimaginable advances on the part of the masses (see *Essay*, 148). For Godwin's return bout with Malthus, see William Godwin, *Of Population* (London: Longmans, 1820), especially book 6, chapters 2 and 5. For the controversy surrounding Malthus and sexuality, see James, *Population Malthus*, 121–26.

11. See M. de Condorcet, *Outlines of an Historical View of the Progress of the Human Mind* (London: J. Johnson, 1795), 347: "that premature destruction, so contrary to nature and to social prosperity, of a portion of the beings who may have received life"; see also James, *Population Malthus*, 60–61.

12. See James, *Population Malthus*, 98–102, 160–68 for Malthus's own marriage.

13. Godwin, *Of Population*, 582. Compare Southey's remark that Malthus "writes advice to the poor for the rich to read"; see *Annual Review* 2 (1804): 301.

14. See Frances Ferguson, "Malthus, Godwin, Wordsworth, and the Spirit of Solitude," in *Literature and the Body* (Baltimore and London: Johns Hopkins University Press, 1988), 116–18; as Ferguson points out, "The central fact about this example of misery is that it has nothing at all to do with the kind of misery involved in the prospect of imminent starvation" (p. 117).

15. MS Morgan; quoted by William St. Clair, *The Godwins and the Shelleys: The Biography of a Family* (New York and London: W. W. Norton & Company, 1989), 465; for Frances Place's promotion of the sponge in the 1820s, see James, *Population Malthus*, 386.

16. See, for instance, W. Petersen, "Malthus and the Intellectuals," in *Thomas Robert Malthus: Critical Reassessments*, ed. John Cunningham Wood (London: Croom Helm, 1986), 1:367–68.

17. Even Malthus's own version of utopia—the equalization of property—cannot prevent the perception on his part that "in every civilized state a class of proprietors and a class of labourers must exist" (*Essay*, 198).

18. See Catherine Gallagher, "The Body Versus the Social Body in the Works of Thomas Malthus and Henry Mayhew," in *The Making of the Modern Body: Sexuality and Society in the Nineteenth Century*, ed. Catherine Gallagher and Thomas Laqueur (Berkeley, Los Angeles, and London: University of California Press, 1987), 83–106, especially 91–97 for Malthus's objection to the labor theory of value because of its conflation of value and exchange value.

19. For the bullion controversy and Malthus's argument with Ricardo, see James, *Population Malthus*, 190–212.

20. *Edinburgh Review* 17 (February 1811): 341; see James, *Population Malthus*, 200–207.

21. *The Letters of Mary Wollstonecraft Shelley*, ed. Betty T. Bennett (Baltimore and London: Johns Hopkins University Press, 1980–83), 1: 136.

22. In Malthus's *Essay*, the city makes only one major appearance, in connection with a passage in which Price, apopros of the respective life expectancies in town and country, refers to great cities as "the graves of mankind" (*Essay*, 196); Malthus takes Price to task for imagining that rural life is the guarantee of health, happiness, and longevity.

23. "Some women insert sponges into the vagina's interior; these, intercepting the sperm, prevent it from springing into the vessel where generation occurs. Others oblige their fuckers to make use of a little sack of Venetian skin, in the vulgate called a condom, which the semen fills and where it is prevented from flowing farther" (*Philosophy in the Bedroom*, 230).

24. Julia Kristeva, *Powers of Horror: An Essay on Abjection*, trans. Leon S. Roudiez (New York: Columbia University Press, 1982), 53.

25. Ibid., 54.

26. Ibid., 35.

27. AIDS itself can be seen (or constructed as) "an epidemic of signification," pervading the linguistic and figurative dimensions of AIDS discourse much as it pervades population discourse; see Paula A. Treichler, "AIDS, Homophobia, and Biomedical Discourse: An Epidemic of Signification," in *AIDS: Cultural Analysis, Cultural Activism*, ed. Douglas Crimp (Cambridge, MA, and London: MIT Press, 1988), 31–70.

28. See William Hazlitt, "Mr. Malthus," in *The Spirit of the Age*, ed. E. D. Mackerness (London and Glasgow: Collins, 1969), 170: "In order to quell and frighten away the bugbear of Modern Philosophy, he was obliged to make a sort of monster of the principle of population." For Hazlitt's sustained polemical response to Malthus (as well as to Godwin), see *Reply to the Essay on Population* (1807); and, for Hazlitt's political views and their relation to Malthusianism, see John Kinnaird, *William Hazlitt: Critic of Power* (New York: Columbia University Press, 1978), 114–24, 393 nn. 36–39.

29. Michel Foucault, *The History of Sexuality, vol. 1*, trans. R. Hurley (New York: Vintage Books, 1980), 139.

6

Replacing the Race of Mothers
AIDS and *The Last Man*

With ills the land is rife, with ills the sea,
Diseases haunt our frail humanity,
Through noon, through night, on casual wing they glide,
Silent,—a voice the power all-wise denied.

—Hesiod, *Works and Days*, ll.139-42[1]

AIDS has now spread its shadow round the globe. By the year 2000,
the World Health Organization recently calculated, some 40 million
people will be infected with the AIDS virus.

—*New York Times*, June 3,1991[2]

THE EXPONENTIAL CALCULATIONS brought to bear on forecasting the global spread of AIDS replicate Malthusian panic in the face of unlimited population growth. The complementary faces of apocalyptic epidemiology are the unchecked spread of infection and an escalating death rate. Grim reminders about the length of the shadow cast around the globe by AIDS tend to give rise to a number of nightmarish apprehensions—for instance, that AIDS knows no external limits, whether national or ethnic; or that, although it may at first have seemed to endanger certain groups more than others, internal boundaries are equally porous. Hence the new prominence, in the intimate realm, of the condom—not just as a physical barrier to the exchange of body fluids, but as a symbolic boundary. But there is more to it than the construction of the modern, prophylactic form of intimacy known as "safe sex" (as opposed to "unsafe sex," or sex without border controls or barriers). When AIDS can no longer be posed as a problem that only affects other people, or other peoples, plague-thinking becomes the order of the day. AIDS phobia, typically, is the fear of limits unwittingly transgressed—raising questions about the safety of health care itself (and even so-called safe sex). But these questions rapidly become diffused as a generalized anxiety. Can one ever be truly safe, when the boundaries of bodies and persons are so permeable—not only by body fluids, but by the psychic erosion of identities risked in any encounter with another? For the anxious reader, the writing on the wall seems to say, not so much—or not only—that "Silence is Death" (the slogan effectively mobilized by the AIDS activist organization, ACT UP), but, more insidiously, that intimacy itself can be fatal.

So it should not be surprising to find stable monogamy being promoted as a prophylactic against AIDS in the initial, heterosexist phases of preventive education, much as Malthus had installed the "restraint" of marriage as the archregulator of populations. Nor should it be surprising to find that—just as the family turns out to be a problematic solution for Malthus—sexual abstinence might start to look like the only certain prophylactic. But an abstinent population is doomed to extinction anyway. This is the desolate, futuristic fable of *The Last Man* (1826), where Mary Godwin Shelley empties the entire world of its population, leaving one, solitary man to foretell the ending of his own story.[3] Two decades after the publication of Malthus's *Essay on the Principle of Population*, Godwin took up the relation between population and plague once more in *Of Population* (1820), subtitled, indefatigably, *An Enquiry concerning the Power of Increase on the Numbers of Mankind, being an Answer to Mr. Malthus's Essay on that Subject*. In the face of Malthus's calculations about population growth, Godwin proposes the novel idea that "there can be no real increase of population, but by an increase of the number of women capable of child-bearing." Arguing against the received notion that a society takes only a decade to recover from the devastations of plague, Godwin calculates that it would take twice as long before there were enough women of childbearing age "to replace the race of mothers"—"A portentous gap," he observes, a trifle melodramatically, "that might almost make us tremble for the continuance of the race."[4] Godwin's argument against the Malthusian principle of unlimited proliferation turns on the scarcity of mothers, the race that ensures "the continuance of the race." In her apocalyptic novel, Mary Shelley joins the Malthus controversy on her own account, rewriting the "dismal theorum" from the perspective of a woman who also happens to be not only a mother, but the mother of dead children. Hers, I want to suggest, is the "unmanly" or feminized face of melancholia that is consigned to silence by Malthusian discourse.[5]

The central character of *The Last Man*, Lionel Verney, is ostensibly just that— the last man on earth. We know that Shelley called herself "the last man" and identified with "that solitary being's feelings, feeling myself," she wrote eloquently in her journal, "as the last relic of a beloved race, my companions, extinct before me—."[6] Her letters to Jane Williams in the early 1820s testify to "a melancholy & misery no human words can describe and no human mind long support," referring to the "chaos of melancholy in which I lived so long."[7] She began *The Last Man* in 1824 and ended it in 1825, writing it in the shadow of profound personal bereavement after the drowning of Percy Shelley in 1822 and then the death of Byron at Missolonghi in 1824, as well as the earlier deaths of two out of her three surviving children.[8] Haunted by the horror of disease, the novel is suffused with maternal mourning as well as survivor guilt; well might Mary Shelley—the daughter of a dead mother—have felt herself to be "the last relic" of a beloved race of mothers. But however tempting it is to read *The Last Man* in autobiographical terms, I want to broaden the terms of the inquiry. To invoke Freud's distinction between mourning and melancholia once more, melancholia characterizes a failure to complete the work of mourning. Suggestively linking reproduction and authorship, *The Last Man* prompts one to ask, not so much whether melancholia is a peculiarly feminine liability (as Kristeva, for instance, would argue), but what consolation writing might hold for the melancholic, and in what ways the writing of melancholia might effect the consolidation of authorial identity, making it possible to mourn, and hence, memorialize the dead.

Beginning her book with an elaborate hoax about its find in the cave of the Cumaean Sibyl identifies Shelley not just with the last woman, but with the last woman writer. Much has been made of her reading of Mary Wollstonecraft's writing, and her reconstruction of the primal scene of her own conception in a morbid pre-enactment of Woolf's twentieth-century injunction to read back through our mothers. We know that Mary and Percy Shelley held their trysts on the grave of Mary Wollstonecraft, and that Mary Shelley was familiar with the love letters of her mother and William Godwin (from which she could calculate, almost to the day, the date of her own conception).[9] But it is less often pointed out that for Shelley—and for Woolf too, perhaps—this reading back through a dead mother may have been a problematic form of maternal identification.[10] By setting the novel's primal scene of writing in the cave of the Cumaean Sibyl, *The Last Man* seems to say that its melancholy comes from a difficulty in conceiving of oneself apart from a dead mother. This is the ambivalent tie to the past that Freud identifies with melancholia, and Kristeva, in *Black Sun: Depression and Melancholia*, with the chaotic, pre-objectal, maternal "Thing." Shelley's letters during this period describe how silenced affect gave rise to the compensatory activity she calls "scribbling." In a letter of 1822 to Jane Williams, she calls herself "the silent Mary": "You will think that I make up for my silence in speech by my garrulity on paper—& so indeed it is—I can speak of nothing but the one train of feeling which engrosses me—I can*not speak* of that—but I *can write*, & so I scribble."[11] Volume 3 of Shelley's plague novel begins with the quotation from Hesiod which forms the first of my two epigraphs. "Our enemy," recounts the narrator, "trod our hearts, and no sound was echoed from her steps—. . . . Diseases haunt our frail humanity . . . *Silent, —a voice the power all-wise denied*" (p. 229; my italics). As a figure for silenced grief, or grief denied a voice, plague becomes a symptom of the melancholia that Kristeva calls "an abyss of sorrow, a noncommunicable grief."[12] If *The Last Man* attempts to voice this noncommunicable grief, it also invites us to ask how language, "voice," and writing function in the novel's imaginary. I want to argue that structures associated with identificaton, as well as phobia, characterize the writing of melancholy in *The Last Man*. These structures turn out to be not so different from the ones involved in the communication of any literary affect, while lending themselves to being figured as infection.

i: "Diseases Haunt our Frail Humanity"

The *Last Man* dooms its readers to extinction in the year 2100. Written in the wake of a cholera epidemic which had begun in Calcutta in 1817 and seemed to be rapidly approaching the borders of Europe, the novel imagines an end to national, political, and family life. The spread of global infection mapped the paths of improved communications as well as contemporary imperial and commercial activity—military campaigns, trade, immigration, and even tourism (travels much like Shelley's own in Italy)—not to mention the Greek Wars of Independence, which provides the bridgehead for the transmission of plague from east to west in *The Last Man*. Unlike previous epidemics, which confined their impact to the pilgrim routes, this early-nineteenth-century cholera epidemic spread by way of British soldiers engaged in campaigns on India's northern frontier and on board ships bound for Southeast Asia. The first epidemic was arrested on the shores of the

Caspian because the winter of 1823–24 was unusually severe. But for observers in Europe it must have seemed as though the march of cholera toward Europe was unstoppable, as it later proved to be. In 1826, the same year that Mary Shelley published *The Last Man*, a fresh epidemic in Bengal once again reached Russia, spread by way of Russian military campaigns against Persia, Turkey, and Poland, and crossed the Baltic by ship to England in 1831. It reached Ireland the next year, Irish immigrants brought it to Canada, and the epidemic spread to the United States and Mexico during the early 1830s.[13] The sources of infection remained mysterious, since the connection with infected water supplies was not established until the 1840s, when urban sanitation became the key to disease prevention. The cholera baccillus itself remained unidentified until the late nineteenth century.

Historicizing *The Last Man* as Shelley's response to an actual cholera epidemic may account for its fictional retreat to an island fastness: "I am the native of a sea-surrounded nook" (p. 5)—so Verney, the last man, begins his narrative. But plague knows no boundaries, and England (especially rural England) provides only a temporary haven for the novel's tightly knit family of characters. Disease makes the world smaller, attacking island mentality, penetrating the geopolitical defenses of national identity, and above all striking at the heart of the family. *The Last Man* is often read as a political roman à clef—either as a critique of the (masculine) Romanticism represented by Shelley and Byron, or as a dystopic novel, caught in the ebb tide of post-French Revolutionary disillusion, that refuses both the *telos* of historical progress and Godwinian perfectibility.[14] Unlike Volney's *Ruins of Empire*, which inspired its vision of a ruined, postimperial civilization, Shelley's futuristic novel imagines no revolutionary rebirth of history, only an end to reproduction altogether.[15] The *topos* of plague—already central to the Malthus-Godwin debate—becomes a means of testing reformist politics to their breaking point. Shelley's imaginary English republic or "protectorate" provides an anatomy of contemporary social thought, in a spectrum ranging from hapless Godwinian utopianism (Merrival) to Cobbett's pessimistic pragmaticism (Ryland). Above all, the novel contrasts the imperial ambitions of a Byronic egoist (Lord Raymond) with the altruism of an idealized, socially responsible, republican Percy Shelley (Adrian). Mary Shelley's distinctive contribution to the recently revived Godwin-Malthus controversy was to expose the weakness of both Godwinian and Malthusian perspectives in the face of world-historical disaster. Whether or not Percy Shelley, in the guise of Adrian, offers a viable reformist alternative to Godwinian perfectibility, on one hand, or Malthusian *laissez-faire* on the other, intellectual debate in the novel is overtaken by an epidemic which threatens to make *all* political arguments, *all* political institutions, irrelevant to human survival. In *The Last Man*, no attempt to transform systems of government, to reform social institutions, or even to alleviate suffering on a local level, can finally withstand the devastations of plague or mitigate their effects on individuals.

Disaster on the scale imagined by *The Last Man* raises questions not just about the efficacy of competing philosophies, but about *any* system of meaningful difference. The imperial depredations of plague are presaged by a solar eclipse, which induces panic throughout Asia:

> On the twenty-first of June, it was said that an hour before noon, a black sun arose: an orb, the size of that luminary, but dark, defined, whose beams were shadows, ascended from the west; in about an hour it reached the meridian, and eclipsed the bright parent of day. Night fell upon every country, night, sudden, rayless, entire. The stars came out, shedding their ineffectual glimmerings on the light-widowed earth. But soon the dim orb passed from over the sun, and lingered down the eastern heaven. . . . Gradually the object of fear sank beneath the horizon, and to the last shot up shadowy beams into the otherwise radiant air. Such was the tale sent us from Asia, from the eastern extremity of Europe, and from Africa as far west as the Golden coast. (p. 162)

The negative light of this black sun swallows up everything else—even the idea of plague itself—in the shadow of a "new fear which the black sun had spread" (p. 163). What is this "new fear?" A Kristevan etiology for plague suggests itself. Viewed as a sign-system—a disease of communication, as well as a communicable disease— "plague" becomes a figure for the elaboration of phobic defenses in the face of a new fear; or rather, an old one. To put it another way, plague could be read as the phobic proto-writing or metaphoric elaboration of melancholia. In the opening pages of *Black Sun: Depression and Melancholia*, Kristeva asks: "Where does this black sun come from? Out of what eerie galaxy do its invisible, lethargic rays reach me . . . ?"[16] For Kristeva, the black sun that irradiates the existence of the depressed person (Nerval's "light without representation . . . an imagined sun, bright and black at the same time") is a refraction of uncompleted mourning for the pre-objectal mother—the sign of a depressed narcissist who mourns not an object, but the

"Thing."[17] The symptom of this impossible mourning for an unrepresentable maternal "Thing" is not only the elaborate, ventriloquized effects of Shelley's (Verney's) and Kristeva's (the depressed person's) prose, but the melancholy subject's identification with death.

What would the rhetorical manifestations of such an identification look like? The penultimate chapter of *The Last Man* begins by invoking "black Melancholy." Melancholia sets its imprint on the written page not only in the form of literary allusion (inevitably, to Milton's *Il Penseroso*), but also as the rhetorical trope of personification. The only surviving character, Shelley's narrator-hero, Verney, grandiosely demands whether he can sustain the novel's apocalyptic ending: "Can I accomplish my task? Can I streak my paper with words capacious of the grand conclusion?" (p. 318). To increase his verbal capacity, he calls on an uncreating mother named Melancholy:

> Arise, black Melancholy! quit thy Cimmerian solitude! Bring with thee murky fogs from hell, which may drink up the day; bring blights and pestiferous exhalations, which, entering the hollow caverns and breathing places of earth, may fill her stony veins with corruption, so that not only herbage may no longer flourish, the trees may rot, and the rivers run with gall—but the everlasting mountains be decomposed, and the mighty deep putrify, and the genial atmosphere which clips the globe, lose all powers of generation and sustenance. *Do this, sad visaged power, while I write, while eyes read these pages.* (p. 318; my italics)

Verney's invocation—or rather, curse—negates the creator's command ("be fruitful and multiply"); he imposes a reproductive ban on the atmosphere itself ("lose all powers of generation and sustenance"). Shelley imagines the failure of reproduction in terms of the waste and abjection—rotting trees, undrinkable rivers, decomposing mountains—which for Kristeva implicate the melancholic's maternal "Thing" ("the recipient that contains my dejecta . . . a waste with which, in my sadness, I merge. It is Job's ashpit in the Bible").[18] But the "clipping" embrace of a dead mother has as its payoff the saving identification with maternal sadness that Kristeva—and apparently Shelley too—associates with the turn to signs: "Do this, sad visaged power, while I *write*, while eyes read these pages" (p. 318; my italics). Verney's invocation to Melancholy enacts the psychic process of identification.

111

Capacious words "streak" the paper, giving the author the "sad visaged," unmanly face of Melancholy, and answering Verney's question ("And who will read them?") by posing the reader herself as dead: "beware, fair being . . . beware lest the cheerful current of thy blood be checked . . . ." (p. 318). If plague means the collapse of civilization, and melancholia a lack of meaning that is glaring, phobic writing (i.e., melancholy figures) could be said to effect a saving identification between "green" Verney and "black Melancholy." This maternal identification stands between the dejected subject and the waste or emptiness within; but the price Verney/Shelley must pay is to identify with the oxymoron of nonreproductive life.

"Let not day look on these lines, lest garish day waste, turn pale, and die" (p. 318). "These lines"—Verney's lines—lay waste the world; day does look on them and turns into a black sun. The onset of night returns *The Last Man* to its shadowy beginnings in the Cumaean cave. Ventriloquizing maternal Melancholy, Verney enjoins himself to "seek some cave, deep embowered in earth's dark entrails, where no light will penetrate, save that which struggles, red and flickering, through a single fissure, staining thy page with grimmest livery of death" (p. 318). This is the cave of the Cumaean Sibyl where, in the fiction of the novel's own finding, Shelley, as editor, deciphers and translates the obscure and chaotic tracings of her own unacted future: "Sometimes," she writes, "I have thought that, obscure and chaotic as they are, they owe their present form to me, their decipherer" (p. 4). She has the same ventriloquistic relation to Verney's prophetic "exclamations of exultation or woe" (p. 3) as Verney has to the language of Melancholy. At this point it seems worth posing again the question that Shelley herself asks at the start of her novel: "Will my readers ask how I could find solace from the narration of misery and woeful change? This is one of the mysteries of our nature, which holds full sway over me, and from whose influence I cannot escape. I confess, that I have not been unmoved by the development of the tale, and that I have been depressed, nay agonized, at some parts of the recital, which I have faithfully transcribed from my materials" (p. 4). Kristeva calls writing (writing springing out of that very melancholia) the only counter depressant. Verney's daylight-extinguishing lines at the end of *The Last Man* are rewritten in the cave of the Cumaean Sibyl as the fragments that give coherence to a chaotic identity. Or, as Kristeva puts it, "sadness reconstitutes an affective cohesion of the self."[19] Affect is the glue that makes the chaos and obscurity of melancholia cohere for the signifying subject. Because literary creation (in Kristeva's words) "bears witness to the affect" and at the same time to the "imprint of separation and beginning of the symbol's sway," Verney's identification with maternal sadness—his ventriloquization of Melancholy—provides an organizing identity for the bereaved author-daughter.

When he takes up his pen at the end of the novel, Verney is a solitary man without friend or partner. The "dedication" that he carves on the ruins of imperial Rome—". . . TO THE ILLUSTRIOUS DEAD. / SHADOWS, ARISE, AND READ YOUR FALL! / BEHOLD THE HISTORY OF THE / LAST MAN" (p. 339)—wishfully creates an all-male readership; the illustrious dead are his dead men friends, Adrian and Lord Raymond. As the manly perpetrator of signs, Verney reveals that the Kristevan "cure" of writing demands the elimination of the mother. Significantly, the last surviving form of the reproductive family—consisting of Verney himself, his friend Adrian, and his niece Clara—becomes extinct with the drowning of Adrian and Clara, who represent the only prospect of a nonincestuous, potentially reproductive couple. But the final casualty of the novel is not just the reproductive couple; it is the last of the Shelleyan race of mothers. In the face-off between the grandeur of Verney's dedication among the ruins of masculine, imperial culture and the novel's fictive provenance in the cave of the Cumaean Sibyl, the mother is both lost and wishfully found in the "elsewhere" of signs. Shelley's implied dedication to the Last Woman might read something like this, as ventriloquized by Kristeva: "'I have lost an essential object that happens to be, in the final analysis, my mother,' is what the speaking being seems to be saying. 'But no, I have found her again in signs, or rather, since I consent to lose her, I have not lost her (that is the negation), I can recover her in language.'" [20] This elaborate disavowal, viewed as a negation of loss, opens up a potential cure for melancholia—but at a price; it means surrendering the fantasy of a (deathly) maternal embrace, in contrast to the depressed person's nostalgic clinging to "the real object (the Thing) of their loss." The bleak inscription on which Verney founds a motherless postimperial culture is the manoeuver that posits authorship on the (de)negation (*Verneinung*) of maternal archaeology. Turning the tables to read Kristeva in the light of *The Last Man* reveals the negation of the mother, posited on the arbitrariness of meaning, as the necessary sacrifice that Kristeva must make in the interests of her theory of signs. The daughter has to take her mother's place as the author of meaning, as Shelley does in her "Author's Introduction" when she claims to have bestowed her powers "in giving form and substance to the frail and attenuated Leaves of the Sibyl" (p. 4).

ii. "The Modern Exstasy of Violent Sorrow"

Sadness is catching; reading can make you ill (and might even prove fatal). Or so Shelley implies of the transfer of affect involved in both melancholia and reading. Plague in *The Last Man* first enters the novel as a word that has no meaning: "That word . . . was PLAGUE" (p. 127). As it approaches England, it takes the form of whispers and obscure mentions in newspapers, mutating from rumor into the full-blown apocalyptic inscription of a modern print-culture:

> Before it had been a rumour; but now in words unerasable, in def-
> inite and undeniable print, the knowledge went forth. Its obscurity
> of situation rendered it the more conspicuous: the diminutive let-
> ters grew gigantic to the bewildered eye of fear: they seemed graven
> with a pen of iron, impressed by fire, woven in the clouds, stamped
> on the very front of the universe. (p. 171)

"Graven," "impressed," "woven," "stamped on the very front of the universe," the imprint of plague-writing constructs a face. Like Melancholy, this is a personification; the next time we see pestilence writ so large, it is "above the dome of St. Sophia," where "the superstitious Greek saw Pestilence" (p. 139). The symptom of plague is textual infection—the italicized, unpronounceable word that hovers on Verney's lips: "I dared not pronounce the word *plague*, that hovered on my lips," he confesses, "lest they [my friends] should construe my perturbed looks into a symptom, and see infection in my languor" (p. 174). Ryland, the erstwhile "powerful, ironical, seemingly fearless canvasser for the first rank among Englishmen," is infected by word of mouth: "his joints were unknit, his limbs would not support him; his face was contracted, his eye wandering. . . . In answer to our eager questions, one word alone fell, as it were involuntarily, from his convulsed lips: *The Plague*." (p. 175). Sick with fear, Ryland infects the entire world ("Ryland's words rang in my ears; all the world was infected"; p. 176). At once a sign and a state of mind, plague travels from lip to lip like a communicable disease, or an epidemic of signification.[21] Plague-talk collapses the difference between signs and bodies; the mouth that speaks is both the site of infection and the means of its communication to others.

In *The Last Man*, the family is the most prized idyllic enclave in the novel, the most vulnerable, and the one most charged with affect. International disaster is swiftly recoded as a national nightmare, and then as the deaths of loved ones, especially women and children. As Verney puts it, "universal misery assumed concentration and shape, when I looked on my wife and children" (p. 180). England—the last bastion of civilization—shrinks to an island prison ("the sea, late our defence, seems our prison bound") and then into a tomb ("little England become a wide, wide tomb"). London becomes a plague-city. In this literary and metropolitan plague center, the linguistic communication of affect occurs with special virulence and ease. When Verney visits London in the midst of the plague, he attends a performance of *Macbeth*. As Shelley reproduces Shakespeare's regicide tragedy, the deaths of mothers and children move to the center of the stage; cosmic and political chaos become metaphors for all-encompassing disease. Shakespeare's lines lamenting Scotland—"It cannot / Be called our mother, but our grave"—create in the audience a shock of recognition, "like the swift passing of an electric shock":

> Alas, poor country;
> Almost afraid to know itself! It cannot
> Be called our mother, but our grave: where nothing,
> But who knows nothing, is once seen to smile;
> Where signs, and groans, and shrieks that rent the air,
> Are made, not marked; where violent sorrow seems
> A modern exstasy. (p. 204; *Macbeth* 4.3.164–70)

Wrested from their Shakespearean context, "Each word struck the sense, as our life's passing bell" (here Shelley's—or Verney's—"lines" lapse into Shakespearean pastiche); the onlookers gaze at the stage "as if our eyes could fall innocuous on that alone." The actor playing Ross stalls in announcing the death of Macduff's family, fearing an uncontrollable outbreak of grief on the part of his audience. In turn, his "show of terror increased ours, we gasped with him . . . each face changed with the actor's changes." And finally, with Macduff's exclamation—

> All my pretty ones?
> Did you say all?—O hell kite! All?
> What! all my pretty chickens, and their dam,
> At one fell swoop! (p. 204; *Macbeth* 4.3.216–19)

—"a burst of despair was echoed from every lip." As Verney puts it, "I had been absorbed by the terrors of Rosse [sic]—I re-echoed the cry of Macduff. . . ." Plague is catching, and so are Macduff's cries.[22]

Absorption and reecho perform the symptoms of literary identification—the transmission of affect from actor to audience, or from page to reader. In the audience's response to *Macbeth*, Shelley suggests not only the difficulty of separating our words from another's, our feelings from someone else's, but also the way in which language itself might be said to generate the plague of affect. Earlier in the novel, when Adrian describes his youthful alienation in a fragment of supposedly autobiographical writing, Shelley has him reflect on life in this fashion: "We go on, each thought linked to the one which was its parent, each act to a previous act. No joy or sorrow dies barren of progeny, which for ever generated and generating, weaves the chain that make [sic] our life" (p. 32). Adrian illustrates his thought with a quotation that implicates exclamatory language in the generation and transmission of affect: "Un dia llama à otro dia / y ass i llama, y encadema / llanto à llanto, y pena à pena"; Shelley's own footnote translates as follows: "One day calls to another, / and in that manner is linked / a cry to a cry and a sorrow to a sorrow" (p. 32 and n).[23] Her quotation anticipates the scene of Shelley's later "production" of *Macbeth*. Linking a cry to a cry, *Macbeth* weaves the chain that binds affect to language. Plague becomes a figure for literary identification, now defined as both absorption by other people's feelings and the reechoing of their words. But it also suggests that not just phobic language but *all* language may serve to bind affect, via the identificatory mechanisms of its performance. If "the modern exstasy of violent sorrow" is characterized by its transferability, the binding of affect to language also consolidates the identity of the sorrowing audience. Just as Verney's saving invocation to black Melancholy identifies him with the sad-visaged power he invokes, *Macbeth* permits the audience a consoling identification—and, in doing so, gives them a "voice." This is the one form of reproduction permitted in *The Last Man*: "No joy or sorrow dies barren of progeny"; thoughts and feelings give birth to others. But there is a further, more disturbing implication in Shelley's appropriation of *Macbeth*. The moment of absorption and reecho can be experienced as annihilating as well as consolidating or consoling. In the final shipwreck at the end of *The Last Man*, from which Verney emerges as the only survivor, "Ocean drank in, and absorbed [his] feeble voice, replying with pitiless roar" (p. 324).[24] *Macbeth* may give voice to silenced melancholia, but it also risks drowning the melancholic's feeble voice, not in a pitilessly undifferentiated roar, but in a roar of

116

undifferentiated pity. Shelley's "ocean of death" (p. 300) is also an ocean of affect that threatens to swamp her novel.

Affect, Shelley implies, knows no limits where the subject is concerned. In *The Last Man*, the sign of this porousness is a melancholic woman. Verney reels from the theater into a phantasmagoric street scene of drunks and prostitutes—"those melancholy beings to whom the name of home was mockery" (p. 205). The subtext of Shelley's novel associates the disruption of home and nation with the embrace of a fatal woman. Feminized as a death-bearing other—typically, a foreign or racial other—plague conquers nations and effeminizes men. "Plague," Shelley writes, "had become Queen of the World" (p. 252); a sinister imperialist, "she" entwines herself with manliness: "She has invested his form, is incarnate in his flesh, has entwined herself with his being" (p. 229). In Malthus's *Essay*, Cleopatra functions as a figure for the disruptive woman who is never far from the surface in discourses of population and plague.[25] In *The Last Man*, Shelley pinpoints the Nile as the source of the plague ("This enemy to the human race had begun early in June to raise its serpent head on the shores of the Nile," p. 127). Almost in the same breath, Shelley goes on: "It was in Constantinople" (p. 127). There could scarcely be a more appropriate origin for the impending collapse of civilization. As the traditional site for the always permeable boundary between western civilization and its oriental other, Constantinople marks the porous boundaries of national, sexual, and psychic identities. England turns out to be defenseless against this double invasion of foreignness and plague. Usurped by an avenging, feminized melancholia, the imperial subject is similarly unmanned in *The Last Man*.

The English women who figure as partners in Shelley's domestication of the political scene (Perdita, Verney's sister, who marries Lord Raymond; and Idris, the sister of Verney's friend Adrian, who marries Verney himself) are depicted as complex, troubled, but always loving wives and mothers; they pose no threat to men, being victims themselves. By contrast, the sources of political and personal instability in the novel's opening idyll are twofold—at home, Adrian's ambitious and powerful mother, the ex-queen, who schemes unsuccessfully to restore the monarchy; and, abroad, the disruptive Princess Evadne, daughter of the Greek ambassador to England. Evadne's role in Shelley's narrative is that of an outcast who demarcates and undermines the boundaries of national and domestic identities, while functioning as a home breaker—one of "those melancholy beings to whom the name of home was mockery." In the romantic plot of *The Last Man*, the more experienced Evadne has been loved by the youthful Adrian, but herself falls in love with the dominant

Lord Raymond; then suddenly and mysteriously quits England. Adrian, stricken with melancholy on his own account, withdraws from society, while the two couples (Idris and Verney, Perdita and Lord Raymond) establish their domestic idyll against the backdrop of political life. This is how things stand when Evadne suddenly reappears, seven years later, after Lord Raymond (now Lord Protector) tracks her down "to one of the most pernurious streets in the metropolis" (p. 77). A convicted collaborator who has been reduced to poverty and exile after her marriage to a Turk and the intervening Greek Wars of Independence, Evadne is still consumed by her former passion for Lord Raymond. Lord Raymond, in turn, is perversely drawn to the ambiguous underworld she inhabits. Becoming estranged from Perdita, he throws over his marriage and resigns the protectorship, then departs suddenly with Adrian for the Greek wars. The first volume of *The Last Man* thus comes to a close with this dispersal of its extended, utopian family, apparently disrupted by Evadne and all that she represents.

The second volume of *The Last Man* opens with the international scene where plague and the Greek Wars of Independence are intertwined. Evadne reappears near the start, hard on the heels of Shelley's first reference to plague ("This enemy to the human race had begun early in June to raise its serpent-head on the shores of the Nile . . ."). Plague and Evadne are interchangeable in the phantasmagoric scenes that ensue. After a climactic battle in which the Turks are defeated, Verney encounters among the slain a spectral, wounded, and delirious figure, disguised as a soldier. "The lost, the dying Evadne (for it was she)" curses Lord Raymond before she dies, foretelling his death during the siege of Constantinople:

> Many living deaths have I borne for thee, O Raymond, and now I expire, thy victim!—By my death I purchase thee—lo! the instruments of war, fire, the plague are my servitors, I dared, I conquered them all, till now! I have sold myself to death, with the sole condition that thou shouldst follow me—Fire, and war, and plague, unite for thy destruction—O my Raymond, there is no safety for thee! (p. 131)

Evadne's "emaciated form," "sunken cheek," and "sepulchral voice," her hot hand and burning lips, make her the embodiment of the diseased and vengeful femme fatale. After her death, Verney veils "this monument of human passion and human misery" (p. 132), as if the mere sight of her could breed infection. Evadne's curse haunts Lord Raymond as he embarks on the next stage of his campaign, the siege of Constantinople: "'Fire, the sword, and plague! They may all be found in yonder city; on my head alone may they fall!'" What is more, "From this day Raymond's melancholy increased" (p. 134). With the fall of Constantinople, plague does fall on his head, opening the gates to the epidemic that spreads across Europe to England. Lord Raymond speculates that his melancholia emanates from the plague that has already subjugated Constantinople ("perhaps I have imbibed its effluvia—perhaps disease is the real cause of my prognostications," p. 136). But he seems also to recognize that its real source is what he calls "the fatal name of Evadne" and "the strange link that enchains [him] to her." The fatal name of Evadne strikes back against Lord Raymond's imperial power. In the empire of plague, Melancholy has the last word.

iii. "Not What is Commonly Called Contagious"

The power of Evadne's curse to infect Lord Raymond with melancholia bears on the question of immunity. Searching for Lord Raymond's body among the booby-trapped ruins of Constantinople, Verney falls asleep and dreams of him as an angry Timon lobbing after him the vessels from his feast, "surcharged with fetid vapour." In his dream, Lord Raymond's "shape, altered by a thousand distortions, expanded into a gigantic phantom, bearing on its brow the sign of pestilence" (p. 146). Evadne's fatal alias, Pestilence, has becomes Lord Raymond's sign. What is strange about this dream narrative is that Evadne dies of her wound (or else of her thwarted passion), while Lord Raymond is killed by the falling ruins of Constantinople (or else of his thwarted imperial ambition). If Lord Raymond catches anything from Evadne, it is the fatality of his engagement with Greek national struggle—his passion for a feminized ideal (Hellas) whose debased other is the deracinated Evadne. But the paths of transmission lead inexorably from Evadne to Lord Raymond via Constantinople and finally back to the little family circle located in England. When Verney at length reaches home, having buried Lord Raymond and his sister Perdita on the way, he is greeted with the news that a plague-infested vessel from America has recently appeared off the coast of England; a solitary, infected sailor makes it as far as the beach. As he touches land, Verney himself becomes the harbinger of pestilence. Strangely, however, he retains his immunity for much of the novel, eventually becoming the only known instance of a plague-survivor.

As Shelley's text discloses, the mystery of transmission is crucial to plague discourse (and, of course, to the politics of effective prevention):

> That the plague was not what is commonly called contagious, like the scarlet fever, or extinct small-pox, was proved. It was called an epidemic. But the grand question was still unsettled of how this epidemic was generated and increased. If infection depended upon the air, the air was subject to infection. As for instance, a typhus fever has been brought by ships to one sea-port town; yet the very people who brought it there, were incapable of communicating it in a town more fortunately situated. But how are we to judge of airs, and pronounce—in such a city plague will die unproductive; in such another, nature has provided for it a plentiful harvest? In the same way, individuals may escape ninety-nine times, and receive the death-blow at the hundredth; because bodies are sometimes in a state to reject the infection of malady, and at others, thirsty to imbibe it. (pp. 167–68)

Plague becomes the litmus paper not only for political schemes, but for mental health. As we have seen, Ryland (the anti-aristocratic pragmatist who succeeds Lord Raymond as Protector) turns out to be a panic-stricken pessimist who thinks only of his own safety. By contrast, the previously ineffectual Adrian emerges as an energetic and altruistic administrator, successfully advocating measures designed to withstand the plague. Believing that infection thrives on low morale ("He knew that fear and melancholy forebodings were powerful assistants to disease," p. 181), he tries to disguise its symptoms, minimize its progress, and organize a kind of popular grass-roots resistence. Both Adrian and Verney survive the plague, proving Adrian right, up to a point. But their "systematic modes of proceeding" in the face of infection are powerless to prevent (in rapid succession) the collapse of the infrastructure, invasion by the Irish, agricultural failure, social anarchy, and the death of national culture. Above all, it cannot prevent the deaths of the children on whom national identity depends. As Shelley's narrator puts it, "England, no more; for without her children, what name could that barren island claim?" (p. 300). The figure of a dead child turns out to play a crucial part in giving Verney the immunity that condemns him to be the Last Man.

The opening of volume 3 of *The Last Man* marks the point at which Adrian and Verney, along with Verney's wife Idris and their surviving children, quit their barren island ("England, no more") for the restless uncertainties of foreign travel. But before he leaves, Verney has a near-fatal brush with the plague—not his first encounter, but, significantly, the first that proves catching. Returning home to find his wife desperate and his young son dead, Verney tangles in the antechamber with "a negro half clad, writhing under the agony of disease, while he held [him] with a convulsive grasp." At this juncture, Verney's rational humanity—previously evident in all his encounters with the plague-stricken populace—suddenly fails him. Shelley's narrative vividly conveys the disgust of this intimate bodily mingling with a racial other:

> With mixed horror and impatience I strove to disengage myself, and fell on the sufferer; he wound his naked festering arms round me, his face was close to mine, and his breath, death-laden, entered my vitals. For a moment I was overcome, my head was bowed by aching nausea; till, reflection returning, I sprung up, threw the wretch from me, and darting up the staircase, entered the chamber usually inhabited by my family. A dim light showed me Alfred on a couch. . . . . I saw full well that no spark of life existed in that ruined form. . . . (p. 245).[26]

"My child lay dead at home; the seeds of mortal disease had taken root in my bosom" (p. 245). My child lay dead at home *because* the seeds of mortal disease had taken root in my bosom? Verney falls sick, but the real victim is the "ruined" form of a child. This is the price paid for a foreign embrace that is simultaneously repudiated and desired, like Evadne's embrace of Lord Raymond, or the hold of a dead mother. Only a dead child can exorcise the horror of abject mingling, putting an acceptable face on an otherwise outcast illness. Within a few lines of this first, sickening embrace ("he wound his naked festering arms round me"), Verney goes on to embrace his son: "I laid him softly down, kissed his cold little mouth." This is a kiss without risk of sexual exchange. The innocence of the dead child guarantees the possibility of an uncorrupted self, ensuring Verney's otherwise inexplicable recovery. The only person in the entire novel to survive the plague, Verney could be said to make it die "unproductive"; it stops with him, or rather, with the dead child who provides him with his *cordon sanitaire*.

In this moment of vividly rendered homophobic and racist panic, we are reminded that the occluded relation in *The Last Man* is the one between Verney and Adrian (who refers to himself, revealingly, as "the tainted wether of the flock"—alluding to Antonio in *The Merchant of Venice*). The burial of plague in the vale of Chamonix marks the spot as "sterile"—without power either to reproduce or infect. Verney inherits this nonreproductive empire, along with the solitude and silence that Percy Shelley, in "Mont Blanc," had associated with the same landscape ("She [Plague] abdicated her throne, and despoiled herself of her imperial sceptre among the ice rocks that surrounded us. She left solitude and silence co-heirs of her kingdom," p. 310).[27] Earlier, as the little band of survivors had made its way through the relics of western civilization, Verney—now widowed, alone, and increasingly hysterical in relation to Adrian—cried out when he heard Adrian's voice: "O fool! O woman nurtured, effeminate and contemptible being—I heard his voice, and answered it with convulsive shrieks" (p. 294). Verney's "convulsive shrieks" and "girlish exstacies" recall the "modern exstasy of violent sorrow" transmitted from actor to audience by the actor in *Macbeth*. His responsiveness to a voice—here, a man's voice—feminizes him in relation to Adrian. One could speculate that this homoeroticized relation to Adrian stands in for Mary Shelley's own relation to her dead husband's poetry; Adrian, after all, is the covering Shelley-poet in a novel whose cries are linked to his cries, and sorrows to his sorrows. His voice is the one Mary Shelley imagines as poetry. When Verney dedicates his narrative "TO THE ILLUSTRIOUS DEAD," he commits himself to a dead poets' society—all that is left to him. If plague and melancholia are the intertwined "diseases [that] haunt our frail humanity" in *The Last Man*, poetry (Percy Shelley's poetry) becomes the voice of the silenced dead; it provides, as it were, the only cure. Shelley writes in her "Author's Introduction," "*Di mie tenere frondi altro lavoro / Credea mostrarte*" ("From my tender leaves I expected to present another work to you," p. 3 and n). The last woman—"the last relic of a beloved race"—could be said to write from a sterile place where the mother is buried and literary transmission involves preserving the corpus of a dead poet (the labor to which Mary Shelley had dedicated herself in the wake of Shelley's death). The work she presents to Percy Shelley in place of a child renounces not only the fantasy of a maternal embrace, but the hope of a reproductive future, and along with it, the fantasy that words and bodies are interchangeable. *The Last Man* seems to say that, for Mary Shelley at least, the writing-cure involved a sacrifice that could be figured by a child (the future of reproduction) as much as a mother.

*　　　　*　　　　*

The Last Man calls out to be read as a prophetic commentary on the modern epidemic that seemed initially to exclude women and has only more recently come to be seen as putting them at risk too. With hindsight, the most homophobic aspect of early epidemiological constructions of AIDS was the insistence on the absolute differences between men and women (or their sexual practices), accompanied by a mistaken emphasis on homosexual transmission—with what devastating effects both for gay men and for women we now know. The invisibility of women in medical definitions of AIDS still decreases their chances of early diagnosis and treatment, and therefore of long-term survival.[28] But women are specifically at risk in the reproductive realm—as the mothers (and infectors) of HIV-positive children. A chilling but insufficiently disseminated statistic is that most women with AIDS are mothers.[29] What does it mean to give birth to infection, when the life expectancy of the AIDS-infected mother herself is so drastically reduced? What does it mean, for that matter, to outlive an AIDS-infected child? The Last Man, although it cannot answer questions like these, does speak indirectly to the silenced mourning of a modern race of mothers, while at the same time uncovering the deadly psychic structures that underpin past and present constructions of plague—the phobic dread of a breached cordon sanitaire; the abjecting of an imagined racial or sexual other; the morbid preoccupation with "innocent" victims (children, for instance) whose deaths permit the subject to sustain the illusion of a discrete, impregnable identity. Shelley's novel tells the one story that no one can bear to read, because it writes us out of the story altogether: the only good reader is a dead reader.[30] But in a moment of denial or optimism, Verney ends by speculating about a world "re-peopled . . . [by] the children of a saved pair of lovers" (p. 339), seeking to learn the history of their ante-pestilential race. The Last Man can be read not only as a monument to lost millennarial hopes and to the illustrious dead, but as a memorial to the future of those unborn "children of a saved pair of lovers" who may or may not inherit a post-plague future that lies beyond our present imagining.

1. Mary Shelley, *The Last Man*, ed. Hugh J. Luke (Lincoln: University of Nebraska Press, 1993), 229; subsequent page references in the text are to this edition. Mary Shelley footnotes Elton's translation, where lines ll.141–42 read "Self-wandering through the noon, the night they glide, / Voiceless—a voice the power all-wise denied"; see Mary Shelley, *The Last Man*, ed. Morton D. Paley (Oxford and New York: Oxford University Press, 1994), 477 n.

2. Successive estimates are higher; see, for instance, a report cited in the *Guardian*, January 28, 1993, under the headline "Spread of Aids may be out of control"—"By 1995, 20 million will be infected with HIV . . . By 2000 there may be 38–110 million adults with the virus and more than 10 million children."

3. The relevance of Mary Shelley's plague novel to contemporary discussions of AIDS has been made recently by Anne K. Mellor in her introduction to *The Last Man*, xxii–v, and by Audrey A. Fisch, "Plaguing Politics: AIDS, Deconstruction, and *The Last Man*," in *The Other Mary Shelley: Beyond Frankenstein*, ed. Audrey A. Fisch, Anne K. Mellor, and Esther H. Schor (New York and Oxford: Oxford University Press, 1993), 267–86; Fisch's reading links politics, plague, and deconstruction in particularly interesting ways.

4. William Godwin, *Of Population* (London: Longman's, 1820), 241. Apropos of Shelley's novel, Barbara Johnson raises the question, "Why couldn't such a story be entitled *The Last Woman?* . . . Would the idea that humanity could not end with a woman have something to do with the ends of *man?*"; see "The Last Man," in *The Other Mary Shelley*, 262.

5. See "Malthus, Matricide, and the Marquis de Sade," chapter 5 above.

6. May 14, 1824; *The Journals of Mary Shelley 1814–1844*, ed. Paula R. Feldman and Diana Scott-Kilvert (Oxford: Clarendon Press, 1987), 2: 476–77.

7. *The Letters of Mary Wollstonecraft Shelley*, ed. Betty T. Bennett (Baltimore and London: Johns Hopkins University Press, 1980–83), 1: 263, 503.

8. Mary Shelley's daughter Clara and her son William died in 1818 and 1819, respectively.

9. See, for instance, Marc A. Rubenstein, "'My Accursed Origin': The Search for the Mother in *Frankenstein*," *Studies in Romanticism* 15 (1976): 165–94.

10. For a different but related view of the problems of maternal identification in relation to Mary Shelley's melancholy incest novel, *Matilda*—begun after the death of her son William in 1819—see Terence Harpold, "'Did you get Mathilda from Papa?': Seduction Fantasy and the Circulation of Mary Shelley's *Mathilda*," *Studies in Romanticism* 28 (1989): 49–67.

11. *The Letters of Shelley*, 1: 297

12. Julia Kristeva, *Black Sun: Depression and Melancholia*, trans. Leon S. Roudiez (New York: Columbia University Press, 1989), 3: "For those who are racked by melancholia, writing about it would have meaning only if writing sprang out of that very melancholia. I am trying to address an abyss of sorrow, a noncommunicable grief that at times, and often on a long-term basis, lays claims upon us to the extent of having us lose all interest in words, actions, and even life itself."

13. See William H. McNeill, *Plagues and Peoples* (New York: Doubleday, 1977), 231–33.

14. See, for instance, Anne K. Mellor, *Mary Shelley: Her Life, Her Fiction, Her Monsters* (New York and London: Routledge, 1988); and Lee Sterrenburg, "The Last Man: Anatomy of Failed Revolutions," *Nineteenth Century Fiction* 33 (1978): 324–47.

15. Mary Shelley's reading of Volney's *Ruins* (included in the reading-list of Frankenstein's monster) may have been mediated by Percy Shelley's; see *Mary Shelley*, 45, 232 n.

16. Kristeva, *Black Sun*, 3.

17. *Ibid.*, 13.

18. *Ibid.*, 15.

19. *Ibid.*, 19.

20. *Ibid.*, 43.

21. See Paula A. Treichler, "AIDS, Homophobia, and Biomedical Discourse: An Epidemic of Signification," in *AIDS: Cultural Analysis, Cultural Activism*, ed. Douglas Crimp (Cambridge, MA, and London: MIT Press, 1988), 31–70. Interestingly, contemporary reviewers castigated *The Last Man* itself as "the product of a diseased imagination and a polluted taste," as if the novel itself were infectious; see Elizabeth Nitchie, *Mary Shelley: Author of Frankenstein* (New Brunswick, NJ: Rutgers University Press, 1953), 151.

22. See Joseph W. Donoghue, *Dramatic Character in the English Romantic Age* (Princeton: Princeton University Press, 1970), 336–43, for Hazlitt's account of Kean's 1814 debut as Macbeth, which Mary Shelley may have in mind.

23. Calderon, *El Principe Constante*, act 2; *Calderon: Obras Completas* (Madrid: Aguilar, 1966), 1.261

24. Compare the same language at the end of *The Last Man*, when "the great sea of calamity" (271) overwhelms its few survivors, and "generation after generation flowing on ceaselessly . . . swept onwards towards the absorbing ocean," disappearing into the "ocean of death" (300).

25. See, for instance, Sander L. Gilman, "AIDS and Syphilis: The Iconography of Disease," in *AIDS: Cultural Analysis, Cultural Activism*, ed. Crimp, 87–107, and "Seeing the AIDS Patient," in *Disease and Representation: Images of Illness from Madness to AIDS* (Ithaca and London: Cornell University Press, 1988), 245–72.

26. Compare the exotic body of the African (man or woman), which is often seen as the origin and site for the transmission of AIDS; see, for instance, Cindy Patton, *Inventing AIDS* (New York and London: Routledge, 1990), 78–97.

27. "And what were thou . . . If to the human mind's imaginings / Silence and solitude were vacancy?" ("Mont Blanc" [1816] ll.142–44).

28. See, for instance, The ACT UP/New York Women and AIDS Book Group, *Women, AIDS, and Activism* (Boston, MA: South End Press, 1990); and, for women's own accounts, *Positive Women: Voices of Women with AIDS*, ed. Andrea Rudd and Darien Taylor (Toronto: Second Story Press, 1992).

29. See Judith Walker, "Mothers and Children," in *Women, AIDS, and Activism*, 165–71.

30. As Barbara Johnson points out, "The end of man . . . will always already have coincided with the moment of predicting"; see "The Last Man," 266.

Part III

The Origin of Signs

7

"Tea Daddy"

Poor Mrs. Klein and the Pencil Shavings

. . . on one occasion, Dick lifted a little toy man to his mouth, gnashed his teeth and said "Tea daddy," by which he meant "Eat daddy."

—Melanie Klein, "The Importance of Symbol
Formation in the Development of the Ego" (1930).[1]

T (ti), the twentieth letter of the English and other modern alphabets, the nineteenth of the ancient Roman alphabet, corresponding in form to the Greek T . . . in Phoenician, and originally also in Greek, the last letter of the alphabet. It represents the point-breath-stop of Bell's "visible speech," or surd dental mute, so called, but in English is gingival or alveolar rather than dental.

—*Oxford English Dictionary*

ONE RESPONSE to the current return to Klein: it feels like eating one's words. Psychoanalytic feminism has been so thoroughly immersed in Lacanian theory for the past decade that taking Klein at her word—reading her literally, as she asks to be read—seems to risk a kind of theoretical regression. Can one renege on Lacan's "return to Freud," not to mention the entire freight of post-Saussurean linguistics that it brings in its train? Klein, it goes without saying, lacks any adequate account of the relation between language and the unconscious ("incapable of even so much as suspecting the existence of the category of the signifier"—Lacan's verdict on the Kleinian school).[2] Moving with untroubled literalness between phantasy and its objects, her writing resists the very aspect of Lacanian theory that has made it so inviting to literary theorists and to feminists in quest of a language-based account of the relations between sexuality and subjectivity. Hence, for Lacan himself, Klein's interest lies primarily in the account she gives of what he would call "the domain of the imaginary" (i.e., "the interplay of projections, introjections, expulsions, reintrojections of bad objects" which underpins object-relations theory), rather than in any account of what she, in his terms, miscalls the "symbolic"—the realm that Lacan himself identifies with language.[3]

But Klein holds special interest to feminists for her emphasis on the early relations of mother and infant, especially for reconceptualizing the shadowy, so-called preoedipal domain surmised (but tantalizingly unexplored) by Freud, and more recently theorized in the work of Kristeva. This is the domain that psychoanalytic feminism in search of an alternative to the Freudian Oedipus complex or the Lacanian Law of the Father has often nostalgically invoked. Klein's focus on the mother and her theories of "prematurity"—her insistence on infant phantasies coterminous with the earliest instinctual experience—offers psychoanalytic feminism a way to rethink both the Oedipus complex and the preoedipal domain (no longer properly "pre" in Klein, to the extent that the oedipal itself is characterized for her by its prematurity).[4] Lacan describes Klein as "working on the child at the very limit of the appearance of language."[5] I want to explore this limit in the case history of little Dick recounted by Klein's 1930 essay, "The Importance of Symbol Formation in the Development of the Ego," along with Lacan's later rereading of it in his two seminars of 1954, "Discourse Analysis and Ego Analysis" and "The Topic of the Imaginary." At the same time, I will try to triangulate the relation between Klein and Lacan by introducing Kristeva's essay, "Freud and Love: Treatment and its Discontents."[6] The Kristevan account of abjection and its relation to transference-love—both processes which she views as intimately connected with the early relations of mother and child and with the beginnings of signification—allows for the grafting of language onto Kleinian theory at the very limit of its appearance.

Psychoanalytic feminists tend to come to Klein today by way of Lacan and Kristeva, with a hindsight or *après coup* that has more to do with working back than nostalgia; and so the turn (the spin) I will be giving to "return" in this essay is necessarily retrospective. I would like to suggest that the alliance of Klein and Kristeva may allow psychoanalytic feminists, so to speak, to eat their words and have them too, refocusing the question of the "literal" that teasingly plays in the misplaced T of "Tea daddy" as (misplaced) metaphor. Perhaps, then, there is a sense in which the theoretical regression I invoked at the outset mimes its theoretical object. We may be confronting the difficult crossover between, on one hand, a Kristevan account of signification that is necessarily post-Lacanian, even in its divergence from Lacan, in its insistence on the missing, unsuspected category of the signifier as a necessary condition for the emergence of the subject; and, on the other hand, what Lacan himself views as regressive, a Kleinian account of eating (cannibalism, even), incorporation, and primary identification, or what Klein herself (in the elaborated sense peculiar to her) calls "projective identification," which is ambiguously poised on the borderline of instinct and ego.[7] A borderline case—the border between the regressive and the "premature," the literal and the metaphorical, or instinct and signification—aptly prompts a return to the scene of symbolic arrest that Klein presents in her case history of little Dick, a four-year-old psychotic characterized by his simultaneous failure to develop in the area of object relations and language. I began this essay intending to explore the possibility of grafting language onto Kleinian theory. As I wrote, however, a different question began to emerge: what role does Klein play for both Lacan and Kristeva? How does theory swallow up or disgorge its others (its "objects")? Finally, in what ways might a Kristevan "return to Klein" permit us to hear the "literal" of the Kleinian text with an ear attuned to metaphor?

i. "Dick is inside dark mummy"

In Lacan's reading, Klein offers little Dick words, simultaneously locating him in language and in a system of symbolic relations. As Klein herself presents it, the case history of little Dick traces the confused beginnings of symbol formation in a child who would now be regarded as autistic, but whom Klein thought of as schizophrenic.[8] Little Dick exemplifies for her the aggressivity of the early oral-sadistic phase, with its focus on biting and devouring the mother's body; a phase which also introduces the Oedipus conflict. The child's phantasized attack on the maternal body—imagined as a container for the father's penis, for excrement, and for children—has as its object both mother and father, and gives rise to intense anxiety. As Klein writes, "The object of attack becomes a source of danger because the subject fears similar, retaliatory attacks from it." Anxiety sets going the mechanism of identification (with the persecutory penis, vagina, and breast), and at the same time fuels the symbolic process—the ever mobile symbolic equations or displaced identifications which Klein views in the light of defenses: "This anxiety contributes to make [the child] equate the organs in question with other things; owing to this equation these in their turn become objects of anxiety, and so he is impelled constantly to make other and new equations . . ."(p. 97). Providing the basis for phantasy, Klein's symbolic equations also provide the basis for subsequent relations to, and mastery of, reality.[9] By contrast, a failure in symbol formation—too much anxiety too soon, or the inability to tolerate it—brings to a standstill the child's relation to objects (mother and father), and hence, in Klein's terms, to both language and reality. This is the case with little Dick.

Klein begins by observing that little Dick is indifferent to the presence or absence of his mother or nurse, doesn't play, and has no contact with his environment; he strings sounds together in a meaningless way, constantly repeats certain noises, and uses his small vocabulary incorrectly. Whether obedient or disobedient, he seems to lack affect. On his first visit to Klein, he runs about aimlessly in her room and treats her like a piece of furniture, as well as displaying a striking absence of anxiety. Klein concludes that little Dick's arrest is a consequence, among other things, of a difficulty in tolerating anxiety which she attributes to the premature awakening in him of genitality. This prematurity has caused "a premature and exaggerated identification with the object attacked"; hence his too-early, too-successful defenses against that identification, and the arrest of symbol formation. She relates his early difficulties in nursing, like his later refusal to bite up food, to the cessation of phantasy life defensively mobilized against his own sadistic relation to the mother's body. Anxiety has backfired. The very defense that should have opened the doors has closed them, leaving him in a void, without either "objects" or symbolic representations. But although little Dick is indifferent to his surroundings in general, Klein tells us that there is nonetheless some significant symbolic traffic: "he was interested in trains and stations and also in door-handles, doors and the opening and shutting of them" (p. 101). With characteristic literalness, she interprets these interests as having to do with penetration into the maternal body (doors and locks are the ways in and out) and dread of what would be done to him after he had succeeded, especially by the father's penis (door handles stand for the father's penis and his own). Little Dick's literalness—what Hanna Segal calls the "concrete thinking" characteristic of psychosis—colludes with Klein's to give her an opening.[10]

The difficulty in analyzing little Dick, for Klein, lies in the absence of symbolic representations. When she plays trains with him, Klein gives him representation, names, signs in exchange for toys. Although Klein herself doesn't put it like this, inserting a difference between symbol and thing gives rise to a traffic in what is nonidentical; the very sameness-and-difference that distinguishes big and little trains can be thought of as characterizing the relations—the play—of signs:

> I took a big train and put it beside a smaller one and called them "Daddy-train" and "Dick-train." Thereupon he picked up the train I called "Dick" and made it roll to the window and said "Station." I explained: "The station is mummy; Dick is going into mummy." He left the train, ran into the space between the outer and inner doors of the room, shut himself in, saying "dark" and ran out again directly. He went through this performance several times. I explained to him: "It is dark inside mummy. Dick is inside dark mummy." Meantime he picked up the train again, but soon ran back into the space between the doors. While I was saying that he was going into dark mummy, he said twice in a questioning way: "Nurse?" I answered: "Nurse is soon coming," and this he repeated and used the words later quite correctly, retaining them in his mind. (p. 102)

On later visits little Dick again puts the train in the hall, calls for his nurse, and finally, seized with acute anxiety, calls for Melanie Klein herself. In Klein's account, we see that the nonidentity of symbols and the thing symbolized leads him simultaneously to anxiety, to object-relations, and to language.[11] It also leads to the surfacing of his sadism against the mother's body; he tries to cut the toy coal out of the toy coal cart ("Cut"), throws the damaged cart in a drawer ("Gone"), and scratches with his nails on the door of the entrance hall, "showing that he identified the space with the cart and both with the mother's body, which he was attacking" (p. 103). Little Dick's "cut" and "gone" recapitulate both his sadism and his defense against it. The dark space that little Dick inhabits between the two doors is the blank space within the maternal body, emptied of its threatening contents.

Dick, writes Klein, "cut himself off from reality and brought his phantasy life to a standstill by taking refuge in the phantasies of a dark, empty, vague womb" (p. 105). In terms more Kristevan than Kleinian, one could say that his aggressivity turns to dread of the unnameable. Klein initiates the process of symbolization, not so much by restoring the womb's injurious contents (feces, urine, penis) as by answering his call with her name-calling. When he attacks a cupboard with spoon and knife, he also "asked what the different parts were called." His interest in "the things themselves" is transformed into an interest in the naming of parts: "The words which before he had heard and disregarded he now remembered and applied correctly" (pp. 105–106). One intriguing form taken by little Dick's symptomatic misspeech can be glimpsed in the earlier moment in Klein's account when a linguistic inversion—a slip, a misplaced letter or "literal"—has him literally eating his words, or rather, the toy man that stands for his all-devouring, Saturn-like father (fig. 1):

> We came to recognize the father's penis and a growing feeling of aggression against it in many forms, the desire to eat and destroy it being specially prominent. For example, on one occasion, Dick lifted a little toy man to his mouth, gnashed his teeth and said "Tea daddy," by which he meant "Eat daddy," He then asked for a drink of water. The introjection of the father's penis proved to be associated with the dread both of it, as of a primitive, harm-inflicting super-ego, and of being punished by the mother thus robbed: dread, that is, of the external and the introjected objects. (p. 104)

Here little Dick, in Lacanian terms, acts out his foreclosure of "the Name of the Father," the big Dick of language. For little Dick, the paternal phallus is a penile body part—a part that he wants to eat whole. Making a meal of the phallus, instead of naming the father, little Dick seems to say, in this primitive psychic gesture: I am both little Dick and daddy Dick, Saturn's child and Saturn himself. The undifferentiated little Dick and daddy Dick constitute a primitive, devouring identity.

Psychosis could be defined as a letter that has mistaken its place. The first (most literal) sense of "literal" listed in the *Oxford English Dictionary* (hereafter *OED*) is "of or pertaining to the letters of the alphabet." Little Dick has grasped the principle of linguistic difference (to a T), without being able to apply it to his own condition. The slippage from "Eat" to "Tea" sketches this failure to differentiate at the level of the letter; taken literally, taken internally (*à la lettre*), words lapse regressively into the nonsense of psychosis. The world of little Dick is a world equally without difference and affect. As Lacan will write, "Everything is equally real for him, equally indifferent" (p. 81). His use of language as repetition-without-difference tells the same story (as Klein recounts, "sometimes he would repeat the words correctly, but would go on repeating them in an incessant, mechanical way," p. 99). We could call this failure to differentiate "literalness," a fixation at the level

Fig. 1. Goya, *Saturn Devouring
his Infants* (1821–23).
Museo del Prado, Madrid.

of the letter; or, alternatively, mistaken identification with the mechanical aspect
of language. But mistaken identification also characterizes the vestigial depressive
position—associated with the ability to see wholes instead of empty holes (or body
parts)—that coexists with little Dick's schizophrenia. Along with his sadism, little
Dick shows moments of "remorse, pity, and a feeling that he must make restitution":

> Thus he would proceed to place the little toy men on my lap or in my
> hand, put everything back in the drawer, and so on. . . . This early
> identification with the object could not as yet be brought into relation
> with reality. For instance, once when Dick saw some pencil shavings
> on my lap he said, "Poor Mrs Klein." But on a similar occasion he said
> in just the same way, "Poor curtain." Side by side with his incapacity
> for tolerating axiety, this premature *empathy* became a decisive factor
> in his warding-off of all destructive impulses. (pp. 104–105)

Mrs Klein and the furnishings are all one to little Dick; from treating her like the furniture, he moves to treating the curtains like her and wanting to repair them. For little Dick, there is no difference between objects and "objects." Psychosis, then, could also be defined as empathy that has mistaken its place. To which one might add that the characteristic of Kleinian psychoanalysis is its empathy with—its feeling for—psychosis, its willingness to accompany the regress of the subject's phantasies and projective identifications to the very limit of their appearance.

ii. "A very elementary key"

What did Klein do for little Dick? Lacan would reply: she gave him an Oedipus complex. His "return to Klein" uses her work as the occasion to develop his own ideas about the relations of imaginary and symbolic registers. He first broaches Klein's essay in "Discourse analysis and ego analysis," where Anna Freud stands in for "discourse analysis," while Melanie Klein represents the analysis of contents ("ego analysis"). Intrigued as he is by her technique—"as a result of this interpretation something happens"—Lacan repeatedly, strikingly, characterizes Klein's literal-minded application of the Oedipus complex as "brutal":

> She slams the symbolism on him with complete brutality, does Melanie Klein, on little Dick! Straight away she starts off hitting him large-scale interpretations. She hits him a brutal verbalisation of the Oedipal myth, almost as revolting for us as for any reader—"*You are the little train, you want to fuck your mother.*" (p. 68)

Little Dick is "eyeball to eyeball with reality," as Lacan puts it ("The space between the two doors is the body of his mother," p. 69). Or, a child for whom "the real and the imaginary are equivalent" (p. 84) is eyeball to eyeball with Mrs. Klein, for whom, similarly, "everything takes place on a plane of equal reality—of unreal reality, as she puts it" (p. 82). The two meet in the empty space between the two doors, the space of the maternal body, where Melanie Klein, "with her animal instinct . . . dares to speak to him" (p. 69). In doing so, Lacan observes, she provokes a response; little Dick's anxiety is translated into a call: "Nurse!," "Mrs Klein!"

Properly speaking, for Lacan, little Dick hasn't attained speech: "Speech has not come to him. Language didn't stick to his imaginary system" (p. 84). Thus he remains "at the level of the call." Klein's analytic intervention "literally gives names" to what was before "neither nameable nor named," but "just a reality pure and simple" (p. 69); in Lacan's ventriloquization, "I won't beat about the bush, I just tell him—*Dick little train, big train daddy-train*" (p. 85). This all-too-literal naming is the glue that makes language "stick" to the trains, door handles, and "*dark*" of little Dick's imaginary. Klein's words "graft" the Oedipus complex onto little Dick's arrested symbol-making capacity: "Melanie Klein's discourse . . . brutally grafts the primary symbolisations of the Oedipal situation onto the initial ego-related [*moïque*] inertia of the child" (p. 85). Lacan locates as the "Crucial moment, when the sticking of language to the subject's imaginary begins to sketch itself," little Dick's one word: "Station" (p. 85). Only connect. Klein's brutality, a kind of arbitrariness that takes for granted both the unconscious and the Oedipus complex, "out of habit," allows her to "bring in verbalisation"; in so doing, she symbolizes "an effective relationship, that of one named being with another" (p. 85). "The brutal verbalization of the Oedipus myth" is for Lacan the enabling fiction—the brutal graft—which makes it possible for little Dick to enter into a symbolic network of relations and signifiers.[12] Now he can name the father instead of eating him.

When Lacan calls the Oedipus complex "this nucleus, this little palpitating cell of symbolism" and "the key—a very elementary key" (pp. 85, 86), he insists that little Dick's access to "genuine speech" is nonetheless "not any old speech." The key fits; Klein's oedipal story sticks. But not, in Lacan's book, "literally." The nucleus or metaphor for all complex structures, the Oedipus complex, according to Lacan, surfaces "through a kind of internal force" (p. 65); it too is brutal. What is "brutal" in Klein (i.e., arbitrary, informed by sheer habit) becomes Lacan's own brutal (i.e., highly theorized, deliberate) insistence on the necessity for the subject's integration into a symbolic system, "not any old" system, but one that is always encoded ahead of time, for which the Oedipus complex is a kind of short-hand or synecdoche (part for whole). At once arbitrary and inevitable, the Oedipus complex is less an explanation than a (linguistic) structure, one that Lacan describes as "already established, typical and significant." Or, as he puts it, "When we get on the trail of the unconscious, what we encounter are structured, organised, complex situations. Freud gave us the first model of it, its standard, in the Oedipus complex" (p. 65). Lacan, then, seems to say that Klein's brutal Band-Aid, her "plastering on" of the Oedipus complex ("She plastered on the symbolisation of the Oedipal myth," p. 85) is therapeutic *because* both arbitrary and preordained ("already established"); like metaphor, the oedipal graft initiates a transfer or carry-over of meaning—in this case, from the (literal) object to the "object"; from the little train that is little Dick to the daddy-train that is the big Dick.

Lacan sees Klein as gaining access to little Dick's unconscious by means of forcible entry with a crudely oedipal key; Lacan translates it as "*avoir ouvert les portes de son inconscient*" (p. 85 n). Klein's own account of little Dick, however, suggests that something else may also be at stake. Her unthinking attribution of an unconscious to little Dick resembles the "premature *empathy*" that Dick himself uses to ward off or repair destructiveness ("brutality"): "Poor Mrs Klein," "Poor curtain" (and poor little Dick). I want to backtrack in order to pursue the idea of prematurity for a moment—the prematurity that for Klein is the very hallmark of the Oedipus complex. Klein suggests that little Dick's backwardness in symbol formation is paradoxically associated with what she sees as his premature genitality, and, consequently, his "premature and exaggerated identification with the object attacked" (p. 101)—the mother, "Poor Mrs Klein," the furnishings in her room. Lacan ventriloquizes this prematurity as Klein's own "brutal verbalisation," an assault on little Dick and on her readers that he glosses in words "almost as revolting for us as for any reader"; namely "*you want to fuck your mother*" (p. 68)—alternatively, in his parodying of Klein's nursery talk, "*Dick little train, big train daddy-train*," or, later, in his glossing of "dangerous objects" as "poo-poo" (p. 82). Here the prematurity or sexual precosity is Lacan's own, like the nursery talk; the child attacked by revoltingly adult language (or is the adult attacked by revolting nursery language?) is actually "any reader" assaulted by the mother-fucker in Lacan himself who pooh-poohs (for instance) the ego psychologists. The scapegoat for Lacanian brutality, not surprisingly, is Melanie Klein.

For Klein, little Dick's "Poor Mrs Klein" indicates his too-early identification with the object (the mother whom he fears to destroy and whom he fears will destroy him). Klein, we might note, also empathizes, finding in little Dick's empathy not only a defense against his aggressive impulses, but the basis for reparative symbol formation. The "premature" genitality that Lacan turns into a pre-mature, back-dated version of adult sexuality becomes, for Klein, a pre-mature version of psychoanalytic empathy, read back onto the child by what amounts to an act of too-great imaginative projection, a misidentification. Lacan puts brutally literal words into Klein's mouth (and into little Dick's too, as when he insists that "There is a subject here who *quite literally* does not reply" (p. 84; my italics): Klein puts meaning into Dick's words (the meaning that Lacan finds all too literal), thereby creating—loosely speaking, projecting—a subject who can reply to her where none is (yet). This form of projection at once resembles and differs from an allied process, projection in its full, psychoanalytic sense—the sense in which "projective identification" precedes the "empathy" which in Klein's scheme it enables. Here is the neat anecdote by which Laplanche and Pontalis, in *The Language of Psycho-Analysis*, illustrate the difference between projection in "the ordinary psychological sense" and "projection in the Freudian sense" (i.e., as they would wish the term to be understood): "'Surely we have the same position?'" says one philosopher to another; "'I hope not'" he replies, in "a radical rejection of his opponent's ideas—ideas which he is afraid to discover in himself."[13] What is brutal in Lacan's attribution to Klein of these "revoltingly" literal words corresponds not only to what is unthinking in Klein, and not only to what is instinctual in little Dick, but to the primary and negative nature of projection itself as a form of rejection—to processes fleetingly glimpsed in these moments of projection and negation in Lacan's own text. As Lacan remarks apropos of projection, "Here, we are in the mirror relation" (p. 3)—a remark that opens, dizzyingly, onto the imaginary of psychoanalytic theory, where Klein, a theoretical "mother," constitutes Lacan's "object" of inquiry.

iii. "A Brutal Verbalisation"

Lacan is a master of the "I hope not" gesture of brutal theoretical self-differentiation that involves radical rejection of his opponent's ideas ("ideas which he is afraid to discover in himself"). "Brutal," the OED tells us, brings with it connotations of animality rather than humanity; want of intelligence or reasoning power; animal or sensual nature; rudeness, coarseness, or lack of refinement; and inhumanity in the sense of cruelty, savagery, or ferocity. If Klein is for Lacan deficient on a theoretical level—"Melanie Klein has neither a theory of the imaginary nor a theory of the *ego*" (p. 82)—Lacan's own writing is often marked, as we have seen, by the polemical deployment of unrefined coarseness (*"you want to fuck your mother"*). And if Klein is the theorist of the instincts and their manifestation in the sadism—the cruelty, savagery, and ferocity—of the small child's phantasies about the maternal body, Lacan is the rigorous theorist of the linguistic unconscious whose classic formula *"the unconscious is the discourse of the other"* receives its most spectacular demonstration in the case of little Dick. "Brutal," then, suggests the ways in which Lacan (an analyst not known for pulling his punches) uses Klein's theoretical deficiency—her arrested development—to fuel his own theoretical engine. But Lacan's insistence on Klein's brutality might make us ask: what Kleinian ideas— what aspect of Kleinian theory—may Lacan be afraid to discover in his own? The Klein who becomes Lacan's little Dick ("incapable of even so much as suspecting the existence of the category of the signifier") also strikingly exemplifies the problematic "place of the imaginary in the symbolic structure" (p. 73) that provides the starting point for "The Topic of the Imaginary."[14] Lacan's sustained meditation on what, in Klein's case history, "cannot be understood" reminds us that the door to analytic understanding is opened on "the basis of a kind of refusal of understanding" (p. 73). A difficulty in understanding (in Klein's understanding) provides the key.

Melanie Klein's brutality—her literal application of the Oedipus complex, her failure to suspect "the existence of the category of the signifier"—is central to the problem that Lacan poses in "The topic of the imaginary." I have already indicated how, for Lacan, Klein's sense of "reality" scarcely differs from little Dick's. As Klein "grafts" what she calls the symbolic onto little Dick, so Lacan in turn grafts what *he* calls the symbolic onto Klein—not only to reveal her collusion with the nonsense of little Dick's psychosis ("what, in this text, cannot be understood"), but also to effect a forcible cure of her defective, psychotic theory by way of his language. But the graft takes because there is something to get a handle on in Klein, just as there is something in little Dick's psychosis for Klein herself to get a handle on. A residual theory of the imaginary is already present in Klein, just as (Lacan points out) "the child already has his own system of language" (p. 83). What is it, then, that Lacan may fear to discover in his own ideas? Surely nothing other than the crucial role of the imaginary, the domain which Lacan associates loosely with Klein's account of projective identification and its allied processes, but which in his system is subordinated to the symbolic and to language. To put it another way, if little Dick, lost in the chaos of an unorganized imaginary, stands in Lacan's account for Klein's concept of projective identification and her inability to distinguish between real and unreal (or literal and metaphoric), we could also speculate that it is the troubling presence of Kleinian object-relations that Lacanian theory is reluctant to acknowledge ("I hope not," we overhear him say).

We have already seen how both Lacan and Klein, in opening the doors of the unconscious, blur the boundaries between one unconscious and another—using psychosis (what Lacan calls "too real a relation to reality," p. 87) and empathy (too great an identification with the object) as a means to posit the existence of another subjectivity in their own theoretical writing. And we have seen too that a degree of negation or rejection ("projection" proper) attends the elaboration of Lacanian theory; perhaps any theory. It is just this difficulty in distinguishing what is inside from what is outside that Laplanche and Pontalis, in their dictionary entry for "Projective Identification," point to as a theoretical difficulty in the Kleinian concept itself: "This approach [i.e., Klein's] fails to tackle the problem of whether there is a valid distinction to be made, within the category of identification, between those modes of the process where the subject makes himself one with the other person and those where he makes the other person one with himself."[15] "Here, we are in the mirror relation" indeed—faced with a confused category of identification which problematizes the process of differentiation in very much the way in which it is problematic for little Dick (and, one might add, in a way which points to the Kristevan category of preoedipal, pre-objectival identification to which I will return). In this connection, it's worth mentioning Lacan's own deployment, elsewhere, of a topos that has neither an inside nor an outside (and a hole in the middle): the Klein bottle.[16] Kleinian theory has everything to do with containers and what they contain (the mother's body and its *contenu*). What may well be disturbing to Lacan is the possibility of slippage—the possibility, for instance, of not being able to tell the difference between his theory and hers. Swallowing too much Klein may be what is making Lacan gag.

Lacan claims that the "elementary key" provided by Klein unlocks not just the less complex structure—the less complex "complex"—but also the more complex "complexes," or what Lacan calls "a set of relations between subjects of a wealth and complexity besides which the Oedipus complex seems only to be so abridged an edition that in the end it cannot always be used" (p. 86). An abridged edition (shrink-lit, so to speak), the Oedipus complex provides an elementary handbook for analytic technique. For Lacan, the unabridged (unshrunk) edition is language itself. But in this essay, Lacan famously makes his point by appealing not to language but to optics. Calling Klein's case history "the write-up of an experiment" (p. 80), he invokes "the experiment of the inverted bouquet" as a stand-in for the mirror phase (fig. 2). Lacan's point is that in order to see the bouquet reflected in the pot you have to have a subject-position (a position that only language—the symbolic—provides). Without it, he says, all you have is "a sad, empty pot, or some lonesome flowers, depending on the case" (p. 80). Poor curtain . . . with this comical flicker of misplaced empathy, Lacan returns us to little Dick, for whom

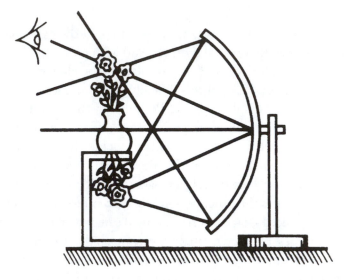

Fig. 2. Lacan, *The experiment of the inverted bouquet* ("a sad, empty pot, or some lonesome flowers"). *The Seminars of Jaques Lacan*, Book 1, ed. Jacques-Alain MIller, trans. John Forrester (Cambridge: Cambridge University Press, 1988), 78, 80. Reprinted with the permission of Cambridge University Press.

the pot is always sad, and the flowers lonesome, since "in his case, the bouquet and the vase cannot both be there at the same time. That is the key" (p. 82). Without the Kleinian "symbolic formations" that Lacan redefines as "imaginative interplay," all Dick has is the naked reality of objects. In "the experiment of the inverted bouquet," the vase is visible, while the hidden bouquet takes its place in the vase by way of an optical illusion, as a reflection of something actually hidden from view (or *vice versa*; in a bit of play on his own account, Lacan suggests that inverting the pot would work just as well): "let us say that the image of the body . . . is like the imaginary vase which contains the bouquet of real flowers" (p. 79). These are the topsy-turvy, always unstable relations of real and imaginary that only the symbolic can put in their proper place.

For Lacan, the reason little Dick can't put the flowers in the vase is that, while he can *project*, he can't *introject*. Here Lacan pauses to insist on a crucial (linguistic) difference. For him—as opposed to Klein—"Introjection is always the introjection of the speech of the other, which introduces an entirely different dimension from that of projection" (p. 83). But at this point, Lacan takes an unexpected tack. He points out that little Dick can play after all, and not only with "the container and the contained" (p. 82); he plays with language ("He even makes use of it to play a game of opposition against the adults' attempts to intrude," p. 83). "It isn't language that I am covertly slipping in," says Lacan—taking by surprise an audience all set to say *"Of course, being Doctor Lacan, he uses this to go on about language again"* (to which he replies, a bit too emphatically: "I hope not"). It is not even, he asserts, "a higher level of language. It is in fact beneath language, if we're talking of levels" (p. 84), wherever that level might be. Lack ("it lacks") is what even "a being deprived of language"—a pet, Lacan suggests, but it could be a baby, for that matter—communicates when it calls its owner. The brute wants to be fed. The call implies a possibility of refusal, a demand beyond need. But it is also, deep down ("beneath language"), an instinctual call: "Feed me, feed me," the theme song of the all-devouring plant in *Little Shop of Horrors*. When little Dick says "station" and "everything starts firing," we find that what Melanie Klein really did was not feed him, but feed him *lines*. As Lacan puts it, *"The station is mummy. Dick is going into mummy* . . . . She'll only feed him these kinds of lines" (p. 85). These kinds of lines are a starvation diet. Offering him words in place of instinctual satisfaction, Klein recodes the initial failure of little Dick's nursing as normative. Klein's lines cure.

By transforming an expression of brute need into one of "lack," Klein's lines not only fire the machinery of the Oedipus complex; they also initiate a series of substitutions. Or, as Lacan puts it, startlingly, "[Little Dick] is swallowed up in a series of equivalences, in a system in which objects are substituted one for the other" (p. 86). In the great oedipal timetable, little Dick becomes de Saussure's famous 8:45 Geneva-Paris train.[17] The key is not the line so much as the series of equivalences. But what has happened in Lacan's own linguistic train of thought? Voracious little Dick, who exists in "too real a relation to reality," gets swallowed up by the very system of equivalences that is supposed to feed him. "It lacks": by an inversion like that of the vase and the bouquet, the call of the pet becomes for Lacan the clamor of a hungry system of equivalences in search of a derailed subject. In this moment of slippage, the insistence of Lacanian theory—*"Of course, being Doctor Lacan, he uses this to go on about language again"*—surfaces as the "core of this observation" concerning optics, fuelled by its own linguistic drive. What we glimpse, *pace* Lacan himself, is not so much "the possibility of defining the contained [*contenu*] and the non-contained [*non-contenu*]" (p. 86) which the symbolic gives little Dick, but rather the Klein bottle (the up-ended vase), which has neither inside nor outside—the difficulty of separating imaginary and symbolic in the very machinery of language itself. We might say, then, that where Melanie Klein brutally verbalizes, little Dick gets chewed up in Lacan's pet theory. The corollary of this process is that Kleinian affect and Kleinian instinct ("with her animal instinct") get spat up on the mat. We could call the spit-up "brutality," the animal instinct which is the underside of Kleinian empathy. This is the brute that Lacan is afraid to find driving the machine of language.

Fig. 3. "It was very painful when I was sharpened for the first time." Marcello Minale, *The Black Pencil* (London: Dobson Books, 1968).

iv. "Poor Melanie Klein"

Lacan construes little Dick's greater-than normal potential for empathy as fear of fragmentation: "When he sees little pencil shavings on Melanie Klein's blouse, the result of a fragmentation, he says—*Poor Melanie Klein*" (p. 70). Or, as Hanna Segal glosses this moment of pathos, "To him the shavings were Mrs Klein cut into bits."[18] But this *corps morcelé* also suggests the detritus of a cast-out mother. For Kristeva, abjecting the mother is the condition for self-differentiation on the part of a not-yet-subject or "abject"—the "abject" being at once little Dick himself and the body of a maternal stand-in, the Kleinian not-yet-object (fig. 3). Kristeva's "Freud and Love: Treatment and its Discontents" invokes "*Einfühlung* (the assimilation of other people's feelings)" as a means of exploring both analytical trans-ference-love and the pre-objectal, primary identification which (Kristeva argues) is correlative to the abjection of the mother.[19] Probing beyond Lacan's question ("how does the imaginary gives rise to the symbolic?"), Kristeva asks instead: "what are the conditions for the emergence of the imaginary?" She insists on the preexistence of a symbolic function and on "*various dispositions* giving access to that function" (p. 44). Klein writes that little Dick had cut himself off from reality "by taking refuge in the phantasies of a dark, empty, vague womb" (p. 105). Lacan reformulates this "reality which knows no development" as "a single and unique primary identification, with the following names—the *void*, the *dark*." He goes on: "This gap is precisely what is human in the structure peculiar to the subject" (pp. 69–70). Kristeva glosses Lacan's gap—a "*gaping hole*" that can also be equated with the arbitrariness of the Saussurean sign—as "this notion of emptiness, which is at the root of the human psyche" (p. 23).[20] She speculates that "the *emptiness* that is intrinsic to the beginnings of the symbolic function appears as the first separation between what is not yet an *Ego* and what is not yet an *object*" (i.e., an "abject"). Primary narcissism, she suggests, may be the defense designed to protect this "emptiness . . . intrinsic to the symbolic function," introducing the minimal difference without which "chaos would sweep away any possibility of distinction, trace and symbolization" (p. 24). Identifying with the gap makes signification possible.

The child, writes Kristeva,

> with all due respect to Lacan, not only *needs* the real and the symbolic—it signifies itself as child, in other words as the subject that it is, and neither as a psychotic nor as an adult, precisely in that zone where *emptiness and narcissism*, the one upholding the other, constitute the zero degree of imagination. (p. 24)

Revising "The Mirror-Phase," Kristeva posits narcissism as an already ternary, "complex" structure prior even to the complex structure of oedipalization, and then asks: what preserves or structures narcissistic emptiness? Her answer is "identification," which—following Freud's discussion of identification in *Group Psychology and the Analysis of the Ego* (1921)—she refers to as *Einfühlung*, or empathy. Reflecting on the ambivalence of identification, Freud derives it from the oral phase "in which the object that we long for and prize is assimilated by eating and is in that way annihilated as such"(*SE* 18.105). Shades of "Tea daddy," as well as his Kristevan alter ego in the case history appended to "Freud and Love," "Matthew or the Walkman against Saturn" (Matthew wields his ubiquitous headset as a defense against "the image of a devouring father . . . eating, voracious, insatiable," p. 54). Properly speaking, this archaic, oral identification, "where what I incorporate is what I become, where *having* amounts to *being*" (p. 25), precedes identification with an object. Contrasting pre-objectal (preoedipal) identification with the metonymic structure of Lacanian (oedipal) desire, Kristeva equates it with metaphor, especially as it appears in analytical transference and in "the internal, recursive, redundant logic of discourse, which is accessible within the 'afterspeech'" (p. 25); that is, in what I have called "the brute in the machine"—the drive and affect that, for Kristeva, as for André Green, Lacan's vision of language occludes.[21]

References to Klein—"a theoretician of gratitude seen as 'an important offshoot of the capacity for love'" (p. 27)—surface insistently in "Freud and Love." In "The Origins of Transference" (1952), Klein herself had argued that analytical transference recapitulates the earliest processes of object relations. Anticipating the trajectory of "Freud and Love," Klein broaches the matter of transference by way of autoerotic and narcissistic "states" (as opposed to Freud's "stages"), and points to an equivocation in Freud's own thinking; might object relations—a more than merely physical relation to the mother's breast—even precede narcissism? Klein goes on to remind her readers of Freud's remarks in *The Ego and the Id* about the first and most important identification with the father of personal prehistory. In a footnote, she draws attention to Freud's suggestion "that these first identifications . . . are a direct and immediate identification which takes place earlier than any object cathexis. This suggestion seems to imply that introjection even precedes object-relations."[22] Klein's tactic here is to suggest that Freud had not yet made up his mind on the question. Kristeva, in turn, builds on Freud's equivocation when she calls "incorporating and introjecting orality's function . . . the essential substratum of what constitutes man's being, namely *language*" (p. 26). She equates introjection of the speech of the other with identification: "In being able to receive the other's words, to assimilate, repeat, and reproduce them, I become like him: One. A subject of enunciation. Through psychic osmosis/identification. Through love" (p. 26). This loving, preoedipal, nonobjectal identification, a psychic "osmosis/identification" that "lets one hold onto the joys of chewing, swallowing, nourishing oneself . . . with words," reappears in transference-love. In Kristeva's account, as in Klein's, the third term that structures metaphoric identification is Freud's "father in individual prehistory."

Is this third term the father, or the mother's desire for the father (or perhaps, "a coagulation of the mother and her desire" p. 41)? For Klein, the preoedipal relation is by definition a "relation between *two* people into which no other object enters,"[23] even if a phantasized penis or part-object is included in the maternal relation. Or, as Kristeva puts it, "Melanie Klein's gratitude is nevertheless and at the same time directed towards the maternal object in its entirety" (p. 28). Kristeva acknowledges that "*empirically*, the first affections, the first imitations and the first vocalizations as well are directed towards the mother." Thus, for her, the assumption of any primary identification with Freud's "father in individual prehistory" on the part of the child "is tenable only if one conceives of *identification* as being always already within the symbolic orbit, under the sway of language" (p. 27). Here Kristeva goes out of her way to point to a contradiction in Klein. For Klein, love is apparently innate (an instinctual response to the satisfaction at the breast); yet it also functions as a defense, and must therefore belong to the realm of ego-related activities (as an idealization of the "good" breast that stems from persecution by the "bad" breast). How are we to explain the contradictory origin of love in both instinct and idealization? In Kristeva's words, "By what miracle is that possible, in a Kleinian life where two live without a third party other than a persecuting or fascinating penis?" (p. 28). Klein notices an equivocation in Freud: Kristeva opens the fault line in Klein's equivocation over "good breast" versus "idealized" object (what is innate as opposed to ego-related, hence involving some form of object relations). Kristeva's lever is the symbolic third term provided by Freud's "father of individual prehistory."

By a double movement, Kristeva at once distances herself from what she calls "Lacanian notions of an always-already-there of language" and inserts a diacritical mark of difference into the space occupied by the preoedipal mother. What Kristeva calls "the archaic inscription of the father" becomes the sign of the mother's lack of plenitude—a "Third Party" that prevents her from "playing at the phallus game all by herself," as Kristeva puts it, in the back room of Kleinian theory (the space between Klein's two doors):

> In contrast with Melanie Klein's "projective identification," the proposition I am offering here has the advantage of pointing to, even before the Oedipal triangle and within a specific disposition, the place of the Third Party; without the latter, the phase Melanie Klein calls "schizo-paranoid" could not become a "depressive"

phase and thus could not carry the "symbolic equivalences" to the level of linguistic "signs." The archaic inscription of the father seems to me a way of modifying the fantasy of a phallic mother playing at the phallus game all by herself, alone and complete, in the back room of Kleinism and post-Kleinism. (p. 44)

The problem that troubles some feminist readers of Kristeva's more recent work—how does this appeal to the "father of individual pre-history" differ from Lacan's Name of the Father?—is a nonissue for Kristeva herself; as she poses it, the problem is rather how to avoid the regressive fantasy (or rather, the Kleinian "phantasy") of a phallic mother. Accordingly she can dismiss as unimportant the question "Who might be the object of primary identification, daddy or mummy?" (in any case the answer is: "both"). Instead, Kristeva asks, apropos of the analytic situation, "of what value would the question be when it actually bears on states existing on the border between the psychic and the somatic, idealization and eroticism . . . ?" (p. 28). This is the borderline where transference-love appears, and where "one hears the discourse that is performed there starting with that limit of advent-and-loss of the subject—which is *Einfühlung*." The "archaic inscription of the father" enters the picture as a question. What in the mother exceeds her desire for the child, creating the gap (the "Not I") with which the *infans* can identify?

The "limit of advent-and-loss of the subject" is played out in the analytical discourse as empathy, the (mistaken) identification which allows metaphor—rather than the mother—to emerge from the vestibule of the unreal-real. For Kristeva, as for Klein, the analyst is also an empathizer, accompanying the patient in a regress "as far as the limits and accidents of his object relations," and deciphering a discourse that exists (to rephrase Lacan) at the very limits and accidents of the appearance of language:

The *Einfühlung* gives the language signifier exchanged during treatment a heterogeneous, drive-affected dimension. It loads it with something preverbal, or even nonrepresentable that needs to be deciphered while taking into account the more precise articulations of discourse (style, grammar, phonetics), and at the same time while cutting through language, in the direction of the unspeakable, indicated by fantasies and "insight" narratives as well as by symptomatic misspeech (slips of the tongue, illogical statements, etc.). (p. 29)

Commenting elsewhere on the heterogeneity of the semiotic, Kristeva corrects any misunderstanding that her aim is "to integrate some alleged concreteness, brute corporality, or energy-in-itself into a language suspected of being too abstract."[24] For her it is not, and never can be, a matter of turning back to the mother-as-origin, as a literal reading of Klein might tempt us to turn back or regress (the semiotic, Kristeva reminds us, "is without primacy and has no place as origin").[25] Rather, we should attend to this work of deciphering the unspeakable within speech—attend, that is, to little Dick's "literal" ("Dick . . . gnashed his teeth and said 'Tea daddy,' by which he meant 'Eat daddy'"). Little Dick's "symptomatic misspeech," his slip of the tongue (which is also, as the *OED* illustrates at length, a slip implicating the teeth), is an illogical statement that partakes of "the internal, recursive, redundant logic of discourse." Lacan would see in it little Dick's foreclosure of the Name of the Father. Kristeva, by constrast, suggests that we should view little Dick's oral incorporation as primary identification. We could redefine this identification as the "heterogeneity" of metaphor.

"Tea daddy"—the A to T (as the *OED* has it, "originally . . . the last letter of the [Greek] alphabet") or Alpha and Omega of all identifications—conjoins the oral drive (biting) to its fathering metaphor (the Saturnine devourer) on the borderline between "incorporating and introjecting orality's function" that Kristeva defines as the essential substratum of language. In "Freud and Love," Kristeva dissociates metaphor from "the classical rhetorical trope (*figurative* v. *plain*)." Instead she allies it with "the modern theories of metaphor that decipher within it an indefinite jamming of semantic features one in to the other, a meaning being acted out," and with "the drifting of heterogeneity within a heterogeneous psychic apparatus, going from drives and sensations to signifier and conversely" (p. 37). This semantic jamming, with its acting out of meaning and its oscillation between drives and signifiers, serves as a reminder that nothing can ever really be "literal," even for little Dick (even for Melanie Klein). The Lacanian insistence of the letter in the unconscious becomes for Kristeva, by way of a Kleinian back-formation, the heterogeneous drift that links drives and signs in the metaphoric structures of transferential discourse. Klein's "Premature *empathy*" (*Einfühlung*)—what might be called "pathetic fallacy"—represents the first positing of the subject in language, or a founding figural moment, by means of a misplaced identification; it is less a matter of naming (as Lacan had argued) than of misnaming. When little Dick spots the pencil shavings on Melanie Klein's lap, and says "Poor Mrs Klein" (or even "Poor curtain"), a Kristevan gloss might run something like this: "in abjecting the mother, I (mis)identify or metaphorize myself."

* * *

Little Dick reminds us that where we have our words, we (once and still) imagine eating them too; but he also reminds us that "having" and "eating"—like "having" and "being"—delineate the borderline or point of slippage between incorporation and introjection that is constitutive not only of language but of the capacity for linguistic play ("the joys of chewing, swallowing, nourishing oneself . . . with words"). Klein's oedipal lines feed brutal joys, the oral play which accompanies little Dick's symbolic eating (for tea) of Freud's "father of individual prehistory." If Little Dick bit off more than he could chew, so—at least according to Lacan and Kristeva—did Klein herself. The Lacanian reading brutalizes Klein: the Kristevan reading has an empathetic feel. Rereading Klein's lines with Kristevan hindsight allows us at least to credit them with their prematurity or "anticipation"—their prior understanding—of the ways in which we might now wish to digest them rather than losing them altogether. I want to end with Klein's brief, early note on "The Importance of Words in Early Analysis" (1927), in which she relates a game with a child involving a Mr. Cookey-Caker (the name represented, she says, "the making of children in an oral and anal way"): "The word 'Cookey-Caker' is the bridge to reality which the child avoids as long as he brings forth his phantasies only by playing." She concludes: "It always means progress when the child has to acknowledge the reality of the objects through his own words."[26] Lacan's unsuspected "category of the signifier" turns out to have been a guest at little Dick's tea party all along. I started by associating the risk of regression in reading Klein with taking her literally. I will end by suggesting that rather than eating Klein's words, we might chew on the play of metaphor that little Dick's unspeakable slip (the meeting point of teeth, tongue, and T) inscribes in the "literal" of Klein's lines.

"Tea Daddy"

1. *The Selected Melanie Klein*, ed. Juliet Mitchell (Harmondsworth, UK: Penguin, 1986), 104. Subsequent page references in the text are to this edition.

2. *Ecrits: A Selection*, trans. Alan Sheridan (New York: Norton, 1977), 272.

3. See *The Seminar of Jacques Lacan: Book 1*, ed. Jacques-Alain Miller, trans. John Forrester (Cambridge: Cambridge University Press, 1988), 74; subsequent page references in the text are to this edition. Compare Hanna Segal's definition of symbol formation as "an activity of the ego attempting to deal with the anxieties stirred by its relation to the object"; see "Notes on Symbol Formation," in *Melanie Klein Today*, ed. Elizabeth Bott Spillius (London: Routledge, 1988), 1: 163.

4. See "Early Stages of the Oedipus Conflict" (1928): "I have repeatedly alluded to the conclusion that the Oedipus complex comes into operation earlier than is usually supposed"; *The Selected Melanie Klein*, 89.

5. Lacan, *Ecrits*, 20.

6. Originally published in a shorter version as "L'abjet d'amour," in *Tel Quel* 91 (1982), "Freud and Love" forms chapter 1 of *Tales of Love*, trans. Leon S. Roudiez (New York: Columbia University Press, 1987). Subsequent page references in the text are to this edition.

7. "In projective identification, the subject in phantasy projects large parts of himself into the object, and the object becomes identified with the parts of the self that it is felt to contain. Similarly, internal objects are projected outside and identified with parts of the external world which come to represent them. These first projections and identifications are the beginnings of the process of symbol formation" (Segal, "Notes on Symbol Formation," *Melanie Klein Today*, 1.164).

8. See *The Selected Melanie Klein*, 95; see also Phyllis Grosskurth, *Melanie Klein: Her World and her Work* (Cambridge, MA: Harvard University Press, 1987), 185–88.

9. See Jacqueline Rose, *Sexuality in the Field of Vision* (London: Verso, 1986), 54–55 and n, for a succinct summary of the difference between Klein's account of symbolization as both an effect of anxiety and a means of transcending it in the interests of mastering reality, and Lacan's emphasis on "the structure of metaphor (or substitution) which lies at the root of, and is endlessly repeated within, subjectivity in its relation to the unconscious"— displacing the subject and making "the real" an endlessly returning "moment of impossibility" onto which symbolic and imaginary are grafted.

10. See Segal, "Notes on Symbol Formation," 163.

11. I am endebted to Shoshana Felman's reading of the Lacanian reading of the case history of little Dick. Felman writes: "Anxiety is linked to the Symbolic. . . . The rising anxiety in Dick embodies his nascent intuition that, in a symbolic system, any element or change has repercussions in the whole. Dick thus develops anxiety, as he passes from *indifference* (everything is equally real) to *difference* (everything is not equally real) . . ."; see *Jacques Lacan and the Adventure of Insight* (Cambridge, MA: Harvard University Press, 1987), 116. Despite not pursuing the "adventure of insight" beyond Lacan's own, Felman's is the most persuasive reading of Lacan's two seminars on Klein currently available.

12. See Felman, *Jacques Lacan and the Adventure of Insight*, especially 117–28 for an extended Lacanian reading of the narrative dimensions of the Oedipus myth.

13. J. Laplanche and J.-B. Pontalis, *The Language of Psycho-Analysis* (New York: Norton, 1973),

355.

14. For an extended discussion of the Lacanian imaginary, see Rose, "The Imaginary," in *Sexuality in the Field of Vision*, 167–97.

15. Laplanche and Pontalis, *The Language of Psycho-Analysis*, 357.

16. For Lacan's use of mathematical and geometrical models, see Catherine Clément, *The Lives and Legends of Jacques Lacan* (New York: Columbia University Press, 1983), 160, 161: "Then there were odd looking bottles with no inside or outside, what mathematicians call Klein bottles. . . . Lacan's mathematical objects gave him the means to represent forms without insides or outsides, forms without boundaries or simple separations, forms of which a hole is a constitutive part." See also Victor Burgin, "Geometry and Abjection," in *Abjection, Melancholia, and Love: The Work of Julia Kristeva* (London: Routledge, 1990), 104–23.

17. "The example drawn on here is de Saussure's 8.45 Geneva-Paris express, which, although it can manifestly be a different train from that of the previous day, is yet identifiable as the same since it is different in function from the rest" (Rose, *Sexuality in the Field of Vision*, 184).

18. Segal, "Notes on Symbol Formation," 165.

19. For related readings of "Freud and Love," see also Cynthia Chase, "Desire and Identification in Lacan and Kristeva," in *Feminism and Psychoanalysis*, ed. Richard Feldstein and Judith Roof (Ithaca, NY: Cornell University Press, 1989), 65–83, and "Primary Narcissism and the Giving of Figure: Kristeva with Hertz and de Man," in *Abjection, Melancholia and Love*, 124–36. Neil Hertz has also developed a reading of "L'Abjet d'amour" ("Freud and Love") that tallies with his invention of a structure that he calls, appropriately for my purposes, "a sort of capital T lying on its side"; see *The End of the Line* (New York: Columbia University Press, 1985), 217–39, especially 231–32.

20. Kristeva acknowledges her indebtedness for the notion of "emptiness" to André Green's *Narcissisme de vie, narcissisme de mort* (Paris: Minuit, 1983).

21. See Rose, *Sexuality in the Field of Vision*, 152.

22. *The Selected Melanie Klein*, 205, 240 n. See also Jean Laplanche, *New Foundations for Psychoanalysis*, trans. David Macey (Oxford: Blackwell, 1989), 80–81 and 166 n, for a pithy discussion of "the Kleinians" and a reference to this 1952 paper.

23. *The Selected Melanie Klein*, 49 n.

24. Rose, *Sexuality in the Field of Vision*, 152, quoted from "Il n'y a pas de maître à langage," in *Nouvelle Revue de Psychanalyse* 20 (Autumn 1979): 130–31.

25. See Rose, *Sexuality in the Field of Vision*, 152.

26. Melanie Klein, *Envy and Gratitude* (London: Virago Press, 1988), 314.

8

"'Cos of the Horse"
The Origin of Questions

HANS: *"Because they kept on saying ''cos of the horse,' ''cos of the horse'"* *(he put a stress on the ''cos'); "so perhaps I got the nonsense because they talked liked that; ''cos of the horse.'"*

—Sigmund Freud, *Analysis of a Phobia in a Five-Year-Old Boy,* 1909 (SE 10.59)

To the question, "How is a person made?" his mother once more repeated the explanation given him often before. This time [Fritz] became more talkative and told her that the governess had told him . . . that the stork brought babies. "That is only a story," said his mother.

—Melanie Klein, "The Development of a Child" (1921)[1]

QUESTS FOR ORIGINS, it goes without saying, are attempts to create founding myths or stories, and all such quests are bound to come up against an originating epistemological uncertainty. But I want to pay attention to the questioning as well as to the quest—to the specifically linguistic and rhetorical aspects of questions. To risk a question of my own (and there will be more): what is the origin of questions? By way of an answer, I want to explore two accounts of children's attempts to answer what Freud regards as the original—the abiding—question: "the great riddle of where babies come from," which he calls "the first problem to engage a child's mental powers" (SE 10.133). Freud's own question—what is the origin of phobia?— becomes the vehicle for a psychoanalytic account of the origin of the gendered, heterosexual subject in oedipal structures; but it also turns out to bear on language.

153

In an infinite regress, it opens not only onto the realm of object relations that would be for Freud himself preoedipal, such as those explored by Melanie Klein (and later by Julie Kristeva), but onto the earliest signifying structures in which the infant is installed via the intersubjective dialogue with his or her "objects" (what Kristeva calls "abjects"). Both the Freudian and the Kleinian versions of this story—not to mention Kristeva's—turn out to implicate the origin of signs as well as the origin of babies; but only Klein and Kristeva redefine these preoccupations so as to suggest that one function of the oedipal story is to determine meanings that would otherwise be troublingly indeterminate—an indeterminacy they identify, implicitly or explicitly, with maternal absence, and, in Kristeva's case, with the "frailty" (her term) of signifying systems.

Freud's *Analysis of a Phobia in a Five-Year-Old Boy* (1909) accidentally gives rise to the speculation that the origin of little Hans's horse phobia may lie in a verbal resemblance or propinquity—in "nonsense"—as much as in the castration anxiety of an oedipal scenario.[2] Melanie Klein's early essay, "The Development of a Child" (1921), points to the seemingly unstoppable rhetorical movement of questions, and the "stories" or phantasies to which they give rise, even as she herself assumes that sexual enlightenment, by providing an answer to the child's questions, will bring them to a halt and relieve the compulsion to know. Freud's retelling of the Oedipus story—the founding pre-text for psychoanalysis—might be said to provide an origin for Klein's account of little Fritz; but Klein's essay is also a rereading of Freud which anticipates the alternative theory of origins provided by Kristeva's subsequent reading of the little Hans case in *Powers of Horror* (1980). Despite Klein's oedipal blueprint, she implicates the maternal body as a crucial, imaginary point of origin, and not just as the initiating site for heterosexualizing oedipal desire. The mother whom Freud represents as an already oedipal object is glimpsed as a lost object—as the site of an archaic, pre-objectal relation. It is here, for Kristeva, that metaphor gets posited in the form of the necessary third term that she calls "the paternal metaphor," or identification with signs; this is the identification that initiates symbolic activity and enables later oedipal structures. If the Freudian narrative retrospectively fixes meanings by way of the oedipal narrative, Kristeva's preoedipal narrative looks back to their fragile beginnings in signification, tending to associate this fragility with the mother. On this backward-looking note, I will begin at the end with Freud's little Oedipus—the child who is the founding father of the man in Freudian theory.

i. Little Hans's Nonsense

Consider Little Hans's own explanation of his horse phobia, his "nonsense" (as he calls it)—that it has its origins in the rhetoric of explanation: "*Because,*" he says, "they [the other children, his holiday playmates] kept on saying ' 'cos of the horse,' . . . so perhaps I got the nonsense *because* they talked like that'" (*SE* 10.59; my italics). The logic that drives little Hans's explanation ("*Because*") is the logic of inquiry set in motion by his father and, at one remove, by the professor, Freud himself; like little Hans, they too are always asking "why?" Along with many an exasperated parent (and many a baffled child), little Hans is reduced to answering "Because"—"just *because*"—as if to put a stop to the innumerable questions that beset him. It is no accident, then, that the case of little Hans unfolds by way of the strenuous question and answer sessions between the little boy and his father later recounted to the professor; and no accident either that little Hans himself is especially preoccupied by the possibility of vehicular breakdown—he himself traces the onset of his phobic "nonsense" back to an upset involving a horse-drawn bus ("*Because* once a horse in a bus fell down," *SE* 10.49; my italics). Without the smooth traffic or transfer of meaning from one place to another, and without the logic of cause and effect which ensures that one thing follows predictably after another, both language and inquiry grind to a halt. "That was when I got the nonsense" (*SE* 10.50), Hans asserts. A fallen horse is the stumbling block, causing a general collapse of sense into nonsense. In the face of this collapse, psychoanalysis becomes complicit with nonsense, by putting the cart before the horse.

Linguistic accident generates the traffic in meaning with which Freud's "little enquirer" precociously collides. The only language without ambiguity, or without the risk of misnaming, would be the language of things, which is no language at all; or else the "language" of psychosis. Signification depends on nonidentity and on the differential movement structured by multiple symbolic substitutions for which—at least since Lacan—the Oedipus story has been read as a shorthand. The bringing to light of this accident-prone traffic might be regarded as little Hans's most profound discovery. As Freud himself writes elsewhere, in *The Interpretation of Dreams* (1900), "Words, since they are the nodal points of numerous ideas, may be regarded as predestined to ambiguity." (*SE* 5.340). In much the same way that language is "predestined" to ambiguity, little Hans is predestined to assume his place in Freud's oedipal family: "Long before he was in the world . . . [Freud] had known that a little Hans would come who would be so fond of his mother that he would be bound to feel afraid of his father because of it . . ." (*SE* 10.42). So fond . . . that he would be *bound* to feel afraid ("because of it"): Freud's logic assumes that fundamental affects (fondness or fear) are "bound" to the meaning provided by the oedipal plot. As Freud lets us know, in his role of the one who foreknows the whole story, the predestined collision of ambiguous words and oedipal structures also constitutes a "nodal point," not only for signification but for the subject. This is the collision that assigns little Hans his meaning within Freudian theory, making him the subject of Freud's previously told oedipal story. The site of the collision marks the convergence of the two questions about origins which not only perplex little Hans himself but turn out to constitute him as an oedipal subject. These two questions—"what is my connection with my father and mother?" and "what is my connection with words?"— point to the mapping of subjectivity onto language which the oedipal plot fixes, retrospectively providing the answer to the riddle of little Hans's (little man's) existence.

Like Freud himself, who is also preoccupied by the question of sexual difference, little Hans keeps asking: "where do babies come from?" Freud puts it in the heroic terms of his own (similarly oedipal) inquiry, the riddle of the Sphinx: "faced with the great riddle of where babies come from," Hans wrestles with a problem "of which the riddle of the Theban Sphinx is probably no more than a distorted version" (*SE* 10.168). A little Prometheus as well as a little Oedipus, little Hans is visibly dissatisfied with the explanations handed down by his altogether too knowing father, and sometimes even moved to sullen revolt: "*You know everything; I don't know anything*" (*SE* 10.90; Freud's italics), he complains. Freud's always evident affection for little Hans makes him the little actor of his own rebellious researches; he too is attempting to wrest the enigma of oedipal subjectivity from the anti-psychoanalytic taxonomy which would label little Hans as just a little nut (neurotically predisposed to phobia by bad heredity or bad character). But Hans's inquiry impinges on another story altogether, that of the origins of language. This is the story of desire driving language, but also, as we learn from little Hans himself, the story of how language gets in the driver's seat. Simultaneously sign and symptom of phobia, the collision-prone vehicle of language conducts Hans metonymically through the streets where he encounters the fear against which (so Kristeva would argue) language provides his only refuge—standing as it does between him and the nothingness he fears. Freud names this fear as the fear of his father, or castrating progenitor; Lacan, in his account of the case, as fear of the castration signified by his mother.[3] But it can also be named as fear of what Kristeva would call the unnameable—the lost maternal object which predates the onset of both language and oedipality. This lost nonobject which phobia inscribes would be not the mother's missing phallus, but an impossible unity posited (and mourned for) at the imaginary origin of the not-yet-subject. Long before he was "so fond" of his mother, long before he was afraid of his father, little Hans was afraid of missing the bus altogether—afraid of finding no meaning at all. The implication of Kristeva's argument is that fear of no-meaning predates fear of the father. Uncovering his origins may be little Hans's Freudian (oedipal) project; but finding the meanings with which to identify—the meanings that identify him—is his Kristevan (preoedipal) project.

The origins of language and the origins of babies coincide in one of Freud's footnotes, when little Hans, glimpsing the mysteries of the paternal role in his own birth, dreams of a plumber who came and unscrewed the bath and stuck a "borer" into his stomach. "Perhaps," writes Freud in a telling footnote, "the word 'borer' ['*Bohrer*'] was not chosen without regard for its connection with 'born' ['*geboren*'] and 'birth' ['*Geburt*']. If so the child could have made no distinction between 'bored' ['*gebohrt*'] and 'born' ['*geboren*']." Freud concludes with a telling *aporia*: "I am not in a position to say whether we have before us here a deep and universal connection between the two ideas or merely the employment of a verbal coincidence peculiar to German [and English]" (*SE* 10.98 n). If Freud is "not in a position to say," what position can there be for little Hans as he tries to answer the riddle of his own origins? Freud ends by observing that "Prometheus (Pramantha), the creator of man, is also etymologically 'the borer'" (*SE* 10.98 n). We can see how Hans's version of the creation myth makes necessity (the universal plumber) the father of invention. The doses of sexual enlightenment given to him in response to his own unfolding theory of origins (at first his father fobs him off with some "nonsense" of his own about a stork) only help him to refine a story which he has guessed at all along. As befits a little Prometheus, he is a self-made man. For Freud, every mannikin—every little man—is his own maker, at once playing out his predestined part and stumbling by accident on the truth of a creation myth which he invents to explain his existence. In Freud's disclaimer ("I am not in a position to say . . ."), we glimpse the ambiguity that always attends this birthing, which is also an accession to subjecthood. Is little Hans engendered by a great fore-Borer or born of an arbitrary linguistic law? Does oedipal desire make him keep asking where babies come from, or does the logic of explanation drive him on to the answers that (like Freud before him) he foreknows? Caught between "a deep and universal connection" and "a verbal coincidence," little Hans finds himself face to face with a now familiar version of the riddle of the Sphinx: what does it mean to be at once a little man and an effect of language?

Freud's own telling installs little Hans in a retroactive narrative whereby meaning always comes afterwards while seeming to have come before. It's not just that the sexual enlightenment of children is a superogatory activity in the face of the knowledge they already have (but resist). Rather, Freud's own discovery is that the logic of explanation works backwards, making nonsense of the procedures of inquiry that he himself has set in motion. Causality is the apple cart upset by the case of little Hans. In another revealing footnote, Freud glosses the phrase used by little Hans's playmates, "*Wegen dem Pferd*," ("'cos of the horse") with the following explanation:

> I may at the same time complete what the child was unable to express, and add that the little word "*wegen*" ["because of," "'cos of'] was the means of enabling the phobia to extend from horses on to "*Wagen*" ["vehicles"] or, as Hans was accustomed to pronounce the word and hear it pronounced, "*Wägen*" [pronounced exactly like "*wegen*"]. It must never be forgotten how much more concretely children treat words than grown-up people do, and consequently how much more significant for them are similarities of sound in words. (*SE* 10.59 n.)

Here Freud comes close to identifying "the little word '*wegen*'" ("'cos of") as the cause of all the nonsense. Not a wagon, still less the horse that draws it, but a conjunction—a little word that yokes one thing to another. Or, as Lacan puts it, terming *wägen/wegen* "la métonymie originelle," the horse becomes the signifier around which little Hans constructs his system: "C'est parce que [because] le poids de *wegen* est transféré par métonymie à ce qui vient juste après (cheval) que le cheval va assumer en lui tous les espoirs de solution." Before being a horse, Lacan goes on, it is something that links and coordinates; its mediating function comes first. Earlier in the same footnote, Freud suggests that this was not the time when Hans originally acquired his "nonsense," but rather that he acquired it "*in that connection*" (Freud's italics). The causality involved isn't one of origins, but rather one of conjunction, or "connection" (as in "A deep and universal *connection* between the two ideas"). With Freudian hindsight, one might be tempted to gloss "connection" as "association," the metonymic movement whereby one thing leads to another—conducting the passenger from *wegen* to *wagon*, from horse to bus, and so to a variety of accidents, transports, and vehicular containers (stork-boxes or stomachs). As little Hans discovers in the tendency of his horse phobia to spread to other traffic, to street life, eventually engulfing the entire outdoor world, the effects of such connections are difficult to halt.

The collision of a deep and universal connection and a verbal coincidence is an apt description for the overdetermined workings of language as Freud describes them not only in little Hans's "nonsense," but elsewhere; for instance, in the realms of dreaming and jokes. Two paths, one dictated by the laws of the unconscious, the other by the arbitrary laws of language, may lead to the same place. Apropos of the "concreteness" of words—their materiality ("similarities of sounds in words")— Freud observes in *The Interpretation of Dreams* that "The linguistic tricks performed by children, who sometimes actually treat words as though they were objects and moreover invent new languages and artificial syntactic forms, are the common source of [nonsensical verbal forms] in dreams and psychoneuroses alike" (*SE* 4.303). Just as the word "horse" can stand for different things (for Hans's angry father, for his pregnant mother, and even for little Hans himself), so little Hans's "nonsense"— produced as it is in obedience to the dictates of free association— can mean different things in differing contexts: a form of defensive or pleasurable wordplay, an expression of Promethean inquiry or revolt, or an illustration of the movements of condensation and displacement that also operate in dreaming. But it is also a strange kind of verbal "object"—symbolic activity itself; or, as Kristeva puts it succinctly, "There is language instead of the good breast."[4] Little Hans's "nonsense" (his horse phobia), standing in for something that can't be named at all, reveals an archaic trace unsettling the oedipal drama which is supposed to have produced it. In *Jokes and their Relation to the Unconscious* (1905), Freud attributes "pleasure in nonsense" to a child's forbidden experiments in the acquisition of its mother tongue: "He puts words together without regard to the condition that they should make sense, in order to obtain from them the pleasurable effect of rhythm or rhyme. Little by little he is forbidden this enjoyment, till all that remains permitted to him are significant combinations of words" (*SE* 8.125). Freud suggests that this prohibition on polymorphously perverse linguistic nonsense operates in the interests of the symbolic ("significant combinations of words"); as such, it is an oedipal prohibition. We could call this non-sense "the semiotic," associating it, in Kristevan fashion, with the preoedipal subject of abjection whose "symptom," she says apropos of little Hans, "is the rejection and reconstruction of languages."[5]

Although little Hans is frightened by his phobic "nonsense," both his pleasure in nonsense talk and the forbidden uses to which he puts it (to outwit his father, for instance) mark his rebellion against "making sense." Nonsense becomes his means of resistance, specifically resistance to the oedipal narrative forced on him by his insistent father. Bouts of nonsense talk usually occur between little Hans and his father when little Hans is either being pressed too hard for an answer, or else getting back at his father for misleading him about the origin of babies (the stork-box theory): "What can be the meaning of the boy's obstinate persistence in all this nonsense? Oh no," writes Freud, "it was no nonsense: it was parody, it was Hans's revenge upon his father" (*SE* 10.70). Verbal nonsense is resistance disguised as parody. In the case of little Hans, semiotic pleasure takes the form of regressive wordplay focussed, often in collusion with his father (as well as with Freud), on the bodily functions which provide the basis for his excremental theory of the origin of babies (babies=*lumf*, as Freud reminds us; see *SE* 10.87, 95). As the body bears *Lumf* (feces) or the cart lets fall its load, so a mother bears her child—the same word, "*niederkommen*," Freud notes, signifies both the fall of a horse and the delivery of a woman (*SE* 10.96 and n). *Lumpf* is like *Strumpf* (stocking) and also, in one wild conversation between Hans and his father, like a "Saffaladi" or "Soffilodi" (his great aunt's name for a saveloy; see *SE* 10.95); carts are greeted as "lumfy" (a term of endearment apparently—compare the cousin affectionately known as "Wumfy"); a little girl whom Hans calls Lodi instead of Lotti becomes a "Schokolodi" (here, at his father's instigation); and, in another particularly inspired piece of nonsense (and translation), mischievous little Hans himself becomes, by analogy with a furniture van (*Möbelwagon*), "a scallywaggon" in stead of a "scallywag" (*SE* 10.79; in German, *Ein Gesindelwerkwagen*), bearing his load of nonsense—his naughtily parodic elaboration on the stork-box theory.[6] Little Hans's nonsense is at once the vehicle for oedipal rebellion, the symptom of his resistance to his father's Freudian intervention, and the trace of a preoedipal nonobject, the absent mother.

As the semiotic residue of the preoedipal ("the pleasurable effect of rhythm or rhyme"), nonsense could be said to keep an avenue open to the mother tongue. In the same way—again according to *Jokes and their Relation to the Unconscious*—a child at a later stage finds pleasure in verbal games because they are forbidden by repressive reason ("He now uses games in order to withdraw from the pressure of critical reason"). Sweepingly, Freud goes on to include all imaginative activity under the heading of "rebellion against the compulsion of logic and reality" (*SE* 8.126). As the power of criticism increases, "liberated nonsense" only dares to show itself indirectly. In little Hans, we see not only the liberating effects of non-sense on a child, but the liberation that it affords to Freud as a creative thinker; little Hans allows him to introduce a little nonsense into psychoanlaytic theory. Freud's own revolt, after all, was against "the compulsion of logic and reality" imposed by the scientific inquiry and empiricism of his times. Logical thinking (the logic of cause and effect) works against the strange form of imaginative activity involved in psychoanalysis, the *post hoc ergo propter hoc* explanation of the origins of psychic life. If a movement between words generated by the accident of proximity (*wägen/wegen*) is the first discovery that emerges from Freud's inquiry, the second is the retroactive effect of meaning, the working back that fixes linguistic ambiguity as oedipal traffic. As Freud writes, "what emerges from the unconscious is to be understood in the light not of what goes before but of what comes after" (*SE* 10.66; compare Lacan's formulation of the relation of horse and cart)—what it brings in its train. Meaning, like the wagon, comes afterwards, and yet it is what gives priority to the phobic horse, putting it back in its predestined place. The tracing back of a phobia to its roots, therefore, involves a redefinition of the "radical" in terms of the load of nonsense that comes after. If speculation about an engendering cause or root word is predestined to end in uncertainty, then one function of Freud's oedipal story may be to defend against the no-meaning that gives rise to phobia by insisting, retrospectively, on a meaning that is always prior. The horse permits the reconstitution of an entire system around it (the Oedipus complex with its freight of castration anxiety). But as Freud himself reveals, the collision of *wägen* with *wegen*— the persistence of nonsense—unsettles (or rather, parodies) the creation myth of psychoanalysis at its linguistic point of origin.

ii: Little Fritz's Stories

In Melanie Klein's account of little Fritz (actually her four-year-old son Eric), questions engulf existence as phobia engulfs the world of little Hans. Fritz's first question, "How is a person made?" swiftly gives rise to others, such as: "How is a chair made?" "Is it only a story that God makes the rain?" and so on. Disabused of the stork-box theory parodically elaborated by little Hans, little Fritz gives up, in quick succession, the story of the Easter hare, the story of Father Christmas, the story of angels, and the story of God himself. From the question, "How is a person made?" he moves to what Klein calls "more specialized problems," viz: "'How can a person move, move his feet, touch something? How does the blood get inside him? How does a person's skin come on him? How does anything grow at all, how can a person work and make things,' etc.?" (p. 9). As Klein puts it, little Fritz's curiosity reflects "the need to examine what interests him to the very bottom, to penetrate into the depths." Like little Hans, he has a special interest in bathrooms and plumbing arrangements (recall little Hans's dream of the great borer). Another Promethean inquirer, little Fritz is thus a fitting hero for Klein's story of progressive psychoanalytic enlightenment and the prophylactic effects of early analysis on children in liberating energy and affect from the inhibiting effects of repression.

But little Fritz's questioning of origins also puts Klein's own story in question. His first, pressing demand for knowledge, "How is a person made?" generates a litany of questions that Klein represents as "an inquiry concerning existence in general," as if, once one question had been asked, no answer—no "story"—could ever arrest either the epistemophilic quest or the rhetoric of inquiry:

> I give a selection from the wealth of questions of this kind asked in these weeks. How teeth grow, how eyes stay in (in the orbit), how the lines on the hand are made, how trees, flowers, woods etc. grow, whether the stalk of the cherry grows with it from the beginning, whether unripe cherries ripen inside the stomach, whether picked flowers can be replanted, whether seed gathered unripe ripens afterwards, how a spring is made, how a river is made, how ships get on to the Danube, how dust is made; further, about the manufacture of the most various articles, stuffs and materials. (pp. 8–9)

And so on. Klein associates this "wealth of questions" with the freeing up of repressed energy effected by Fritz's sexual enlightenment; apparently a rather slow child, he is stimulated to ardent intellectual efforts by being given an answer to his insistent question, "How is a person made?" But in its compulsive rhythms and tendency to give rise to endless other questions—in the restless transfer of curiosity from one object to another—the movement of inquiry resembles the progress of little Hans's phobia, which extends "on to horses and on to carts, on to the fact that horses fall down and that they bite, on to horses of a particular character, onto carts that are heavily loaded" (*SE* 10.51). There is something altogether too mobile about Fritz's questioning to imagine that sexual enlightenment alone could ever arrest it (or—for that matter—that unsatisfied sexual curiosity could ever generate it). Similarly, little Hans's overdetermined imagination, "coloured by images derived from traffic, and . . . advancing systematically from horses, which draw vehicles, to railways," runs on tracks that have no terminus. As Freud observes, "a railway phobia eventually becomes associated with every street-phobia" (*SE* 10.84), finally attaching itself to movement in general. Bearing in mind Freud's definition, apropos of little Hans, of the common characteristic of all instincts—"their capacity for initiating movement" (*SE* 10.140–41)[7]—I will risk a question of my own: what is driving little Fritz's quest for knowledge? Does inquiry have an object; or is it rather the trace of what Kristeva calls, apropos of little Hans's phobia, a "*drive economy in want of an object*"?[8]—the narcissistic unleashing of drive that threatens identity itself.

One way to put it might be to say that, like sexuality, the epistemophilic drive is at once without an object and retrospectively bound by oedipal structures to metonymic desire (desire that shifts, in a fairy-tale manner, from the mother to the beautiful girl in her image whom he will one day marry). Klein parenthetically acknowledges the pleasure of inquiry as an end in itself when she speculates that repression might "bind" what she calls "the uninhibited pleasure in asking about these forbidden things (and with it the pleasure of interrogation in general, the quantity of the investigating impulse)" (p. 20). This repressive binding, she suggests, provides the precondition for lack of interest, perhaps eventually putting a stop to questions altogether, or else creating the "researcher" type who devotes his energies to a few problems—just as little Hans's phobia, once it has become associated with the transfer of movement, the vehicular metaphor of metaphor itself (*metaphorein* = transfer), forbids him even a child's pleasure in movement. Klein's "investigating impulse" sounds like a drive in its own right. One wants to ask, in turn: could inquiry have its origins in a pleasurable drive *without* an object, before becoming a drive that has pleasure as its object? Can pleasure in the forbidden (that is, oedipal pleasure) be distinguished from a form of pleasurable inquiry that has not yet found an oedipal object? Is the quest for forbidden knowledge a specifically oedipal form of a preexisting epistemophilic drive, or is "the pleasure of interrogation in general" a pleasure always retrospectively transferred from "forbidden things"? And finally: do all questions really mean (originate in) the question "Where do babies come from?" or do they really "mean" the sheer, meaningless pleasure of asking them? Apropos of little Hans's phobia, Kristeva quotes Freud's "Instincts and their Vicissitudes" (1915) on the object of an instinct—"the thing in regard to which or through which the instinct is able to achieve its aim." This thing, Freud suggests, "is what is most variable about an instinct and is not originally connected with it, but becomes assigned to it only in consequence of being particularly fitted to make satisfaction possible" (SE 14.122).[9] This is where the Oedipus story comes in—the one story that Klein asks little Fritz (and us) to believe in. Unlike the story of the Easter hare or Father Christmas, the story of Oedipus is supposed to answer the question of origins so as to convert epistemophilic drive without an object into the oedipal desire that is assigned to it in order "to make satisfaction possible."

Klein is at a loss to explain why her utopian scheme fails; why, for all the enlightenment she provides for little Fritz, repression has to take its course, bringing inquiry to a standstill for a time. Despite his kind and liberal upbringing, little Fritz (who, unlike little Hans, is never threatened with castration by his mother) shows a marked castration complex. Klein is baffled: "in this complex and indeed in complex-formation in general," she admits, "the roots lie too deep for us to be able to penetrate down to them" (p. 48). Possessing the same agenda as little Fritz ("the need to examine what interests him to the very bottom, to penetrate into the depths"), she is confronted by seeming impenetrability; knowledge fails her. Klein discovers that resistance persists in little Fritz as "an absolute unwillingness to know." This unwillingness to know at times "appears as a displaced interest in something else which is often marked by a compulsive character" (p. 27). For instance: "'What is the door made of?'—'What is the bed made of?'—'How is wood made?'—'How is glass made?'—[and again] 'How is the chair made?'" Standing in for the overwhelming question that Fritz cannot ask, these questions (like little Hans's nonsense) become a form of resistance or willed refusal to know; Klein tells us that Fritz is just "torment[ing] his environment with his often apparently quite meaningless questions" and that he was "was really indifferent about the answers" (p. 28). The pleasure of interrogation gives way to indifference, intellectual inquiry to meaningless (but tormenting) questions. In this context, Klein puzzlingly speaks both of the "binding" of uninhibited pleasure by repression, and of the binding of "the energy undergoing repression" (pp. 19, 20). Repression, it seems, binds uninhibited pleasure by creating a reserve of the forbidden, equated as it is with oedipal desire. It at once marks the site of forbidden pleasure and becomes the symptom of energy in bondage. But we know from Freud that only the binding of the drive to polymorphous pleasure by oedipal prohibition produces desire. At this point, I am driven to ask whether the repression Klein wants to lift is constitutive of the unconscious, just as an oedipal structure is the necessary constitutive of desire. Is there, however, a form of fantasy—a form of pleasure—that might predate the oedipal story and its forbidden object? Klein's own account suggests that this is indeed the case.

Little Fritz's inhibition, Klein tells us, spreads from inquiry to the stories his mother tells him. Resisting the one story he has been told to believe in—the Oedipus story—he will have no stories at all. His mother shrewdly recaptures his imaginative interest by offering him a sweet as bait, with a story attached to it "about the woman upon whose nose a sausage grew at her husband's wish" (p. 30). This is the Perault story called "The Ridiculous Wishes," in which a poor woodcutter who has been granted three wishes squanders the first on wishing for a sausage, then—when his wife scolds him for wasting his first wish—wastes the second on wishing it hung on his wife's nose; and finally has to use up his last wish putting his wife's face to rights again. Kristeva speaks of the phobic object as, on one level, the "*hallucination of nothing*," reminding us that Lacan names this "non-thing" as "the maternal phallus, which *is not*"[10]—an impossible maternal object which the Oedipus story transforms into "a fantasy of desire." If maternal absence initiates the quest for metaphor—"The metaphor that is taxed with representing *want itself*"[11]— phobia is a metaphor of want derailed into the material of drives. Perault's story is an allegory of the phobic subject in want of metaphoricity ("Incapable of producing metaphors by means of signs alone, he produces them in the very material of drives").[12] On one level, this story of oral satisfaction coincides with an imaginary, fetishistic restoration and removal of the missing (but defacing) phallus. On another level, it turns metaphor into materiality and back again. The story nicely succeeds in allaying little Fritz's anxiety, unleashing a renewed flood, not of questions, but of fantasies—this time, stories told by Fritz to his mother, Klein says, with "enormous zest." Cows, devils, Tom Thumb's castle, a version of Sleeping Beauty, soldiers, death—the stuff of folk tales or the Brothers Grimm. Simultaneously, Klein tells us, little Fritz loses his inhibition on play. Now his games consist of hanging, hitting, imprisonment, or coming to life again, and they show just the right mix of oedipal aggression toward his father and passion for his mother. All Fritz's pleasure is derived not from investigation, but from narratives involving big and little cars, soldiers, the reconstitution of the oedipal family with himself as his mother's husband, and his siblings as their children. His previously compulsive games of "chauffeur, coachman, etc." (vehicular movement or "conjunction" for its own sake) fall into disuse. Like Prometheus with his clay mannikin, Fritz makes dough-babies, showing that he has at least a rudimentary awareness (and an excremental theory) of the answer to his opening question, "How is a person made?" As his questions are moulded into stories, compulsion becomes creativity, providing an embryonic theory of the origin of the "works of art" that, in one of his fantasies, two people are making together in a closet. Making babies and making stories turn out to be connected activities, the one a sublimation of the other. If little Fritz is forbidden to make babies with his mother, at least he will tell her tall stories.

And now for the preoedipal narrative. Storytime holds a special position in the Kleinian household. For Klein herself, little Fritz's fantasies were clearly rich with analytic possibility. But the Brothers Grimm also make several appearances in "The Development of a Child," serving as an index of little Fritz's "development" under the influence of early analysis. Noting that prior to analysis, little Fritz has a strong dislike of Grimm's fairy tales, Klein says that he later came to show a marked preference for them (see p. 40 n). Listening to Grimm's tales provides the occasion for a release of fear and anxiety. He is especially afraid of one story,

> the tale of a witch who offers a man poisoned food but he hands it on to his horse who dies of it. The child said that he was afraid of witches because, all the same, it might be that it wasn't true what he had been told about there not being any witches really. There are queens also who are beautiful and yet who are witches too, and he would very much like to know what poison looks like, whether it is solid or fluid. When I asked him why he was afraid of anything so bad from his mother, what had he done to her or wished about her, he admitted that when he was angry he had wished that she as well as his papa might die and that he had on occasion thought to himself "dirty mamma." (pp. 41–42)

At the very end of her own story of little Fritz, Klein prescribes Grimm's fairy tales as the litmus test for whether or not early analysis will benefit a child, and "as a standard and an expedient" for making manifest children's latent fears. The happily adjusted oedipal child, she says, will be able to tolerate Grimm without anxiety. But, she insists, "I have particularly selected listening to Grimm's tales without anxiety-manifestations as an indication of the mental health of children, because of all the various children known to me there are only very few who do so" (p. 52). This is a test of normalcy that the normal child is bound to fail. Although she invokes Grimm's tales specifically in the context of the oedipal content of children's anxieties, the story she cites—with its motif of persecution and poisoning by the witch queen in revenge for bad things wished or done by the child—suggests that Klein has already glimpsed the mechanisms of projective identification, splitting, and paranoia which are to become the distinctive features of her account of the child's early object relations, specifically as they involve the child's unconscious fantasies about the maternal body.

"Dirty mamma" suggests a mamma injured by little Fritz's hostile "kakis," and threatening injury in return. But it also suggests a maternal body associated with the "kakis" (feces) that little Fritz makes and thinks of as his children, perhaps even as himself. If we ask what body part stands for "dirty mamma" in little Fritz's fantasy, it turns out to be her all-engulfing stomach. Klein tells us that "the stomach had a peculiar significance for this child." Not only does he cling to the idea "that children grow in the mother's stomach" (that children are made of food, like "kakis"), but, Klein tells us,

> in other ways too the stomach had a peculiar affective meaning for him. He would retort with "stomach" in an apparently senseless way on all occasions. For instance, when another child said to him, "Go into the garden," he answered, "Go into your stomach." He brought reproof upon himself because he repeatedly replied to the servants when they asked him where something was, "In your stomach." He would sometimes too complain at meal-times, though not often, of "cold in the stomach," and declared it was from the cold water. (pp. 32–33)

"Stomach" becomes an all-purpose, portmanteau word, "apparently senseless" (another case of the "nonsense"?) located anywhere and nowhere—in the garden, in the mother and also in the child's inside. "Stomach," then, doesn't just mean what all questions mean ("Where do babies come from?"), but has what Klein calls "a peculiar affective meaning" of its own. One could gloss this affective meaning as a problem about differentiation—no longer about the difference between a person and a chair, but about the difference between "mother" and "me." When he uses the word "stomach" to mean everything and nothing, little Fritz seems to be saying: "I'm in the mother and the mother's in me"—rather like Mickey, the jubilant hero of another incorporatory fantasy, Sendak's *In the Night Kitchen* ("I'm in the milk and the milk's in me"). A persistent questioning of origins turns out to have as its lining a difficulty about distinguishing oneself clearly enough from an imaginary origin;

abjecting the maternal body is a way to settle the question of boundaries. Earlier, Klein tells us that Fritz calls "every defining edge, all boundaries in general, for instance the knee-joint, a 'border'" (p. 12). The stomach is the bodily sign of a confused and fluid internal boundary. As Kristeva puts it, "The body's inside . . . shows up in order to compensate for the collapse of the border between inside and outside . . . as if the skin, a fragile container, no longer guaranteed the integrity of one's 'own and clean self'."[13] "Stomach" bears the trace of an abject(ed) mother. Like little Hans's "nonsense," little Fritz's "in your stomach" points to the collapse of the border between inside and outside (perhaps this is the anxiety underlying Fritz's earlier question, "How does a person's skin come on him?").

The link between the "peculiar affective meaning" attached to the maternal stomach and inquiry itself suggests a way to define the status of questions and epistemophilia in general; they constitute a kind of boundary or demarcation of borders. Little Fritz's voyeurism allows us a glimpse of how the "stomach" as signifier of abjection underlies the "stomach" as question—translated, that is, from a confused body space inside one's inside (a place still marked by traces of somatic drives) into the taxonomy of the maternal body initiated by oedipal curiosity.[14] Apropos of "stomach," Klein continues:

> About this time he expressed a curiosity to see his mother quite naked. Immediately afterwards he remarked, "I would like to see your stomach too and the picture that is in your stomach." To her question, "Do you mean the place inside which you were?" he replied "Yes! I would like to look inside your stomach and see whether there isn't a child there." Somewhat later he remarked, "I am very curious, I would like to know everything in the world." To the question what it was he so very much wanted to know, he said, "What your wiwi and your kaki-hole are like. I would like (laughing) "to look inside when you are on the closet without your knowing and see your wiwi and your kaki-hole." (p. 33)[15]

Little Fritz's wish to see his mother "quite naked" (her outside) rapidly reveals itself as a wish to see her inside, and not only that, but himself inside her ("the picture that is in your stomach"). Curiosity—wanting "to know everything in the world"—turns out, predictably enough, to mean wanting to "know" the entrances to the inside of mother's body. We shouldn't be surprised to find that the maternal bowels (her wiwis and kakis) become the object of little Fritz's desire, as they do for little Hans (perhaps even reassuring him that he himself is "clean" rather than "dirty"). But it is striking that when we penetrate with little Fritz "to the bottom" ("the need to examine what interests him to the very bottom"), wanting to *know* (epistemophilia) is predicated on wanting to *look* (scopophilia); and behind scopophilia lies the narcissistic wish to see oneself (specifically, as the object of the mother's imagined "look"). "I would like to look inside" becomes "I would like to look inside and find myself there." Apropos of little Hans, who has a similar wish to see his mother without her shift, Kristeva writes: "Voyeurism is a structural necessity in the constitution of object relations, showing up every time the object shifts towards the abject."[16] What she calls a *"representation"* or *"seeing"*— a visual hallucination ("the picture that is in your stomach")—stands in the place of an absent object and allows the archaic nonobject to be fleetingly grasped as a sign or image. Identifying with the empty space within the mother (her "stomach"), little Fritz identifies himself with her image, the image of her look.

*   *   *

Mapped onto the abjection of the mother ("dirty mamma") is a movement, via narcissism, to the object-relations that will become the basis for the oedipal. The child in the imaginary stomach resolves the narcissistic crisis that for Kristeva precedes the oedipal crisis. Fritz, a subject still beset by queasy traces of the "abject," suffers at mealtimes from "cold in the stomach." Language—displaced orality—comes to his rescue, not only in the stories he tells but in his production of phobic, meaningless signifiers ("in your stomach") and meaningless questions. These signifiers "mean" that he misses his mother while trying to digest her; for Kristeva, " *any* verbalizing activity, whether or not it names a phobic object related to orality, is an attempt to introject the incorporated items."[17] Viewed as an attempt to appropriate an elusive oral object, verbal activity for its own sake—activity of the kind that we see in both little Hans's "nonsense" and little Fritz's questions—bears the traces of this abject origin. Underlying little Hans's and little Fritz's oedipal eroticization of the maternal body or universal stomach is a differentiating, not-yet oedipal answer to the question: "How is a person made?" Kristeva's story uncovers the maternal body as the improper abject, rather than the proper object, of inquiry. Read like this, the case of little Fritz tells us a story made up of the not-yet questions asked of a not-yet object of inquiry.

Up until now, I have avoided putting Kristeva's own story in question. Kristeva harnesses Freud's project to hers at the point where it collides with her inquiry into the origin of signs. I want to ask a final question of my own: what is at stake for her in the ever-present risk of collapse, "the frailty of the signifying system that forces metaphor to turn into drive and conversely [drive into metaphor]"[18] that she sees played out in the case history of little Hans? Coincidentally (or perhaps not), Kristeva refers to "the somewhat elusive, somewhat frail presence of [Hans's] mother."[19] Freud actually calls her "beautiful," but not frail. The want or lack that drives language—the want that metaphor is taxed with representing in Kristeva's system—is at once the frailty of signification and "what seems to be lacking in [Hans's] mother," whatever that is. As for the father, in an attempt to account for little Hans's phobia, Kristeva speculates: "Does Hans's father not play a bit too much the role of the mother whom he thrusts into the shadows?" In Hans's case, "if phobia is a metaphor that has mistaken its place . . . it is because a father does not hold his own."[20] Here too, we find Kristeva refering to an inherent "instability of the paternal metaphor."[21] Kristeva claims that Freud understood this failure of the paternal placeholder to "hold its own"—hence his advice to little Hans's father to take the horse's place, installing himself as the key term in the phobic system. Playing along with the substitution, little Hans is apparently able to divert phobia into the linguistic activity that Kristeva calls "the only 'know-how' where phobia is concerned"—"our ultimate and inseparable fetish," namely, the pursuit of signs.[22] In its refusal of logic (its open admission that "the sign is not the thing, but just the same"), the fetishism of language becomes for Kristeva the ground zero of meaning: "Because of its founding status, the fetishism of 'language' is perhaps the only one that is unanalyzable." *Because of?* Kristeva's explanation, like little Hans's ("'Cos of the horse") is no explanation at all. The failure of analysis confronted by the resistance of language marks a founding impasse; language is the fetish (the negation or denial or loss) that cannot be given up.

It is, of course, language that emerges as the hero of Kristeva's story. The risk of signifying collapse in the face of a parental metaphor consisting of a frail mother and an unstable paternal identification is the tendency averted by phobic signs. In other words, the story that Kristeva tells is the story of resourceful little Hans who saves himself from asymbolia or psychosis via symbolic elaboration. Or, in Bruno Bettelheim's version, Grimm's stories "tell the child that he will succeed only because hardships force him to develop his ingenuity, initiative, and independence. . . . Painful as is the process of separation and individuation, fairy tales assure the child that it is a necessary and inescapable developmental task. . . . "[23] Freud's case history is the founding myth that Kristeva uses to arrest questions about the unknown maternal origin she is reduced to calling "the Thing"—substituting, however, her own developmental narrative about the painful process of psychic separation and individuation. Kristeva seems to say that the origin of questions is an impossible demand made by a not-yet-subject of an unconstituted object. But perhaps Klein has the answer after all: ask me a phobic question, and I'll tell you a Grimm story.

1. Melanie Klein, *Love, Guilt and Reparation* (London: Virago Press, 1988), 4. Subsequent references in the text are to this edition.

2. One critique of the "The Case of Little Hans" draws attention, inadvertently, to this arbitrariness: "We will show that . . . there is no scientifically acceptable evidence showing any connection between [sexual behavior on the part of Hans] and the child's phobia for horses; that the assertion of such connection is pure assumption; and that the case affords no factual support for any of the concepts listed [by classical Freudian psychoanalysis]"; see Joseph Wolpe and Stanley Rachman, "Psychoanalytic Evidence: A Critique based on Freud's Case of Little Hans," in *Critical Essays on Psychoanalysis*, ed. Stanley Rachman (New York: Macmillan, 1963), 199. For a very different account of Hans's "nonsense," see Catherine Belsey, "The Romantic Construction of the Unconscious," in *Literature, Politics and Theory: Papers from the Essex Conference 1976–84*, ed. Francis Barker, Peter Hulme, et al. (London and New York: Methuen, 1986), 57–76, especially 62–65.

3. Jacques Lacan, Seminar of March–April and May–July 1957, "La relation d'objet et les structures freudiennes," *Bulletin de Psychologie* 10 (June 1957): 851–54, and 11 (September 1957): 31–34.

4. Julie Kristeva, *Powers of Horror: An Essay on Abjection*, trans. Leon S. Roudiez (New York: Columbia University Press, 1982), 45.

5. Ibid., 45.

6. See Sigmund Freud, *Gesammelte Werke*, (Frankfurt: S. Fischer, 1960), 7:314; *Gesindelwerk* is defined by the dictionary as *Schimpfwort* [term of abuse] *für unartige Kinder*.

7. Here Freud is taking issue with Adler, who had attempted to distinguish "agressive instinct" from "what is in reality a universal and indispensible attribute of *all* instincts—their instinctual [*triebhaft*] and 'pressing' character, which might be described as their capacity for initiating movement" (*SE* 10.140–41).

8. Kristeva, *Powers of Horror*, 35; see also 44: "what is called 'narcissism' . . . becomes the unleashing of drive as such, without object, threatening all identity, including that of the subject itself."

9. Ibid., 44.

10. Ibid., 42.

11. Ibid., 35.

12. Ibid., 37.

13. Ibid., 53.

14. Mary Kelly, in *Post-Partum Document*, documents this stage in the acquisition of language and oedipality as the interrogatory "weh" that is the forerunner of the grammatically transformed "wh-question" ("the archetypal expression of the unconditional element of demand"; the child's questions mean "I want," or a demand for recurrence); see *Post-Partum Document* (London: Routledge & Kegan Paul, 1983), 46. Mary Kelly's Lacanian (and, to an extent, Kleinian) inquiry into the relation of child and mother in which both are constituted (as oedipal child and as "mother" respectively) makes her the third of the three K's who inform this essay (Klein, Kristeva, Kelly). Kelly's work is unique in positing the mother's unspoken and unconscious question, "What am I?" as the counterpart to the child's epistemophilic quest.

15. Elsewhere, Fritz phantasizes the stomach as a fully furnished house, equipped with bath and soap dish, or as a ruined room, destroyed by his aggressivity; see *Love, Guilt, and Reparation*, 35, 41.

16. Kristeva, *Powers of Horror*, 46.

17. Ibid., 41.

18. Ibid., 35

19. Ibid., 34.

20. Ibid., 35.

21. Ibid., 44.

22. Ibid., 37–38.

23. *German Fairy Tales: Jacob and Wilhelm Grimm and Others*, ed. Helmut Brackert and Volkmar Sander, forward by Bruno Bettelheim (New York: Continuum, 1985), xvi.

9

Portrait of the Artist as a Young Dog

It can be repeatedly demonstrated in analyses of children that behind drawing, painting, and photography there lies a much deeper unconscious activity: it is the procreation and production in the unconscious of the object represented.

—Melanie Klein, "The Rôle of the School in the Libidinal Development of the Child" (1923)[1]

It requires an immense shift in one's view of the world to think that the outside world is essentially meaningless and unknowable, that one perceives the forms but must attribute the meaning. Philosophically, this is the great problem in coming to grips with Kleinian thought and its implications.

—Donald Meltzer, *Richard Week-by-Week* (1978)[2]

THE FIRST OF THESE TWO QUOTATIONS, from Melanie Klein's early essay, "The Rôle of the School in the Libidinal Development of the Child" (1923), uses the metaphor of procreation to effect a passage from artistic practice to psychic process—some would say, altogether too unmediated a passage. Klein's essay deals with the phantasies surrounding the child's acquisition of the three Rs (reading, writing, and arithmetic), arguing that the unconscious plays a part in graphic activity of all kinds; drawing, writing, and even sums, are all libidinally cathected. The second quotation, from Donald Meltzer's sustained attempt to come to grips with Klein's *Narrative of a Child Analysis* (1961) (in *Richard Week-by-Week*, part 2 of *The Kleinian*

Development), raises the question of meaning that troubles Klein's seemingly literal interpretive procedures at all levels. Klein's epic 450-page *Narrative*—the longest case history in the annals of psychoanalysis—contains as its central exhibit a series of seventy-four drawings by her young patient Richard.[3] Klein has tantalizingly little to say about his drawings as a form of artistic production in their own right, interpreting them largely in terms of her own preconceived psychoanalytic plot. But Richard's drawings unfold another narrative altogether. This is the story that Klein herself could not tell. Retrieving a fractured, infantile image of the mother from the vantage point of a ten-year-old, they uncover both an archaeology of the subject and an archaeology of signs. Their backward-looking, regressive trajectory seems to locate the origin of signs in the dismantling of the maternal body. Lacan refers to Klein as "working on the child at the very limit of the appearance of language." In the *Narrative*, she is also working on the child at the very limit of the appearance of signs; or, as Lacan puts it, "through her we have the cartography, drawn by the children's own hands, of the mother's internal empire, the historical atlas of the intestinal divisions in which the *imagos* of the father and brothers (real or virtual), in which the voracious aggression of the subject himself, dispute their deleterious dominance over her sacred regions."[4] For all the seeming reductiveness of Klein's interpretative method, I want to read the *Narrative* as her enquiry into the relation between the origins of signification and the maternal body, a contested site that is also, in this case, a historical atlas of World War II.

"That unique and fairly unread masterpiece," as Donald Meltzer calls it, reads very differently from Klein's other essays and case histories.[5] The *Narrative* offers an almost daily account of the four-month analytical relationship between a ten-year-old boy and the grandmotherly Klein (by then almost sixty). Richard's growing affection for Klein and his impending separation from her (as well as her half-glimpsed affection for him) provides the connecting thread of the *Narrative*; Klein will return to the bombing raids of wartime London, leaving Richard the uncertain benefits of short-term analysis. Despite Klein's personal reticence, her portrait of the brief wartime relationship between older woman and boy is touching not only for what it tells us about Richard's feelings, but for what it tells us about Klein's. The *Narrative* can be read as an autobiography as well as a case history. One strand of the story concerns a distressed, precocious evacuee, displaced from home and family by the outbreak of war (he and his mother are living in a hotel while his father works elsewhere). The other story concerns an elderly Jewish psychoanalyst, who was herself an exile from Hitler's Germany, working in a xenophobic Britain that often found it hard to distinguish Austrian refugees from the Austrian Hitler (as hard as Richard himself finds it). Revealing both the impressive particularity and the curious blind spots of Klein's analytic technique and persona, the *Narrative* maps Klein's complex, displaced identity as a foreigner, a woman, and a psychoanalyst onto the inner life of her young patient, whose overwhelming preoccupation is with the war. Klein's self-portrait of the analyst as an old woman is superimposed on a portrait of the child artist. But the story told by his drawings is also, by implication, the untold narrative of Klein's relation to Freudian theory. This is partly the story of the child's infantile phantasies about the maternal body, but partly the story of Klein's own position as a woman analyst in the ongoing narrative of psychoanalysis.[6]

i. The Artist as a Young Dog

Early on during the *Narrative*, Richard mentions "Bobby, his spaniel, who always gave Richard a welcome and loved him more than it loved anyone else in the family (his eyes shone when he said this)" (p. 26). Bobby the spaniel resembles Larry the Lamb, the character in the wartime BBC Children's Hour program "Toy Town," with whose not-so-innocent slyness Richard identifies; war babies may recall Larry the Lamb's coconspirator, Dennis the Dachshund—the brains of the pair and (like Klein herself) a European refugee displaced to a provincial setting. Bobby still jumps on Richard's lap, and, much to his satisfaction, usurps his father's chair when he gets a chance. Needless to say, Richard is jealous of his father. Predictably, but not entirely humorlessly, Klein "interprets"—her favorite analytic verb—as follows: "Bobby stood for his child and . . . he, Richard, overcame his jealousy and resentment by putting himself in the place of Mummy." But, Klein goes on, "when Bobby welcomed and loved him best of all, he, Richard, was the child who was loved by Mummy, and Bobby stood for Mummy" (p. 26). As for the oedipal drama, "His dog Bobby stood for himself wanting to take his father's place with Mummy (the armchair standing for the bed)" (p. 28). Klein's invariably substitutive mode of interpretation is confirmed when Richard "smiled agreement at Mrs K.'s saying that the dog stood for himself."[7] As this brief canine sample suggests, Klein's reading of the Bobby subplot establishes a shared interpretive lexicon from the outset. Bobby is more than a metaphor; he is a member of the cast. "Mrs K." (the character who appears in Klein's *Narrative*, as distinct from Klein the analyst) relies heavily in her dealing with Richard on the characters, human and animal, real and imaginary, that make up his everyday world, along with an assortment of toys and "found" objects. This is the northern world of a small Scottish village, Pitlochrie (disguised as a Welsh village for the purposes of the *Narrative*), where Klein and her young patient found themselves as a result of the bombing raids in the South.

Inevitably, it is not only Bobby but the anxieties and trauma of war that "stand for" Richard's inner life. The time is spring and summer, 1941, the months when England (and Klein too) was consumed with anxiety about air raids and invasion. Crete and Russia were invaded by Germany in May and June, and London was being heavily bombed while the RAF raided Berlin and fought the Battle of Britain in the South of England.[8] Richard himself, who "read three newspapers every day and listened to all the news on the wireless" (p. 24), is notably preoccupied by the progress of the war and especially by the fate of the Allied forces on land, at sea, and in the air. His own home has narrowly escaped a direct hit and his older brother has been called up, while his father continues his essential work elsewhere. The unconventional scene for his analysis with Klein is an improvised playroom, a community hall that is also used as a Girl Guide meeting room, littered with the insignia of empire—including a Union Jack and maps on which Richard can follow the fate of European countries as they fall before the invading German army. Apart from the toy trains and figures provided by Klein herself, Richard's toys are replicas of the British, German, and Japanese warships—the *Nelson*, the *Bismarck*, and so on; his own code name is the *Vampire* ("The *Vampire* usually stood for Richard," Klein notes, p. 403). Klein makes little overt acknowledgement that Richard's problems might be linked to anxieties about the war actually being waged between German and the Allied forces at the time, not only on land, at sea, and in the air, but on the radio, via BBC broadcasts and the voice of Lord Haw-Haw (whom Richard at one point ventriloquizes, much as he sometimes impersonates Hitler). When Richard turns to the map to express his fears about the blockading of British battleships in the Mediterranean or the fate of the British troops in Greece, Klein routinely "interprets" his anxieties as referring to the fate of Daddy when he puts his genital into Mummy. Military campaigns and propaganda wars become code names for an interior struggle—much as Richard, in taking *Vampire* as his code name, equates himself and a (naval) "destroyer." Hearing in his anxious grasp of current affairs and his knowledge of the shifting map of Europe only a displaced allegory of parental sexual intercourse, Klein risks making infantile phantasy the real referent of contemporary historical events, denying both the child's subjectivity and the reality of his situation.

Yet war is crucial to Klein's psychoanalytic campaign, if only because of its immutable violence and the question it poses for relations between the social and the psychic.[9] Among other things, the *Narrative* can be read as a historical novel. Donald Meltzer reports Henry Reed as saying that Klein's *Narrative* stood on his shelf beside Tolstoy's *War and Peace*, in which the larger movements of history similarly unfold alongside individual development, making love and war intertwined aspects of the same national drama. The density and specificity of Klein's record of the almost daily meetings between herself and Richard makes this the *War and Peace* of case histories; but the war waged here is confined to a provincial theater. For Meltzer, the *Narrative* opens with all the economy of a Chekhov play ("immediately all the characters are introduced and all the themes and subplots are hinted at"). Here is his conveniently compressed account of the initial mise-en-scène:

> Immediately the stage is filled with characters: the primal scene is introduced and the cast builds up through the next three sessions—there is mummy, daddy, brother Paul, Richard; there is Bobby the dog; somewhere there is "Cook," Johnny Wilson, his analytical rival; and somewhere there is Mr Klein, who is not dead despite Richard knowing very well that he was, and there is Mrs Klein's son. And in the background of the stage set is the war situation with accomodating maps on the wall and all the other paraphernalia of the Girl Guides' room.[10]

(We could add to this cast bit players such as Mr. Smith the grocer, a red-haired girl whom Richard particularly dislikes, a string of bus conductresses; not to mention Hitler, Rippentrop, Lord Haw-Haw, and, of course, Larry the Lamb). Above all, there is "Mrs Klein"—the "Sweet Mrs Klein" or "Lovely Mrs Klein" of Richard's last drawings, in her red jacket and purple dress, who is also at times Hitler, and to whom Richard attributes an improbably active love life with a variety of rivals as well as a living husband. Even the weather plays its part, along with the Scottish landscape to which Richard himself is vividly responsive. Stage props include the contents of the improvised playroom (the piano, the kitchen with its water tank, the sooty old stove) as well as the contents of Mrs K.'s bag, whose insides Richard vigorously investigates from time to time as part of his inquiry into the maternal body.

As a Kleinian himself, Meltzer offers a sympathetic (although not entirely uncritical) overview of Klein's *Narrative*. When the analysis opens, Richard is a child who fears other children so much that he is unable to go to school; the primal scene is represented by Richard's fear that "a nasty man—a kind of tramp—would come and kidnap Mummy during the night" (p. 20). Musically gifted, articulate, and charming ("pseudo-charming," according to Meltzer), he lags behind in his development and shows a variety of depressive and persecutory symptoms. He is fearful of being spied on or poisoned, while all the time conducting a devastatingly destructive interior campaign of his own. During the course of the analysis, in Meltzer's account, the transferential relation between Klein and Richard reveals seduction and voyeuristic jealousy on his part, and a struggle with rivals for possession of the mother. The background to this lively psychodrama is intense distrust of the mother herself and confusion between good and bad objects at the oral level, which Richard is partially able to resolve during the course of his analysis with Klein. A move toward acceptance of the breast as a combined object—the image that comes to hand is Mrs K.'s umbrella ("The open umbrella stood for the breast, but the stick in it stood for Mr K.'s genital," p. 456)—allows Richard to overcome his internal struggle and achieve a more friendly relation with the other babies, whom he starts out wanting to kill. His murderous jealousy lies behind both his hostility toward children and his school-refusal. As Meltzer sees it, Klein was able to respond to the helpless baby in Richard—giving him the opportunity not only to attack or to cling to the breast, but to achieve some hope about its (and his own) basic internal goodness. This is the legacy she leaves him when she returns to London.

Klein's method of one-to-one substitutions on the level of "Bobby stood for himself" (or, for that matter, the symbolism provided by Mrs K.'s "British Made" umbrella) has been criticized as a random "translation" of Richard's communications.[11] The effect is to move the analysis inexorably along tracks that are to a large extent predetermined by Klein's psychoanalytic master plot; the attribution of meaning often appears quite arbitrary, since Klein simply substitutes her own terms for Richard's on the assumption that "interpreting" his unconscious phantasies (however crudely) will lead to a reduction in anxiety. As the primary psychoanalytic and therapeutic intervention, interpretation, according to Klein, enables Richard, "to integrate the split-off parts of his mind so that the effects of the different phantasy situations which arise through splitting may be mitigated" (p. 300).

At the same time, interpretation provides a vehicle for the overarching metanarrative developed by Klein's commentary on each session. In its original inception, the *Narrative* had marked a theoretical departure from Freud's understanding of the Oedipus complex, which Klein, unlike Freud, saw as being resolved by way of the child's growing capacity to love both parents; this theoretical development emerges in her earlier paper based (for the boy) on Richard's analysis, "The Oedipus Complex in the Light of Early Anxieties" (1945).[12] Richard, according to this story, comes to love his father as well as his mother, while at the same time gaining greater trust in a good maternal object (for Klein, we should remember, "the good breast [is] the core of the ego," p. 434). Ostensibly, his shift from uncertainty and suspicion about the maternal breast to a growing ability to reconcile himself with a combined object (the umbrella again) is the main psychoanalytic narrative sketched by Klein's case history.

By the time Klein came to reorganize her case material at the end of her life, in the late 1950s, her theoretical emphasis had shifted to ideas she had developed meanwhile—ideas about reparation, splitting, projective identification, persecutory anxiety, and paranoia. But even in the full-length case history as finally published, theoretical discussion is relatively curtailed. As Meltzer puts it, making a canine distinction between Freud and Klein: "Where the theoretical tail wags the clinical dog with him, hardly any theoretical tail exists to be wagged with her."[13] In quest of this theoretical "tail," Meltzer attempts to graft Klein's technique in her work with Richard onto the unfolding of her theoretical ideas between the time of the analysis in1941 and the late 1950s. His mission in performing this graft is partly to rescue Klein's work from the hostility of those put off by "poor communication," "linguistic snarles" [sic], and "the dogmatic demeanour" of her writing (note how Klein herself has become the dog); and partly to "dis-mantle" the Kleinian myth—his pun, intentional this time. For Meltzer, the *Narrative* tells us about the Melanie beneath the mantle, rendering her insights more accessible and humanizing her analytic practice, while providing a watchful commentary on the turns and developments, the analytical choices, interventions, and mistakes of the day-by-day analysis she recounts. What he calls the "concreteness" of her thinking, and specifically, her concept of the concreteness of psychic reality, is for him the quintessential "Kleinian development" unfolded in Richard's case history. As he puts it, "Objects are really damaged in the inner world: they really become persecutory; they really do have to be repaired."[14] This shift—effectively removing Freud's distinction between phantasy and reality—does more than acknowledge the centrality of psychic life; it also bears on the conditions of meaning. The issue of meaning comes up most acutely in connection with the wartime imagery that saturates Richard's daily life, his inner drama, his play therapy, and his drawings.

Meltzer's crucial insight provides the basis for a response of sorts to the criticism that Klein refuses to acknowledge the actual historical issues at stake for both Richard and herself. In particular, the Jewish Melanie Klein risks being seen as depriving Richard of the right to his own politics. Elisabeth Geleerd, taking the position of a classical (Anna) Freudian analyst in her contemporary review of the *Narrative*, makes a related objection when she complains about the forcible annexing of Richard by Kleinian interpretation, at least at the level of the transference, much as smaller countries were being overwhelmed by Germany at the time ("how long can a helpless person keep from being invaded and overpowered by a stronger one?").[15] For Geleerd, Klein is an analytic bully. For Klein herself, however, the relation between inside and outside—or, for that matter, between "British made" and "Foreign"—may have been more complicated.[16] Meltzer observes, apropos of a very "concrete" piece of acting out by Richard involving his penknife, that dangerous problems can arise, "If, when infantile problems are stirred up . . . they then encounter fortuitous events in the outside world which set up a terrible reverberation."[17] Danger threatens the psyche when inner and outer dramas appear to converge, as they do for Richard—not only in the case of bad war news, but when he finds his father having a heart attack on the bathroom floor (a sufficiently devastating experience for a ten-year-old boy, one might think). The intensity of the child's anxiety or fear, Klein suggests, is in direct proportion to the extent to which infantile dramas have been reactivated by external events.[18] The interior action is never just a reaction to the external drama; on the contrary, it is what gives the external drama its ever-present psychic meaning. Klein allows herself the crucial reminder that "we were living in constant actual danger" and that Richard's anxieties increased when the war news was bad (he goes so far as to contemplate suicide if Britain loses the war). But she insists that "fears of external dangers are intensified by anxieties arising in the earliest stages" (p. 217)—and hence that psychoanalysis can diminish the anxiety produced by actual dangers.[19] Richard's psychic life is hazardous, in other words, because he fears that he really could destroy his inner objects. Whether in war or peace, inner life is already fraught with danger and destruction; intrapsychic sources can fuel unlimited war anxiety.

The Kleinian child's perception of external reality is always colored by phantasized attacks. While Klein's refusal to acknowledge the trauma of war may be dismaying today, in the wake of what we know of its effects on the children of Belfast or Bosnia, she incidentally reveals that—for adults as well as children—a fantasmatic war is always being waged alongside the historical one, like the propaganda war that also plays its part in her *Narrative*. In telling the day-to-day story, not just of the Allied struggle with Germany, but of a struggle shaped by the production of wartime news and by national paranoia, Klein narrates the contours of contemporary world-historical events as they exist in the realm of the imaginary. Richard's head is occupied by demonic Hitler and treacherous Lord Haw-Haw, not to mention a positive epidemic of spy mania (leading Richard, at one point, to improbable suspicions of the family cook), as well as suspicions about the existence of a mysterious "secret weapon" (pp. 441, 454, 456). In this phantasized narrative, saturated as it is with violence, persecution, and paranoia—a subjective world shaped by the Kleinian processes of splitting, projection, and identification—the individual can easily turn out to be on both sides at once. Mrs K. may figure as the good mother or as Hitler by turns. Richard becomes an airplane bombing his own toy fleets (whether British or German), launching his assaults from an imaginary arsenal against the hostile forces projected onto his mother or Mrs K., or onto the bad Hitler-father and foreign spy (the deceased Mr. Klein) whom he locates within them. War gives Richard a language for the destructiveness that, for Klein, in any case characterizes the young child's inner world—reminding us that our access to the "reality" of contemporary events is mediated by something that is never simply attributable to either the sociopolitical or the death instinct. The terrible meaning of Hitler is neither ahistorical nor apolitical, but (qua meaning) freighted from the outset with this cargo of infantile anxiety. To insist that Hitler is always only Hitler is to deny the power of splitting and projective identification, to whose mechanisms Klein gives center stage; it is also to attribute unique human agency to an individual, when the phenomenon of "Hitler" is inseparable from what is negative in the human psyche .

According to Laplanche and Pontalis, defining Klein's concept of projective identification, "the phantasized projection of split-off parts of the subject's own self . . . into the interior of the mother's body, so as to injure and control the mother from within . . . lies at the root of such anxieties as the fear of being imprisoned and persecuted within the mother's body."[20] We have seen the peculiar form of identification that involves aggression against the mother at work elsewhere (most notoriously, in Sade's writing).[21] Splitting and projective identification may provide the basis for actual persecution based on specific ideologies of nation, race, or gender, as the recent course of European history amply illustrates. And as Klein wittily reveals, even the "Made in Britain" logo—an attempt to identify manufactured origins with patriotism or national pride—is underpinned by the xenophobic and matriphobic traits exemplified by Richard himself (for whom a foreign-made umbrella would automatically be suspect). Klein's practice and her implied theoretical stance emphasize, simultaneously, the arbitrariness by which meaning is assigned to the world and the predetermined nature of those meanings given the workings of the unconscious. Klein's limited interpretive repertoire was a matter of some amusement to Richard himself in later life; he recalled that "She would often talk about the 'big Mummy genital' and the 'big Daddy genital,' or the 'good Mummy genital' or the 'bad Daddy genital.' . . . It was very much a strong interest in genitalia."[22] But for Klein there is nothing natural or pre-given about the relation between umbrella and breast, stick, or penis. As Meltzer writes, "It requires an immense shift in one's view of the world to think that . . . one perceives the forms but must attribute the meaning."[23] The meaning of something that "stands for" something else is always divided against itself, bearing the marks of having been produced rather than originating in any externally pre-existing order of things. Significantly, the mechanism that Klein herself saw as fundamental to psychic processes was splitting, partly as a defense against this troubling ambiguity—so that in making one breast good and the other bad, for instance, at least part of the mother could be saved.[24] Kleinian meaning is less self-identical, and Kleinian "interpretation" less literal, than either of them look at first sight. This is nowhere clearer than in what the mother herself will "stand for" in Richard's drawings, the nonverbal signs that occupy the central exhibition space of Klein's *Narrative*.

ii. Dismantling the Mother

The central exhibit of Klein's *Narrative* is the series of seventy-four drawings (most, but not all of his output) made by Richard during his four-month analysis. The themes and images of these drawings loop back—in a movement at once recapitulatory and regressive—to a phantasized primal object, as Richard brings to bear the images and techniques of a younger and younger child on the contested meanings of the maternal body. Later on in the progress of her *Narrative*, Klein has Richard show her his wartime identity card in its waterproof case: "Had Mrs K. got the same waterproof case for her identity card?" he asks, slipping it in and out—and then proceeds to read her excerpts from his diary. Klein interprets the play with the identity card as genital play. But the ID card (and its case) can be read as an allegory of Richard's accession to a discrete identity by way of a distinct and bounded image—not only his own, but the mother's, or her Kleinian stand-in. Perhaps this is why Richard can read from his diary. His drawings chart the basis for his production as the subject in and of (his own) representation. The chief metaphors for this process of self-representation—involving as it does both annexation and separation—are imperial (or maritime) aggression, and what I will call, after Meltzer, the dismantling of the mother. Richard's artistic production has four overlapping yet distinct phases or sequences. First come marine or submarine drawings involving U-boats and destroyers; next come empire drawings that map the power struggle over contested territory; then railway drawings that lay out the track of imaginary bodies in connection with one another; and finally the increasingly fragmented, abstract, or symbolic representations of the maternal body itself—Richard's masterpieces of modernist abstraction. By means of her "retrospective" (the backward-looking trajectory provided by her exhibition of Richard's collected drawings), Klein implicates the origin of signs in the child's first attempts to delineate the maternal body.

Although this trajectory is sometimes overlapping and confused, the unfolding order of Richard's drawings makes it possible to delineate its main phases. At the outset, Richard draws a set of U-boats that quickly mutate into a more elaborate series of eight drawings involving destroyers or ships above the waterline, and U-boats, mother fishes, plants, starfish, and octopi (for Klein, the bad father and his genital) attacking them below the waterline.[25] Drawing nos. 3 and 6 (figs. 1 and 2) provide a confused example of this above the line / below the line structure, showing (Klein suggests) two states simultaneously existing; the greedy starfish baby is Richard himself—the subject of the visual narrative encoded in his pictures. The starfish baby ushers in the second series of twenty-five abstract drawings, the "empire" drawings—evolutions from the jagged outline of the starfish, some of them framed (like the identity card in its case) with an enclosing line.[26] The spiky edges and internal divisions of these empire drawings point to the warring, fractured, but distinctive outlines of an emerging self—as if a simple outline had opened up to reveal the ever-changing map of contested inner space. Drawings such as nos. 9 and 14 (figs. 3 and 4) represent versions of a psychic empire made up of the competing and struggling forces variously identified with Richard's mother, father, brother, and Richard himself. In his own elaborate color-coding, red stands for Richard (as it stood for the British Empire in generations of school atlases), black

Fig. 1. Richard, drawing 3

Fig. 2. Richard, drawing 6

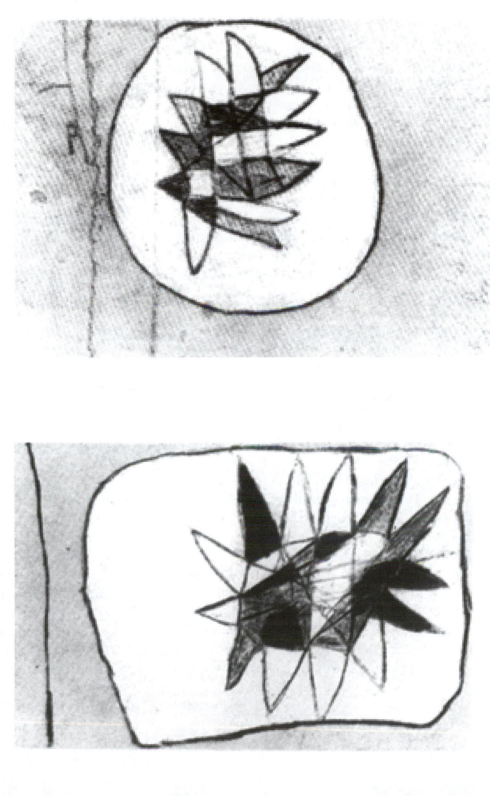

for his father, light blue for his mother (as opposed to the menacing, bad, dark blue mother), and so on. Like Hitler, Richard has a tendency to annex more and more countries for himself, waging war against the mother with the "secret weapon" of his inflamed genital (Klein's interpretation, needless to say); for Klein, this hidden weapon is always present in the empire drawings.

At this point, a sequence of eight "railway" drawings emerges, interspersed and overlapping with a number of drawings representing air bombardment and submarine warfare.[27] A drawing such as no. 39, with its branching, multidirectional curves, involves a different mapping of Richard's psychic geography onto the comings and goings in his life (both real and imaginary) and the phantasized scene of parental intercourse (Klein again), while the anti-aircraft gun of no. 43 implicates a new and significant target—a circle with a dot in the middle, which Klein identifies with the maternal breast (figs. 5 and 6). This new form marks a crucial transition, about two thirds of the way through the series, as the railway drawings merge ambiguously with Richard's schematic representations of the maternal body—or rather, his representations of Klein herself, for instance in drawings nos. 66 and 67 (figs. 7 and 8).[28] Initiating the final phase of Richard's artistic production, these drawings of the maternal body ultimately regress until they are no more than a series of abstract scribbles, squiggles, circles, and dots (both nipples and, for Klein, furious attacks peppering the breast).[29] At the same time they bear a variety of inscriptions explicitly identifying them as portraits of Klein—the "Lovely Mrs Klein" and "Sweet Mrs Klein" of nos. 66 and 67, or the "Sweet Mrs Klein" ("Lovely eyes") and "Darling Mrs Klein" of nos. 68 and 70 (figs. 9 and 10). The culminating pair of the entire series, drawings no. 73 and 74, puts the airplane in which Richard and Mrs K. are flying to London beside the wonderfully achieved, rhythmic drawing—somewhere between a Picasso and a Henry Moore—which is Richard's culminating masterpiece of abstraction (figs. 11 and 12). From images keyed to war (representations of U-boats, submarines, airplanes, and bombardment), Richard has "regressed" via his jagged, symbolic empire drawings and railway drawings to the child's earliest graphic inscriptions (squiggles, circles, dots). The minimalist abstractions of his "late period" involve an increasingly self-conscious symbolic representation of the maternal body, alias "Mrs M. Klein." But even as he recovers this earliest relation to the maternal body, the imaginary breast-mother is irrecoverably fragmented and divided.

Klein asserts that "the drawings meant to Richard his relation with Mrs K. and her inside" (p. 361).[30] Richard frequently bites his pencils, sticks them in his

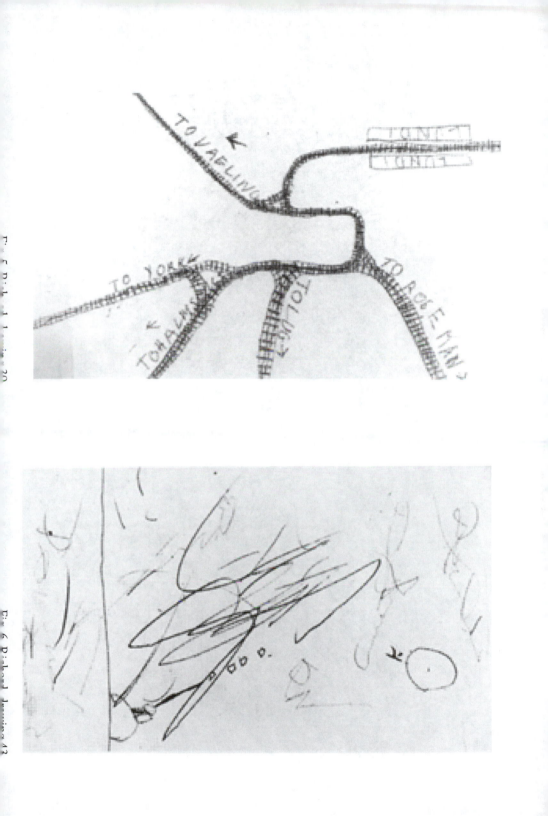

Fig 5. Richard. Jennings 30.

Fig 6. Richard. Jennings 43.

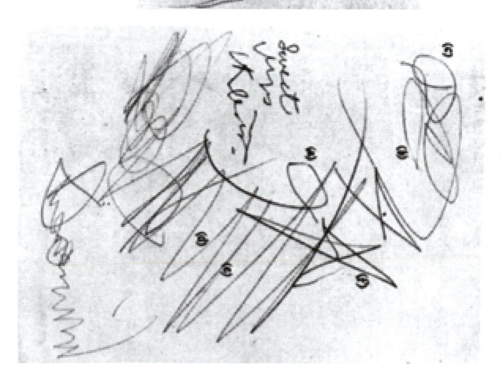

Fig. 7. Richard, drawing 66

Fig. 8. Richard, drawing 67

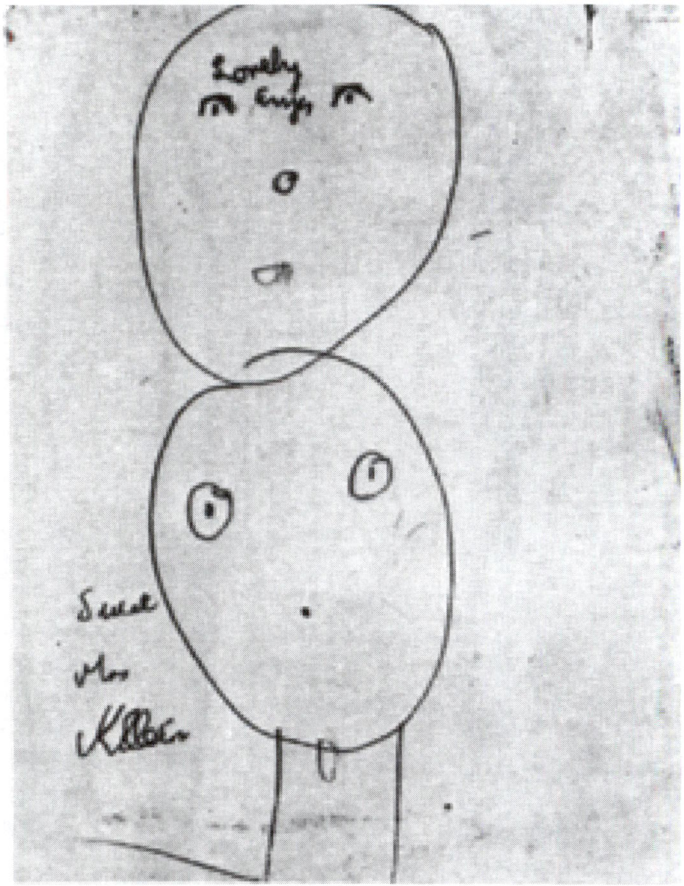

Fig. 9. Richard, drawing 68

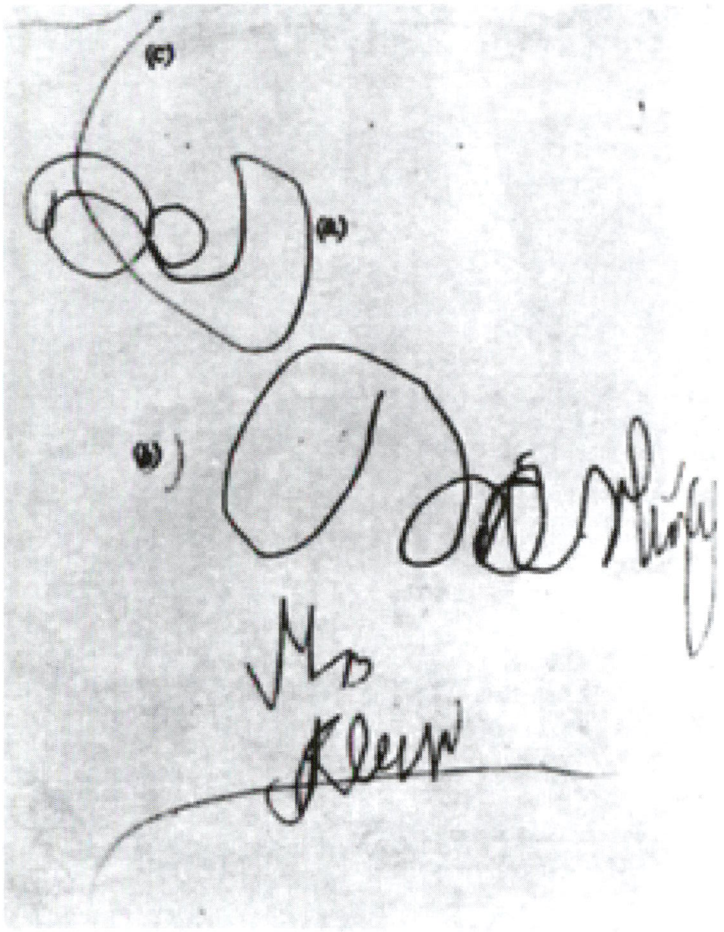

Fig. 10. Richard, drawing 70

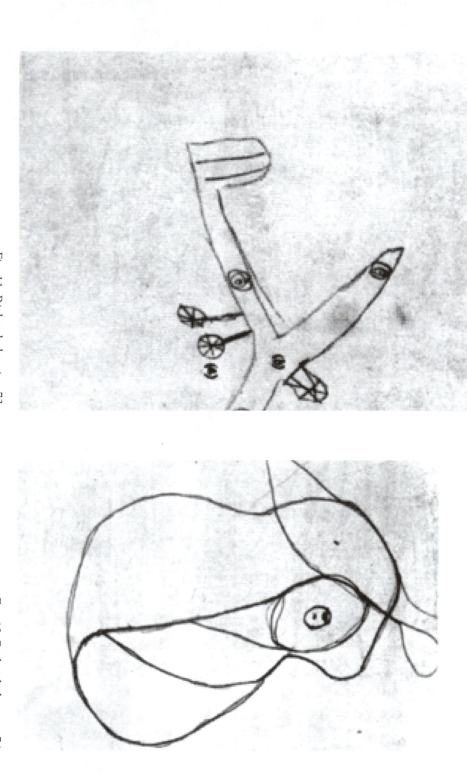

Fig. 11. Richard, drawing 73

Fig. 12. Richard, drawing 74

mouth, attacks them, or makes them attack his paper (scribbling on the pages of his drawing book or violently marking them with dots); breasts dotted like strawberries become exploding landmines in one trio of drawings.[31] But by far the most striking illustration of the "concreteness" of Richard's art is the drawing pad itself. At one point, when Richard finishes a pad, Mrs K. produces a new one that is yellowish instead of white, reminding him of being sick (p. 262; earlier, the xenophobic "yellow peril" has been identified with bad inside things). Klein "interprets" that "the pad with the white pages stands for her good breast, her good milk—the Milky Way on her dress [a dress with white spots that Richard has identified with the Milky Way]; the yellowish pages which reminded him of being sick made him feel that he had soiled the breast" (p. 264). Next time, Klein has a new, white pad, but when she forgets it the following session, Richard turns white with misery and anger. Klein sugggests that his feelings recollect those of the baby who didn't get enough from his mother's breasts and who was angry and disappointed at being fobbed off with a bottle; first he gets the wrong pad, then no pad at all. Richard responds with a dark, abstract drawing of an eagle in a rage ("Richard pulled up his coat over his ears, leaving only part of his face uncovered, and said this was what the eagle was doing," p. 276)—representing, according to Klein, Richard inside Mrs K. and his mother, hurting and devouring them in revenge for their withdrawal of nourishment.[32] Klein concludes this sequence involving the drawing pad by observing that "the deep disappointment and anxiety aroused by the yellow pad had shown the longing, never overcome, for the mother's good breast (the white pad, the 'Milky Way' on [her] dress)" (p. 278).[33] Pad equals breast; an injury to one constitutes an injury to the other in the concrete world of Richard's unconscious phantasies.[34]

Significantly, these sessions coincide with a decisive shift in Richard's drawings toward the iconography of breasts. Developing a hint from Meltzer that the evolution of Richard's drawings can be compared to the different periods in an artist's oeuvre, I want to look more closely at the transition from railway drawings to breast images. Juxtaposing two seemingly contrasting drawings, nos. 54 and 55 (figs. 13 and 14), a map of Richard's clockwork train track and the first portrait of Klein ("Mrs M. Klein"), Meltzer points out that "the same phantasy has many different iconographic representations"—

There was probably no secret intention [on Klein's part] in putting [these] drawings . . . on the same page, but one of the things that

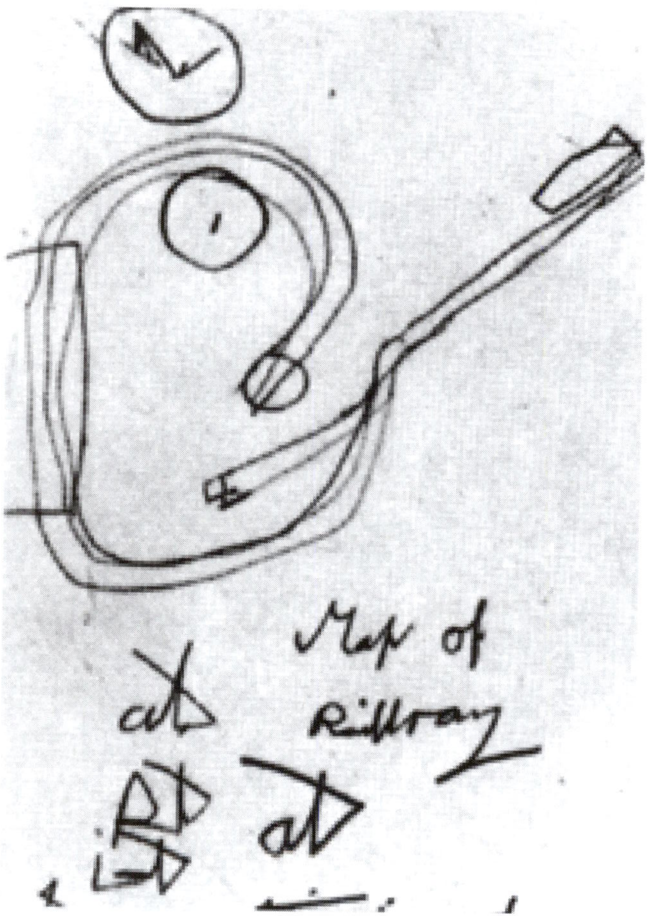

Fig. 13. Richard, drawing 54

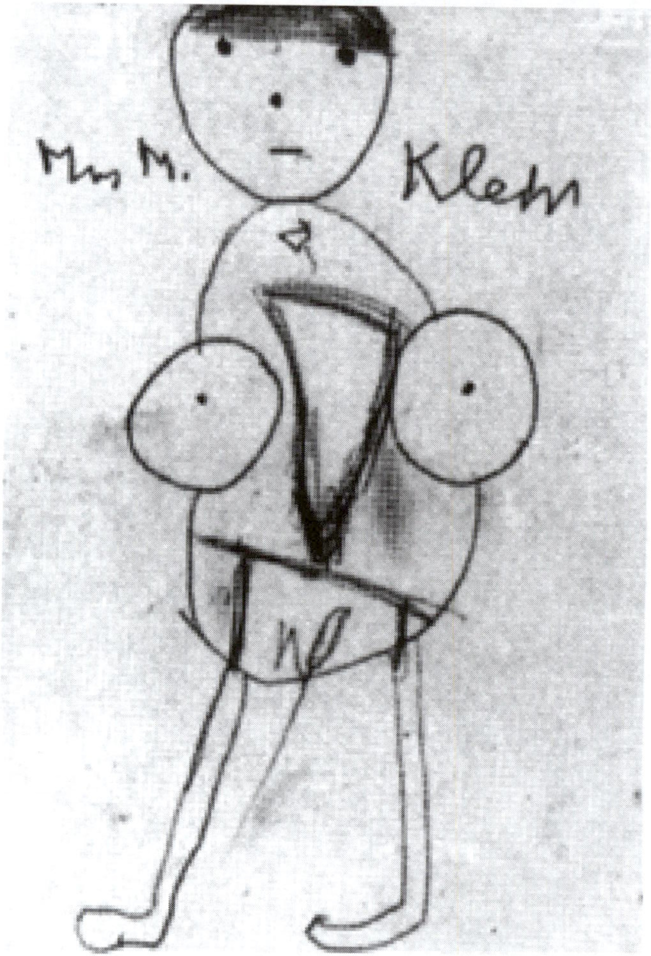

Fig. 14. Richard, drawing 55

they illustrate is the strong artistic similarity they bear to one another—as, for instance, in different periods of Picasso's work—the realistic drawings of the Blue Period and suddenly the Cubism. Drawings nos. 54 and 55 have a very strong relationship to one another, one abstract and the other representational. The two smaller circles of the railway drawing turn into the head and breasts of the portait of Mrs Klein. The railways have a link back to the recent series of railway drawings, but the circle also has a reference back to the antiaircraft gun which was firing into the air in drawing 43. . . .[35]

The rich associative detail of Klein's own account makes this conjunction especially illuminating. When Richard embarks on the first drawing, of a railway track, he has just been reunited with the clockwork train that he connects with early happy memories of his former home. His picture represents what he calls "a map" of the clockwork train track: "One circle represented a chair, round which were lines standing for rails. He did not explain the circle above it" (p. 316). As he draws, Richard makes engine noises and talks enthusiastically about its strength and speed. Zeroing in on the unexplained second circle, Klein "interprets" that Richard is glad to have his toy train back, "not only because he liked playing with it, but also because it stood for himself—the little Richard who was alive and feeding from Mummy's breasts—the two circles" (p. 317). Klein's notes add that the happy memories associated with the train are themselves "cover memories" for feelings of well-being which she dates back to his infancy (p. 318).

We could read the train drawing itself as a "cover" for the maternal breast. Noting the abstract iconography of breasts that is hidden in one picture, but explicit in the other ("Mrs M. Klein"), Meltzer points to the way in which the circles with a dot in the middle recall the earlier, more confused drawing no. 43 (fig. 6) in which an anti-aircraft gun is jealously shooting at "Mummy's and Mrs K.'s breast, the circle with the dot in the middle," while "the scribbles on the same page represented his mother's body" (p. 259).[36] Significantly, Richard's first portrait of "Mrs M. Klein," no. 55 (fig. 14), also includes an allusion to the iconography of war—an incomplete triangle which Richard later identifies as the victory sign ("V for Victory"): "The top line of the triangle and the line leading to the genital were added later. Richard explained that the two sides of the triangle were bones. Before he made the additions, he picked up the drawing suddenly and put his lips to one breast" (p. 323). Klein interprets this battle as the one that is going on, not only inside Mrs K., but inside Richard (at this point in the analysis, he is angry with Mrs Klein for depriving him of his Sunday session). Hitler has won the bigger victory within him. Richard follows up his kiss by looking fondly at Klein: "I love you," he tells her (p. 324). This is the first occasion on which Richard has drawn Mrs K. or made a declaration of love. Yet although Klein herself chooses not to mention it in connection with this particular drawing, the maternal body contains, icono-graphically, a quite different face (as Richard's phantasies so often do): that of Hitler, whose goggle eyes, triangular nose, and residual moustache are startlingly propped on Klein's legs and topped with her head. A similar instance of the confusion and coexistence of Mrs K. and the Hitler inside her occurs in a tumultuous, dramatically underdocumented session for which Klein's detailed notes are miss-ing. This session, toward the end of Richard's analysis, is remarkable both for its emotional intensity and for its frenzied productivity; Richard draws at least a dozen pictures, of which Klein reproduces only six.[37] Although it is hardly possible to do justice to the density of Klein's material for this session, I want to try to reca-pitulate its major themes since it brings to light in a particularly graphic way what Lacan calls "the cartography . . . of the mother's internal empire."

During the previous session, Richard has become increasingly aggressive—attacking the piano, which he associates with his mother, and enveloping himself in the Union Jack, while noisily singing the National Anthem (as Klein shrewdly observes of the flushed and shouting boy, "trying to counteract anger and hostil-ity by loyalty," p. 416); we have already seen how easily the swastika can turn into a Union Jack—and vice versa.[38] During the next session Richard becomes impos-sible to control, hammering on the floor, spilling water, and cutting the table with his knife. Unusually for her, Mrs K. loses patience with him. When they meet again, Richard counters her interpretation that "she had changed into the 'wicked brute' [Hitler] by being impatient with him" with the sarcastic comment: "Hitler said, 'My patience is exhausted'" (p. 420)—a devastating moment of historical quotation. Klein contents herself with observing in response that "she had, in his mind, completely changed into Hitler. He felt that she contained Hitler" (p. 420). Almost immediately afterwards, Richard draws nos. 67 and 68 (figs. 8 and 9). The first drawing, no. 67, is the strikingly fragmented and scribbled representation of Mrs K., of which Richard remarks that "she was underneath the scribble," and Klein, that she "seemed to be in little bits." The second drawing, no. 68, prompts Klein to "interpret" that "her tummy was also a face—actually Hitler's—inside her, and that the penis he had added seemed to be Hitler's" (p. 421). This is the troublingly composite image that Richard wrestles with throughout. Mrs M. Klein always contains the bad Hitler (alias Mr K.), just as Richard, with his angry goosestepping, constantly risks becoming a little Hitler draped in a swastika, forever annexing other countries to his own greedy empire ("whatever he consciously intended, it always turned out that he had more countries than anybody else," p. 466). Richard associates the impossibility of ever knowing whose side anyone is on in this war with the "not proper," "muddled and mixed up" map of Hitler's Europe (pp. 34-35). At one point, he also repeats a *risqué* joke of his father's: "he pointed at Brest and said Daddy had made a joke about Brest: he said something about the Germans going on to attack the legs now they had started with the breast" (p. 41).[39] The mixed-up map is a sexualized version of the body symbolically carved up by Richard's own maternal iconography. Like Sendak, whose wild child Max in *Where the Wild Things Are* is sent to his room for menacing his mother ("I'll eat you up"), both Richard and his father implicitly recognize that loving onslaughts on the breast-mother are lined with infantile aggression.

During this session, Klein notes the artificiality and insincerity of Richard's professions of love for her. While scribbling drawing no. 67 ("Sweet Mrs Klein," fig. 8), Richard had spoken of "the sweet Mrs K.," and while making drawing no. 68 (fig. 9), Klein tells us, he "leaned forward, looking into Mrs K.'s eyes, and said that she had such lovely eyes." (p. 421). But as she relates, "While he was speaking of the 'sweet' Mrs K., my 'lovely eyes,' and so on, he was at the same time destroying me in the drawing" (pp. 425–26). In another drawing, no. 69 (fig. 15, the only one of a related trio which Klein reproduces), Mrs K. is again in bits, with her lovely eyes, her nose, her stomach, and her breasts disconnected except by the enraged scribble that (as we know from the earlier drawing no. 43) represents the maternal body.[40] Klein reports: "his rage was increasing, his face was red and his eyes flashing, from time to time he ground his teeth and bit the pencil hard, particularly when talking about breasts or drawing circles representing them" (p. 421). Recognizing his rage as the symbolic need to tear out bits of her, Klein has "the feeling that he had regressed to the attempts of young children who are unable to draw a complete figure, for complex reasons, such as lack of skill, lack of integration, and feelings of guilt about having torn to bits the mother's breast" (p. 420). Regressing to infantile rage, Richard goes to pieces as an artist, and so does the mother. The "Darling Mrs Klein" of drawing no. 70 (fig. 10) mutates into a related drawing of the full moon containing a quarter moon being shot at by an airplane ("Mrs

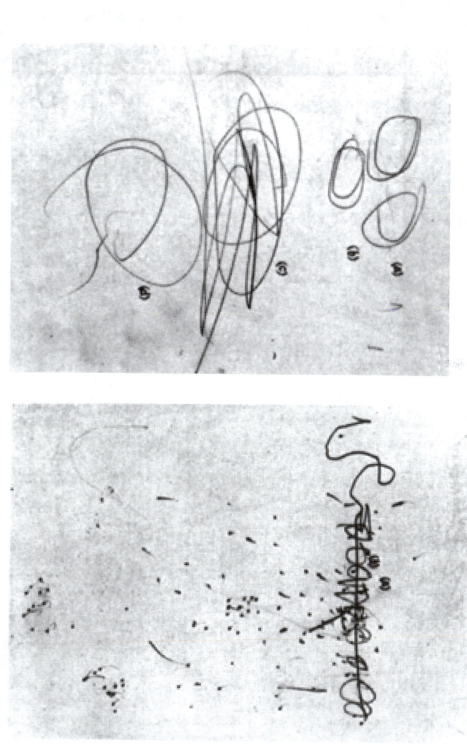

Fig. 15. Richard, drawing 69

Fig. 16. Richard, drawing 72

K. interpreted that the full moon was herself and the quarter moon was Mr K.'s genital inside her. . . . Richard was shooting at both her and Mr K. together," pp. 422–23).[41] The session culminates in drawing no. 72 (fig. 16), representing the train in which Mrs K. is going to travel to London. Richard systematically bombs it, carefully at first, but "in the end, getting into a real frenzy, [he] said the whole train was bombed and destroyed" (p. 423). Klein interprets Richard's rage and despair in the context of her impending departure as fear that she actually will be bombed in London ("Since he felt that he could not save her, he had to attack and destroy her," p. 423). Finally, Richard melodramatically enacts the shooting of Hitler, who turns out to be standing just where Mrs K. herself is standing. Then he draws two white buckets of water from the kitchen tank, "said that he was getting his milk and it looked very nice," and leaves—so Klein narrates—in a composed and friendly mood.[42]

The going-to-pieces of Richard's art uncovers both an archeology of signs and an archeology of subject formation. The casting out of the maternal body as a crucial stage in the formation of the "imperial" subject is a now-familiar aspect of psychic development in accounts such as Kristeva's. Richard's last, reparative pair of drawings—illustrating, for Klein, his wish "to keep Mrs K. as a live and good Mummy inside him" (p. 450)—gather up and connect the fragments. Like the companion drawing of a bus (not reproduced by Klein), drawing no. 73 (fig. 11) involves a journey. He and Mrs K. will sit side by side on an airplane that "looks like a person" (according to Richard) and whose landing wheels are her two breasts. Just as the bus "is taking her away with him, inside himself" (p. 451), the airplane "stands for" Richard, with Mrs K. preserved inside him (her breasts go air freight). According to Richard himself, the other drawing, no. 74 (fig. 12), is also a travel drawing: "He said it was a railway line and made his pencil go over it repeatedly; this stood for a train travelling. He mentioned that he would like to become an explorer and to read books about travel" (p. 451).[43] Klein, right on cue, "interpreted the exploration of Mummy's (now Mrs K.'s) inside and pointed out that the drawing of the railway line was in the shape of a female body" (p. 451). As if tracing or caressing this shape gives him pleasure, Richard keeps making his pencil travel over it, then "pointed to the circle near the top and said that this was the breast. The smaller circle was the nipple. He suddenly pounced on it with his pencil, making the dot in the centre, but at once restrained himself from making further dots—obviously preventing himself from destroying Mrs K.'s breast and body" (p. 451). The looping, aesthetically satisfying shapes of Richard's drawing—

197

at once breast, body, and railway track—bring together his entire artistic oeuvre, combining visual pleasure in the line with the sheer repetitive pleasure of tracing it, while holding destructiveness (as it were) within bounds. Klein observes that Richard was very sad during this session, repeatedly touching her arm or hand and wanting to be caressed and cuddled by her. The drawing puts him in touch with her—literally, if we are to believe Klein's own claim, in "The Rôle of the School in the Libidinal Development of the Child" about "the maternal significance of . . . everything that can be written upon;"[44] the outline "stands for" her body—a body permanently on the line.

In the second-to-last session, a lost drawing of submarine warfare forlornly quotes Richard's first marine drawings. But now "Richard said that he did not want to look under the surface of the drawing (which meant beneath the line)" (p. 460). Richard refuses Klein's "interpreting." But not wanting to look at what lies beneath the line also suggests that Richard needs to cling to a whole and complete image. His last graphic work traces the outline of Klein's hand on a piece of paper: "On the same paper he had previously drawn the outline of his own hand. This piece of paper he took with him" (p. 363). Klein sees his drawing as "another way of keeping her inside him." But much earlier, Richard had switched suddenly from drawing exploding strawberry-breasts to outlining Klein's india-rubber eraser on his pad: "Then he made two horizontal lines across the paper and a vertical line which cut the drawing of the rubber in half, and said that these lines were bars. It was a prison" (p. 336). Klein "interprets" that the india rubber stands for "Mr K.'s or rather Daddy's genital"; Richard "wished to make sure about it and therefore he drew the outline" (pp. 336–37), imprisoning it in his own inside (in Klein's—as opposed to Lacan's—nonverbal sense of the word, "introjecting" it) "for the purpose of controlling it and preventing it from doing harm" (p. 337).[45] Apropos of the eraser, Klein identifies reproduction as a defense against ambiguity: "The urge to make an exact reproduction of the object links with the uncertainty about internal happenings and objects, which contributes to the obsessional need to cling to exact descriptions, be it by writing, drawing, or other means" (p. 339); and presumably, even by means of critical rereading. Richard's two-handed drawing ("another way of keeping her inside him") imprisons Klein as well as keeping her safe—simultaneously covering and recovering her beneath-the-line significance. In the same session, Richard pretends to be Mrs K. "broadcasting to the world. She is saying, 'I shall give the right kind of peace to everybody.'" Still ventriloquizing Klein the peace maker, he adds: "'And Richard is a very nice boy . . .'" (p. 462). Hitler (alias Lord Haw-

Haw) has become Churchill. But we should be wary of imposing an upbeat ending. I want to keep the two images in focus together—the outlined india-rubber eraser and the two hands, big and small, traced side by side on the same piece of paper. Richard's grandiose, manic declaration of world peace is an attempt to hold the line against chaos, a child's single-handed redrawing of the mixed-up map that is modern Europe.

*   *   *

Klein prefaces the *Narrative* by announcing that one of her aims is "to illustrate [her] technique in greater detail" (p. 11). The emphasis on "detail" turns into a claim for "coherence." Klein goes on to insist that "psychoanalysis is a scientific procedure and its technique embodies scientific principles. The assessment and interpretation of the patient's material by the analyst are based on a coherent framework of theory" (p. 12). And finally, "As my account shows, I could penetrate into very deep layers of the mind" (p. 13). Klein's penetration into the depths of Richard's mind "stands for" (as she herself might say) a coherent framework of theory. By making Richard's drawings her central exhibit, she holds up a mirror to her own production (the *Narrative* itself) and makes it whole. Meltzer emphasizes a theoretical lack in Klein's work as compared to Freud's ("Where the theoretical tail wags the clinical dog with him, hardly any theoretical tail exists to be wagged with her"). The Freudian "tail" that is missing in Klein's work takes on gender-specific significance—both the mark of a missing body of theory and the sign of lack associated with femininity (like the short-tailed Manx cat in Woolf's *A Room of One's Own*). The masculine associations of theory and the imaginary construction of women's special relation to the empirical and the body raise questions about the "concreteness" that Meltzer singles out as the essential "Kleinian development" (the title of his book on the relation between Kleinian psychoanalysis and its Freudian foundations). Literalness—the literalness of the body—is a traditional metaphor for femininity. Does Klein embody just a little development, a little addition, to the symbolic and necessarily phallic attributes of Freudian theory? Can enough hands-on technique (enough detail) compensate for, or develop, what is theoretically lacking? Klein's missing tail—that old Freudian lack—gets redefined as a bit of a fetish (in her own writing as well as in Freud's, and perhaps in Meltzer's account too).

In "The Rôle of the School in the Libidinal Development of the Child," Klein writes of a child's drawings as "a 'magic gesture,'" by which he can realise the omnipotence of his thought," as well as a destructive and depreciatory act.[46] Richard's drawings offer a simultaneously wishful and fragmented representation of the maternal body; on one hand, there is "Lovely Mrs K.," and on the other, his furious, destructive scribbles. If Klein conceived of the *Narrative* not only as a way to prove her point that analyzing a child frees his phantasy life, but also as a way to make herself theoretically complete, it succeeds in doing so not because Richard, as a boy child, "stands for" the fetish of theory demanded of a woman analyst in the continuing struggle with, and over, Freud; rather, it does so because Richard's graphic art ultimately exceeds the terms of Klein's psychoanalytic theory as well as her technique. Standing for the no-thing of maternal origin, Richard's drawings sketch the incomplete outlines of Klein's missing theory of signs.[47] Her portrait of the artist as a young dog connects the mother's formation, deformation, and reformation with the "magic gesture" of sign-making, whose cultural ambiguity gets historically inscribed in the *Narrative* as the vexed relation between art and war, or the drawing, redrawing, and crossing of lines.

1. Melanie Klein, *Love, Guilt and Reparation* (London: Virago Press, 1988), 72.

2. Donald Meltzer, *Richard Week-by-Week*, *The Kleinian Development*, part 2 (Perthshire: Clunie Press, 1978), 86. Meltzer, collaborating with Hanna Segal, was also the coauthor of one of two important review articles of Klein's *Narrative* when it first appeared; see Hanna Segal and Donald Meltzer, "Narrative of a Child Analysis," *International Journal of Psycho-Analysis* 44 (October 1963): 507–13.

3. See Melanie Klein, *Narrative of a Child Analysis* (London: Virago Press, 1989). The drawings, illustrated in black and white in the Virago edition, were accompanied by the following authorial note in the original Hogarth Press edition of 1961: "The illustrations are photographs of Richard's original drawings, some in pencil and some in crayon. They have been photographed and slightly reduced in size: all originally measuring approximately 7 inches by $4^{1/2}$ inches." Klein altered the drawings only to emphasize or black out details such as names or to insert letters referring to parts of a drawing. Subsequent page references and numbers in the text refer to the text and drawings of the Virago edition.

4. Jacques Lacan, *Ecrits*, trans. Alan Sheridan (New York and London: W. W. Norton & Company, 1977), 20, 20–21.

5. Meltzer, *Richard Week-by-Week*, 1.

6. For the struggles between Kleinians and (Anna) Freudians in wartime London, see *The Freud-Klein Controversies 1941–45*, ed. Pearl King and Riccardo Steiner (London and New York:

Tavistock/Routledge, 1991); and Phyllis Grosskurth, *Melanie Klein: Her World and Her Work* (Cambridge, MA, and London: Harvard University Press, 1987), 279–362. For an intelligent discussion of the insights and difficulties posed by Kleinian theory in the context of the "Controversial Discussions," see also Jacqueline Rose's essays, "Negativity in the Work of Melanie Klein," and "War in the Nursery," in *Why War?* (Oxford: Blackwell, 1993), 137–90, 191–230.

7. There is more in the same vein; it appears that in the doggy realm, "Bobby would like to have a wife and babies, but Mummy did not want two dogs in the house." Again Mrs K. "interprets" that "Bobby stood for himself: it was he who wanted to be independent, have a wife and babies" (*Narrative*, 29). Much later in the analysis, another dog called James appears in one of Richard's dreams, now standing for "the attractive Daddy-genital" inside the mother (*Narrative*, 404).

8. See Grosskurth, *Melanie Klein*, 266. Grosskurth's account of Richard's analysis with Klein suggests the degree of Klein's own anxiety about an invasion; see *Melanie Klein*, 262–77, especially 271.

9. Compare Rose, *Why War?* 137–38, speculating on "some seemingly irreducible negativity, bearer of a violence sanctioned . . . by State and subjects, setting the parameters of our being-in-the-social, confronting us with something at the limits of psyche and social alike."

10. Meltzer, *Richard Week-by-Week*, 3, 4.

11. See, for instance, Elisabeth Geleerd, "Evaluation of Melanie Klein's 'Narrative of a Child Analysis,'" *International Journal of Psycho-Analysis* 44 (October 1963): 493–506. Geleerd's is the first part of a two-part consideration of the *Narrative*, the first a critique by a non-Kleinian or "classical" analyst, the second by Hanna Segal and Donald Meltzer, who answer Geleerd's specific criticism—"the giving of so-called 'deep' interpretations from the start"—by arguing that "the analytic situation is most securely established by the interpretation of the most pressing anxieties regardless of their developmental level"; see Segal and Meltzer, "Narrative," 511.

12. See Klein, *Love, Guilt and Reparation*, 370–97.

13. Meltzer, *Richard Day-by-Day*, 1.

14. Ibid., 81–82.

15. Geleerd, "Evaluation," 501, 502: "just as the small European countries were helpless against the German armies . . . how long can a helpless person keep from being invaded and overpowered by a stronger one? . . . Mrs Klein is seen as a strong person who will overpower the patient." See also Gilles Deleuze on the "forcing" of Richard in Gilles Deleuze and Claire Parnet, *Dialogues*, trans. Hugh Tomlinson and Barbara Habberjam (New York: Columbia University Press, 1987), 81.

16. See, for instance, Melanie Klein, "On the Theory of Anxiety and Guilt" (1948), in *Envy and Gratitude* (London: Virago Press, 1988), 40: "the young child's perception of external reality and external objects is perpetually influenced and coloured by his phantasies, and . . . this in some measure continues throughout life. External experiences which rouse anxiety at once activate even in normal persons anxiety derived from intrapsychic sources. The interaction between objective anxiety and neurotic anxiety—or, to express it in other words, the inter-action between anxiety arising from external and from internal sources—corresponds to the interaction between external reality and psychic reality."

17. Meltzer, *Richard Week-by-Week*, 80.

18. See Klein, "On the Theory of Anxiety and Guilt," 32: "External dangers are experienced in the light of internal dangers and are therefore intensified; on the other hand, any danger threatening from outside intensifies the perpetual inner danger-situation."

19. Klein also argues "that during the war even children who were exposed to the greatest dangers in war time could bear them if their relation with their parents . . . was sufficiently secure," concluding that "external dangers can be borne if a good internal object is securely enough established" (*Narrative*, 447).

20. J. Laplanche and J.-B. Pontalis, *The Language of Psycho-Analysis* (New York: W. W. Norton & Company, 1973), 356.

21. See chapter 5 above for Sade and attacks on the mother.

22. See Grosskurth, *Melanie Klein*, 273.

23. Meltzer, *Richard Week-by-Week*, 86.

24. So, for instance, "By keeping one breast good and one bad, [Richard] was attempting to keep one part of Mummy all right" (*Narrative*, 396).

25. This first nautical phase, starting with the U-boats of nos. 1 and 2, gives way to the combinations of destroyers, U-boats, mother fish, starfish, and octopi of nos. 3, 4, 6–8, and 10, with later recurrences of the submarine motif in nos. 21 and 29.

26. The empire drawings comprise nos. 9, 11–15, 17–20, 22–28, 30, 32–34, 36, and three late, isolated recurrences, nos. 45, 48, and 64; an isolated variant appears in no. 49 (see n. 32 below).

27. The railway drawings comprise nos. 37–39, 50, 52–54, and 57, interspersed and overlapping with a number of drawings involving air-bombardment and submarine warfare, nos. 40–43, 46, 47, and 51.

28. The drawings of Klein ("Mrs Klein") comprise nos. 55, 60–62, 63, and 66–68.

29. As Klein puts it, of drawing no. 43, "The scribbles . . . represented his mother's body, her inside which contained Daddy's genital, and the babies."

30. Compare "The Rôle of the School in the Libidinal Development of the Child," where Klein draws attention to "The maternal significance of . . . everything that can be written upon" (*Love, Guilt and Reparation*, 60 n.).

31. The strawberry landmines are represented by nos. 60–62; see *Narrative*, 336–37 for Klein's interpretation.

32. For the angry eagle, see the dark, atypical drawing no. 49.

33. Later on, Klein produces another drawing pad, "but it was not quite the same, though it was not a yellow one" (*Narrative*, 346). She interprets that he wants an inexhaustible supply of pads of the same kind—like good, uninjured, and inexhaustible breasts. And finally she produces a third pad, a new one ("not quite the kind he liked, but [he] preferred it to the thin yellowish paper Mrs K. had brought on a previous occasion and which had not been used since"; *Narrative*, 352). Hence the importance of the envelope in which his drawings are kept. Mrs Klein has brought a new envelope since the old one had got wet in the rain; Klein notes: "The old envelope had acquired a particular importance because it was so closely linked with his relation to the analyst and in some sense also represented the analyst herself" (*Narrative*, 325). She goes on to associate these transferential feelings with "his deep attachment to his

first objects" such as "the old deserted house which stood for the lonely and deserted mother and was linked with all his early memories" (*Narrative*, 325). Is there a hint of counter-transferential feeling in Klein's own association?

34. Words themselves may have the same concreteness; at one point Richard sneezes and says, "half to himself: 'He knows his blows,' meaning to say, 'He blows his nose,' and was very amused when Mrs K. drew attention to this slip of the tongue" (*Narrative*, 34). Klein interprets his fear of a cold as "something bad inside him, hence the blows." Words can also turn bad and make one sick, like a cold; thus Richard can say "He was sick of what Mrs K. was saying" and Klein points out in return "that he had used the word 'sick' because he felt that Mrs K.'s words were now the same as the poisonous food which the maids—actually Mummy—would put into him as a punishment for his poisoning them" (*Narrative*, 133–34). Klein footnotes the connection with a later session when Richard announces that he has a pain in his tummy and says that he is "fed up with psychoanalysis"; she points out that "he had used the expression 'fed up' because that was what he felt at that moment: it seemed to him that he had actually eaten up everybody, and that Mrs K. was feeding him with frightening words" (*Narrative*, 145 and n).

35. Meltzer, *Richard Day-by-Day*, 83–84.

36. Compare also no. 57, another train-track drawing, whose figure-of-eight loops Klein interprets as Richard running between the two breasts, as well as between his mother and Mrs K. (see *Narrative*, 329 and n).

37. Of the dozen drawings produced in this tumultuous session, the six represented are nos. 67–72.

38. "[Richard] scribbled something on another page and showed it to Mrs K., saying, as he had done formerly, that it was easy to change a swastika into a Union Jack" (*Narrative*, 412).

39. Compare Grosskurth, *Melanie Klein*, 273, for Richard's own comical recollection: "'I remember going on about the fact that we were going to bomb the Germans, and seize Berlin, and so on and so on and then Brest. Melanie seized on b-r-e-a-s-t, which of course was very much her angle.'"

40. Other drawings in this series (nos. 70–72) recollect earlier iconographic and associative material, such as the banana-shaped "genital" of drawing no. 63, or the lobster that Richard has been carting about in his suitcase as a gift to his family—his own secret weapon "to fight the bad Mummy containing Hitler," says Klein (*Narrative*, 422).

41. See no. 71 for this related drawing.

42. Between this session and the one that produces Richard's last drawings is a session focussed on a particularly graphic dream for which Richard does an illustration—a picture that is unfortunately missing, Klein reports; for the dream and the drawing, see *Narrative*, 430–31.

43. The adult Richard really did become an explorer in his work, "travel[ling] widely, usually to remote places covered most of the year in snow, under which lie extinct volcanoes"; see Grosskurth, *Melanie Klein*, 272.

44. Klein, *Love, Guilt and Reparation*, 60 n.

45. This is the reverse of projective identification (i.e., the phantasized projection of split-off parts of the self into the mother's body for the purpose of doing harm).

46. Klein, *Love, Guilt and Reparation*, 72.

47. Compare Mary Kelly in *Post-Partum Document*—an artist's investigation into the relation between her own artistic production and that of her son—for whom a child's art, like the unconscious, is a place "where the eccentricity and extravagance of anatomical transformation is not bounded by logic or by the specular image"; see *Post-Partum Document* (London: Routledge & Kegan Paul, 1983), 114. Drawing on Klein as well as Lacan, *Post-Partum Document* is also an inquiry into "the possibility of female fetishism" in which the mother's fetishization of the child's memorabilia (his first words, drawings, writings) is displaced onto the work of art in such a way as to "question the fetishistic nature of representation itself" (*Post-Partum Document*, xv, xvi).

Part IV

Theory at the Breast

10

Incorruptible Milk
Breast-feeding and the French Revolution

IN 1791, THE WOMEN CITIZENS of Clermont-Ferrand wrote to the French National Assembly: "Nous faisons sucer à nos enfants un lait incorruptible et que nous clarifions à cet effet avec l'esprit naturel et agréable de la liberté (*Applaudissements*)."[1] From the vantage point of the bicentennial of the French Revolution, we might ponder the politicization of what has come to seem so private a matter. But to place maternal nurture—that is, breast-feeding—unequivocally in the personal domain is to forget that, for the eighteenth century at least, wet-nursing was both a social institution and a state-regulated industry. My concern, however, is not so much with changing definitions of public and private that coincided with the French Revolution, nor with the ideological situating of women vis-à-vis either domain, as with what might be called the semiotics of maternal breast-feeding. The history that interests me is the history of Revolutionary signs, and the sign that interests me here is the figure of the breast-feeding mother.

What light does this patriotic communiqué from the women of Clermont-Ferrand shed on the meaning of mother's milk during the French Revolution? And if liberty's milk is incorruptible, what does that make the milk of the ancien régime? In Enlightenment writing about maternal breast-feeding, the imaginary source of spoilt or adulterated milk is invariably the wet-nurse. Serving as the figure for a generalized maternal alienation and neglect associated with the ancien régime, the wet-nurse is often paired with her opposite, the woman of society who refuses to nurse her own child—although we should remember that, in reality, the institution of wet-nursing had as much to do with the economics of a hard-pressed urban artisan class, who could not afford to keep their infants at home when both parents had to work for the family to survive at all.[2] Enlightenment advocacy of maternal breast-feeding in France should therefore be read as at least as much an expression of changing cultural attitudes toward mother-infant relations and the family as an informed social critique; significantly, enlightened women of the middle and upper classes (who could afford to do so) rather than of the lower classes (who could not) typically responded to the call to nurse their own children in the decades leading up to the French Revolution.[3] But the advocacy of maternal breast-feeding represented, for instance, by Rousseau can also be read as extending into the symbolic realm where the dominant allegories of the French Revolution were themselves played out. In this realm, questions about the relations of specific historical practices and cultural formations to seemingly transhistorical psychic mechanisms are likely to arise in their most perplexing form. I want to address at least some of these questions in what follows, specifically as they relate to the symbolic ordering of gender during the French Revolution.

As a start, I will begin by asking the meaning of mother's milk in Enlightenment writing about maternal breast-feeding, and go on to argue that the Rousseauian sexual ideology associated with it leads to unresolved problems in Revolutionary thinking about women. In addition, I will sketch a semiotic reading of the representations of the Republic as a nursing mother that figure in the festivals and allegories of the French Revolution, where anxieties about controlling women intersect with anxieties about purifying—about revolutionizing—signs themselves. Finally, I will argue that questions involving breast-feeding that present themselves in the body of psychoanalytic writing represented by Freudian theory may also be interestingly related to quite another set of questions—questions, however, that bear on the relationship beween history and psychoanalysis. What, for instance, is the relation between any instinctual satisfaction actually experienced by the baby at the breast and the psychic satisfaction hallucinated by the baby in relation to a symbolic breast? Just as the infant's fantasy of satisfaction is only ever "propped" on the instinctual experience, to use Jean Laplanche's term (*étayage*—itself a translation of Freud's term, *Anlehnung*, or "anaclisis"), so the powerful symbolic domain of public spectacle—one might equally claim—may only ever be propped metonymically on the material practices from which it derives its representations.[4] The relation between the two is neither referential nor causal. That is to say, the deployment of a psychoanalytic reading in the context of the French Revolution does not amount to transferring explanatory power or motivating force from material practices to unconscious phantasy. Rather, the temptation to make this transfer—to view symbolic representations as a reflection of social realities (or more wishfully, to attribute transformative power to symbolic representations)—may in itself be what a psychoanalytic reading of Revolutionary sign-systems most tellingly reveals.

I will be contending, therefore, not only that the discourses of history and psychoanalysis meet, so to speak, at the breast—at once provoking the wish that they should mean each other, and resisting any simple reduction of one to the other; but also that in both Enlightenment writing about maternal breast-feeding and in the festivals of the French Revolution, women are simultaneously viewed as the guarantors of the family and of an incorruptible sign-system. My chief examples will be, first, the most widely influential Enlightenment case for maternal breast-feeding, Rousseau's *Emile* (1762), along with Marie Anel Le Rebours's popular and much reprinted handbook, *Avis aux mères qui veulent nourir leurs enfants* (1767), which raises some of the same issues; and, second, the debates surrounding women's participation in the French Revolution during the late summer and autumn of 1793, along with the allegory of the Republic as breast-feeding mother, or "Nature," which figures prominently in the closely contemporary festival of August 10, 1793. I will be considering both the Enlightenment case for maternal breast-feeding and the historical instance of women's political and symbolic role during the French Revolution in the light of their contradictory and ambivalent deployment of the symbolic figure of the breast-feeding mother. Finally, I will return to the question of the relationship between "history" and "psychoanalysis," and to the possibility that the psychic formations and subjectivity associated with Freudian psychoanalysis are themselves the product of changes in late-eighteenth-century attitudes to the family—or rather, as some critics and theorists of the family would claim, the product of the specific form of the modern family known as "bourgeois," whose emergence arguably coincides with the French Revolution.[5]

i. "L'homme de la nature"; or, Let Them Eat Grass

A popular eighteenth-century engraving depicts Rousseau as *l'homme de la nature* presenting a nosegay to a mother as she nurses her child outside a rustic cottage; nearby, a ewe obligingly suckles her lamb (the caption reads: "*Il rendit les mères à leurs devoirs et les enfants au bonheur*") (fig. 1).[6] In another famous engraving of 1784, Voysard's *L'Alaitement maternel encouragé*, Rousseau figures as "Un Philosophe Sensible" who indicates to charity where she should bestow her bounty, while Comedy, in the guise of Figaro, spills his sack at the feet of breast-feeding mothers (the allusion is to Beaumarchais's offer to contribute the profits from *The*

Fig. 1. Augustin Le Grand, *Jean-Jacques Rousseau ou l'homme de la Nature: "Il rendit les mères à leurs devoirs et les enfants au bonheur."* Photo Claude Caroly.

Fig. 2. Voysard, after Borel, *L'Alaitement maternel encouragé* (1784): "Un Philosophe Sensible indique à la bienfaisance les objets sur les quels elle doit verser ses dons. La Comédie, sous la figure de Figaro, tiens des gros Sacs. Elle en repand un aux pieds de plusiers mères qui donnent le sein à leurs enfants. Au dessus du Philosophe est la Statue de l'humanité, portant ces mots: 'Secours pour les Mères nourices.'" Wellcome Institute, London

Marriage of Figaro to a charity that would enable poor mothers to nurse their own children—an offer taken up by the city of Lyon) (fig. 2).[7] Rousseau's call for a return to breast-feeding in *Emile* is famous for indicting the socialite mother of the upper classes for her irresponsibility and lack of maternal feeling; erasing the economic conditions which actually sustained the institution of wet-nursing in eighteenth-century France as a necessity for the urban artisanal classes, *Emile* replaces the unnatural mother by the figure of a maternal nurse—a figure who stands for an imaginary natural family immune to social forces and cemented by the bonds of mutual love. The case for maternal breast-feeding in Rousseau's writing, however, is complicated by the fact that his own life notoriously embodied a contradiction undermining both his self-representation as man of nature and his ideal of the natural family: his (self-confessed) abandonment at their birth of his five children by Thérèse to the *Enfants trouvés*, or Foundling Hospital.[8]

Rousseau's account in the *Confessions* initiates an argument for the Republic as parent; thus he can claim that he idealistically surrendered his children to the classless parental state embodied by the *Enfants trouvés* and the rural wet-nurse: "by destining them to become workers and peasants instead of adventurers and fortune-hunters, I thought I was acting as a citizen and a father, and looked upon myself as a member of Plato's Republic."[9] When the Republic is imagined as Platonic parent, both the *enfant trouvé* and the culpable father disappear from the record (and so, incidentally, does the mother). But Rousseau's apology contains an unspeakable subtext. Consigning one's children to the *Enfants trouvés* was a solution to which poor parents often resorted in eighteenth-century Paris, especially during the economic crises that preceded the Revolution.[10] As Rousseau himself must have known, the exceptionally high incidence of infant mortality among children thus abandoned (as well as the infant mortality rate associated with wet-nursing generally) was an acknowledged scandal at the time and led to repeated attempts to bring the institution of wet-nursing under state surveillance. Leaving one's children at the *Enfant trouvés* therefore meant not just consigning them to oblivion (still less to imagined rural innocence); it was a form of socially condoned infanticide.[11] In unburdening himself of his children, Rousseau at a stroke ensured a repetition of his own abandonment by the mother who had died at his birth and put a stop to it. When, therefore, he writes in *Emile* that "women have stopped being mothers," he was complaining about a stoppage that intimately concerned himself.[12] His solution was to get rid of the mother as well as the *enfant trouvé*, leaving the educator in charge.

Rousseau's depiction of the wretched infant, in *Emile*, "unhappier than a criminal in irons," reads like a dark parody of Wordsworth's blessed babe in *The Prelude* ("*No* outcast he, bewildered and depressed," *Prelude*, 2.261; my italics). Deprived of freedom at the outset by his swaddling bands, the anti-Rousseauian infant grows up without affect or morality. Pain and suffering are its first sentiments, crying its only means of protest, bondage its legacy—"The first gifts they receive from you are chains."[13] Rousseau attributes the infant's wretched psychic state directly to the connected practices of peasant swaddling and peasant wet-nursing. He blames the wet-nursing system not only for consigning infants to neglect and increased risk of death at the hands of ignorant, unsupervised, and uncaring country wet-nurses, but for preventing maternal attachment ("There is no substitute," he insists, "for maternal solicitude"). As a mother-substitute, the wet-nurse is already by definition suspect for Rousseau, since "She who nurses another's child in place of her own is a bad mother. How will she be a good nurse?"[14] And if attachment should develop between wet-nurse and child (as it must often have done in practice, when the infant survived), then the natural mother must either abdicate her own claim, or else teach her child to look down on and reject the peasant nurse to whom it has become tenderly attached. In Rousseau's account, class division provides the symbolic nexus for institutionalized alienation between mother and child.[15]

Riven by contradictions (the child forms an attachment to a despised mother-substitute, yet can only despise the mother who has failed to nurture it herself), the mother-child bond inscribes for Rousseau an unhealable division traversing both the social and the psychic. To resolve this impasse, the model child of *Emile* is rendered conveniently motherless; a wet-nurse replaces the mother, under the supervision of a Rousseauian "governor."[16] In his exhaustive detailing of the Enlightenment infant-rearing and child-care practices that became associated with him (although, of course, they did not originate with him), Rousseau establishes the nursery as the first site of rational surveillance. In doing so, he anticipates not only the regulatory surveillance actually exercised by the state and the police over the wet-nursing business in an attempt to remedy its haphazard, entrepreneurial workings and high rate of infant mortality, but also, ironically, the later nineteenth-century move to bring the wet-nurse herself under the direct supervision of her employer, a situation represented by the employment of a *nourrice-sur-lieu* within the bourgeois home itself.[17] Emile's wet-nurse is reduced to the sum of her milk, viewed as the product of a carefully regulated system of biological, temperamental, moral, and dietary components. Rousseau's receipe for purifying both milk and morals is pastoralization. Ideally, he says, the wet-nurse should be a healthy peasant woman of good character, living in the country and (this is important) eating a largely vegetarian diet: "The milk of herbivorous females is sweeter and healthier than that of carnivores. Formed of a substance homogeneous with its own, it preserves its nature better and becomes less subject to putrefaction."[18] Meat-eating on the part of the wet-nurse leads to bad morals as well as (so Rousseau believes) intestinal parasites in infants. Since corruption begins at the breast, the only safeguard against moral infection or infestation by worms is to put women out to grass.

In Rousseau's regime, the herbivorous nurse not only comes to occupy the place of any other lactating herbivorous female—that is, the fields—but is also excluded from the realm of reason: "Do not reason with nurses. Give orders."[19] Reason is the necessary dietary supplement supplied by the governor. One might ask what constitutes a natural mother for Rousseau since mothers no longer want to be mothers, and wet-nurses, however carefully selected, rank scarcely above sheep; by his own admission, the natural order has long since been abandoned ("as soon as one leaves the natural order, to do anything well has its complications").[20] There are two obvious implications of Rouseau's argument, the first ideological, the other harder to categorize. On one hand, the effect of *Emile* is less to validate a mother-child bond than to reestablish the status quo along traditional gender lines; the family becomes the place where women nurse and men teach. Even the mother who nurses her own child only does so until it can enter the care of the father ("Let the child pass from the hands of the one into those of the other").[21] Gender hierarchy replaces social division, healing the split at the site of the mother-child relationship, but doing so at the price of relegating the mother to a secondary role, that of nurturer. The other implication is more troubling. *Emile* suggests that every mother is unnatural—either refusing to nurture her own child, like the woman of society, or choosing to nurture someone else's for money in place of her own, like the peasant wet-nurse. No mother can ever be (in Winnicott's phrase) good enough, no milk impervious to corruption. The parasite is endemic to the system.

Emile suggests how Enlightenment advocacy of breast-feeding such as Rousseau's can coincide with conservative views of the family and with a consolidation of women's traditional role within it; bringing up baby—a prelude to educating the natural man—means disciplining the mother. Le Rebours's popular *Avis aux mères*, which was endorsed by Samuel Tissot, the enlightened Swiss doctor, as well as by the Faculty of Medicine of Paris, represents a practical guide to infant care and nursing written by a midwife for women themselves. Consulted by, among others,

Madame Roland, it reads at times like a protofeminist exhortation to women to oppose not only their traditional birth attendants but their husbands in choosing to breast-feed their babies. But Le Rebours also inadvertantly throws light on a problem that arises once more in the place occupied by the mother, and it is this aspect of her manual I want to explore before moving on to the Revolution itself. For Le Rebours, the problem involves the corruption of man's natural, natal nobility by what Le Rebours calls "bastard" milk: "Quel étrange abus est-ce donc de pervertir cette noblesse naturelle de l'homme qui nous vient de nature, de corrompre son corps et son esprit . . . en lui faisant prendre *la nouriture dégénérée d'un lait étranger et bâtard.*"[22] The "strange abuse" is not simply that of perverting nature, but of cor-rupting body and spirit with milk defined as both alien and illegitimate. As well as being bad, ugly, libertine, or drunken, the wet-nurse, according to Le Rebours, might infect the infant with her very blood (a popular belief, this): "Comment souffrons-nous que notre enfant soit infecté d'un sang impur et contagieux."[23] A body fluid credited with almost supernaturally pervasive powers, bastard milk—milk, that is, from outside the family circle—becomes associated with the fear that the child's love for its parents ("ce ciment . . . qui [forme] l'union naturelle des infants et des pères et mères") will be replaced by a love tagged as merely political and cal-culating; or, as we might gloss this concern, "nature" risks exposure as "culture."[24] That blood alone could cease to be an effective guarantor or glue (*ciment*) of family relationships is the unuttered anxiety that gives advocacy of maternal breast-feed-ing its special urgency at a time when, arguably, the family was increasingly under siege, whether for economic reasons or as an institution viewed as politically con-tinuous with the ancien régime, and itself in need of sentimental reform.

Le Rebours reveals the "natural" family as a structure always dependent on the repression or casting out of a debased other—actually the mother, whose blood is necessarily foreign to that of the father, given the laws of exogamy. Once more, the place of this symbolically debased other is occupied by the wet-nurse, who serves as a fantasized conduit for all that is illegitimate or arbitrary in the social order.[25] According to this scheme of things, maternal milk not only gives the family its imag-inary natural identity; it also provides the means by which social relations may be filtered of their impurities. In addition, maternal breast-feeding leads to perma-nent attachment to the mother, giving milk a single, unproblematic referent: "Ceux que ne changent point de mères, conservent leur attachment pour elles toute leur vie."[26] The mother comes to stand for conservation as well as for attachment, pro-viding the ground for signification itself. One might speculate, too, that in the face of the defamiliarizing threats by which the family was assailed during a period of Revolutionary upheaval, she becomes the guarantor of the social order—preserving the inheritance of property by ensuring the legitimacy of the infant's blood. Some historians, indeed, have argued that the principal achievement of the French Revolution was not only to consolidate the emerging bourgeois family as the norm, but to install it in place of the monarchy. Interestingly enough, the fifth edition of *Avis aux mères* (published in Year VII of the Revolution) ends with a verse tribute by a teenage son, specified as being "en âge de raison," to the mother who nursed him with "le nectar le plus doux" ("c'est sur ses genoux / Que j'ai pu savourer le nectar le plus doux").[27] Breast milk becomes the nectar of the Age of Reason. The role of the Republican mother, one might reasonably predict, will be at once to purify the ancien régime and to sweeten or clarify the very disorders (of blood and property) signified by the Revolution itself.

ii. "La France Républicaine"; or, Let Them Eat Signs

I want to turn now to the sign of the breast-feeding mother in French Revolutionary iconography and to the figure she cuts both in debates about the political role of women during the Revolution, and in Revolutionary festivals such as those designed by David, where the issues raised by Rousseau and Le Rebours surface as a concern with the purification of signs. Saint-Just (himself an orphan), whose Republican blueprint for the first five years of the Revolution, *Sur les institutions républicaines*, places maternal breast-feeding at the foundation of the educational system, writes: "The mother who has not nursed her baby ceases to be a mother in the eyes of the fatherland."[28] The breast-feeding mother provides the Revolution with one of its most powerful images of the Republic; in one engraving, "La France Républicaine"—described as "Ouvrant son Sein à tous les Français"(fig. 3)—wears a level to indicate equality of access to the Republican breast. In 1793, the need to consolidate attachment to the Republic at a time when Jacobin centralization had recently been threatened by Girondin federalism coincided with legislation specifically designed to encourage maternal nursing; the National Convention's decree of June 28, 1793 stipulated, for instance, that only mothers who nursed their own children would be eligible for state aid, unless certified as unable to do so by the officer of health.[29] In another engraving apparently dating from around the same time, a young mother nurses a baby (presumably a boy, as we shall see) wearing the red, white, and blue Republican cockade (fig.

Fig. 3. Clément, after Boizot, *La France Républicaine*. *Ouvrant son Sein à tous les Français*. Musée Carnavalet, Paris. Photo Édimédia.

Fig. 4. Anonymous, *Republican Mother and Child* (cc. 1793); Bibliothèque Nationale, Paris. Photo Bibliotèque Nationale

4). As it happens, the cockade that tags maternal nursing with patriotic and nationalist significance came to hold particular meaning for women during 1793, when a contest about the extent to which they might occupy roles other than that of Republican nurse was played out with the cockade as its symbolic stake. This struggle over women's participation in the public political arena came to a head during summer and autumn of 1793 and ended in the dissolution of the Society of Revolutionary Republican Women in October after a series of public disturbances focused on the wearing of the Republican cockade by women, altercations that have come to be known as the "war of the cockades."[30]

The Society of Revolutionary Republican Women defined themselves from the start in terms of their refusal to remain in "the confined sphere of their households."[31] The subsequent exclusion of women from politics has usually been read as the inevitable product of constructing Revolutionary gender ideology on the basis of Rousseauian theory—most recently, for instance, by Joan Landes, who argues that the bourgeois redefinition of the public sphere as essentially masculine led to women's relegation to the home, in contrast to their relative political influence under the ancien régime.[32] But one could also see the confinement of women to their domestic and nurturing function as a punitive response to Revolutionary violence—violence that became associated with the body of the woman, onto which all the turbulence of Revolution could be conveniently projected and then disciplined.[33] In this Revolutionary backlash against women, a sexual order equated with gender hierarchy was substituted for a generalized disorder laid at the mother's door. Two motifs stand out in the campaign against Revolutionary women's groups, which led to the dissolution of the Society of Revolutionary Republican Women: first, the tendency to view women's political participation as inherently dangerous; second, the tendency to locate the threat of disorder generally posed by the Revolution in the confrontation between warring groups of women. In contemporary documents recording the debates about women's participation in Revolutionary politics, the specter of women's association with public disorder goes hand in hand with the fear that the Revolutionary Republican Women were disordering stable distinctions between the sexes.

The Society of Revolutionary Republican Women became an embarrassment for the Montagnards (whose May 1793 coup against the Girondins they initially supported) when they pressed for implementation of a radical Jacobin program of political terror and strict economic controls on the price of necessities (as always, liable to become a women's issue during the Revolutionary period).[34] This legislation, which they successfully pushed through in September 1793, included the particularly troublesome decree of September 21, which involved the compulsory wearing of the Republican cockade by all women and brought the Revolutionary Republican Women into open conflict with the market women, or women of Les Halles (a symbolic and actual force to be reckoned with, and—not surprisingly—committed to the notion of a free-market economy). The struggles between the Society and the market women over the wearing of the cockade gave credibility to the idea that women were responsible for the public disorder that must often have been close to the surface in the streets of Paris at this time. At a meeting of the Jacobin Society on September 16, a citizen attributed to women "all the disorders which have occurred in Paris."[35] A police report of September 21 called the wearing of the cockade "a new apple of discord which the evildoers have thrown among us; they inspire in women the desire to share the political rights of men."[36] The struggle extended to the wearing of the bonnet rouge, which the Society of Revolutionary Republican Women began to adopt but which some women objected to as "only for men to wear."[37] Cockades were snatched, bonnets thrown in the mud; in one dispute, male bystanders joined in, asserting that "it's only men who should wear bonnets de police [bonnets rouge]." The official police procès-verbal concluded that "this recent habit of women wearing bonnets de police can be regarded as a rallying sign or as an occasion for disorder."[38]

The "war of the cockades" underlines the gap between the feminized allegories of the Revolution and the gender ideology actually being played out within Revolutionary organizations and in the marketplace.[39] In other words, the liberty cap became sexually as well as politically transgressive when it moved from the head of "Marianne," the popular embodiment of Liberty, to the heads of actual militant women in the streets. When Amar, on behalf of the Committee of General Security, reported on efforts to deal with "the consequences of disorders" that had broken out at a meeting of the Society shortly before, his account of the immediate issues (which could be summed up as cross-dressing and public disorder) was overshadowed by a general consideration of women's case for involvement in the political sphere. He ruled decisively against women, claiming that since they are disposed to "an over-excitation which would be deadly in public affairs . . . interests of state would soon be sacrificed to everything which ardor in passions can generate in the way of error and disorder."[40] Chaumette, president of the Paris Commune, responded similarly to a women's deputation wearing bonnets rouges by calling for the uproar to be recorded in the procès-verbal ("It is horrible, it is contrary to all the laws of nature for a woman to want to make herself a man"). In an escalating sequence of rhetorical questions, he demanded: "Since when is it permitted to give up one's sex? . . . Is it to men that nature confided domestic cares? *Has she given us breasts to breast-feed our children?*"[41] The threat to public order is swiftly redefined as a breakdown of sexual roles; Chaumette's hysterical demand reveals what is at stake for him when women wear the cockade or *bonnet rouge*: the unmanning of Revolutionary men. If bare-breasted Liberty erupts into marketplace or commune, conversely, men may have to stay home and play the nurse.

The great festivals of the Revolution attempt to channel the spectacle of public disorder into public displays of a different kind. Rational exercises in instant history and mass pedagogy, the official festivals were designed to install the participants in a specular, imaginary relation to the symbolic authority of the Republic; this aim necessarily included the symbolic ordering of gender roles, which, as we can see from the reactions of Amar and Chaumette, were never far from the surface. David's carefully orchestrated Festival of August 10, 1793, the Festival of the Unity and Indivisibility of the Republic, made the image of maternal nature its point of origin by erecting the Fountain of Regeneration on the site of the Bastille (we might note in passing the irony that an opera house was the modern bicentennial tribute to popular and national public spectacle). The festival's other "stations" included a monumental figure of Hercules representing the people crushing federalism, a reference to the unsuccessful Girondin revolt in the summer of 1793. Lynn Hunt has argued that the edging out of Liberty, or "Marianne," by this decisively masculine figure of popular strength during the latter part of 1793 was in part a response to the threat of women's increasing political participation.[42] The commemorative coin struck for the "festival of the Unity and Indivisibility of the Republic" (fig. 5) depicts the first station, where the president of the Convention, followed by the representatives, drank the regenerative waters springing from the breasts of an Egyptian deity representing Nature (seen also in closeup, in an anonymous contemporary engraving) (fig. 6). As one bemused onlooker complained, with a touch of xenophobic chauvinism, "I would like to know why her hair was dressed in that way. We are French, and under the pretext that we have been corrupted in our morals and in our monuments, they want to turn us into Egyptians, Greeks, Etruscans."[43] The president's gesture was accompanied by a speech explaining how nature had made all men free and equal (presumably in their access to the breast), and the fountain bore the inscription "Nous sommes tous ses enfants."[44] But where, one might

Fig. 5. Medal:
*Régéneration française.
10 août 1793.*
Bibliothèque
Nationale, Paris.
Photos Bibliothèque
Nationale.

Fig. 6. Anonymous, *Fontaine
de la Régéneration elevée sur les
Ruine de la Bastille.* [sic]
Bibliothèque Nationale,
Paris. Photos Bibliothèque
Nationale.

220

Fig. 7. Helman, after Monnet, *La Fantaine de la Régéneration*.Bibliothèque Nationale, Paris. Photo Tristant.

Fig. 8. H.-F. Gravelot and C.-N. Cochin, *Charité, Iconologie par figures, ou Traité complet des Allégories, Emblèmes, etc. A L'Usage des Artistes,* 4 vols. (Paris, Lattré, n.d. [1791]), i. 55: "Amour du prochain, vertu bienfaisante qui seule comprend toutes les autres. On la représent sous la figure d'une femme offrant le sein à un enfant, & tenant dans sa main un coeur enflammé. Près de la Charité sont plusieurs autres enfans auxquels elle donne ses soins . . . ." Éditions Minkoff, 1972.

ask, were women positioned (interpellated, in Althuserian terms) in David's elaborately staged tableau of revolutionary ideology?

As the president of the Convention explained to the people when they halted in front of the Hercules, "that giant is you!"[45] But not all of you. In this carefully scripted and choreographed festival, only men drank from the Fountain of Regeneration; the role of the Republican mother was to offer (or to be—to symbolize) the breast. Prominently displayed in the center foreground of Monnet's engraving of the scene is a Republican mother breast-feeding her infant; with her free hand she points to the representatives drinking from the fountain (fig. 7). The meaning of the station (the meaning we, too, as onlookers, are supposed to swallow) lies in that deflection of the gaze from the exemplary Republican mother to the allegory into which she is subsumed—not that of an all-providing Nature, but rather the visually dominant, ideologically charged, abstract image of the State as Mother Republic.[46] Behind the figure of the breast-feeding mother we glimpse the great, failed, Enlightenment project of the French Revolution, the proposed abolition of the poor altogether by way of a system of legislated poor relief, which would have done away with the *enfant trouvé* and the wet-nurse alike.[47] If one iconographic source for Revolutionary images of the Republic as breast-feeding mother is the figure of Nature the Many-breasted, the other is the allegorical figure of the wet-nurse or nursing mother who traditionally represents *Charité*, as she does, for instance, in Gravelot's and Cochin's sourcebook for revolutionary iconography, *Iconologie par Figures* (1791) (fig. 8).[48] Subsumed into an all-encompassing program, state-regulated "Charity" becomes synonymous with the state apparatus that replaces an absolute monarchy. From this angle, Louis XIV's motto, "L'Etat, c'est moi" is the hidden subtext of the motto inscribed on the Fountain of Regeneration ("Nous sommes tous ses enfants").

It could be argued that one motive for official attempts to identify the Republic with an all-nurturing mother was to mystify social relations and mask contemporary political and economic disarray; both Republican unity and basic food supplies were matters of intense political anxiety for the Montagnards during the summer of 1793. But I want instead to consider the very notion of "unity and indivisibility" as it bears both on production (market production, for instance—the matter of supplies) and reproduction (the reproduction of signs and children).[49] For both Rousseau and Le Rebours, maternal breast-feeding supposedly creates a family unit immune to corruption; in Rousseau's imaginary pastoral economy, a pure equivalence of production can be maintained (good diet plus good morals equals good milk), while for Le Rebours, the mother who nurses her own child protects the family from the taint of bastard blood. As the symbol of a closed circulatory system (a system which keeps the transfer of bodily fluids and property within the family), the breast-feeding mother preserves not only the legitimate blood line, but also, more generally, a fantasy of incorruptible signs—of meanings "unified and indivisible"; the meanings that David's elaborate interpretive devices and commentaries sought, prophylactically, to guard against corruption.[50] The Fountain of Regeneration can be read as allegorizing not only the unity of the centralized Jacobin state, but the power of the state to control meanings themselves during the time of state-regulated suspicion and legalized terror that has come to be associated with Robespierre's regime. Not for nothing did Madame Roland nickname Robespierre "the Incorruptible"; what David claimed, on Robespierre's behalf, was nothing short of control over the production of an incorruptible sign-system. David's festival thus attempts to "restore"—to purge—the symbolic system. The breast-feeding mother figures the purification of Liberty's signs. (Swallow that one.)

David's phantasy of a revolution in signs takes us back to the very basis of wish fulfillment as Freud describes it in *The Interpretation of Dreams*, where his example of its infantile origins are the perceptions of the hungry baby. Freud emphasizes not so much the wish as the imaginary nature of its fulfillment. When the hungry baby screams, he explains in a complicated passage, only the "experience of satisfaction" can effect a change; but this experience of satisfaction has as a central component a perception, or mnemic image, associated with the original experience. The re-evoking of the perception amounts to a wish, and the hallucinated reappearance of the perception corresponds to—even brings about—its fulfillment. "Nothing," Freud writes in a startlingly radical speculation, "prevents us from assuming that there was a primitive state of the psychical apparatus in which this path was actually traversed, that is, in which wishing ended in hallucinating" (*SE* 5.567, 565–66). The baby's wish, then, may lead to the hallucination of a satisfaction that involves not milk, but an image of the breast that we might call the "symbolic" breast.[51] The distinction here (between breast as signifier and milk as signified) repeats, on another level, the crucial distinction to which I alluded at the outset between the representations of the Revolution and the material conditions or social practices of the time. What Freud calls "perceptual identity"—the hallucinated oneness and indivisibility of what is seen (the breast as signifier) and the experience of satisfaction (the appeasement of hunger signified by the breast, or rather, by breast milk)—approximates to the wish embodied in David's festival; that is, the wish that the Revolution might be effected on the level of signs. Representations of Revolution, in David's book, amount to the hallucination of material transformation, or at any rate, are guarenteed to bring with them their own satisfaction.

The same hallucination attends any reading of history that treats its discourses and representations as a merely mystified or displaced expression of (for instance) institutionalized wet-nursing or actual hunger—treats them as ultimately referential (as distinct from material in their effects, as such discourses and representations on some level certainly were). If psychoanalysis and social history neither signify nor explain each other, a psychoanalytic reading of the meaning of breast-feeding during the French Revolution, such as the one I have sketched here, would be one that draws attention to the persistence of *our* wish to take the shortcut from hunger to hallucinating the breast; or from material conditions and social practices to the Revolutionary allegories and symbolic systems propped on them at a crucial remove. Indeed, in the current phase of French Revolutionary studies, the breast-feeding mother may even mark the site of a yet more obstinate and startlingly contrary wish: the wish, not so much that the discourses and representations of the Revolution might be rendered transparent to (rather than permeable by) what we are in the habit of calling "history," but rather that we might be allowed to rest content on the symbolic breast of a hallucinatory or "mnemic" image—on rhetoricity, representations, signs; on the analysis of discourses and symbolic systems as if they were the end of the story, just because they constitute a history in and of themselves. But that is another argument altogether.

*　　*　　*

As a footnote to this history of (among other things) the *enfants trouvés* of the French Revolution, I want to invoke a touching piece of propagandist theater involving none other than Chaumette, as recounted in Michelet's *History of the French Revolution*. When a veteran corporal came before Chaumette in the autumn of 1793, wanting to be reassured that in adopting the orphaned baby daughter of a man who had been executed he was not acting against the national interests,

> Chaumette took the little girl in his arms and sat down next to the corporal. "On the contrary," he replied, "What a splendid example of republican virtue you are giving! . . . this is reason snatching innocence from the jaws of vile prejudice. Citizens, join with this

noble old warrior! By your embraces, show this child that she who is an orphan in law is herewith adopted by the Nation."[52]

As a result of this session, Michelet goes on, "the Convention founded an asylum for the 'Children of the Nation,' as the offspring of the condemned were called." As Rousseau himself had fantasized, the Rousseauian Revolution sought to wipe out inherited guilt by substituting a new parent, the Republic, who played the part of both mother and father. In this instant allegory of innocence rescued from vile prejudice by Republican reason, every parentless infant became the Child of the Nation; every orphan, however aristocratic or politically suspect its parents, could be rehabilitated by popular adoption. Autumn 1793 was also the moment that saw the adoption of the new Republican calendar, with its symbolic attempt to wipe out the inscriptions of pre-Revolutionary history. The same utopian narrative of fresh beginnings underpins both the image of the breast-feeding mother whose apotheosis is David's Fountain of Regeneration and the inverted family romance of popular origins which haunts Rousseau's apology for abandoning his children to the *Enfants trouvés*. In the Revolutionary imaginary, the Revolutionary subject— the masculine subject of the French Revolution—finds himself in the bosom of the state, just as he finds inscribed in his own bosom the psychic structures that bind the Freudian unconscious to the emerging bourgeois family; the motto borne by every cockade-bearing man is not *"L'état, c'est moi"* but some variant on it that might be glossed as "I am in-stated." For the Revolutionary woman, by contrast, given a political agenda involving compulsory maternal nurture, the motto may read a little differently: *"Le tit, c'est moi"*—a phrase it seems scarcely necessary to translate.

1. *Adresse des citoyens de Clermont Ferrand à l'Assemblée Législative*, December 7, 1791; quoted in Marc de Villiers, *Histoire des Clubs de femmes et des Légions d'Amazones 1793–1848–1871* (Paris: Plon-Nourrit et Cie, 1910), 97; see also Pierre Trahard, *La Sensibilité Révolutionaire (1789–1794)* (Paris: Boivin & Cie.,1936), 201–202. For other patriotic uses of milk, see also Olwen Hufton, "Women in Revolution 1789–1796," *Past and Present* 53 (1971), 100.

2. See George D. Sussman, *Selling Mother's Milk: The Wet-Nursing Business in France 1715–1914* (Urbana: University of Illinois Press, 1982), 22, for an eloquent breakdown of the figures: "of approximately 20,000 babies born each year in Paris at the end of the Ancien Régime, nearly one-half were placed in the country with rural wet-nurses procured through the Bureau of Wet Nurses, 20 to 25 percent from the wealthiest classes were placed directly by their parents with more highly paid wet nurses closer to Paris, 20 to 25 percent were abandoned with the

foundling administration to die early or be nursed far from Paris by a poorly paid woman, and a small remainder (a few thousand at most) were nursed in their own homes either by their mothers or by live-in wet nurses." Compare Sussman, *Selling Mother's Milk*, 110–11 for the changing trend; by Year X of the Revolution (1801–1802), about half of all Parisian babies were nursed by their own mothers, although the persistence of a state-regulated wet-nursing business right through the nineteenth century makes this the most tenacious of the institutions associated with the ancien régime.

3. See Sussman, *Selling Mother's Milk*, 19–35, for a brief history of wet-nursing and the Enlightenment. For a specimen history of maternal breast-feeding, Mme. Roland's nursing of her baby daughter, see Sussman, 79–86. Valerie Fildes, *Wet Nursing: A History from Antiquity to the Present* (Oxford: Blackwell, 1988), 111–26, also briefly surveys eighteenth-century theory and practice in England and France.

4. See the discussion of "propping," with reference to the infantile origins of sexuality, in Jean Laplanche, *Life and Death in Psychoanalysis*, trans. Jeffrey Mehlman (Baltimore: Johns Hopkins University Press, 1976), 15–18. Laplanche returns to the subject in *New Foundations for Psychoanalysis*, trans. David Macey (Oxford: Blackwell, 1989), 77–78.

5. For this argument, and for an anti-psychoanalytic critique of Freud's concept of the family for his assumption that the "bourgeois" family is an ahistorical norm, see Mark Poster, *Critical Theory of the Family* (New York: Seabury Press, 1978), 1–41, 166–205.

6. I am grateful to Adela Pinch for drawing my attention to this engraving, reproduced here from Fanny Faÿ-Sallois, *Les Nourrices à Paris au XIXᵉ Siècle* (Paris: Payot, 1980), facing 136.

7. See Sussman, *Selling Mother's Milk*, 30; the charity aided nearly 500 Lyonnais mothers beteween 1785 and 1786. In the background of the Voysard engraving is the prison where, in the popular imagination, the many parents who could not afford to pay the rural wet-nurses to whom they had entrusted their babies were imprisoned for debt. In 1791, when the National Assembly pardoned all nursing debts, there were found to be only three such prisoners in Paris, but altogether over 5,000 had judgments outstanding against them, 75 percent of which dated from the economic upheavals of the first three years of the Revolution; see Sussman, *Selling Mother's Milk*, 61–62.

8. See Carol Blum, *Rousseau and the Republic of Virtue: The Language of Politics in the French Revolution* (Ithaca: Cornell University Press, 1986), 74–92 for the debate surrounding Rousseau's abandonment of his children and a reading of Rousseau's defense; Blum reproduces the Voysard engraving (*Rousseau and the Republic of Virtue*, 76) in connection with her discussion of Rousseauian virtue and pity.

9. *The Confessions of Jean-Jacques Rousseau*, trans. J. M. Cohen (Harmondsworth: Penguin, 1953), 333. Or, as he put it elsewhere, "Plato wanted all children raised in the Republic; let each one remain unknown to his father and let all be children of the State"; Jean-Jacques Rousseau, *Oeuvres complètes*, ed. Bernard Gagnebin and Marcel Raymond (Paris: Pléiade, 1959), 1.1431; quoted and trans. Carol Blum, *Rousseau and the Republic of Virtue*, 81.

10. See Sussman, *Selling Mother's Milk*, 22, 62–64, as well as Fildes, *Wet Nursing*, 144–58, for a general account of infant abandonment. For the abandonment of legitimate children by the poor, see O. H. Hufton, *The Poor of Eighteenth-Century France 1750–1789* (Oxford: Oxford University Press, 1974), 329–49; Hufton estimates that in the last decade of the ancien régime, 40,000 children each year were abandoned (see Hufton, 318). Although at an earlier period poor

parents often (as Rousseau did with his first child) enclosed some form of identification so that the child might later be reclaimed, the habit was discouraged by the authorities and died out in the immediately pre-Revolutionary decades (see Hufton, 333).

11.   In 1751, apparently a good year, only 68.5 percent of the children admitted to the Paris Foundling Hospital died under the age of one; but in the second half of 1781, 85.7 percent of newborns died before they were a year old. Infant mortality (lowest for infants nursed by their own mothers) meant that whereas 25–40 percent of infants put out to wet-nurses by their parents died, anything from 65–90 percent of abandoned newborns did not survive their first year; see Sussman, *Selling Mother's Milk*, 66–67. The incidence of infant mortality associated with the Foundling Hospital was accentuated by the scarcity of wet-nurses, delays in placement, and the rigors of the journey to wet-nurses in the provinces (babies were often suckled several to each nurse, increasing the likelihood of cross infection); see Sussman, 22.

12.   Jean-Jacques Rousseau, *Emile, or On Education*, trans. Allan Bloom (New York: Basic Books, 1979), 46.

13.   Ibid., 43.

14.   Ibid., 44–45.

15.   Pierre Rousssel, in his *Système Physique et Moral de la Femme* (1777), saw the argument as going the other way; one benefit of wet-nursing, he claims, may be to teach the nursling not to look down on the class to which he owes his nurture; see *Système Physique et Moral de la Femme*, 6th ed. (Paris: Caille et Ravier, 1813), 210. For the social background of the rural wet–nurse, see Sussman, *Selling Mother's Milk*, 50–56; a substantial body of material—both written and pictorial—attests to the sentimental attachment that must often have existed between nursling and nurse.

16.   Rousseau's model in his overseeing of nurse and child is Cato the Censor, a man of rustic origins associated in Roman history with policies of moral, social, and economic reconstruction, who "himself raised his son from the cradle and with such care that he left everything to be present when the nurse—that is to say, the mother—changed and bathed him" (*Emile*, 61, 49 n).

17.   See Sussman, *Selling Mother's Milk*, 37–44, for successive pre-Revolutionary attempts to bring the wet-nursing bureaus under state control, culminating in the King's declaration of July 24, 1769; and see Fay-Sallois, *Les Nourrices à Paris*, 193–239, for the combined privileging and surveillance of the *nourrice-sur-lieu* in the late nineteenth-century bourgeois family, as well as Sussman, *Selling Mothers' Milk*, 153–55.

18.   Rousseau, *Emile*, 57–58. For debates about the merits of city vs. country for the welfare of the nursing infant, see Marie-France Morel, "City and Country in Eighteenth-Century Medical Discussions about Early Childhood," in *Medicine and Society in France: Selections from the Annales*, eds. Robert Foster and Orest Ranum, trans. Elborg Forster and Patricia M. Ranum (Baltimore: Johns Hopkins University Press, 1980), 6: 48–65.

19.   Rousseau, *Emile*, 61.

20.   Ibid., 57. Rousseau's comment occurs in the context of his insistence that the nurse's milk should be new—that is, she should recently have given birth to a child of her own.

21.   Ibid., 48.

22.   Le Rebours, *Avis aux mères qui veulent nourir leurs enfants*, 5th ed. (Paris: Th. Barrois père, 1799), 66–67; my italics. See also Sussman, *Selling Mother's Milk*, 28, 89–90.

23. Le Rebours, *Avis aux mères*, 66. In fact, although a syphilitic nurse might in theory infect her nursling, infection usually travelled the other way—from syphilitic city baby to rural nurse; for syphilis as an occupational disease of wet-nurses, see Fildes, *Wet Nursing*, 238–40.

24. Le Rebours, *Avis aux mères*, 68.

25. See "Below Stairs: The Maid and the Family Romance," in Peter Stallybrass and Allon White, *The Politics and Poetics of Transgression* (Ithaca: Cornell University Press, 1986), 149–70.

26. Le Rebours, *Avis aux mères*, 105.

27. Ibid., 281.

28. See Saint Just, *Oeuvres complètes*, ed. Charles Vellay (Paris: Charpentier and Fasquelle, 1908), 2:516–17; quoted and trans. by Carol Blum, *Rousseau and the Republic of Virtue*, 190. Children were to belong to their mothers until five, and thereafter to the fatherland.

29. Title 1, article 27; see Fay-Sallois, *Les Nourrices à Paris*, [120].

30. I am indebted to the invaluable documentary account of the women of the Revolution provided by *Women in Revolutionary Paris 1789–1795*, ed. Darline Gay Levy, Harriet Branson Applewhite, and Mary Dunham Johnson (Urbana: University of Illinois Press, 1979). For a succinct account of responses to women's activism during the Revolution, see also Harriet B. Applewhite and Darline Gay Levy, "Responses to the Political Activism of the Women of the People in Revolutionary Paris," in *Women and the Structure of Society*, ed. Barbara J. Harris and JoAnn K. McNamara (Durham, NC: Duke University Press, 1984), 215–31. For the history of the Society of Revolutionary Republican women, see Marie Cerati, *Le Club des Citoyennes Républicaines Révolutionaires* (Paris: Éditions Sociales, 1966), Paule-Marie Duhet, *Les Femmes et la Révolution 1789–1794* (Paris: Julliard, 1971), 135–60, and Marc de Villiers, *Histoire des Clubs de femmes*, 223–74.

31. See Levy, Applewhite, and Johnson, *Women in Revolutionary Paris*, 176.

32. See Joan B. Landes, *Women and the Public Sphere in the Age of the French Revolution* (Ithaca: Cornell University Press, 1988). For this particular chapter of the history of women during the Revolution, as well as for Revolutionary motherhood in general, see Landes, *Women and the Public Sphere*, 93–151, especially 139–46; and see also the account given by Blum, *Rousseau and the Republic of Virtue*, 204–15.

33. In contemporary representations of Revolutionary anti-clericism, what Michel Vovelle calls "*la caricature incendiaire*" occupies a special place—caricatures incendiary not only in their politics, but as as a form of pornography that involves disciplining women's bodies. "La Discipline patriotique or le fanatisme corrigé," for instance, represents a sequence of salacious pictures based on an incident during Passion Week 1791, in which the women of les Halles took it on themselves to chastise nuns for their religious fanaticism—a visual encounter or exposé of Revolutionary satire; see Michel Vovelle, *La Révolution Française: Images et Récit 1789–1799* (Paris: Messidor/Diderot, 1986), 2: 268, fig. 4.

34. See Levy, Applewhite, and Johnson, *Women in Revolutionary Paris*, 145–47; the program included legalized terror, the creation of an *armée populaire*, the notorious Law of Suspects, and strict controls on the price of necessities (a woman's issue throughout the Revolutionary period).

35. Ibid., 183.

36. Ibid., 199–200.

37. Ibid., 205–207.

38. Ibid., 207–208.

39. For the feminized allegories of the Revolution and their permutations, see Maurice Agulhon, *Marianne into Battle: Republican Imagery and Symbolism in France, 1789–1880*, trans. Janet Lloyd (Cambridge: Cambridge University Press, 1981), especially 11–37; and Lynn Hunt, *Politics, Culture, and Class in the French Revolution* (Berkeley: University of California Press, 1984), 87–119.

40. Levy, Applewhite, and Johnson, *Women in Revolutionary Paris*, 215–16.

41. Ibid., 219; my italics.

42. See Hunt, *Politics, Culture, and Class in the French Revolution*, 94-117, especially 94–98 for the dominance of Hercules as opposed to Marianne, and his emergence in the context of the festival of August 10, 1793: "The masculinity of Hercules," she argues, "reflected indirectly on the deputies themselves . . . [and] served to distance the deputies from the growing mobilization of women into active politics" (104). For a critique of the same festival, see also Mona Ozouf, *Festivals and the French Revolution*, trans. Alan Sheridan (Cambridge, MA: Harvard University Press, 1988), 154–57.

43. Quoted in Ozouf, *Festivals and the French Revolution*, 314.

44. See Judith Schlanger, "Le Peuple au front gravé," *L'Enjeu et le débat: les Passés Intellectuels* (Paris: Denoel/Gontier, 1979), 160.

45. See Hunt, *Politics, Culture, and Class in the French Revolution*, 107, 104–110, and see also Schlanger, *L'Enjeu et le débat: les Passés Intellectuels*, 155–68, for an account of David's plan to inscribe allegorical ideas in the form of words on the figure of Hercules itself.

46. See Marina Warner, *Monuments and Maidens: The Allegory of the Female Form* (New York: Atheneum, 1985), 281–82, for a suggestive formulation of the ways in which Liberty's exposed breast might mutate into the breast of Tyche, matron and nurturer, as a type of the caregiving state.

47. For the difficulties in implementing this project—chiefly, the numbers of poor involved and the inadequate financial resources for dealing with them, especially once the war began to take its full toll—see Hufton, "Women in Revolution 1789–1796," *Past and Present* 53 (1971): 90–108, especially 97–98. As Hufton points out, women (and, of course, children) were those most directly affected by the economic dislocations of the French Revolution.

48. See Agulhon, *Marianne into Battle*, 11–13.

49. For an interesting account of related issues in connection with representations of Revolution, see Neil Hertz, "Medusa's Head: Male Hysteria under Political Pressure," in *The End of the Line: Essays on Psychoanalysis and the Sublime* (New York: Columbia University Press, 1985), 161–91, especially 173–75; and see also the response by Catherine Gallagher, ibid, 194–96.

50. See Ozouf, *Festivals and the French Revolution*: "Images seem to be so threatened by ambiguity that they need the reassurance of commentary. . . . It was the task of this commentary to provide a fixed translation, capable of restraining the uncontrolled movement of meaning and of limiting severely the room for interpretation" (214).

51. As Laplanche and Pontalis comment apropos of this passage, "How . . . can an infant *feed itself* on wind alone? The Freudian model is incomprehensible unless one understands that it is

not the real object, but the lost object; not the milk, but the breast as a signifier, which is the object of the primal hallucination"; see Jean Laplanche and J.-B. Pontalis, "Fantasy and the Origins of Sexuality," *International Journal of Psycho-analysis* 49 (1968): 15 n. See also Laplanche, *New Foundations for Psychoanalysis*, 77–78: "in the prototypical example, the almost fictive model of suckling, breast and milk do not coincide; there is a displacement from breast to milk. The 'hallucination' does not substitute an imaginary real for the real, or one form of food for another."

52. Jules Michelet, *History of the French Revolution*, trans. Keith Botsford, (Wynnewood, PA: Livingston Publishing Co., 1973), 7: 31.

11

Baring the Breast
Mastectomy and the Surgical Analogy

I have often in my own mind compared cathartic psychotherapy with surgical intervention. I have described my treatments as psychotherapeutic operations; and I have brought out their analogy with the opening up of a cavity filled with pus, the scraping out of a carious region, etc. An analogy of this kind finds its justification not so much in the removal of what is pathological as in the establishment of conditions that are more likely to lead the course of the process in the direction of recovery.

—Sigmund Freud, *Studies on Hysteria*, 1895 (SE 2.305)

MASTECTOMY IS A CRUEL SUBJECT. Psychoanalysis, too, has a cutting edge. In 1895, Freud concluded *Studies on Hysteria* with his vivid, uncomfortable analogy between "cathartic psychotherapy" and surgery. Freud's radical intervention in the emerging field of psychoanalysis during the 1880s is often contrasted with that of his Philadelphia contemporary Weir Mitchell (whose notorious rest cure Freud himself employed alongside the talking cure during the early phase of his work with hysterics).[1] The enforced passivity of the Weir Mitchell rest cure has long since been discredited. But despite his later evolution of concepts such as resistance, transference, and psychical working through, Freud's belief in the curative effects of catharsis remains foundational. Although hypnosis and the laying-on of hands has been replaced by free association and suspended attention, the cathartic treatment that achieved its fullest expression in *Studies on Hysteria* continues to underlie much contemporary psychoanalytic practice.

But in the wake of recent, and especially, post-Kleinian developments, the surgical analogy has lost some of its edge. Where Freud stressed transference as an analytic tool as well as a symptomatic neurosis, contemporary object-relations is as likely to emphasize the uses of counter-transference (rather than, or as well as, its abuses). The talking cure has become the listening profession, the surgeon a radio receiver—sometimes a radio transmitter too. In "Recommendations to Physicians Practising Psycho-Analysis" (1912), Freud had advised analysts to arm themselves with surgical detatchment:

> I cannot advise my colleagues too urgently to model themselves during psycho-analytic treatment on the surgeon, who puts aside all his feelings, even his human sympathy, and concentrates his mental forces on the single aim of performing the operation as skilfully as possible. . . . The justification for requiring this emotional coldness in the analyst is that it creates the most advantageous conditions for both parties: for the doctor a desirable protection for his emotional life and for the patient the largest amount of help that we can give him to-day. (SE 12. 115)

(Interestingly, Freud regards the analyst's own emotional life as in need of protection). But in the same essay, using a strikingly contemporary analogy drawn from communications technology, Freud goes on to compare the unconscious of the analyst to a telephone receiver, turned "like a receptive organ towards the transmitting unconscious of the patient" (SE 12.115). Sensitively attuned to the transmitting unconscious, the post-Freudian analyst is all ears.

The purgative effects of pity and fear have well-known literary antecedents; Freud was writing in the wake of influential nineteenth-century theories of tragedy. Why then the specifically surgical analogy? (Why not, for instance, a dramatic one?) The answer may lie in the medical context from which modern psychoanalysis emerged. Freud's allusion to "the removal of what is pathological" depends on another late-nineteenth-century development that was foundational to the history of medicine: the development of surgery itself. In France and Germany, surgery achieved its apotheosis during the period that also gave rise to Freudian psychoanalysis. The growing understanding of asepsis during the 1880s transformed surgical intervention from a life-threatening trauma to the art of saving lives; it became at once the most refined and the most sophisticated branch of medicine available to the ambitious medical practitioner.[2] Significantly, surgery was also the branch of medicine to which Freud most frequently compared psychoanalysis, insisting on the need for equally rigorous training even as he tried to wrest it from the grip of the medical profession.[3] When Freud wrote in 1923 that "Analytic technique has attained a certainty and delicacy rivalling that of surgery" (*SE* 18.249), he was claiming for his own more recently established discipline the status accorded to the most prestigious medical specialty of his formative years.

The history of mastectomy is as gender- and period-specific as the invention of the talking cure. In its modern form, it entered medical practice at exactly the same moment, during the late 1880s and early 1890s. Surgical intervention only came to offer a real prospect of cure for breast cancer when wholesale excision— the so-called radical mastectomy—emerged (so to speak) at the cutting edge of treatment for malignant breast tumors. At the forefront in surgical innovation, German doctors pioneered the operation for breast cancer, which remained standard in America for the next seventy-five years. In the annals of breast cancer, the "radical" mastectomy figures as the life-saving art of preservation through drastic cutting. Only in the last few decades has this "radical" (and radically disfiguring) operation given way, not just to the "modified radical" but to more conservative (i.e., preservative) surgical approaches. The surgeon no longer makes a lightning decision on the operating table over the unconscious, anaestheticized body of a woman (the dreaded "one-step" procedure); instead, modern breast-cancer patients, in America at least, have the legal right to demand consultation and the two-step procedure (biopsy followed later by mastectomy) before going under the knife.[4]

The competing and complementary models of surgery and receptivity—in tension with each other, yet inseparably knotted together in the history of psychoanalytic theory and practice—continue to inform the modern talking cure. A pathology to be excised with the clinical detachment of the trained practitioner? Or a communications system, attuned to the unconscious, two-way transmissions of the analytic wave-band? To consider mastectomy as a metaphor for psychoanalysis would be to ignore its painful materiality and its pressing immediacy for women themselves. Instead, I want to explore the representation of mastectomy for what it can tell us about the knot of psychic life—and about representation too. Viewed apart from other subjectivities, psychic life tends to emphasize pathology; the subject's personal history is purged in isolation. But viewed as a process that involves the subject's earliest relations to its objects, psychic life invites the metaphor of repair work—the work of restoring missing connections in the wake of an early psychic catastrophe (one that typically involves the mother). In the last resort, it may be the inextricability of aggressivity and reparation, cutting and linking, that is at stake not only in the discourse of psychoanalysis, but in critical inquiry too. Acts of analytic investigation involve probing as well as untying—both cutting and suturing. In the representation of mastectomy, one might say that pathology arises at the point where the surgical analogy colludes with surgical heroism (i.e., the infliction of unspeakably painful or disfiguring treatments in the interests or hope of cure); where sadism is disavowed, along with pain. My example of this collusion will be Thomas Eakins's painting of a mastectomy operation, *The Agnew Clinic* (1889)— a painting which centers less on the fate of the woman patient than on that of the aging surgeon.[5] Looked at in this light, the "subject" of mastectomy is not the unconscious woman on the operating table, but the gladiatorial doctor (and perhaps the artist) who assumes her unconscious *agon*.

By contrast, contemporary poetry by breast cancer sufferers and survivors reflects the common cultural assumption that articulating pain and loss brings relief and healing to the subject. In mastectomy poetry, baring the breast—giving voice to the unconscious, or expressing undischarged emotions—has uncontested therapeutic value. Writing makes you better (so the unstated message goes); survivor discourse is supposed to be a form of therapy, and not only for the survivor. In the case of mastectomy, Freud's surgical analogy is dramatically literalized. But rather than surgical heroism or its obverse, surgical heroinism (the endurance of unspeakably painful or extreme treatments in the hope of cure), women's writing in the wake of breast surgery tends to be characterized by mourning, anger, and protest. In the interior world of the breast cancer survivor, the surgeon is the sadist whose cut has grotesquely disfiguring consequences for the patient. But the subject of postmastectomy poetry is not simply the cancer survivor, not simply her mutilation; it includes the entire range of her objects and attachments—her breast, her mother, *the* breast, along with the fantasies of attack and fullness that tend to accompany breast-thinking. These are at once the object-relations in and by which the mastectomy survivor is constituted, and the lost part (or part object) with which she seeks renewed connection. Ostensibly, the enabling figure in postmastectomy poetry may be baring the breast—giving voice to loss (whether loss of wholeness or self-loss). But its psychic landscape is shaped by tenacious attachment to, and mourning for, a past symbolized both by the absent breast and by the maternal body. Standing in for the missing breast, mastectomy poetry tries to shape a space in which to contain, not only sadistic attack, but a repaired relation to this past. The therapy offered by mastectomy poetry is less what it shares than what it holds.

i. "Minerva Medica"

"O, stately Mistress of our sacred Art,
  Changeless and beautiful, and wise and brave . . ."
  —Dr. S. Weir Mitchell, "Minerva Medica"[6]

Fig. 1a. Thomas Eakins, *The Agnew Clinic* (1889).
Courtesy of the University of Pennsylvania School of Medicine.

Eakins's representation of Agnew entails the simultaneous denial of the patient's pain and the subliming of the surgeon-hero. *The Agnew Clinic* (fig. 1a) depicts the final stages of a mastectomy operation. The only breast we can actually see is the unmutilated one that lolls softly on the chest of a woman from whose other breast, hidden from view, a tumor has just been surgically excised. This missing breast has been probed in ways we are not allowed to glimpse, although the assisting surgeon's busy hands, suturing the wound, invite us to guess. The dissociated pain in the picture (for, like Mrs. Gradgrind's, it must be somewhere in the room) lies out of sight, but not out of mind. In some sense, it lies in the imagined removal of the mammary curve that Eakins renders with such loving realism in the surviving breast. This is a wound not so much to the unconscious woman patient as to the vision (and perhaps the unconscious too) of the onlookers who register her disfigurement: the team of medical attendants, the audience of medical students; even viewers of the picture, positioned as we are beneath and in front of this huge canvas—at the precise intersection of the imaginary lines extending downward from Agnew's scalpel, on one hand, and on the other, the diagonal rail that directs our eyes like a pointer to the hidden site of the operation.

A curve and a cut: these are the visual inscriptions or codes that dominate the design of Eakins's picture, with the ellipse of the operating-theater rail to the left (repeated in the curve of the seat beyond) and the single, pronounced diagonal of the raked amphitheater to the right. The curved rail embraces not only the cluster of medical attendants around the patient, but the luminous figure of Agnew himself at its apex. Eakins's elliptical design cordons off the highlighted surgical arena from the circle of student spectators, establishing a visual asepsis that accentuates the separation between the white-gowned medical attendants and the dark-suited audience. But the design also represents a startling visual pun—a displacement that repeats another, less visible displacement in Eakins's picture: that of the mastectomy operation itself. Inserted bodily into the ellipse, Agnew stands with his scalpel in his unbloodied left hand; he was ambidextrous as a result of a boyhood accident and retained a special fondness for using his left hand, as Eakins had observed while attending his clinics.[7] Agnew's hagiographic biographer and son-in-law, J. Howe Adams (occupying the exact center of the picture, above and to the left of the anaesthetist), records that Agnew himself insisted on Eakins's removing the blood from his hands—a cleanup that seems to have had as much to do with propriety as asepsis. As Adams writes: "The criticism is made that surgeons grow brutal, but here was a surgeon, who had been accustomed to working in blood for fifty years, who had not had his sense of propriety blunted in the least" (a sense of propriety as acute and delicate as his scalpel, presumably).[8] Now look at the right hand of the assisting surgeon, busy with the wound (fig. 1b). The bloody instrument stands in relation to the incision just as the aseptic figure of Agnew stands in relation to the elliptical space of the operating ring, and at precisely the same angle. White-

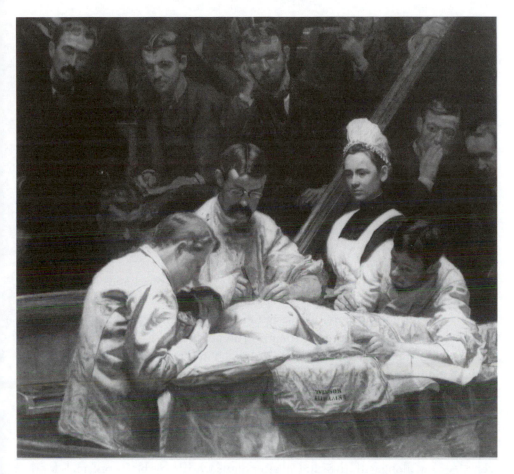

Fig. 1b. Thomas Eakins, *The Agnew Clinic* (1889), detail.
Courtesy of the University of Pennsylvania School of Medicine.

clad, white-haired, upright, Agnew is a figure, not just for the saving art of surgery, but for the surgical instrument he holds in one hand as he gestures with the other—at once surgeon and teacher, as Adams faithfully records ("By long training he was able to lecture on the case and operate at the same time").[9] Whether the scalpel is a metonymy for the surgeon, or the surgeon a figure for the scalpel, Agnew, for all his luminous apartness, is in it up to his knees.

In *The Agnew Clinic*, doctor's orders wiped the blood from the surgeon's hands and scalpel, "despite the artist's protests for fidelity to nature" (Adams again).[10] There was to be no offensive repetition of the bloody hand in *The Gross Clinic*

(1875), Eakins's portrait of Agnew's great surgical predecessor, Samuel Gross.[11] The removal of blood reveals, for Adams, one of Agnew's so-called "peculiarities"—namely, his "sense of propriety." Perhaps blood, especially female blood, is always improper. Be that as it may, Agnew was evidently only able to authorize the spectacle of himself at work on a woman's body if his scalpel was clean. Something had to be erased—whether that something was the impropriety of female blood, or the problem of mutilation which one modern observer of the surgical scene has adduced to explain the male doctor's defensive lack of empathy for his mastectomy patient. As Oliver Cope writes, "The only adequate explanation for his lack of feeling is that the problem of mutilation is too much for him to manage. Only when mutilation is put to him in terms of an analogy—the loss of masculinity— does he react to it."[12] In *The Agnew Clinic*, Eakins portrays the management of mutilation (understood as fears about loss of masculinity) in the guise of modern patient management. The absence of blood on the surgeon's hands is paired with his patient's lack of consciousness. The approximate center of *The Agnew Clinic* foregrounds another intent figure whose presence had become inseparable from the late-nineteenth-century surgical theater: the anaesthetist, whose ministrations make possible the practice of modern surgery. Thanks to him, Agnew's noble, pedagogical, humane calm—"his wonderful tranquility of mind and confidence while operating"[13]—could banish the spectacle of unallieviated female suffering. This calm face (not the patient's, but the doctor's) that turns the other cheek to suffering is the painting's displaced focus. If there is a pain in the room at all, it is registered in *The Agnew Clinic* by the serene medical overview that orders and transcends the scene. Agnew, along with the surgical attendants who do his busywork, feels for the patient—but at a sublimely Olympian remove.

The dispersal of pained consciousness takes a specific form in Eakins's picture, that of a repeated figure of attentive looking—displaced, however, from Agnew himself to his colleagues: the intent, downward, bespectacled look of the surgeon at work on the wound; the nurse's steady and unflinching watchfulness; the rapt concentration of the anaesthetist as he administers the ether cone. Overarching their concentrated acts of attention is Agnew's abstracted and unseeing gaze as he stands apart from his handiwork to pronounce on its meaning. Behind all these bearers of the look (the look that manages and diffuses pain under the sign of humane medical practice) the all-male surgery class whom Agnew called "the boys" sit, lounge, or lean, with varying degrees and poses of absorbed attention and inattention.[14] Among them the artist included himself, painted by his artist wife (Susan

Macdowell Eakins), marginally but still discernably present on the extreme left-hand edge of the canvas. As the impressario of this theater of medically managed pain, Agnew—the artist's surrogate in a picture necessarily pervaded by the analogy between surgeon and painter—is a teacher of souls as well as a healer of bodies. His teaching allows us to view the art of cutting as the art of healing, while compelling identification with the surgeon's sublime patience. But in this scenario, the body of a woman provides the necessary ground for both surgery and painting. Playing the part the female nude has always played in classical painting, she is the blank page or canvas on which Agnew and Eakins inscribe their meaning.[15] If Agnew's aesthetic morality required the excision of feminine consciousness along with the expunging of blood, Eakins's art seems to demand as its necessary sacrifice the sculptured immobilization of a young (and apparently beautiful) woman. Laid out on the operating couch, not so much naked as classically draped, the female patient is at once the focus of medical attention and the object of the most profound avoidance. With Agnew himself, we look away into a distance where the question of her survival is diminished by the long perspective of medical progress.

Paradoxically, however, it was for the unconscious patient's benefit that the entire spectacle was mounted. The unacknowledged scandal of *The Agnew Clinic* is that Agnew regarded operations for breast cancer as likely to shorten rather than prolong life, and as having little or no impact on the chances of recurrence. The mastectomy operation with which Eakins chose to honor Agnew's retirement turns out to be a medical charade. As so often in the history of medicine, caring for the patient means knowing better than she knows. Agnew's humane art, in other words, involved a lie—at best, a killing kindness.[16] According to William Halsted, "Hayes Agnew stated in a lecture a very short time before his death that he operated on breast cancers solely for the moral effect on the patients, that he believed the operation shortened rather than prolonged life."[17] Since the patient herself is unconscious, it must be the onlookers who register the effect of an operation that may well be hastening the death of the very woman it is supposed to save. Victim of the medical wisdom from which she is herself debarred, the woman patient becomes a site for its production. As the inverted lettering on the surgical sheet reminds us, this is a "UNIVERSITY HOSPITAL."[18] Looked at this way, Agnew's heroism was to insist that humanity came before truth; his teaching showed medical students how to master the art of moral effects. At least one modern doctor is on record as responding, in answer to the breast cancer sufferer's question "Why did you lie to me?" with the excuse: "I didn't want to hurt you."[19] In this substitutition, pity masks a too-dangerous identification (and feminine to-be-hurtness, a covertly sadistic fantasy). The analogous moral effect of *The Agnew Clinic* is to subsume its viewers into the pained overview signalled by Agnew's upright stance, his didactic gesture, and the sobriety of his tranquil facial expression—his double consciousness that there is more to be known and seen than either we or the patient can bear to know and see. This double consciousness is the burden Agnew bears so heroically and so alone. But it is also what shields him from the threat embodied by his unconscious patient. His oversight is a kind of blindness, or scotomization, that protects him from the threat of mutilation.

Perhaps that is why the nurse, Mary Clymer (the first in her class, as we know her to have been) appears strikingly impassive in the face of the female wound which she—unlike Agnew—confronts directly in her line of vision. As the only woman in the picture besides the patient, Nurse Clymer provides an important clue to the gender-relations that structure its production. Her job is to be calm, obedient, and at hand—but not to let herself know (let alone know better). Nurse Clymer wrote in her diary, "Never be curious. Be watchful but not officious."[20] She is the incurious onlooker, her watchfulness subordinated to the superior knowledge of her medical overseers. Eakins interposes her presence between the patient's nudity and the all-male surgical team as the obstacle that precludes a sexual relation between them, while at the same time ensuring that the bonds between medical men are cemented by their exclusive knowledge.[21] In this scene of aestheticized labor, the masculine appropriative look has been deflected and sublimated as the art of surgery or painting represented, respectively, by Agnew and Eakins. Paying tribute to Agnew's surgical skill, Adams wrote: "without a flourish or a sweep, his knife sank with unerring quickness to the exact depth he intended, and as quickly was withdrawn."[22] That Eakins identified with the act of surgery has been argued, fascinatingly and at length, in Michael Fried's study of Eakins, *Realism, Writing, Disfiguration* (1987), which takes both writing and its analogue, anatomical dissection, as the overarching figure for Eakins's troubled realism. Eakins himself—whose father was a writing master—studied and taught anatomy and dissection during the course of his own career. The overdetermined analogies between surgery, sculpture, and writing are concentrated in the inscription carved into the wooden frame of *The Agnew Clinic*: "CHIRURGUS PERITISSIMUS; SCRIPTOR ET DOCTOR CLARISSIMUS; VIR VENERATUS ET CARISSIMUS."[23] Predictably, Fried's psychoanalytic reading of Eakins's art emphasizes the thematics of castration anxiety, or (in figurative terms) "disfiguration." The father is necessarily the central figure in both the oedipal scenario and its paranoic versions; the subject's successful or failed identification with the father within a legible specular structure allows for the production of a unified self (or, conversely, forestalls it).[24] But although Fried argues that writing threatens constantly to undo this specular structure, the threat of mutilation implied by mastectomy hardly earns a mention. Instead, his reading of Eakins takes as its visual point of reference the bloody hand of Samuel Gross in *The Gross Clinic*; Fried's underlying psychoanalytic premise is Eakins's relation to a father not so much *"veneratus et carissimus"* as paranoiacally loved and feared.[25] When it comes to sexual difference, even Fried might be said to avert his eyes. Nurse Clymer not only clinches the sexual division of labor in the medical arena; she also reaffirms the power of the masculine surgeon-artist (and even the psychoanalytic art historian) to be the arbiter of a meaning which consigns her to the margins.

The Agnew Clinic can be read as a willed refusal of, or deliberate blindness to, sexual difference. To identify with the feminine position risks the collapse of the exclusively masculine and oedipal identification on which Eakins predicates his portrait of Agnew. Appropriately, it was received on behalf of the University of Pennsylvania Medical School by none other than Weir Mitchell. Treating feminine "neurasthenia" with total rest, immobilization, and seclusion, the Weir Mitchell rest cure replicated an extreme version of nineteenth-century middle-class domestic ideology, particularly prohibiting a woman's use of her hands (significantly, both the patient's and Nurse Clymer's hands are hidden).[26] Agnew, too, "believed that the ideal place for women was at home." Although "not opposed to the higher education of women," he did oppose their admission to surgery classes alongside men, and his biographer records his "deep, insurmountable mistrust in the ability to train the special talents of woman into the attributes of the really successful *practising* physician."[27] But tempting as it is to read both the etherized patient and Nurse Clymer's professional impassivity as refractions of a conservative gender ideology, the medical literature of the time suggests another, more pathological reading. In an article published in the *Medical Record* in 1894, Willy Meyer proposed "An Improved Method of the Radical Operation for Carcinoma of the Breast." He closes what is one of the 1890s' two ground-breaking reports on mastectomy (the other is Halsted's) with the hope that "this terrible foe of suffering mankind, this dread especially of the female sex, [will] become oftner silenced and made more submissive to the surgeon's knife."[28] In Meyer's fantasized construction, the silencing and submission of the female body before the surgeon's knife in Eakins's painting becomes an allegory of the defeat of breast cancer. In this allegory, the surgeon (or his scalpel) stands in for the art of surgery, while the woman (or her breast) stands in for the "terrible foe of suffering mankind," cancer itself. Cancer—synonymous with the disease of femininity—becomes the recalcitrant enemy against which the crusading surgeon-soldier does battle. The dread of cancer is embodied as the dread of woman.

In the aftermath of his painting, Eakins lamented: "They call me a butcher, and all I was trying to do was to picture the soul of a great surgeon." His portrait of a surgeon's soul had failed to obscure the relation between sublimation and violence ("butchery"). Significantly, *The Agnew Clinic* was thought "not cheerful" for ladies to look at, and, to Eakins's chagrin, it was declined for exhibition by the Philadelphia Academy on a technicality.[29] Medical history has also been hard on Agnew. *The Agnew Clinic* turns out to be situated on the cusp of the change in the treatment of breast cancer which was to transform medical practice in the 1890s. A surgeon of the old school, Agnew (in the words of his faithful biographer) was "fearless, yet conservative; not shrinking from any operation . . . but never eager to operate."[30] In particular—as Halsted notes—mastectomy was not an operation that Agnew favored, believing as he did that it shortened rather than prolonged life. In line with the conservative approach of other surgical predecessors (including Samuel Gross), he practiced a modified form of mastectomy that was associated with a high risk of recurrence. His three-volume *The Principles and Practice of Surgery*, published in Philadelphia between 1878 and 1883, devotes considerable space to the prognosis for breast cancer. Agnew takes the traditional medical view that the operation, at best, could do little more than postpone the patient's death for a year or two. Cautiously assessing the evidence of his own cases and those of his predecessors, he writes:

> I should hesitate . . . to claim a single case of absolute cure where the diagnosis of carcinoma had been verified by microscopic examination. The almost uniform history has been death from return of the disease within two or two and a half years. . . . I do not despair of carcinoma being cured somewhere in the future, but this blessed achievement will, I believe, never be wrought by the knife of the surgeon.[31]

Agnew can only look to a deferred future or chemical treatments for the "blessed achievement" of a cancer cure; breast cancer had defeated the surgeon's knife. The history presided over by Agnew ("SCRIPTOR ET DOCTOR CLARISSIMUS") is "the almost uniform history" of death, as Eakins must surely have known.

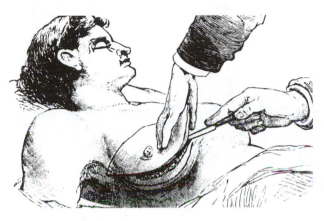

Fig. 2. "Lower incision made and gland being separated from the pectoral muscle," D. Hayes Agnew, *The Principles and Practice of Surgery*, 3 vols. (Philadelphia: J. B. Lippencott & Co., 1878–83).

Agnew's *The Principles and Practice of Surgery* also provides the missing visual subtext to *The Agnew Clinic*. If—as seems likely—Eakins consulted Agnew's surgical textbook, he would have found illustrated in it the view of the patient's breast that is screened from us in *The Agnew Clinic* itself (fig. 2). In Agnew's illustration, the surgeon's knife—indeed, his hand (fingers, according to Agnew, were the best instrument for removing diseased lymph nodes)—is in the wound. But Eakins would certainly have known other surgical illustrations of mastectomy operations besides Agnew's. Early in his own career, he had studied anatomy with Joseph Pancoast at Jefferson Medical College in Philadelphia.[32] Pancoast's 1844 *Treatise on Operative Surgery*, beautifying the patient as a neoclassical torso, displays the wound with graphic precision, along with the surgeon's and his assistant's intrusive hands (fig. 3);[33] Pancoast's detailed instructions for *"The form of cutaneous incision"* include not only the shape, specified as "the elliptic" ("The long axis of the ellipse should be directed from below outwards and upwards towards the armpit"), but the angle and direction of the cut and how to make it ("rapidly and by long sweeps").[34] These instructions would not have been lost on the dissecting sculptor-painter Eakins. The wound itself may be hidden from view in *The Agnew Clinic*, but the medical iconography of mastectomy—the elliptical curve of the cut, the angle of the surgeon's scalpel (or even fingers) in the incision—underpins the entire design of Eakins's picture. Eakins's visual punning on the ellipse of the operating theater

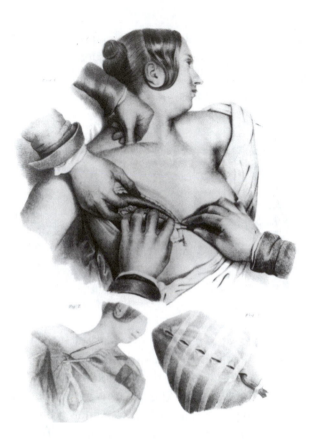

Fig. 3. "Extirpation of the mammary gland," Joseph Pancoast, *Treatise on Operative Surgery* (Philadelphia: Carey and Hart, 1844). The Wellcome Institute Library, London.

and the intersecting angle of the diagonal can be read as inscribing the unseen agon between painting (the specular art) and drawing/writing (inscription) elaborated in Fried's account of his painting; as in *The Gross Clinic*, the association between scalpel and pen threatens to destabilize the specular scenario and fragment the unified self ("the soul of a great surgeon") that is predicated on successful negotiation of the oedipal sublime.

But Fried might have brought his account closer to home. By 1889—the date of Eakins's picture, and the year when Halsted became chief of surgery at Johns Hopkins, the rival institution to the University of Pennsylvania Hospital—Agnew's conservative procedures were already outmoded. Halsted pioneered the surgical methods that he had seen practiced from the mid-1870s onwards by von Volkmann and Heidenhain during the the period of his studies in Germany.[35] The "radical" mastectomy introduced by Halsted from Germany was still being performed at the

Johns Hopkins Hospital as late as the 1960s.[36] His results, achieved between 1889 and 1894, dramatically transformed the statistics for the recurrence of breast cancer.[37] Whereas in the past, Hasted says, "The conscientious physician could not under the circumstances advise his patient to be operated upon . . . we can state positively that cancer of the breast is a curable disease if operated upon properly and in time."[38] The new approach to mastectomy can be seen in the drawings that illustrated both Meyer's and Halsted's operating procedures—the long line of an incision reaching up beyond the armpit; the wholesale carving out of the breast and underlying pectoral muscles; and above all, the absence of the surgeon's intrusive fingers (figs. 4a and b, fig. 5). Both Willy Meyer and William Halsted went on record in the mid-1890s as saying that the handling of the tumor by the surgeon and his assistant's tools was a major cause of the dissemination of cancer cells in and from the site of the wound itself. Their "radical" procedure involved working well beyond the cancer site, in order (in Meyer's words) "*to extirpate the breast, the contents of the axillary and of the sub- and infra-clavicular region, and the pectoral muscles, in one mass.*"[39] This new hands-off approach also coincided with the surgeon's preparedness to overlook what Halsted calls, with chilling understatement, "the disability which might result from removing a little more tissue here and there."[40] Surgeons, he advises, should practice the operation on cadavers; significantly, it is a female cadaver—her face covered, her entire chest scooped out, that we see in Halsted's surgical illustration (fig. 6).

The Agnew Clinic is sometimes adduced to illustrate the modernization of aseptic surgical practice that had taken place since the bloody days of *The Gross Clinic* in the 1870s.[41] But it would be more accurate to see it as the swansong of the kinder, gentler art of surgery embodied by the aging Agnew. In the last resort, Eakins's painting records the passing of a great surgeon who had met his match, not in the female cancer patient but in another allegorical female figure: death. Adams's biography (published in 1892, shortly after Agnew's death) gives a detailed account of the spring 1888 retirement banquet at which Weir Mitchell read a seriocomic poem in honor of Agnew's "jubilee," his fifty years of dedication to surgery; the money raised by this subscription banquet was used to commission Eakins's portrait. The context in which Eakins painted *The Agnew Clinic* suggests that Agnew's impending death, not just his imminent retirement, colored his portrait of the surgeon-hero. Weir Mitchell's jocular doggerel poem in honor of the occasion contains, inset, a poetic biography (an "elegy," almost) entitled "Minerva Medica." Medical wisdom is "the tranquil goddess" who singles out "one shy, grave lad" (Agnew) in

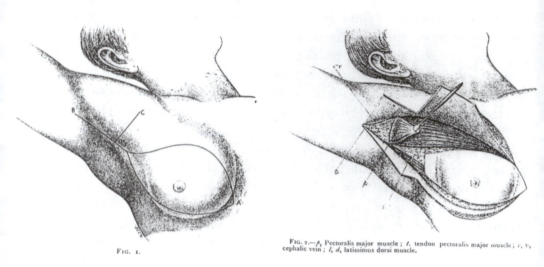

FIG. 1.

FIG. 2.—*A*, Pectoralis major muscle ; *t*, tendon pectoralis major muscle ; *c*, *v*, cephalic vein ; *l*, *d*, latissimus dorsi muscle.

Fig. 4a and b. Willy Meyer, "An Improved Method of the Radical Operation for Carcinoma of the Breast," *Medical Record,* 46 (1894), p. 747, fig. 1, 2.

his youth. "Be mine," she whispers, claiming him with a kiss. Having long ago won, or been claimed by, "the Mistress of our Art," Agnew now celebrates the golden jubilee of their faithful marriage. She still stands by his side, "The gracious woman, strong and tender-eyed . . . . Changeless and beautiful, and wise and brave." This is her valediction:

> For as the sculptor years shall chisel deep
>   The lines of pity 'neath the brow of thought,
> Below your whitening hair the hurt shall read
>   How well you learned what I my best have taught![42]

Eakins's attraction to portraying old age is well documented,[43] and these lines— the lines of poetic inscription and pity—must surely have appealed to the sculptor in him. The suggestion that ill health shadowed the presentation of Eakins's portrait the following year is present in Adams's account; when Agnew staggered after his speech, Adams records, "A thrill of horror ran through the house."[44] Identifying

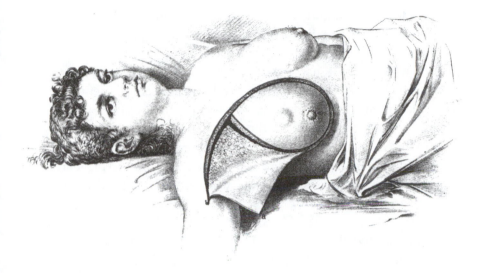

Fig. 5. William S. Halsted, "Operations for the Cure of Cancer of the Breast," *Johns Hopkins Hospital Reports*, 4 (1894), plate X; reprinted in William S. Halstead, *Surgical Papers*, 2 vols (Baltimore: Johns Hopkins Press, 1924). The Wellcome Institute Library, London.

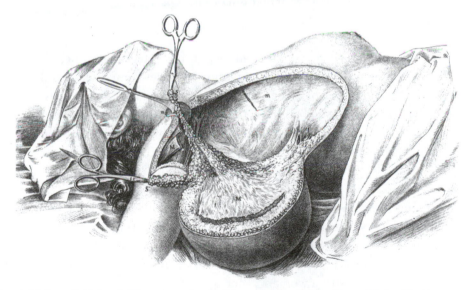

Fig. 6. William S. Halsted, "Operations for the Cure of Cancer of the Breast," *Johns Hopkins Hospital Reports*, 4 (1894), plate XI; reprinted in William S. Halstead, *Surgical Papers*, 2 vols (Baltimore: Johns Hopkins Press, 1924). The Wellcome Institute Library, London.

with Agnew's fictive foreknowledge, his biographer writes of surgery as at once a cruel mistress and an all-wise Providence:

> [Agnew] knew well that surgery is a cruel mistress; he knew that when her servants grow old, their minds less active, and their fingers less nimble, she holds these failings up to the pitiless gaze of all . . . . she is as relentless to the old, tried follower of fifty years as to the newest tyro of to-day. This is one of nature's cruel but necessary provisions. Nothing earthly is as precious as human life; but when the operator grows unfit for his work, an All-wise Providence proclaims it widely.[45]

In other words, not just Agnew but his biographer—and (why not?) his painter, Eakins—knew he was past it. Perhaps this was the knowledge that burdened the abstracted surgeon in the midst of his teaching. It is he, not the anaesthetized patient, whom surgery holds up to "the pitiless gaze of all," immobilized in his posture of forethought.

Adams's biographical account of Agnew's last lecture to the medical school sheds a different light on the the surgical heroism of *The Agnew Clinic*. The operating arena becomes that of the dying gladiator saluting his profession for the last time:

> This modern gladiator, who had fought the better fight for health and happiness, who had wrung many victories from disease and death, as hard fought as that of Hercules for the life of Alcestis, must have felt, as he gazed on those tiers of benches,—so singularly suggestive of the old Roman arena and amphitheatre,—like the gladiators of old, as they gazed on Caesar with the cry on their lips, "Those who are about to die, salute you."[46]

In this fantasmatic arena, there are, in fact, not just two women (the unconscious patient and the watchful Nurse Clymer), but three. The third woman is "Minerva Medica" herself—or rather, the death she prefigures. With the help of "The Theme of The Three Caskets" (1913), we can identify her with "the three inevitable relations that a man has with a woman"; that is, the woman who bears him, the woman who is his mate and the woman who destroys him; . . . they are the three forms taken by the figure of the mother in the course of a man's life—the mother herself, the beloved one who is chosen after her pattern, and lastly the Mother Earth who receives him once more. But it is in vain that an old man yearns for the love of woman as he had it first from his mother; the third of the Fates alone, the silent Goddess of Death, will take him into her arms. (SE 12.301)

Freud's yearning fantasy, as he entered what he thought of as his old age, underpins the pathos of Agnew's last salute to "the boys" as Adams tells it. Whether or not *The Agnew Clinic* participates in Adams's medical hero worship ("To the American world, who dearly loves a hero, [Agnew] stood the ideal of the prowess of the American surgeon"),[47] Eakins's painting takes on new meaning. A death-bearing woman—Freud's silent Goddess of Death—teaches the saintly old surgeon how to die. This consoling scenario requires his submission to a mother's embrace rather than to a father. If death is embodied as a cancerous woman, no wonder he has to avert his gaze; keeping "Minerva Medica" in his and our mind's eye (rather than focussing on the cancer patient) defends against the threat to the surgeon's own life.

Agnew's outmoded surgical practice was overtaken by Nature's "cruel but necessary provisions," as well as the ironies of medical history. But perhaps Eakins himself knew the cruelty of surgery. The lines that extend downwards from Agnew's scalpel and the pointer-like diagonal rail intersect at the site of an imaginary onlooker's breast. That subject—an imaginary, doubled point of psychic identification and corporeal entry—can only be femininized. This is the feminine position that the entire painting has tried to foreclose, occluding as it does the patient's threat to the specular and psychic economies of the artist-surgeon. By installing the viewer in his painting, Eakins indirectly discloses mastectomy as a wound to the seeing on which masculine subjectivity is predicated in *The Agnew Clinic*.

ii. The Missing Breast

To return to health, I had to scrutinize my life, root out the destructive elements, be surgeon and seer to my own psyche. . . . I had to see the disease as metaphor. . . . I learned to distinguish the external and

249

internal enemies, to define all my allies. I mobilized a healing commu-
nity, and finally I used the imagination as a major tool for healing.
—Deena Metzger, Her Soul beneath the Bone (1988)[48]

A hundred years after Eakins's painting, the forward to an anthology of mastectomy poetry, *Her Soul beneath the Bone: Women's Poetry on Breast Cancer* (1988),
emphasizes women's "desperate need to share their feelings with others"—feelings
not only of pain and loss, but of anger and protest, if not at a duping doctor, still
at "breast cancer as a disease whose treatment requires tearing a woman's breast from
her body" (pp. xiii-xv). Faced by the poems in *Her Soul beneath the Bone*, the veteran breast cancer activist, Rose Kushner, tries to read them "with a poet's eyes"
(through the "eyes" of writing?) but all she can think of is the Vietnam War, "where
the enemy could not be identified and where it was often necessary to destroy a village in order to save it" (p. xvi). The lies and betrayal of military official-speak
persisted even in what Kushner identifies as "the current Enlightened Era" of the
1980s, when the one-stage biopsy-mastectomy and the dreaded "radical" had for
some time ceased to be the norm. The editor's preface, by Leatrice Lifshitz, herself
a poet, goes on to emphasize not only the motif of shared experience as "a way to
make vital connections and a way to survive" but the need to break silence: "This
anthology is a wail—a long, sharp, piercing wail; but it is more. If it moans, it also
hopes. If it screams, it also quietly reflects" (p. xvii). The hopeful moan or reflective scream—an oxymoronic utterance "on the edge of tomorrow"—testifies to
the excruciated consciousness of the cancer survivor in the wake of psychic catastrophe, facing an uncertain future.

The introduction to *Her Soul beneath the Bone*, by yet another poet, Phyllis
Hoge Thompson, identifies breast cancer as "a rich and natural mine for metaphor."
(Perhaps this is what it means to "read with a poet's eyes.") Interestingly, Thompson
goes on to describe both the volume ("a somewhat peculiar book") and breast
cancer itself as (respectively) "bizarre" and "outré." These foreign phrases signal the
presence of otherness and pathology at the heart of familiar, domestic, or maternal identities. Mastectomy poetry is at once close to home and an alien
invasion—altogether too close to the bone. What Wilfred Bion calls "the bizarre
object" names a pathological response to persecutory anxiety. The bizarre object,
he writes, emerges at the point where an intolerable threat to survival produces splitting and fragmentation in the subject. This is the sense of chaotic depersonalization
that characterizes the imaginative world of the psychotic. Bion associates psy-

chotic states with a form of splitting that involves the expulsion of fragments of the personality "so that they enter into or engulf their objects." The prototype for such splitting is Klein's account of the phantasied attacks made by the infant on the breast during the paranoid-schizoid phase. In these "sadistic splitting eviscerating attacks," mental functions are "expelled from the personality to penetrate, or encyst, the objects." These are the penetrated or encysted objects that Bion calls "bizarre objects":

> Each particle is felt to consist of a real object which is encapsulated in a piece of personality that has engulfed it. The nature of this complete particle will depend partly on the character of the real object, say a gramophone, and partly on the character of the part of personality that engulfs it. If the piece of personality is concerned with sight, the gramophone when played is felt to be watching the patient; if with hearing, then the gramophone when played is felt to be listening to the patient. The object, angry at being engulfed, swells up, so to speak, and suffuses and controls the piece of personality that engulfs it: to that extent the particle of personality has become a thing.[49]

As a consequence of fragmentation, "the patient feels surrounded by minute objects which, being impregnated now with cruelty, link objects together cruelly," attacking thought itself. The very possibility of linking ("that-which-links") is jeopardized, while "sense impressions appear to have suffered mutilation of a kind which would be appropriate had they been attacked as the breast is felt to be attacked in the sadistic phantasies of the infant."[50] Eyes and ears—indeed, all organs of sight, insight, and awareness—become simultaneously the objects of sadistic attack, and themselves the attackers.

At the start of *Her Soul beneath the Bone*, in her prose-poem "Healing," Deena Metzger writes: "I had to scrutinize my life, root out the destructive elements, be surgeon and seer to my own psyche. . . . I used the imagination as a major tool for healing" (p. 1). The surgical analogy invokes a therapeutic process in which scrutinization, radical probing, and surgery characterize the imagination—defined not only as a mode of insight, but as the ability to metaphorize and to distingish external from internal ("to see the disease as metaphor" and "to distinguish the external and internal enemies"). But as well as cutting, there is linking: "There's a connection / that I need to make again" ("Before Surgery," p. 8), writes Jeanne Lohmann. This connection is often represented in terms of the mother, whose body is both inside and outside the woman poet ("My bones that formed in you / My breast that they will take," p. 8)—but also in terms of the relation between inner and outer worlds. Like the psychotic in "dread of imminent annihilation" (Bion again),[51] the breast-cancer sufferer confronts the unbearable anxiety of her own dying. Inner and outer become confused as the patient splits and fragments a hated reality, precluding the basis of self-understanding or thinking. For Bion, one source of psychosis is the failure or inability of the mother to allow ingress to the infant's projections. Hence the psychotic's increasingly violent and desperate attacks on the imaginary body of the mother, which becomes the representative of a hostile, defensive reality. The patient's recognition of his or her own psychosis provides the basis for getting better (as Edna O'Shaughnessy puts it, "once he gains insight into the fact that he is ill he may begin to get well").[52] But the beginnings of thinking—the beginnings of linking—made possible by the analyst's receptiveness to the psychotic's projections are themselves often experienced by the patient as an assault. The perceptions and projections that are now permitted entry return as blows or wounds to the body; the patient, writes O'Shaughnessy, "feels struck in the eye."[53] Not just seeing, but insight itself becomes a mode of attack.

In *Her Soul beneath the Bone*, the surgeon and the tools or machines of medical practice are the assault weapons. Patricia Goedicke's "In the Hospital," for instance, contains a catalogue of such weapons—"sharp knives," "inquisitive glances," "harsh hands" (p. 2). In "One More Time," Goedicke makes the crackling cold of the X-ray center's "polished steel table" the site for an out-of-body experience of depersonalized looking: "Suspended in icy silence / I look at myself from far off" (p.3). The figure of attentive, clinical looking in Eakins's *The Agnew Clinic* turns into this look that penetrates, freezes, and silences the cancer patient. In Terry Kennedy's "Mammogram," the X-ray machine—"the god-eye-ball test / (checking your soul)" (p. 4)—clicks its picture in the writer's own brain, making her do the job of the omniscient camera. In Kennedy's "For Hatfield, the Radiologist"—the radiologist whose vocation is "reading women like a book . . . seeing through their breasts / into that pea-sized death"—the poet's own eying of her breasts assumes the radiologist's voyeurism ("your eyes, those two blue prophets, / peering past flesh / into the source of milk," p. 5). Hatfield's masculine gaze finds death there ("uncover[s] the hours left"), but the cruel insight is the poet's own. In Joan Halperin's disbelieving "Diagnosis," "the blunt forefinger of a doctor / pokes at a tumour / he says is in my breast" (p. 7). These figures of intrusive looking or sadistic poking—the inquisitive glances and peering eyes, the sharp knives and blunt forefingers—project onto the medical arena the imaginative probing that Metzger claims as her "major tool for healing." Subjected to an arsenal of insight, the cancerous body and, above all, death itself take on the role of bizarre objects: "The metal teeth of Death bite / But spit me out" ("One More Time," p. 3). At once bitten and biting, the cancer-patient experiences the metal-toothed enemy, Death, as an enemy who is both inside and outside. Or, as Jana Harris puts it, "the worst betrayal is when / your own body / turns on you, not / the male radiologist" ("The Lump/The Swelling/The Possibility of Cancer: Notes from the Oncology Clinic," p. 25).

Faced with surgical attack from outside and betrayal from within, the cancer patient is divided against herself. How can she define her allies? She must either dissociate in order to survive—surrendering her breast and identifying, as it were, with the aggressor ("When they took off my right breast / I gave it to them," "In the Hospital," p. 2); or else she must go painfully to pieces: "Now strangers take parts of you away. / Bit by bit / you disintegrate in pain" (Miriam Krasno, "Separation," p. 17).[54] Threatened not only by the army of "surgeons [who] whet their knives" in secret, but by "great companies of diseased cells / Looming on every horizon," the cancer patient exists "in the heart of the war zone" (Patricia Goedicke, "100,000 upon 100,000," p. 61); her body is at once the battlefield, the sacrificial victim, and the enemy. Breast cancer becomes "the new dragon, / The one with a thousand eyes" (p. 61) who demands modern sacrifice in the form of virgins and wives. In this mythic realm, poetry is wielded as "a weapon / against loss," like the hateful, prosthetic breast-ball given to the postmastectomy patient to clutch and release (Tammy Mae Chapman, "Woman's Barter"). Reconnecting the pain-fragmented patient with herself, her poem becomes a kind of breast-ball—"breast with concave nipple / something of her own / to hold" ("Woman's Barter," p. 30). The patient who had refused to play ball as a child must now play for her life. Mimicking, parodying, reversing, and satirizing the terms of medical discourse, the language of women's mastectomy poetry transforms a piercing wail into an arsenal of analytic defiance: "The doctor calls the cutting / he will do / 'modified' and 'radical,' / twin words, a pair / that break on one another" ("Before Surgery," p. 8). Like breast and ball—another non-equivalent pair—the cancer-poet, marooned in a "war zone" of contradictory meanings, turns the language of betrayal back on the aggressor ("it was often necessary to destroy a village in order to save it," p. xvi). Instead of prosthesis, a poem: "something of her own / to hold"—a language-weapon that is also a container.

What form of holding does this poetic receptacle provide for the postmastectomy patient's anguished morselling of consciousness ("Bit by bit")? How can a poem contain the cell-like proliferations of projective identification, and in what sense is a poem like a breast—or, for that matter, a mother? A surprising number of poems in *Her Soul beneath the Bone* look into "the source of milk" and find the mother there. Sometimes the pain of bit-by-bit separation is imagined as the mother's loss of her daughter (as in "Separation"—"your lips no longer press her forehead. / Your body is ripped apart," p. 17); but more often the daughter's loss of her mother gives shape to her disconnection. The missing link is the mother's holding: "There's a connection / That I need to make again. . . . Your death is at a distance, Mother. / Come here, and hold me now" ("Before Surgery," p 8). Men "say they 'know' us" but although "Our daughters know" (p. 8), only the dead or absent mother can truly know, and repair, the damage. Leatrice Lifshitz's "Ma" reproaches the mother for having let her down ("Ma, you should have fixed it") because the daughter has been left "with dumb skin / instead of a breast" (p. 9). The mother's broken promise ("that I am in your image"), the daughter's defiant assertion of the rights of nipples ("a nipple / has a right"), provide the occasion for an indirect, nostalgic tribute to the mother's imaginary healing power and maternal omniscience ("You should have fixed it, Ma / kissed it and made it better / like a knee or elbow," p. 9). Elegies like Julie Landsman's "To Mother" mourn the mother's emptied breast as the place of lost plenitude ("I wanted to be as full as you"). Even when breast feeding her own child, the daughter "felt your fullness then," rather than her own (pp. 10, 11). In Emily Sims's "Complications," the daughter is "a small replica"; the same, but different, she is less a replacement than an irritant to her anguished father as he waits out his wife's time in intensive care. The daughter-poet—at once replica and irritant, like a breast-ball—becomes the source of this scared and angry poetry.

The breast-ball in "Women's Barter" belongs to a system of exchange with zero returns. In Patricia Goedicke's "Once There Was a Woman," the catalogue of asymmetrical pairs ("a woman with one round breast / And one flat one . . . a woman with two tears / Of self-pity in each eye") refuses to add up to a rounded total. Even "love becomes lopsided" (Pat Gray, "Cancer in the Breast," p. 36). There is always something missing, something empty where once there was once the fantasy of fullness. What is that something missing?—that lopsided, sinister remainder, as Lorraine Vernon puts it gappily, "transforming Woman / with the little /   / (left" ("Slant," p. 34). In Goedicke's "Now Only One of Us Remains," the stranger "washing up and down the shore" is a corpselike woman who has lost her feelings. In Marian Irwin's "Post Mastectomy—Week One," the postmastec- tomy patient is "my own unknown," at once lost to herself and weeping for a loss that is absolute and unqualified: "Unsure of where I am / I weep the loss" (p. 32). The loss of the mother's holding fullness makes it impossible to locate either one- self or one's pain. This is a kind of self-loss that Tess Enroth's "Consultation" associates with the helpless cry of an abandoned baby:

> Try now to locate the pain.
> Describe its nature,
> intensity, duration.
> We can, you know, alleviate,
> sometimes can eradicate
>   what is
> essentially a symptom.
> Pain can't tell us
>   everything
> Grave and mortal ills
> often do not hurt.
> But pain can tell us
>   something.
> It may, like a baby's cry, mean
>   anything.
> Try now to tell us
> where and when the pain is most severe;
> —Inside in darkness and alone—
> tell us
>   nothing.   (p. 31)

How can a self that is not yet a self—a traumatized self, struggling to survive and voice a psychic catastophe—respond to the doctor's diagnostic questioning except with this wail that means at the same time "anything" and "nothing"?

What Leatrice Lifshitz calls "a long, sharp, piercing wail" (p. xvii) can be read as the primitive form of the daughter's cry for her missing mother. The baby's cry is not about pain, which might "tell us / something"; not about where and how it hurts. Nor is it about a "grave and mortal ill" as understood by an adult who understands the meaning of death. The cry comes from a parenthetical interior where the mother is not ("—Inside in darkness and alone—"). Absence, not just war, characterizes the landscape of this primitive outcry. Patricia Goedicke calls it "White as the inside of an onion" ("That Was the Fruit of My Orchard," p. 20). Not a nightmare, but a place where "I, who was not there" casts no shadow—a "shadowless country of loss" where loss itself is a "cry / Without sound" (pp. 20, 21). Who or what is this "I, who was not there"?—not the dissociated, etherized patient on the polished steel X-ray table, but an "I" without the guarantee of maternal presence, gripped by the terror and negativity of "nothing" (p. 31). The fantasmatic space vacated by the mother is represented by the space of the phantom breast, where a drink of water "curves / filling up the hole / —phantom nerves, they say" ("The Lump/The Swelling/The Possibility of Cancer," p. 29). "The hole" is the imaginary plentitude represented by the missing breast—not just phantom nerves, but an object that is not (or no longer) there. The same hallucination of plenitude figures, this time ironically, in Joanne Seltzer's "Breasts"—"What's a breast? Illusion. / An object for sending milk to babies" (p. 55). Here the illusory maternal "object" is charged with the infant's fantasmatic longing: "you burn / up for milk. This is the way of mammals: / we suck and we suck and we don't feel full." At once anything and nothing, like the meaning of the baby's cry, the breast becomes the repository for impossible wanting, unassuageable demand—for a lack that is not so much symbolically engendered as previously installed in the problematics of desperate infantile need. It is this prior lack that is provoked by the trauma of mastectomy.

But the absent mother also signifies what Bion, in "A Theory of Thinking," calls the "no-breast" or "'absent' breast inside"—the breast that may become a thought if the idea of a bad breast (a frustrating no-breast) can give way, through satisfaction, or through the ability to tolerate frustration, to the idea of a missing breast: "the 'no-breast' inside becomes a thought and an apparatus for 'thinking' it develops."[55] The possibility of thinking the missing breast—metaphorizing it—is the mastectomy poet's lifeline, her (missing) connection. If mastectomy painfully recapitulates the infant's long-ago phantasized, envious attacks on the breast, making it the prototype of all attacks on linking, writing may restore the lost connection; it becomes a form of reparation or repair work, at once a mode of linking and of thinking (in Bion's terms, the empty thought turns into a conception). Sally Allen

McNall's surreal humor, in "Poem for the Woman Who Filled a Prosthesis with Birdseed, and Others," juxtaposes memories of weaning her own daughter ("for days I dripped / milk, tears, milk, tears— / dreamed I was / a bottle") with grief for her mother's "modified" radical mastectomy. She wakes from a dream talking nonsense ("I woke up saying / 'in a modified raspberry / garden,'" p. 66). But the image of "red bumpy berries/full of seeds" (p. 68) evokes both the granular texture of the breast and the birdseed-filled prosthesis of her title. Visceral and abundant ("simply soak the earth / the air / the page"), the breast-poem becomes the source of sensation and inundation in which milk, blood, tears, words, and ink are indiscriminately mingled—"we burn, we leak, we ooze blood, / tears, words, ink, milk" (p. 67). Fecundated by the metaphor of maternal juice ("we're ripe gardens now"), the poem's liquid mix (abject or healing? mourning or celebratory?) posits an imaginary, mammary source for writing. This daughter, thinking about her mother's mastectomy, demands: "hold me"—hold the collapsed bottle she once held and dreamed she was ("the kind / that collapses, / inside a stiff, white frame," p. 66). The poem's submerged, dreamlike connections trace a pattern in which "real" feeling, bodily touching ("it feels quite real, feel"; "I'd felt the / scar, already, for fever," p. 67) metaphorize not only the feel of feeling (the feel of a prosthesis), but the feel of being in touch. In touch, too, with the "Others" of its title ("Poem for the Woman Who Filled a Prosthesis with Birdseed, *and Others*"; my italics). Holding its imaginings to the shape of an uncollapsed bottle or a birdseed-filled prosthesis, the poem answers its implicit demand with a substitute plenitude. Poetry is the supplement for mother's milk.

In *Her Soul beneath the Bone*, scar tissue comes to figure writing. Each woman's scar is a material inscription on her body. Sometimes the meaning of this curving scar is not yet apparent—"The hard new path / I follow curves from sight" ("Post-Mastectomy—Week One," p. 32). Sometimes the scar is a violent, ugly slash—"a fierce horizontal slash / rounding your chest to the arm— / puckered and red as a rapist's mouth" ("Cancer in the Breast," p. 36); here the red mouth, angry and puckered with distaste, voices anger at a surgical attack that feels as brutal as a rape. Sometimes the scar is a sinister sign of deformity—"The scar snakes hard / across the hollowed plain" (F. M. Bancroft, "elegy," p. 38), leaving the survivor of the pair as innocent and bereft as a baby: "My fingers knead the survivor like a baby" (here the survivor is both the lover, with her kneading hands, and the surviving breast). Elsewhere, the curve of "S-shaped stitches" sketches "the way a hand / curved my breast" (Alice Davis, "After Surgery," p. 42), evoking the memory of an erotic gesture from the past. In "Scars," Elizabeth Lincoln contrasts "a white crooked scar / at the bend of my left thumb"—"the unnecessary wound" that marks the date of another's death—with the wound under her blouse where "a ridge of scar / molds on a field of bone" (p. 69). This (necessary?) wounding by "the motions / of the surgeon's knife, / its dull and futile dance" can be mastered ("I try to master it with art"). But the other scar, "the cosmic one," is "the one / I can't conquer." The two incommensurate scars of the poem's title ("Scars") delineate "the jagged edges we live on," poised between living and dying. No art can fully master the bewildering cosmic accident of death.

Yet the scar tissue of mastectomy-poetry is mastered as an art-form in its own right. The radiologist of Jane Harris's "The Lump / The Swelling / The Possibility of Cancer" had been equipped "with blue-green felt-tipped / Crayolas" ("he draws on her lump / following the / paint-by-number / nuclear medicine / chart on the wall," p. 27). In contrast to this rote nuclear painting-by-numbers, Joan Halperin develops "artist's fingers / that trace the contours of my breast" ("Injunctions," p. 19). In "I Am No Longer Afraid," the volume's closing poem, Deena Metzger transforms her fear into a journey and her scar into a leaf-covered branch: "There was a fine red line across my chest where a knife entered, but now / a branch winds about the scar and travels from arm to heart" (p. 71). This is a path that knows its destination. The body becomes at once map and manuscript, at once book and the sign of a tree—a word picture that grows on her: "I have designed my chest with the care given to an illuminated manuscript . . . . On the book of my body, I have permanently inscribed a tree" (p. 71). Turning her body into performance art, Metzger makes her scar a signifier for a self divided. In Joan Halperin's "A Single Pearl," the aestheticized, lost object (at once breast and tear) reappears as a pearl, "pulled toward the heart of the moon" (p. 70). The elusive pearl—so hard and round, so self-contained and undissolving ("The pearl repels touch")—finds its idealized other in a moon that has a heart. This imagined confluence of mourning and pleasure ("The pearl drops like a tear / allows me to mourn and caress both sides") restores imagined fullness to an emptied out self: "The pearl fills cavities / enters voids. / . . . seeds the barren places" (p. 70). The poem—a pearl secreted in response to the irritant of cancer—stands in for something that can be taken back into the self. Not a tumor, not a hated breast-ball, not a prosthesis, it becomes a metaphor for the missing breast—a good object, a thought, holding and, finally, held. As pearl is to moon, so poem is to the self rerounded by writing. The tear held together by its own surface tension can be allowed to fall in the shape of a poem.

Baring the Breast

The trajectory charted by *Her Soul beneath the Bone* makes the dissociated, affectless patient the artist of her own recovery. The scalpel's transfer from surgeon to patient raises the issue of aggressivity, whether in art or analysis. Where does the sadism go when women take up the scalpel to probe their own pain? Metzger asks, in effect, whether there can be cure without enduring or inflicting psychic wounds, or at least owning an aggressivity that is directed as much towards the self as towards its objects. But, by the same token, can there be cure without analytic love?[56] Women's literary representations of mastectomy create a space in which to imagine not only eviscerating attack, trauma, and psychic catastrophe, but a reconstituted relation to the self—in particular, a repaired relation to the maternal past signified by the missing breast. In this sense, writing not only puts women in possession of their pain but allows them to redefine the terms of their treatment and cure; it hands over the scalpel as pen, reappropriating the imagination as a weapon. Paradoxically, the mastectomy patient must be a bad patient, or at least a resisting one in order to heal herself (and others). The Amazon bared her breast in battle, wearing her scar as a badge of militant courage and defiance. But this is not to idealize self-inflicted breast mutilation or the scars of the cancer survivor. Rather, the Amazonian metaphor that often surfaces in representations of mastectomy allows women to identify with survival, as it does in the final poem in the collection, Deena Metzger's celebratory "I Am No Longer Afraid" ("I have the body of a warrior who does not kill or wound," p. 71). The post-mastectomy poet flaunts her wound as writing—a scar that traces the site of meaning taken into the self, a loss accepted and deeply understood. Theorizing her relation to the breast even as she mourns it, the mastectomy poet attempts not only to analyze or unloose her ties to what is lost, but to recontain and rethink it. If one figure for this holding operation is the missing breast, another is her poem.

*   *   *

I want to end by reflecting on the question of the "radical" in psychoanalysis, and in psychoanalytically inflected art history too. The cover of Michael Fried's *Realism, Writing, Disfiguration* sports an appreciation by Janet Malcolm, a writer distinguished by the exceptional bleakness of her account of the contemporary practice of psychoanalysis. "Criticism as radical as this is rare," she writes,

but only when criticism is radical does it stand a chance of being
something more than a pale reflection of the work of art that is its
subject. By disfiguring the work of art almost beyond recognition,
Fried forces us to imagine it anew.[57]

Malcolm's play on the term "radical" makes striking use of the surgical analogy, and
with it the clashing senses of a word to which both psychoanalysis and mastectomy
have given new meanings.[58] Halsted's "radical" mastectomy went to the root of cancer,
but at the price of hideous mutilation that changed the shape of the female body
"almost beyond recognition," and, with the passing of time, came to seem a form
of needless surgical violence against women. In Malcolm's agonistic appreciation,
Fried as hero forces us to reimagine Eakins's realism by deploying the weapons of
psychoanalysis; Fried's reading of Eakins is not "a pale reflection of the work of
art" but a radically renewing disfiguration. Malcolm implicitly equates the surgical heroism of psychoanalytic reading with the threat to wholeness involved in
castration theory. Fried's analysis—or so Malcolm's appreciation suggests—is like
Freud's in defamiliarizing not just the body but its comforting representations (representations associated with the practice of "realism"); in particular, Fried estranges
us from the appearance of reality in Eakins's realism, dependent as it is on representations of the (normative, masculine) body. In its place Fried introduces the textual
system of language and the unconscious—the post-Freudian scene of writing as
developed by Derrida. For Fried, in fact, the surgical scalpel is more than a bloody
allusion to painting and sculpture (or, by extension, inscription). It becomes a
figure for an art "excruciated" (the term is Fried's) between competing systems of
representation—painting on one hand versus drawing/writing on the other.

But how radical is Fried's psychoanalytic reading of Eakins? Freud, after all,
had his own blind spot, envisaging as he did a feminine body that was psychically
indifferent yet paradoxically differentiated by an invisible mutilation (the problematic
"nothing to see" of feminine castration, as viewed by the little boy). Freud's difficulty in imagining psychic life in terms other than constructed by the Oedipus
complex is replicated in Fried's apparent reluctance to reimagine the issue of disfiguration when it comes to *The Agnew Clinic* (significantly, his most sustained
discussion of the painting occurs in a footnote about inscription). Contrary to
Malcolm's claim, this is a picture for which an oedipal thematics of castration does
indeed offer only "a pale reflection" of an already masculine fantasy—Freud's, in
which the visual representation (the look) of "man" involves rendering "woman"

invisible; the only mutilation worth talking about is the one that can be thematized as the effect of feminine lack on a masculine subject, that is, castration anxiety. One project of a feminist reading might be to understand *The Agnew Clinic*, as Marcia Pointon has done in her critique of Fried, as a painting that "address[es] for a male audience the crisis of sexual difference and the crisis of Realism by assigning to woman the specific role of lack."[59] Another feminist project might involve the recovery of a historically situated female body; in the case of mastectomy, after all, masculine castration anxiety bandages a female wound that is situated in the real—in the materiality of the female body as well as the symbolic realm of lack. But perhaps there is room for a psychoanalytically inflected reading that takes things beyond both Fried and Freud.

In *Naked Authority*, Pointon argues that Fried's oedipal and paranoic scenario not only makes the mother the scapegoat, but effectively relegates her to the pre-oedipal and to "an ungendered condition of negativity."[60] It is this negativity that makes it possible to break with the predictable binarism of woman's association with lack and man's with the specular regime of looking while retaining the scopic implications of the figure of looking (and looking away) in *The Agnew Clinic*. The over-determined violence of wounding and looking seems to require the situating of the mother ("Minerva Medica" in her third, death-dealing form) in the field of unconscious phantasy where the earliest anxieties are psychotic in content. It is, of course, Melanie Klein who has most to say about the infant's phantasized attacks on the breast of the mother during the paranoid-schizoid phase—about the mechanisms of splitting and projective identification which operate as defenses against these violent onslaughts. One might expect the representation of a wound to the breast to bring just such unconscious phantasies into play even before castration-anxiety enters the picture. Among the concentrated acts of looking that multiply all over Eakins's canvas so that only Agnew himself seems to look away, the most concentrated of all is that of the bespectacled surgeon at work on the unseen breast. As Pointon observes of the all-male audience, "these men are masters of the scopic";[61] after all, what does mastery of the scopic mean if not the marshalling of defences against being unmastered? Like other members of the audience (half a dozen including the surgeon himself), the surgeon wears glasses—objects nearly as bizarre, yet as realistically appropriate, as the anaesthetist's ether cone or Nurse Clymer's strange breast-shaped starched cap (captured with equal meticulousness as a kind of displaced mammary fetish).

Significantly, for my purposes anyway, Bion's clinical example of the agglomeration of bizarre objects produced by projective identification is a pair of dark glasses—two glasses, he says, "thus resembling the breast"; made of glass to pay the patient out "for trying to see through them when they were breasts," and "felt as a conscience that punished [the patient], partly for getting rid of them to avoid pain."[62] Bion tells his patient, "Your sight has come back into you but splits your head; you feel it is very bad sight because of what you have done to it."[63] The multiplication of the look in *The Agnew Clinic* that finds its focus in the surgeon's glasses contains the painting's unconscious meaning. By way of closure, I want to introduce another bizarre object (for Freud, the most disquieting of all). I have already suggested that the phantasmal missing breast can be glimpsed in the design of Eakins's painting, with its allusion to medical illustrations of mastectomy operations in Agnew's and others' text-books. But another clue to the wound Eakins turned away from lies in what it is tempting to call the upward displacement of his picture. Where women were concerned, Agnew was an experienced practitioner, not of the operation for breast cancer, which he believed to shorten life, but of operations for "surgical diseases of women" that are illustrated with graphic fullness in Agnew's *Principles and Practice of Surgery*. Take a look, for instance, at this: "Closing up the vagina: edges pared and sutures introduced" (fig. 7)—an object, if ever there was one, with what Bion, in "A Theory of Thinking," calls "the characteristics of a greedy vagina-like 'breast' that strips of its goodness all that the infant gives or receives leaving only degenerate objects."[64] In the imaginary eye of such a wound—if such an eye could see—both the work of art and the female body are indeed "disfigur[ed] almost beyond recognition."

If the forced and forceful reimagining of art is one aspect of the disfiguration involved in any radical analytic project, the other aspect of such reimagining is the repair work that belongs to the depressive position—for Klein, the knot that reties the negativity of psychoanalysis.[65] Like the history of breast cancer, the medical history of mastectomy is, and remains, a history of sexual politics. The representation of mastectomy teaches the continued need for medical activism on the part of women. But it also reveals the possibility for connection—for retying aggressivity and love, or linking the surgical analogy of psychoanalysis with analytic empathy. Together, *The Agnew Clinic* and the poems in *Her Soul beneath the Bone* pose the subject of mastectomy at the site where this seeing split in the integrity of the body and the subject is at once probed and sutured; where the surgical analogy turns into something like a receptive organ attuned to the transmitting uncon-

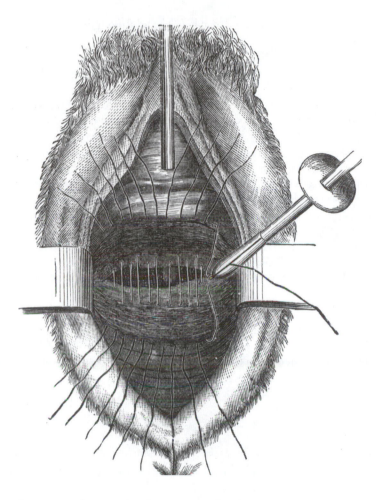

Fig. 7. "Closing up the vagina: edges pared and sutures introduced," D. Hayes Agnew, *The Principles and Practice of Surgery*, 3 vols. (Philadelphia: J. B. Lippincott & Co., 1878–83). The Wellcome Institute Library, London.

scious, and the negativity of psychoanalysis is yoked to "that-which-links." Baring the breast—laying a wound open to the imagination—allows us to register not only disfiguration but the power of figures to provide an apparatus for "thinking" the missing breast.

FIRST THINGS

This essay is dedicated to my friends Zillah and Alison, to my mother, and others.

1. For Freud's 1887 review of a translation of Weir Mitchell, see *SE* 1.35.

2. See, for instance, Richard Hardaway Meade, *An Introduction to the History of General Surgery* (Philadelphia: W. B. Saunders Company, 1968).

3. For instance, in "The Question of Lay Analysis" (1926), Freud turns the question of professionalism back against the doctors themselves, who "frequently practise analytic treatment without having learnt it" (*SE* 20.230).

4. By 1982, the one-stage biopsy/radical mastectomy was no longer routine in the United States; by 1988, fifteen states had laws requiring doctors to inform breast-cancer patients about alternatives to mastectomy. See *Her Soul beneath the Bone: Women's Poetry on Breast Cancer*, ed. Leatrice H. Lifshitz (Urbana and Chicago: University of Illinois Press, 1988), xv.

5. Recent extended art-historical discussions of *The Agnew Clinic* can be found in Lloyd Goodrich, *Thomas Eakins*, 2 vols. (Cambridge, MA, and London: Harvard University Press, 1982), 39–51; David M. Lubin, *Acts of Portrayal: Eakins, Sargent, James* (New Haven and London: Yale University Press, 1985), 27–82, and, from a specifically feminist perspective, Marcia Pointon, *The Body in Western Painting 1830–1908* (Cambridge: Cambridge University Press, 1990), 35–58.

6. J. Howe Adams, *History of the Life of D. Hayes Agnew* (Philadelphia and London: F. A. Davis and Co., 1892), 312.

7. See Adams, *History of the Life of D. Hayes Agnew*, 170–71: "Mr. Eakins, who had been attending his cliniques for several months to get his characteristic attitudes and methods of operating, recognized at once this peculiarity."

8. Adams, *History of the Life of D. Hayes Agnew*, 334.

9. Ibid., 166.

10. Ibid., 333.

11. For the reception of *The Gross Clinic*, see Goodrich, *Thomas Eakins*, 1: 130-37.

12. Oliver Cope, "Breast Cancer—Has the Time Come for a Less Mutilating Treatment?" *Psychiatry in Medicine* 2 (1971): 268.

13. Adams, *History of the Life of D. Hayes Agnew*, 166: "His tall and erect figure was always the first object which caught the eye of the incomer into these clinics. It is impossible to express his wonderful tranquility of mind and confidence while operating . . . he never imparted any sense of uneasiness to spectators or friends."

14. Ibid., 334.

15. As Pointon observes: "Two discourses of power, that of Art and that of Medicine, intersect at the moment of high Realism over the incapacitated body of a semi-naked woman" (*The Body in Western Painting*, 58).

16. See Diana Long Hall, "Eakins's Agnew Clinic: The Medical World in Transition," *Transactions and Studies of the College of Physicians of Philadelphia* 7 (1985): 26–32 for a succinct assessment of Agnew's "humane" and "palliative" surgical philosophy.

17. See William S. Halsted, "The Results of operations for the cure of cancer of the Breast Performed at the Johns Hopkins Hospital from June 1889 to January 1894," *Johns Hopkins*

Hospital Reports 4, no. 6 (1894): 7; reprinted in William S. Halsted, *Surgical Papers*, 2 vols. (Baltimore: Johns Hopkins University, 1924). Both Meyer's and Halsted's reports are reprinted in *Silvergirl's Surgery: The Breast*, ed. Guy F. Robbins (Austin, TX: Silvergirl, Inc., 1984), 149; Halsted's article is misleadingly cited as appearing in the *Johns Hopkins Hospital Bulletin*.

18. See Judith Fryer, "'The Body in Pain' in Thomas Eakins's *Agnew Clinic*," in *The Female Body: Figures, Styles, Speculations*, ed. Laurence Goldstein (Ann Arbor: University of Michigan Press, 1991), 140: "the painting can be read as a representation of late nineteenth-century medical practice in which male science seeks to know, so as to master, the female body, which is always other than his own." For Eakins's fascination with lettering and inscription generally, see also Michael Fried, *Realism, Writing, Disfiguration: on Thomas Eakins and Stephen Crane* (Chicago and London: University of Chicago Press, 1987), 27, 177–78.

19. "Elizabeth," in *Breasts: Women Speak about Their Breasts and Their Lives*, ed. Daphna Ayalah and Isaac J. Weinstock (London: Hutchinson, 1980), 223.

20. See Fryer, "The Body in Pain," 242 and n. Fryer, who notices that Nurse Clymer blocks the artist's vision, offers the fullest reading of the ways in which *The Agnew Clinic* concerns not only "the nature of woman and medicine's proper relation to her" but also "the nature of woman and the artist's proper relation to her" ("The Body in Pain," 245, 251–52).

21. For the professional controversy surrounding Eakins's attitude to the use of nude models, see Fried, *Realism, Writing, Disfiguration*, 18 and n. Nurse Clymer's role is also that of the impassive chaperone in Eakins's early and late versions of *William Rush Carving His Allegorical Figure of the Schuylkill River* (1876–77 and 1908).

22. Adams, *History of the Life of D. Hayes Agnew*, 166.

23. In the footnote that contains his most sustained discussion of *The Agnew Clinic*, Fried draws attention to the act of carving thematized within the painting by a student apparently carving with a penknife on the back of a bench and, outside the painting, by the epigraph incised into its frame by Eakins himself; see *Realism, Writing, Disfiguration*, 177–78.

24. See Fried, *Realism, Writing, Disfiguration*, 177.

25. Consequently, as Pointon observes, "woman is effectively expelled from Fried's account" (*The Body in Western Painting*, 48).

26. See Fryer, "The Body in Pain," 242–44. Eakins himself typically depicts women as servants to a higher art even where they are musicians; see, for instance, *Elizabeth Crowell at the Piano* (1875), *The Pathetic Song* (1881), or *The Concert Singer* (1892), where the hand of the male conductor intrudes pointedly from the frame.

27. See Adams, *History of the Life of D. Hayes Agnew*, 148 (his italics); see also Fryer, "The Body in Pain," 244. In 1870, Agnew's introductory address to the incoming class of medical students had gone out of its way to denounce the agitation for Women's Rights generally and, more specifically, women's ambition to enter the medical profession. Should women "implead juries," "mount the political platform," or "amputate limbs," he writes, "let her remember there are laws controlling the social structure of society, the operations of which will disrobe her of all those qualities now the glory of the sex, and will cast her down in the dust of the earth." See D. Hayes Agnew, M.D., *Lecture Introductory to the One Hundredth and Fifth Course of Instruction in the Medical Department of the University of Pennsylvania* (Philadelphia: R. P. King's Sons, 1870), 14–15, 18.

28. Willy Meyer, "An Improved Method of the Radical Operation for Carcinoma of the Breast," *Medical Record* 46 (1894): 749.

29. Goodrich, *Thomas Eakins*, 2: 46, 49.

30. Adams, *History of the Life of D. Hayes Agnew*, 164. For an interesting account of the terms "conservative" and "radical" as applied to surgery, see Gert H. Brieger, "From conservative to radical surgery in late nineteenth-century America," in *Medical Theory, Surgical Practice*, ed. Christopher Lawrence (London and New York: Routledge, 1992), 216–31. For Eakins's relation to these changes in surgical philosophy, see also Gert Brieger, "Sense and Sensibility in Late Nineteenth-century Surgery in America," in *Medicine and the Five Senses*, ed. W. F. Bynum and Roy Porter (Cambridge: Cambridge University Press, 1992), 225–43.

31. D. Hayes Agnew, *The Principles and Practice of Surgery* (Philadelphia: J. B. Lippincott & Co., 1878–83), 3:711.

32. See Elizabeth Johns, *Thomas Eakins: The Heroism of Modern Life* (Princeton: Princeton University Press, 1983), 54–55. Pancoast was one of the few surgeons during the mid-nineteenth century to recommend what later became the standard procedure of wholesale removal of the mammary and axillary glands; see Robbins, *The Breast*, 48.

33. Compare Halsted's criticism of the use of the surgeon's hands for this purpose: "The glands and fat should not be pulled out by the fingers, as advised, I am sorry to say, in modern textbooks and as practiced very often by operators" (Halsted, *Johns Hopkins Hospital Reports* 4, no. 6.12).

34. Joseph Pancoast, *Treatise on Operative Surgery* (Philadelphia: Carey and Hart, 1844); reprinted in Robbins, *The Breast*, 51.

35. See Meade, *An Introduction to the History of General Surgery*, 155.

36. Ibid., 161.

37. Ibid., 156. During the period covered by his report, Halsted performed 76 mastectomies with no deaths from recurrence.

38. Halsted, *Johns Hopkins Hospital Reports* 4, no. 6.16.

39. Meyer, *Medical Record* 46.747.

40. Halsted, *Johns Hopkins Hospital Reports* 4, no. 6.16.

41. See, for instance, Elizabeth Johns, *Thomas Eakins: The Heroism of Modern Life*, 78–79.

42. Adams, *History of the Life of D. Hayes Agnew*, 311–12.

43. See Goodrich, *Thomas Eakins*, 2:59.

44. Adams, *History of the Life of D. Hayes Agnew*, 335.

45. Ibid., 319–20.

46. Ibid., 320.

47. Ibid., 364.

48. *Her Soul beneath the Bone*, 1. Subsequent page references in the text are to this volume.

49. W. R. Bion, "Differentiation of the Psychotic from the Non-Psychotic Personalities," in *Second Thoughts: Selected Papers on Pscyho-Analysis* (London: Karnac Books Ltd., 1990), 43, 47, 47–48. For the history of the term "bizarre," adopted by psychoanalysis from the aesthetic realm, see Sander L. Gilman, *Disease and Representation: Images of Illness from Madness to AIDS* (Ithaca and London:

Cornell University Press, 1988), 231–44.

50. Bion, "Differentiation of the Psychotic," 50, 51.

51. Ibid., 44.

52. See Edna O'Shaughnessy, "Psychosis: Not Thinking in a Bizarre World," in *Clinical Lectures on Klein and Bion*, ed. Robin Anderson (London and New York: Tavistock/Routledge, 1992), 98.

53. O'Shaughnessy, "Psychosis: Not Thinking in a Bizarre World," 97.

54. Perhaps the most vivid account of this process—similarly in a militaristic context—is Fanny Burney's 1812 narrative of the unanaesthetized mastectomy operation performed on her in 1811 by Baron de Larry, a distinguished Parisian surgeon who was a veteran of the Napoleonic battlefields: "Hopeless, then, desperate, & self-given up, I closed once more my Eyes, relinquishing all watching, all resistance, all interference, & sadly resolute to be wholly resigned"; see *The Journals and Letters of Fanny Burney*, ed. Joyce Hemlow (Oxford: Oxford University Press, 1972–84), 6:612. Revealingly, Larry issues his instructions "*en militaire*" and requires the resisting Burney to "submit"; but, as she relates, "the flesh resisted," while the opened breast becomes a kind of sentient organ. In her illuminating reading of Burney's narrative, Julia Epstein compares writing and surgery ("Writing, like the act of surgery, is an invasion of privacy that can be simultaneously wounding and therapeutic") and suggests that "Burney endured the physical pain of writing to exorcise the remembered pain of surgery," replicating the cathartic model of the surgical analogy; see *The Iron Pen: Frances Burney and the Politics of Women's Writing* (Madison: University of Wisconsin Press, 1989), 55, 61.

55. Bion, "A Theory of Thinking," in *Second Thoughts*, 111, 112.

56. For another account of analytic love, or empathy, see Julia Kristeva, "Freud and Love: Treatment and its Discontents," in *Tales of Love*, trans. Leon S. Roudiez (New York: Columbia University Press, 1987), 21–56.

57. Fried, *Realism, Writing, Disfiguration*, back cover. See also Janet Malcolm's *Psychoanalysis: The Impossible Profession* (New York: Knopf, 1981).

58. For the changing meanings of "conservative" and "radical" in surgery itself, see Brieger, "From conservative to radical surgery in late nineteenth-century America," 216–31.

59. Pointon, *The Body in Western Painting*, 58.

60. Ibid., 48. As Fried himself acknowledges, the mother is the ultimate scapegoat of *The Gross Clinic*, "the personage who more than any other has been sacrificed in the interests of representation" (*Realism, Writing, Disfiguration*, 69).

61. "Lolling on their elbows, erect and surveying the scene, leaning back in their seats, resting their heads on each others' shoulders, peering with their heads on one side, these men are masters of the scopic" (Pointon, *The Body in Western Painting*, 52).

62. Bion, "Differentiation of the Psychotic," 57–58.

63. Ibid., 58.

64. Bion, "A Theory of Thinking," 115.

65. For negativity and Klein, see Jacqueline Rose, "Negativity in the Work of Melanie Klein," in *Why War?* (Oxford: Blackwell, 1993), 137–90.

12

Narcissa's Gaze

Berthe Morisot and the Filial Mirror

For both the man and the woman, the maternal body lines the seductive surface of the image, but the body he sees is not the same one she is looking at . . . . Similarly, with regard to the artistic text, and if pleasure is understood in Barthes' sense of the term as a loss of preconceived identity, rather than an instance of repletion, then it is possible to produce a different form of pleasure for the woman by representing a specific loss — the loss of her imagined closeness to the mother's body.

—Mary Kelly, "Desiring Images/Imaging Desire"[1]

AMONG BERTHE MORISOT'S EARLIEST surviving paintings is a female Narcissus, a young woman absorbed in contemplating her own reflection. Known as *Study: At the Water's Edge*, it belongs to 1864 and the period of Morisot's landscape studies with Corot (fig. 1).[2] The decorous pastoral theme signals Morisot's relation to late-nineteenth-century visual culture, where women and mirrors often appear together, as well as her apprentice relation to her teacher, Corot.[3] But it also anticipates the characteristic mood of self-absorption and *rêverie* in Morisot's mature painting. The young woman's elongated pose and foreshortened reflection suggest that Morisot was absorbed by absorption itself, and particularly, from a formal point of view, by the artistic contemplation of what might be called nonidentical forms.[4] Despite the apparent reciprocity of the shady landscape and its watery counterpart, her painting discloses their shifting nonequivalence. The young woman's averted face disappears in shadow, while the light reflected off her forearm is mirrored (yet

Fig. 1. Berthe Morisot, *Study: At the Water's Edge* (1864). Collection Mrs. Fred L. Schoneman, New York, N.Y.

not mirrored exactly) by its foreshortened reflection in the water. An emblem of minimal difference hinges—clumsily but disturbingly—on this white-on-white image of a young woman thinking.

Morisot's studies with Corot taught her to look at, and to love, landscape. *La Penseuse* is nature, waiting to be loved: "Old Corot used to say that nature wanted to be *loved*, that she gave herself only to her true lovers"—so Morisot recalled.[5] But here nature seems to be caught looking at (perhaps even loving) herself; or just lost in a fit of abstraction, reflecting on her reflection. The erotic narrative implied by her classical pose—the nymph's *rêverie* is about to be disturbed by satyr, shepherd, or god, or else nature is about to give herself to her true lover—carries a hidden warning against autoeroticism. Milton's Eve, after all, had to give up her own reflection in favor of Adam;

taught better, she reluctantly surrenders pleasure in herself for pleasure in him (but "He for God only . . ."). This allegory of misdirected desire has its psychoanalytic afterlife in Freud's feminization of the Narcissus story. For Freud, the narcissistic woman is both "the purest and truest one"—the most womanly, and the most erotically alluring.[6] She also represents a notorious impasse. At once the embodiment of self-pleasure and the fascinating object of desire, she threatens to short-circuit the entire system by her self-absorption. No psychic encounter seems possible between the feminine self-admirer and her masculine lover; they remain forever a phase apart, caught in the nonequivalence of masculine and feminine narcissisms.[7]

The Narcissus story has many tellings besides Freud's, not least its allegorical tellings in the context of art appreciation and nature-love. Appropriated as a feminist narrative of the woman painter's relation to the past, it can also become a site for the introduction of feminine difference. Apropos of Morisot's filial relation to Corot and her repetition of the Narcissus theme, Anne Higonnet has suggested that "Morisot's *Study* stands for her antecedents in the history of painting." But, she writes, it also "marks her difference within painting's history."[8] How does a woman painter insert herself into this history, and what might the "mark" of this mark of (feminine) difference be? Can a woman be represented as looking at herself, or at another woman, without being disturbed by a voyeuristic look that is traditionally coded as that of the masculine art-lover? And what visual codes or pleasures are available to the woman painter who wants to use her art to think, and to think about herself and her art, even while tacitly acknowledging her aestheticization and her to-be-looked-at-ness as an inevitable aspect of her cultural construction?[9]

I want to understand this "mark" (of the mark) of feminine difference in Morisot's paintings as a diacritical marking—a visual discourse of nonidentity, played out in the formal and compositional syntax of her canvases. Apropos of Manet, Tamar Garb suggests that a woman's "gaze has . . . always to be contained and turned upon itself" if it is not to disturb the socially and sexually regulated regime of looking.[10] Morisot's painting, on the face of it, seems not to disturb this regime. Yet she tends to deploy the swerve and containment of the look to trouble its seemingly unruffled surface—installing herself in the deflection or reflection of light; or else in the moment when, as the woman painter's gaze turns back on itself, she meets her own eyes in the mirror. The space of feminine intrasubjectivity can be read in Morisot's painting as successful containment, mirroring the apparently unproblematic social and psychic "fit" between the upper-class, nontransgressive, "feminine" Morisot and her late-nineteenth-century frame (too easily equated with the "femininity" of the Impressionism whose values she was thought perfectly to embody).[11] But it can also be read as a mode of resistance to the masculine, appropriative look of the lover, or what Garb calls "the non-innocent look of culture." The Narcissa's gaze of my title, therefore, names neither the privileged self-reflexive subject of consciousness, nor Freud's fantasy of feminine self-sufficiency (so pleasing, in different ways, to both men and women). While narcissism may be defined as amorous capture by an image, I want to risk locating a specifically feminine narcissism (one could call it a mode of identification) in the turning back on itself, or hinge, of object love and autoeroticism.[12] Such narcissism is also available to masculine subjects, it goes without saying. But it is peculiarly liable to be *coded* as feminine and, I would argue, at the end of the nineteenth century it was both culturally available and culturally approved for women in ways that it was not for men (for men, indeed, it would be taken as the sign of homosexuality). Taking one's self or one's image as the object of identification and desire—turning love back toward the self—is the specific form of loving and looking that one finds in Morisot's light-filled paintings of girls and women. For women painters, the hinge of object love and autoeroticism may be the female body cathected as the locus of visual pleasure; or it may be a child, especially a daughter, viewed as a reflection-with-a-difference of the artist-mother (a self that is not quite an other).[13] But while female nudity could be viewed as culturally transgressive for women artists, painting a daughter fell easily into the permitted realm of the maternal imaginary.

Marking the porous boundaries of self and other, a daughter is the privileged object of the mother's narcissistic gaze. Morisot's portraits of her adolescent daughter, Julie Manet, provide a space for negotiating not only the look of a woman artist but her filiation—that is, her filial relation to her past and to the future of painting. In addition, the filial mirror produces an image for the production of mothering itself when the mother is also an artist. Mallarmé's deeply respectful posthumous tribute to Morisot refers to "une ardente flamme maternelle, où se mit, en entier, la créatrice."[14] Did the artist submit to the mother, or the mother submerge herself in the artist? Feminist critics, understandably, have been quick to dismiss family-centered accounts of Morisot such as that of her grandson Denis Rouart, who wrote that "for to her to love was to paint."[15] Too quick, perhaps, since the language of love may have something to tell us, after all. Morisot included Julie in a number of sketched or painted self-portraits of the artist at work, where artist and mother are compositionally twinned.[16] But for the most part Morisot's daughter is rendered as the object of the painter's loving gaze (rather than in terms of the intimate mother-child duo favored by a woman contemporary like Morisot's friend, Mary Cassatt). This distancing of the maternal relation

Fig. 2. Berthe Morisot,
The Wet Nurse (1879).
Private collection,
Washington, D.C.

can be registered as a disturbance in Morisot's enigmatic painting of her infant daughter in the arms of her nurse. *The Wet Nurse* (1879) (fig. 2) blurs everything—including the featureless face of the nurse herself—with the restless flurry of Morisot's brushstrokes. The only image allowed to cohere is the rosy baby at the breast. In this moment of visual pleasure, where looking substitutes for nursing and painting supplements maternal nurture, autoeroticism finds its image in the founding moment of sucking. The infant Julie, her arm raised to fondle the nurse's breast, becomes an emblem of the self-reflexive turn on which both fantasy and sexuality are propped in psychoanalytic accounts of the origins of sexuality at the breast.[17] While on one level *The Wet Nurse* renders back to the viewer the loving maternal gaze that so signally fails to emanate from the sightless face of the wet nurse, on another it destabilizes any reassuring representation of primary maternal preoccupation.[18]

In this essay, however, I want to focus on a group of much later paintings belonging to the 1890s that are similarly both charged and troubled by maternal concerns. Here the coincidence of loving and painting, like the relations of distance and desire, are inflected not only by the biographical circumstances of Julie's adolescence and Morisot's middle age, but by transitions in Morisot's artistic practice. Griselda Pollock has noted Morisot's use of her daughter's life "to produce works remarkable for their concern with female subjectivity especially at critical turning-points of the feminine."[19] And Anne Higonnet has written perceptively that, during the 1890s, "Morisot renewed herself in her paintings of her daughter," just as Renoir turned to the nude or Degas to the dance at the same period.[20] Adolescence itself—whose emergence at the end of the nineteenth century in fin de siècle France gave rise to new literary and artistic concerns—can be seen as inseparable from the rise of early modernism.[21] Morisot's portraits of her adolescent daughter therefore function not only as inquiries into femininity, caught at a moment of crucial transition, but as inquiries into Morisot's evolving artistic concerns, caught at a critical turning point in her own life. The girl adolescent inevitably confronts her middle-aged mother with an image of loss (both her own and her daughter's). But she can also serve as a powerful metaphor for artistic change. These paintings pose the question of narcissism—loving (one's own) image or images—in the context of mother-daughter relations, while also posing the question of femininity in the context of an emergent modernism. I want to suggest that the jeune fille becomes a figure both for Morisot's filial relations to the history of painting, and for artistic filiation more generally. Morisot's distinctiveness as a woman Impressionist is her reinvention of this history as a source of psychic meaning and visual pleasure.

In these late paintings of Julie Manet, the *rêverie* of the adolescent girl provides a potential site of resistance for the woman artist's ideological installation as mother. It also provides a crucial image of modernity, seen through the lens of sexual difference. Griselda Pollock writes of Morisot's "rearticulation of traditional space so that it ceases to function primarily as the space of sight for a mastering gaze," citing the example of Mary Kelly's attempt to repicture or re-fuse "the literal figuration of the woman's body."[22] To rephrase Pollock, one might say that the space of Morisot's painting rearticulates the gaze of nonequivalence, producing (for instance) the image of her daughter as a sign for the differential relationship of femininity to itself. Dissolving the literality of the feminine figure in the play of light and shadow, or abstracting it as pure form, Morisot also demarcates the space of her canvasses as an interstitial space—the space of feminine (self-)difference and self-loss—rather than the space of sight or possession. This liminal space questions not only the limits of maternal preoccupation, but the limits of figuration.

i. The Filial Mirror

In Morisot's portraits of Julie, Narcissa's gaze both finds and loses its first object. Parental love (to revert to Freud's "On Narcissism") "is nothing but the parents' narcissism born again . . . [and] transformed into object-love" (*SE* 14.91). Such born-again, identificatory narcissism, Freud suggests, seizes on the child as an image of what the adult has been forced to renounce in the name of object love. The child's charm, he writes, lies precisely in its narcissism, self-contentment and inaccessibility—in its lack of other objects. By contrast with the image of autoerotic satisfaction represented by the baby, the adolescent, particularly the adolescent girl, represents both a troubled and troubling figure. Freud claims that a girl's narcissism becomes intensified at adolescence in order to compensate for the severe restrictions imposed by heterosexual object choice and the girl's loss of her first love, her mother, which the passage to heterosexuality entails.[23] Poised at the moment when narcissism is at once defensively intensified and assailed, when the body becomes the site and testing ground for her nascent sexual identity, the adolescent girl means not only what she is about to discover, but what she is about to lose. Julie's pensiveness seems to testify to the loss of "repletion" (Kelly's term) that Freud viewed as enforced abandonment of "an unassailable libidinal position" at the time of adolescence (*SE* 14.89). In Morisot's portraits of Julie, the jeune fille brings with her, as a reversed image, the disquieting figure of the *jeune fille mal gardée*. Hence their implicit concern with maternal supervision; hence, too, the pleasure that may be produced by their representation of "a specific loss—the loss of [the woman's] imagined closeness to the mother's body."[24]

The three paintings I want to consider in detail—*Julie Manet and her Greyhound Laertes, Julie Playing the Violin*, and *Julie Daydreaming*—all belonging to 1893–94—represent a triptych of adolescent precoccupation. In all three portraits, Julie appears rather subdued and mournful, or else absorbed and abstracted. Her mood in the two earlier paintings may reflect the death of her father in April 1892, as well as a refraction of what we know to have been Morisot's own feelings at the time as she confronted her widowhood.[25] The eyes of the girl with her greyhound are discolored with circles of shadow; the face of the girl playing the violin is darkened by her bent head; and even the langorous, white-clad daydreamer is pensively shaded by the dark blues and greens of her background. The little girl's happy absorption in her play (a feature of Morisot's earlier portrayals of Julie) gives way to an adolescent lost in her thoughts, her music, or her private *rêverie*. While biographical reasons may account for the change, it is also inscribed in the visual culture of the period; compare, for instance, Munch's *Puberty* (1895), whose vulnerable, naked adolescent is shadowed by the metaphor of approaching sexual danger.[26] For Morisot at least, the jeune fille—on the brink of adult consciousness and sexuality—becomes a potential space for the projection of narcissistic injury, whether her own (projected or actual) or that of her mother.

At the time of Edouard Manet's death in 1883, Morisot wrote that Julie was "all I love, all I have left of youth and beauty." She also described the infant Julie, proudly, as "a Manet to the tips of her fingers." Her name perpetuated that of Manet, with whom, Morisot said, she associated "all the memories of [her] youth."[27] In the light of these associations, it is tempting to see *Julie Manet and her Greyhound Laertes* (1893) (fig. 3) as a reprise of Manet's well-known portrait of Morisot herself as a young woman in *Repose* (1870) (fig. 4), which Morisot tried unsuccessfully to acquire in 1893, the same year that she painted her portrait of Julie.[28] When Manet's *Repose* was first exhibited twenty years before, in 1873, much of the hostility and derision it aroused focused on the figure of Morisot herself, who was taken to personify the malaise of modern painting—moody, slovenly, and tainted with bohemianism.[29] Manet apparently began his painting in Morisot's studio, on a sofa that belonged to her, but he posed her in front of a Japanese print of his own that has been identified as Kuniyoshi's turbulent *The Dragon King Pursuing the Ama with the Sacred Jewel* (ca. 1853).[30] Its threatening waves and writhing dragon coils seem about to overwhelm the half-naked Ama, or fisher-maiden (whose dark tresses, incidentally, resemble Morisot's striking coiffure), just as the reclining Morisot seems about to be engulfed by her billowing sea of skirts—not waving, but drowning.[31] Sometimes thought to capture the conflict and melancholy which apparently characterized Morisot's mood at this time, when she was preoccupied by questions to do with her own professional and marital future, *Repose* also evokes a reticent but powerful sexuality which led viewers of Manet's earlier portrait of her in *The Balcony* (1868–69) to cast the memorably self-contained Morisot (to her amusement) as a femme fatale.[32]

Morisot's painting of Julie, twenty years later, poses her in her mourning dress on a similar sofa, this time in a light-filled room where she provides the sombre accent. By accident or design, Morisot's portrait gives the same central position to an unidentified Japanese print.[33] A kneeling, black-robed woman in the foreground of the print hovers near Julie's shoulder like a reminder of Morisot's recent bereavement, perhaps hinting also at maternal oversight.[34] Julie's flexed pose, echoed in the greyhound's nervous, coiled stance, suggests that she too is poised nervously and might spring up at any moment. The interlocking design of girl and dog implies an affective link between them, knotted together as they are by the crisscross, curving diagonals of the painting's formal composition. A gift from Julie's guardian,

Fig. 3. Berthe Morisot, *Julie Manet with Her Greyhound Laertes* (1893). Musée Marmottan, Paris.

Fig. 4. Édouard Manet, *Repose (Berthe Morisot)* (1870). Museum of Art, Rhode Island School of Design. Bequest of the Estate of Mrs. Edith Stuyvesant Vanderbilt Gerry.

Mallarmé, the greyhound—associated in classical iconography with the virgin huntress Diana—makes an apt companion for a young girl. But the dog could also be read as a reference to Morisot's recent widowhood, since in portraiture it alludes traditionally to a woman's marital fidelity, or to her fidelity to the memory of a dead husband, which Morisot's journal reveals to have been on her mind at the time.[35] Like the monitory kneeling figure above her, Laertes announces the jeune fille as gardée, if not défendue, while also installing her mother indirectly in the painting as its informing, guardian presence.

Unlike Manet's portrait of Morisot in *Repose*, *Julie Manet and her Greyhound Laertes* is also a family portrait—the portrait of a family in mourning. The insubstantial, almost ghostly chair (compositionally paired with Julie on her sofa) gestures toward the otherwise unrepresentable death of her father, Eugène Manet, the previous year. Against this sketchy indication of a too-empty room, Julie's dark silhouette stands out as a displaced figure for her mother's mourning; the bruising shadow round her eyes suggests a girl who mourns without knowing the full meaning of her own (or her mother's) loss. Everything that matters in this painting is contained in silhouette—the contours of Julie's dark dress, with its puffed and ruched sleeves; the silky, sofa-colored dog whose slender curves echo Julie's; the kneeling figure in the Japanese print; and even, as in a negative, the pale, ghostly outlines of an empty chair. The outlines are clear but the meaning is left to be inferred by the viewer, whether Morisot herself or her intimate friends. Significantly, this was the elegiac painting that Monet chose for himself as a memento in 1895, immediately after Morisot's own death.[36] For those who knew Morisot, *Julie Manet and her Greyhound Laertes* was already a memorial portrait—an "impression" of maternal mourning that included the artist as mother.

But this is also a memorial portrait in another sense. What Morisot responded to in the style of Japanese prints—the clarity and simplicity of outline, the "incomparable vitality and lightness of execution"—was also what she most admired in Manet: "only he and they," she wrote, "are capable of suggesting a mouth or ears with a single stroke."[37] Hanging a Japanese print behind Julie could be read as a metonymy for Manet's economy of line, as well as for Morisot's own recent approach to figure painting, evolved in the context of Cassatt's exactly contemporary experiments with line in her own Japanese-influenced color prints of the 1890s.[38] The touches by which Morisot models Julie's face, or outlines the dog's muzzle, are at once an allusion to the Japanese print behind her, and an *hommage* or tribute to Manet—who functions not only as a reminder of the youth and beauty that he had repeatedly commemorated in his portraits of Morisot as a young woman, but as the artist whose interventions and example had been crucial for her own artistic development. For Morisot, Manet remained the great painter of his age, his death the end of a phase in her own life. The figure of Julie Manet can be read as a metonymy for Morisot's artistic affiliations as much as an image of her past and present bereavement. This is a painting about painting as well as mourning; about technique—about line—as well as memory.

During a period of intense grief after the death of Eugène Manet, Morisot wrote: "I say 'I want to die' but it's not true at all; *I want to become younger*."[39] The wish to live one's life over again in one's children must be among the commonest of all maternal fantasies. But the unpreparedness for aging that accompanies the mother's engagement with her daughter's adolescence takes a specific form in Morisot. She wrote: "We arrive unprepared to each of life's ages and we lack experience in spite of our years."[40] Her unpreparedness for aging is displaced onto her daughter's lack of experience. The cliché of the young girl poised on the brink of adulthood allows her to ask what it would mean to *"become younger"*—to be as unprepared for life's ages (or its losses) as Julie. But Julie also provides Morisot with a figure for artistic transition. In her earlier comments on "realism," echoing discussions with Mallarmé, Degas, and Renoir, Morisot associated what she called the reproduction of "an individual in physiognomy and in gesture" with the "literary"—with a too-legible, scientific, realist mode of representation; for her, on the contrary, "Music and painting should never be literary." [41] Her ambition, she wrote in the early 1890s, anticipating Woolf's post-Impressionist experiments with time and memory, was "to *capture something that passes*"—for instance, "A distinctive pose of Julie," or "every once in a while a more vivid reminder of my family."[42] Morisot's focus on the familial and its reminders (its remains) can be read, like Woolf's, as a version of the woman modernist's preoccupation with memorializing the fleeting moments that make up a woman's day—a life, in her case, lived in a cultured domestic interior of which no trace would otherwise be left except a remembered pose or a phrase of music. Music, in fact, provides an apt metaphor for this art of capturing "something that passes" that also functions as an intimate familial reminder or trace of the passing moment. Julie herself, while serving often as her mother's sketching companion, was as much musician as artist.

In *Julie Playing the Violin* (1893) (fig. 5), Morisot invokes painting's fin de siècle analogy with melodic line and harmony; not for nothing had Whistler titled his own paintings of the 1890s "arrangements," "symphonies," "harmonies," and "nocturnes."[43] Mallarmé's Oxford lecture of 1894, "La Musique et les Lettres," develops the longstanding *Symboliste* equation of music and poetry.[44] The same analogy, interestingly, informs the language of Denis Rouart's later account of the evolving technique of Morisot's painting during the 1890s as she turned away from an earlier Impressionist mode. Realizing, he says, that Impressionism had formed "too exclusive an attachment to light at the expense of other qualities . . . she profoundly altered her technique"—not only lengthening her brushstrokes and accentuating her drawing, but subjecting her colors to what he calls "a controlling harmony."[45] In *Julie Playing the Violin*, this controlling harmony is at once the musical metaphor itself and the linear accent of the blue-green girl whose figure provides the vertical compositional line of the painting. "Real painters," Morisot wrote, "understand with a brush in their hand . . . One doesn't train a musician's ear by explaining sound vibrations to him scientifically, any more than one trains a painter's eye by explaining colour relationships and linear harmonies to him."[46] Julie's violin-playing can serve as an analogy for the painter's art and training; her length-

Fig. 5. Berthe Morisot, *Julie Playing the Violin* (1893). Collection Mr. Hermann Mayer.

ened bow stands in for the brush, the flow of her belted dress for the artist's linear harmonies. The visual equivalent of her silent music is the overflow of light, glancing off the surfaces of bowls, mirrors, painted surrounds, even furniture. This play of light, reflected from paint, glass, china, marble, and polished wood, blurs the brushwork below Julie's playing arm and spills out into an imaginary, liminal foreground through the vertical door that frames her. Accentuated by Morisot's lengthened brushstrokes, the flow of Julie's dark skirt is clinched by a white sash, making her a figure of simultaneous overflow and containment; Julie too is a vessel (or even a taut-strung instrument) who may be spilled or broken unless properly cherished.[47]

In *Julie Playing the Violin*, individual physiognomy is subsumed into the musician's expressiveness. Even the lines of Julie's instrument—an impossible object, from the point of view of perspective, so foreshortened as to be unrepresentable—are transposed, reappearing in the curved legs of the table behind her that echo the violin's neck and scroll. Flowers and plants in the background hint at the relation of a musical culture to money and leisure. Julie's music-making, in fact, is the product of a specialized, not to say hot-house education. The three large china bowls in the background suggest both expense and fragility—the brittle vibration of china or glass, and also, metaphorically, the frail china jar of virginity that comes to mind in relation to the education of a young girl of the *haute bourgeoisie* at the turn of the century. Like Eliot's china jar which "still / Moves perpetually in its stillness" ("Not the stillness of the violin, while the note lasts, / Not that only . . ."),[48] Julie is the apotheosis of high culture. At once its bearer and its product—its container—she is defined by the aestheticized objects that surround her as much as by the musical analogy or by the raptness of her music-making. Nurture and culture coincide in Morisot's portrait of the adolescent musician. But this is also a representation of a particular kind of maternal work. While *Julie Playing the Violin* makes visible what it means to understand with a brush in one's hand—the labour of its own cultural production—it also makes visible the work involved in producing the *jeune fille*. This is the peculiarly arduous labor of the mother-artist, one that gives new meaning to Mallarmé's characterization of Morisot's art in terms of "une ardente flamme maternelle, où se mit, en entier, la créatrice."

If we oversee rather than overhear *Julie Playing the Violin*, this overseeing—not voyeurism, but educational, cultural, and social supervision—is the measure of the tyrannical demand made on Morisot as mother.[49] Oversight, rather than the intimate care and nurture of a child's body, provides the precise class inflection of *Julie Playing the Violin*, just as the subtext of Morisot's *The Wet Nurse* had been the cre-

281

ation of a healthy infant, nourished not by her mother's own milk but by the *nourice sur lieu* in the supervisory environment of the bourgeois family. Linda Nochlin has written that the labor of wet-nursing at once parallels and makes possible Morisot's own painting, underpinning the seemingly leisurely scene of the *haute bourgeoise* with the actualities of her Impressionist practice.[50] In *Julie Playing the Violin*, similarly, we glimpse the cultural construction, not only of the fin de siècle domestic interior inhabited by Morisot, but of the jeune fille. Julie's music-making belongs, emphatically, to a private rather than public space of performance—she is anything but a *fille publique* of the kind that inhabits the Baudelairean spaces of modernity and public amusement defined by the free-ranging Impressionism of Morisot's male contemporaries.[51] The salon where Julie plays (whether alone, for her mother, or for an imaginary audience of friends and relatives) is the same intimate space as the salon-studio in which her mother worked and entertained her select circle of literary, musical, and artistic friends.[52] In this class- and gender-inflected representation, the girl musician is at once the bearer of cultural values, and the bearer of a distinguished paternal name—the name which designates her as culturally "at home." But her family line is also Morisot's artistic line; *Julie Playing the Violin* exhibits Julie's genealogy and her mother's side by side. One might say that what Morisot has done in her portrait of Julie is to subsume the labor of the bourgeois mother (the production of a daughter, the maintaining of the family) into the production of music and art. It is this idealization of the bourgeois scene of culture that constitutes, in part, Morisot's recognizable signature.

Morisot characteristically signs *Julie Playing the Violin* by including in it a portrait of herself—Manet's *Berthe Morisot Reclining* (1873), originally a full-length portrait, which is clearly visible over Julie's bow-shoulder. On the other side, a slice of Degas's wedding portrait of Eugène Manet is just visible, providing another clue that this painting presupposes an intimate or familial viewer.[53] Framed by her cultural pedigree, with its doubling of the name and remains of Manet, Julie becomes a rare distillation of art and breeding. Her wealth—her family inheritance—is inscribed in and by her mother's art, with all its rich associations. The marriageability of the jeune fille is revealed to be an inseparable aspect of her cultural construction. Morisot's role as bourgeois mother, after all, was to ensure Julie's insertion into a world where her accomplishments were the measure of her family line. This jeune fille, playing her violin under the supervisory gaze of her loving parents, has been nurtured since infancy for a suitable marriage. Appropriately, Julie (a talented painter as well as musician) married Ernest Rouart, the son of Henri

Rouart, one of Impressionism's most wealthy patrons and collectors, and himself a student of her other guardian, Degas. It would be possible to conclude that the beauty of Morisot's art is inseparable from obscuring the conditions of its own production, along with that of the jeune fille. But I want to take a different tack. Arguably, the price paid for Julie's insertion into Impressionism's line of descent was the deprivation that Kelly refers to as loss of imagined closeness to the mother's body (a disturbance that seems to be registered in *The Wet Nurse*). I want to turn to a third portrait of the adolescent Julie for an image of what that loss of imagined maternal closeness might look like when it is played out in terms of a loss of preconceived identity. If it indeed produces "a different form of pleasure for the woman," how might that differential form of pleasure unsettle an art predicated on the aestheticization of bourgeois ideology?

ii. "In Dreams One is Oneself"

Julie Daydreaming (1894) (fig. 6) is Morisot's most striking image of modernity. Julie is depicted as a young woman poised on the brink of adult sexuality, lost in abstraction, and absorbed in her thoughts. Contemplating her life in the eye of her mother's art, Julie becomes for the first time the subject or bearer, not so much of culture, as of her mother's own introspective gaze. Morisot paints her as if in a mirror image, the close-up devoid of foreground, so that Julie now occupies a private rather than familial space—withdrawn from the space of the salon to the privileged space of adolescent daydreaming (a space that is also, needless to say, a sign of her economic and social privilege).[54] This time *La Penseuse*, or rather, *La Rêveuse*, confronts us directly, eye to unseeing eye. The force and concentration of Rodin's *Penseur* may represent a man's thinking, but the outlines of a woman's thought, in Morisot's painting, are diffused and indefinable; they have less to do with effortful cogitation than with the relaxation of mental activity that is caught in Julie's slack-handed pose. *Julie Daydreaming* shifts the emphasis from agonistic masculinity to feminine indeterminacy. Neither happy nor unhappy, Julie becomes a blank space whose meaning has yet to be revealed. She is the white canvas on which her mother paints; her *rêverie* (like her earlier mourning) can be read as an inquiry into Morisot's art and "thought"—that is, her thinking in her art.

Morisot assimilates Julie to an almost *Symboliste* evocation of mood, abstracting her against a featureless flat background. Nothing stands out except the colours of *rêverie*, the suggestion of sensuality in her chestnut hair, the flowing rhythms of

Fig. 6. Berthe Morisot, *Julie Daydreaming* (1894)
Private collection.
Courtesy Galerie Hopkins-Thomas, Paris.

Fig. 7. Julie Manet, 1894. Private collection. Courtesy Galerie Hopkins-Thomas, Paris.

her white dress and her arms, the finger which lies along her cheek like the lock of hair twisting down beside it. This is an attitude of autoeroticism, as finger and hair suggest—the pleasure of a body discovering itself, or even the imaginary pleasure of a mother caressing her daughter's face, as her brush strokes the surface of the canvas. One might almost say that Julie's creative *rêverie* is the condition of possibility for her mother's art. Morisot lamented that modern adolescence, with its educational and social demands, was no longer a time for leisure—

> no more of those lovely moments of leisure, of that picturesque languor; everyone is restless and fidgety, no one understands that there's nothing like 2 hours reclining on a *chaise longue*—life is a dream—and the dream is more real that the reality; in dreams one is oneself, truly oneself—if one has a soul it's there.[55]

"To think," she wrote on another occasion, "that one has so many fine ideas while lying on the couch or in a trance on the omnibus." Like a number of Morisot's paintings of the 1890s—the erotic *Sleeping Girl* (1892) or the reclining figure of *On the Chaise Longue* (1893)—*Julie Daydreaming* suggests her interest in languorous, in-between, autoerotic states where sexuality and self-sufficiency meet, and fine ideas are born.[56] Whatever the content of Julie's fine ideas may be, we are left to infer them. Perhaps she is thinking of nothing at all; perhaps she is just absentminded.

Photographs of the adolescent Julie (fig. 7) and of Morisot herself accentuate their extreme slenderness.[57] Remarking that "The attitude of her entire life was rather introspective," her brother, Tibburce Morisot, also alluded to her famous undemonstrativeness (except toward her daughter, and possibly her husband); her feelings, he wrote, "were all the more keen for being contained."[58] This containment—the brooding introspection glimpsed in Manet's portraits—suggests that Morisot may have exercised her self-discipline on her body as well as her feelings.[59] She herself wrote of aging—"age which has thought, which has suffered, which has eaten little and drunk little, which glimpses the beyond"—in strikingly ascetic terms.[60] The *rêverie* of the young woman and the asceticism of the older woman represent two sides of the same coin; they suggest that the true life of the self can only be lived outside the body, or perhaps by reabsorbing bodily desire into a form of sensuousness that has no other object than the self. Neither Morisot nor Julie were hysterics (although Morisot's paintings were received as *hysterisées* during her own time by critics hostile to their Impressionism).[61] But spirituality and bodily transcendence might both be thought of as internalizations of the contemporary constraints on female sexuality whose other manifestation during the 1890s was the sexualizing of the hysteric as the woman of excessive libido and uncontrolled sensual appetite. Among the many forms taken by the surveillance and disciplining of women's bodies and minds at the end of the nineteenth century, the mental hospital provided the most graphic instance.[62] The 1880s had seen the height of Charcot's scientific studies of hysterical women at the Salpêtrière; when Freud visited Paris in the mid-1880s, it was to witness the hysteric's somatization at first hand. The bodily manifestations of hysteria—its *crises* and *exstaces*—came under the specular regime of the physician when photography installed the hysteric in the age of mechanical reproduction. As an image rendered simultaneously anonymous and devoid of social context, the hysteric derived her meaning from Charcot's interpretive taxonomy and from her repertoire of formulaic poses. Morisot's portrayals of Julie, by contrast, problematize the relation between women's legibility—their visibility—and an unrepresentable interiority. Julie's opacity constitutes a form of reserve that eludes the regime of the taxonomic gaze.

The same taxonomic impulse that produced the hysteric also gave birth to the modern adolescent. Although Freud himself has comparatively little to say about adolescence (for him the experiences of infantile sexuality are the important ones), Dora's case-history implicitly links hysteria and the crisis of female adolescence. The psychologists of adolescence who came after Freud brought science to bear on what was viewed as the adolescent intensification of imagination, creativity, and sexuality, tending to regard female adolescents as particularly vulnerable to biologically based dangers; C. Stanley Hall was not alone in considering that the onset of menstruation unfitted girls for serious intellectual efforts.[63] Significantly, *rêverie* was the foremost feature of adolescence singled out in Hall's monumental work, *Adolescence: Its Psychology and Its Relations to Physiology, Anthropology, Sociology, Sex, Crime, Religion, and Education* (1904). For Hall, "Puberty is the birthday of the imagination. This has its morning twighlight in *rêverie*." Listing the pathological traits of adolescence in his chapter on "Diseases of Body and Mind," Hall leads off with "Inner absorption and reverie:"

> Who has not had spells of mental involution and absent-mindedness,
> when thoughts went "wool-gathering" and the soul was haunted
> by automatic presentations that take the reins from the will and
> lead us far away in a rapt state, now reminiscent, now anticipatory,

into a world of dreams or ghosts? . . . In these weird seizures, we lose touch with the world and move about "in a world not realized." Sometimes these states suggest the intellectual aura or voluminous mentation of epilepsy and the day-dreamer goes about dazed like a somnambulist, and should be admitted to be legally irresponsible, because every act proves an alibi for attention. This may be the germ of some ancillary personality and lead to a double housekeeping of consciousness, or it may be incipient lunacy. . . .[64]

"The normal soul," he writes, "always soon comes back to the world of reality." For Hall, daydreaming is linked both to poetry and to pathology. What he calls "this subthalamic realm" is at once recapitulatory, like Wordsworthian preexistence ("we seem to lapse into some unknown past that 'hath elsewhere had its setting'"), and contains the seeds of epilepsy, somnambulism, multiple personality syndrome—particularly thought to afflict young women, then as now—or even outright lunacy.[65] Marking the difficult passage from incipent pathology to normalcy, adolescence in Hall's account also effects the transition from polymorphous sexuality to heterosexuality. Heterosexual object choice comes to the rescue of the unfixed aims of adolescence.

Julie Daydreaming serves as a reminder that daydreaming, like hysteria, is a gendered concept, associated not only with adolescence in general but with the adolescent girl in particular; as late as the 1940s, Helene Deutsch could refer to the world of daydreams occupied by the adolescent girl.[66] Images of dreaming or sleeping women are a commonplace of fin de siècle art.[67] What distinguishes Morisot's picture from the cliché of women's "subthalamic" existence, for all its aqueous background, is its abstraction (just as Julie's pose is distinguished from Charcot's photographs by the absence of an interpretive taxonomy). Isolated against a flat, tonal background, no longer framed by her familial genealogy, Julie is rendered as a pure image—in two senses. Morisot's portrait focuses attention on the opacity of her dress, her skin, her expression. Her elusiveness as a subject matches the contentlessness of her *rêverie*. We know nothing of her thoughts and desires, or even whether she thinks and desires at all. Suspended between waking and sleep, she also hovers between latency and sexuality. Her virginal whiteness makes her at once a blank page, as yet to be written on by sexuality and experience, and a site of potential resistence—whether to the inscription of a fully heterosexualized subjectivity, or to the system of social and economic exchange where virginity is destiny. Julie's *rêverie* sketches an imaginary space where the female subject can take refuge from the rigid constraints imposed on both the jeune fille and *chère maman* by the ideological demands of their culture, class, and fin de siècle milieu. This is a portrait in which the maternal *créatrice* finds herself by losing herself in the unfixity of adolescence.

The question, "who is Julie?" (or even "what does Julie want?") is a version of the biographical question, "who is Morisot?" (or even, Freud's perplexed "what does woman want?"). These are impertinent questions, implying as they do the existence of a psychological truth (whether about Morisot or about women). They arise because unreadability in the representation of a woman—as in the case of Manet's enigmatic portraits of the younger Morisot—tends to result in the imposition of a narrative (in her case, implausibly, that of femme fatale). Freud reads hysterical body language as the means by which repressed desire evades the psychic censor. Julie's body, however, gives nothing away but her inattentive, absent gaze; her dreams, by definition, cannot be censored. *Rêverie* constructs an interior space where the psyche (like the somnambulist) "should be admitted to be legally irresponsible," accountable to no one. This interior space has its visual counterpart in the dark and representationally meaningless space of absence between her arms, at the lower center of the painting. But there is somewhere one might look, outside the painting, for a subtext to the enigmatic signifier that is Julie. Morisot's journal (not surprisingly) tells us little about her own sexual desires or conflicts. She does, however, record her sense of professional injustice as a woman painter: "I don't think there has ever been a man who treated a woman as an equal, and that's all I would have asked, for I know I'm worth as much as they."[68] She chose not to associate herself with the *Union des Femmes Peintres et Sculpteurs* which emerged in the 1880s, never exhibiting in the *Salon des femmes*, and distancing herself from the overt feminism of Cassatt.[69] Instead, she became an icon of the refined and rarified artistic femininity to which Mallarmé and *Symboliste* art critics like Théodore de Wyzéwa could appeal during the 1890s.[70] But in 1890 Morisot did read and discuss Marie Bashkirtseff's adolescent journals, which sparked contemporary debate not only about the nature of the jeune fille and about her narcissism (Hall was later to call Bashkirtseff "one of the best types of exaggerated adolescent confessionalists"), but about women's professional and artistic aspirations.[71] As Morisot could hardly have escaped knowing, Bashkirtseff was a respected member of the *Union des Femmes Peintres et Sculpteurs* during the 1880s until her death.[72] Later, Julie herself—for whom artistic ambition was also an issue—read her journals with evident sympathy and identification, recording her comments in her own journal.[73]

Despite the absence of any explicit comment from Morisot, who remained characteristically reticent on the subject, Julie's unacted possibilities pose the adolescent as an unformed question mark over the future of the woman artist. Morisot wrote that she "would like to relive [her] life and comment on it," and that "Remembrance is the only real imperishable life."[74] Painting Julie, I have tried to suggest, was both a mode of memory for Morisot and a means of self-recovery—a way to reflect on her personal and professional history. But her portraits represent more than a memento to lost youth, a remembrance of times past, or even the construction of an artistic genealogy. Instead of the daughter thinking back through her mother (Virginia Woolf's model of literary filiation), we catch a glimpse of the mother thinking forward through her daughter, perhaps to a future demand for equal treatment—or even to the self-reflexive turn taken by the future of painting. Narcissa's gaze, focused on the adolescent girl, defines a new space of modernity, that of the psyche—"an admirable mirror-effect," as Derrida has it, invented in a mirror where two selves never exactly coincide.[75] Julie's impenetrable gaze insists that the mirror never gives back an exact reflection, installing the woman painter as her noncoinciding other in the mirror effects of her art. Curving like a white swan—the *signe* that is also the Mallarméan *cygne*, the sign or cypher—*Julie Daydreaming* gives Morisot's Impressionism the distinctive rhythms of modernism. Julie's whiteness alludes not so much to her ontological status as to the nonidentity of signs. Morisot's filial mirror reinvents modernity in the image of a feminine subject whose self-difference unsettles woman's traditional function of representing, and securing, sexual difference itself.

*   *   *

I want to end by drawing a speculative line of my own from Julie's adolescent *rêverie* back to *The Wet Nurse*, Morisot's painting of Julie as a baby at the breast, and to her early *Study: At the Water's Edge*. At the start, I posed Morisot as a woman painter thinking in and through her art. Wilfred Bion, in "A Theory of Thinking," defines thought as the mating of a preconception (say, the baby's expectation of a breast) with a frustration (the unavailability of the breast for satisfaction, or the absent breast). If the capacity for tolerating frustration is sufficient, Bion suggests, the "no-breast" can become a thought. In this process, the mother's reciprocal capacity for what Bion calls "reverie" plays a crucial part. Receiving the infant's overwhelming projections of frustration or dread, the mother returns them as manageable. Or, in Bion's words, "the mother's capacity for reverie is the receptor organ for the infant's harvest of self-sensations."[76] Through the interplay between the infant's projective identifications and maternal reverie (the imaginary breast), thinking is born. Derrida predicates the invention of the psyche on specular mechanisms involving differential mirror effects and the deferral of meaning. Bion predicates the emergence of thinking on psychic processes involving projective identification—projections returned with a difference. He goes on to consider, not only the expression of thoughts or conceptions in language and signs, but the satisfying truth-effect or "correlation" that is achieved by their communication. The failure of this correlation between thoughts and their expression, he suggests, leads to a mental state "as if starvation of truth were somehow analogous to alimentary starvation."[77] Conversely, a successfully achieved correlation, or fit, between sense-data and their representation might feel like a good feed. The scene of the substitute good feed for Bion is the analytic consulting room. For Morisot, I suggest, it was the salon-studio where she painted. In Bion's sense, *Julie Daydreaming* represents the correlation of Morisot's maternal *rêverie*—giving back, in a managable form, the look which the blank face of the wet-nurse had failed to return. Julie's daydreaming communicates the fantasmatic satisfaction which Julie had been imagined as experiencing at the breast (a reciprocal fantasy of which Morisot, as mother, had herself been deprived). But the pleasure produced by this fantasy is not to be understood, in Kelly's words, as "an instance of repletion." Rather, I suggest, the question of social or ideological "fit" in Morisot's art can be reformulated as the psychic "fit" or "correlation" that generates a particular and characteristic form of pleasure—pleasure that begins at the breast, but ends with Kelly's "loss of preconceived identity . . . [and] imagined closeness to the mother's body." Morisot's painting can be read as a sustained reflection on this pleasurable disturbance to "the seductive surface of the image" and its lining, the maternal imaginary.

1.   "Desiring Images/Imaging Desire," *Wedge* 6 (1984): 9.

2.   *Study: At the Water's Edge* was exhibited in the Salon of 1864. See Charles Stuckey, William Scott, and Suzanne Lindsay, *Berthe Morisot: Impressionist* (New York: Hudson Hills, 1987), 21–22, for the observation that Morisot's painting is echoed by Corot's *The Secret of Love*

(1865), which uses a similar pose but adds a cupid perched suggestively at the girl's head; see also Felix Bracquemond's *Nymph Reclining at the Edge of the Water* (ca. 1864)—perhaps an inspiration for or an *hommage* to Morisot's *Study.*

3. See Bram Dijkstra, *Idols of Perversity: Fantasies of Feminine Evil in Fin-de-Siècle Culture* (New York and Oxford: Oxford University Press, 1986), 143–48, for the argument that feminine narcissism is the invention of fin de siècle visual culture. Morisot's links with a specifically feminine visual culture involving mirrors are also extensively explored by Anne Higonnet in *Berthe Morisot's Images of Women* (Cambridge, MA: Harvard University Press, 1992).

4. For earlier depictions of absorption involving young women in French painting, see also Michael Fried, *Absorption and Theatricality: Painting and the Beholder in the Age of Diderot* (Berkeley and Los Angeles: University of California Press, 1980).

5. See Anne Higonnet, *Berthe Morisot: A Biography* (New York: Harper & Row, 1990), 196.

6. "On Narcissism: An Introduction" (1914); *SE* 14.88.

7. See, however, Mikkel Borch-Jacobsen, *The Freudian Subject*, trans. Catherine Porter (Stanford Stanford University Press, 1988), 112, for the argument that such narcissism is perfectly symmetrical, but inherently homosexual: "each loves him/herself in the other, and since each is speculating on a mirrored love, the other is in each case an other self, a likeness."

8. See Anne Higonnet, *Berthe Morisot's Images of Women*, 254.

9. See also Tamar Garb, "Gender and Representation," in Francis Franscina, Nigel Blake, Briony Fer, et al., *Modernity and Modernism: French Painting in the Nineteenth Century* (New Haven and London: Yale University Press and Open University, 1993), 222: "For feminism the very phrase 'pleasure in looking' raises the questions: whose pleasure and whose looking is at stake? What is the relationship between power and the act of looking or being looked at? Who has the right to look and how is looking legitimated and culturally coded? And crucially for us, how do the processes of representation and the act of looking *at* art or the elaborate conventions by which looking is staged *in* art, relate to the conditions of looking in life for men and women?"

10. Garb, "Gender and Representation," 246.

11. See the introduction by Kathleen Adler and Tamar Garb to *Berthe Morisot: The Correspondence*, ed. Denis Rouart, trans. Betty W. Hubbard (London: Moyer Bell Ltd., 1986), 7–9, for a brief account of assumptions about Morisot's "femininity" and that of the Impressionist movement.

12. For an extended reading of "On Narcissism" in terms of mimetic indentification, see Mikkel Borch-Jacobsen, *The Freudian Subject*, 53–126. Borch-Jacobsen discusses the social dimensions of identificatory narcissism as (male) homosexuality but does not consider its cultural attribution to women.

13. For one influential account of preoedipal mother-daughter relations, see Nancy Chodorow, *The Reproduction of Mothering: The Sociology of Gender* (Berkeley: University of California Press, 1978); Chodorow writes: "Primary identification and symbiosis with daughters tends to be stronger [than with sons] and cathexis of daughters to be based on experiencing a daughter as an extension or double of the mother herself" (Chodorow, 109).

14. "Berthe Morisot," in *Médaillons et Portraits, Oeuvres Complètes de Stéphane Mallarmé* (Paris: Editions Gallimard, 1945), 535. Mallarmé's tribute was written for the catalogue of Morisot's posthumous Durand-Ruel exhibition of 1896.

15. See *Berthe Morisot: An Exhibition of Paintings and Drawings* (Arts Council of Great Britain,

1958), 5.

16. See, for instance, *Self-Portrait with Julie* (1885), *Self-Portrait with Daughter* (1888), and *Berthe Morisot Drawing with her Daughter* (1889); for Morisot's compositional equation of her daughter and her art, see Anne Higonnet, "The Other Side of the Mirror," in *Perspectives on Morisot*, ed. T. J. Edelstein (New York: Hudson Hills Press, 1990), 71–73; and Higonnet, *Berthe Morisot's Images of Women*, 204–10.

17. See, for instance, Jean Laplanche, *Life and Death in Psychoanalysis*, trans. Jeffrey Mehlman (Baltimore and London: Johns Hopkins University Press, 1976), 15–18.

18. For a different reading of *The Wet Nurse* in relation to the construction of work and leisure, see Linda Nochlin, "Morisot's *Wet Nurse*: The Construction of Work and Leisure in Impressionist Painting," in *Perspectives on Morisot*, 91–102.

19. Griselda Pollock, "Modernity and the Spaces of Femininity," in *Vision and Difference: Feminity, Feminism and the Histories of Art* (London and New York: Routledge, 1988), 81.

20. See Higonnet, *Berthe Morisot's Images of Women*, 235–36.

21. For the emergence of adolescence, see Philippe Ariès, *Centuries of Childhood*, trans. Robert Baldick (New York: Vintage Books, 1962), 30; and for the association of adolescence with literary and artistic modernism, see John Neubauer, *The Fin-de-Siècle Culture of Adolescence* (New Haven and London: Yale University Press, 1992).

22. See Pollock, "Modernity and the Spaces of Femininity," 86, 87; and Kelly, "Desiring Images/Imaging Desire": "The (neo-)feminist alternative has been to refuse the literal figuration of the woman's body, creating significance out of its absence. . . . femininity is not seen as a pre-given entity, but as the mapping-out of sexual difference within a definite terrain. . . . With regard to the spectator, it is a tactic of reversal, attempting to produce the woman, through a different form of identification with the image, as the subject of the look" (*Wedge* 6.7).

23. See *SE* 14.88–89. In the same vein, Helene Deutsch proposes: "The question 'Who will love me now?' is answered with 'I, myself'—another incentive to the increase in narcissism"; see Helene Deutsch, *Selected Problems of Adolescence* (London: Hogarth Press, 1968), 27–28.

24. Kelly, *Wedge* 6.9.

25. See Higonnet, *Berthe Morisot*, 208–10.

26. For visual representations of fin de siècle adolescence by Munch and others, see Neubauer, *The Fin-de-siècle Culture of Adolescence*, 92–121; Neubauer does not, however, consider French painting.

27. Rouart, *Berthe Morisot: The Correspondence*, 134, 115, 132.

28. See *Berthe Morisot: The Correspondence*, 205. For the suggestion that Morisot's painting is a *reprise* of Manet's *Repose*, see Stuckey, Scott, and Lindsay, *Berthe Morisot: Impressionist*, 207. Interestingly, a photograph taken of Julie after her marriage not only poses her on what may well be the same sofa as that of Morisot's *Julie Manet and her Greyhound Laertes*, but repeats an almost identical placing of one hand and the arrangement of skirts in Manet's painting; see Julie Manet, *Growing up with the Impressionists: The Diary of Julie Manet*, trans. and ed. Rosalind de Boland Roberts and Jane Roberts (London: Sotheby's Publications, 1987), 181.

29. See Beatrice Farwell, "Manet, Morisot, and Propriety," in *Perspectives on Morisot*, 45–46. Reclining on a sofa or divan would itself have carried suggestions of modernity and bohemi-

anism, if not of the harem. Other critics saw Manet's treatment as itself transgressive in its rendering of a young woman; see Garb, "Gender and Representation," 255.

30. See Kathleen Adler, *Manet* (Oxford: Phaidon, 1986), 148.

31. Interestingly, Mallarmé refers to *Repose* as *Rêverie* in an essay on "The Impressionists and Edouard Manet," published in the *Art Monthly Review* for 1876: "there a young woman reclines on a divan exhaling all the lassitude of summer time; the jalousies of her room are almost closed; the dreamer's face is dim with shadow, but a vague, deadened daylight suffuses her figure and her muslin dress"; see Carl Paul Barbier, *Documents Stéphane Mallarmé* (Paris: Librairie Nizer, 1968), 1.66–86.

32. See Rouart, *Berthe Morisot: The Correspondence*, 36.

33. See Higonnet, *Berthe Morisot's Images of Women*, 189 and n. for Cassatt's and Morisot's Japanese print collection; some of Cassatt's collection survives, but Morisot's was dispersed without records. Their common interest in Japanese prints was sparked by a major exhibition at the Beaux-Arts in 1890.

34. Eugène Manet had died in April 1892; Morisot's sister, Yves, died in June 1893.

35. See James Hall, *Dictionary of Subjects and Symbols in Art* (London: John Murray, 1974), 105. Even the dog's name, chosen by Mallarmé himself, seems to allude in an identificatory fashion to the death of Eugène Manet; in the *Odyssey*, "The old man Laertes," as he is often called, is left grieving in Ithaca for his absent son while watching helplessly over his lonely daughter-in-law, Penelope (Ophelia's brother—left to tell the tale of Hamlet's death—seems a less likely candidate, or at any rate a more morbid one, since he witnesses his sister's decline into madness and suicide). For Morisot's thoughts on her dead husband, see Higonnet, *Berthe Morisot*, 212–13.

36. See Julie Manet, *Growing Up with the Impressionists*, 85; and M. L. Battaille and G. Wildenstein, *Berthe Morisot: Catalogue des peintures, pastels et aquarelles* (Paris: Les Beaux-Arts, 1961), no. 335.

37. Quoted in Higonnet, *Berthe Morisot*, 204

38. See Higonnet, *Berthe Morisot's Images of Women*, 188–93.

39. Quoted in Higonnet, *Berthe Morisot*, 209.

40. Quoted in ibid., 212.

41. See ibid, 195

42. Quoted in ibid., 203–204

43. See Alex Aronson, *Music and the Novel* (Totowa, NJ: Rowman and Littlefield, 1980); and *Artists on Art*, ed. Robert Goldwater and Marco Treves (New York: Pantheon, 1947), 347.

44. See *Oeuvres Complètes de Stéphane Mallarmé*, 642–54: "la Musique et les Lettres sont la face alternative ici élargie vers l'obscur; scintillante là, avec certitude, d'un phénomène, le seul, je l'appelle, l'Idée" (649).

45. Rouart, *Berthe Morisot: An Exhibition of Paintings and Drawings*, 4–5

46. Quoted in Higonnet, *Berthe Morisot*, 219.

47. For contemporary ideas about both the necessity of controlling women and protecting againt the overspill of color by the discipline of line, see Tamar Garb, "Gender and Representation," 286.

48. T. S. Eliot, *Four Quartets*, "Burnt Norton," 142–45.

49. "Motherhood," as Helene Deutsch puts it, "is a tyrannical full-time emotional task"; see *Selected Problems of Adolescence* (London: Hogarth Press, 1968), 130.

50. See Nochlin, "Morisot's *Wet Nurse*," 91–102

51. See T. J. Clark, *The Painting of Modern Life: Paris in the Art of Manet and His Followers* (London: Thames & Hudson, 1984). For a critique of Clark, see Pollock, "Modernity and the Spaces of Femininity," 50–90.

52. For Morisot's negotiation of her socially inscribed gender role as *haute bourgeoise*, see, for instance, Garb, "Gender and Representation," 284–87. For Morisot's actual eagerness to exhibit and find buyers for her paintings, see S. Glover Lindsay, "Berthe Morisot: Nineteenth-Century Woman as Professional," in *Perspectives on Morisot*, 79–90.

53. See Higonnet, "The Other Side of the Mirror," in *Perspectives on Morisot*, 74–75, and *Berthe Morisot's Images of Women*, 244–46, where these two paintings are identified; see also 243 for another painting of Julie playing the violin, *Violin Practice* (1893), which alludes to Manet by including his *Portrait of Isabelle Lemonnier* (1880).

54. See Neubauer, *The Fin-de-siècle Culture of Adolescence*, 67, for the observation that adolescent daydreaming in literature usually occurs in private rooms ("a luxury of the affluent"); theorists of adolescence at the turn of the century were divided over the advantages and dangers of such privacy (Neubauer, 68).

55. Quoted in Higonnet, *Berthe Morisot*, 219; Morisot is echoing the concerns often voiced about adolescent girls at the turn of the century. Did Morisot perhaps recall Mallarmé's description of Manet's *Rêverie* (*Repose*)?—"there a young woman reclines on a divan, exhaling all the lassitude of summer time" (see n. 31 above).

56. For the collapsing or sleeping woman in art and her association with female autoeroticism during the fin de siècle, see Bram Dijkstra, *Idols of Perversity*, 69–82.

57. Compare, for instance, the photograph of Morisot with her husband taken when Julie was a small child, and the photograph of a painfully thin Morisot taken in 1892, after Eugène Manet's death (see Higonnet, *Berthe Morisot*, following 114).

58. See ibid., 188.

59. There is biographical evidence to suggest anorexic episodes earlier in Morisot's life, for instance around the time of the Paris Commune. Higonnet notes, but does not develop, the possibility that Morisot's tendency toward anorexia predated the privations of the siege of Paris in 1870 (*ibid.*, 64).

60. Ibid., 220.

61. See Garb, "Gender and Representation," 287.

62. This disciplining also took the form of debate about the education of girls, often accompanied by denunciation of women's struggles to find a place for themselves outside the domestic and maternal sphere; see Gustave Le Bon, "La psychologie des femmes et les effets de leur éducation actuelle," *Revue Scientifique* 46 (October 11, 1890): 449–60. See also Tamar Garb, "Berthe Morisot and the Feminizing of Impressionism," in *Perspectives on Morisot*, 61–63, and "Gender and Representation," 279–80, for relevant accounts of scientific and medical inscriptions of sexual difference during this period.

63. See Neubauer, *The Fin-de-siècle Culture of Adolescence*, 141–59.

64. C. Stanley Hall, *Adolescence: Its Psychology and Its Relations to Physiology, Anthropology, Sociology, Sex, Crime, Religion, and Education* (New York: Appleton and Co., 1914), 1:311–12.

65. For the relation between trance states and multiple personality syndrome, and its gendered associations with adolescent girls and women, see Ruth Leys's discussion of Morton Prince's *The Dissociation of a Personality* (1905) in "The Real Miss Beauchamp: Gender and the Subject of Imitation," in *Feminists Theorize the Political*, ed. Judith Butler and Joan Scott (London: Routledge, 1992), 167–214.

66. See Teresa Brennan on "the extensive, burdensome, and completely preoccupying phantasy life and world of daydreams occupied by the adolescent girl"; *The Interpretation of the Flesh* (London: Routledge, 1992), 43; Brennan is paraphrasing Helene Deutsch in *The Psychology of Women* (1944).

67. See, for instance, Dijkstra, *Idols of Perversity*, 83–118. Although Morisot's painting has little in common with Dijkstra's overtly sexual catalogue of weightless women and broken-backed nymphs, the slack-handed pose of *Julie Daydreaming* interestingly resembles that of Dante Gabriel Rossetti's *The Day-Dream* (1880). For a psychoanalytic reading of Rossetti's paintings of unseeing women and their relation to the photographic closeup, see also Pollock, "Woman as sign: psychoanalytic readings," 120–54.

68. Quoted in Higonnet, *Berthe Morisot*, 203.

69. See Tamar Garb, *Sisters of the Brush: Women's Artistic Culture in Late Nineteenth-Century Paris* (New Haven and London: Yale University Press, 1994), 38; and, for Morisot's "fulfilment of [a] fantasy of femininity" associated with the feminization of Impressionism itself, *Sisters of the Brush*, 126–27, 157–58.

70. See, for instance, Wyzéwa's "Mme Berthe Morisot," *L'Art dans les deux mondes*, no. 19 (March 28, 1891): 223–24.

71. See Hall, *Adolescence*, 1:355; and *Berthe Morisot: The Correspondence*, 177.

72. See Garb, *Sisters of the Brush*, 53–54, 81–82 for Bashkirtseff's feminism and her contemporary visibility as a woman artist.

73. See Julie Manet, *Growing Up with the Impressionists*, 110–11, 116. Julie, who recalled her parents arguing over Marie Bashkirtseff, thought her book might be better understood "par une jeune fille qui pénètre en l'esprit de celle qui vous raconte sa vie et ses pensées et qui même compare avec ses propres pensées"; see Julie Manet, *Journal (1893–1899): Sa Jeunesse parmi les peintres impressionistes et les hommes des lettres* (Paris: Librairie C. Klincksieck, 1979), 138 for the full text of this entry.

74. Quoted in Higonnet, *Berthe Morisot*, 209–10.

75. See Jacques Derrida, "Psyche: Inventions of the Other" (1987), trans. Catherine Porter, *A Derrida Reader*, ed. Peggy Kamuf (New York and London: Harvester Wheatsheaf, 1991), 215: "Of this relation of the same to the other, we could say, playfully: It is *only* an invention, a mirage, or an admirable mirror effect."

76. W. R. Bion, "A Theory of Thinking," in *Second Thoughts* (London: Heineman, 1967), 116.

77. Ibid., 119.

Index

INDEX